SAM, SIPE, & COMPANY
The Story of the Cleveland Browns

Also by Bill Levy

How Much Is a College Degree Worth to You? (1963)
College Scholarships & Loans: Who Gets Them, How and Why (1964)
Five Star Golf (1964)
Return to Glory: The Story of the Cleveland Browns (1965)
Three Yards and a Cloud of Dust: The Ohio State Football Story (1966)
The Derby (1967)

SAM, SIPE, & COMPANY

THE STORY OF THE CLEVELAND BROWNS

BY

BILL LEVY

Cleveland, Ohio
J. T. Zubal & P. D. Dole, Publishers
A Divison of John T. Zubal, Inc.
1981

Published in the United States of America
J. T. Zubal & P. D. Dole, Publishers
A Division of John T. Zubal, Inc.

ISBN 0-939738-04-X

First Edition

To Jody and Michael

Acknowledgements

This book, the history of the Cleveland Browns from 1946 through 1980, would not have been possible without the help of a number of individuals who gave generously of their time, sources of information and personal observations.

My thanks go to Art Modell, president of the Browns; Peter Hadhazy, former general manager; Nate Wallack, vice president-public relations, Coach Sam Rutigliano and *Plain Dealer* columnist George Condon.

I would be remiss were I not to express my appreciation to those whose assistance was invaluable in gathering information on the years 1946-64, including the late Harold Sauerbrei, general manager of the Browns; Hal Lebovitz, sports editor of *The Plain Dealer,* and Bill Scholl, professional football writer for *The Cleveland Press.*

A special thanks also goes to Tony Tomsic, photographer for *The Cleveland Press* and *Sports Illustrated,* who shot the cover photograph and many of the pictures used in this book.

The material on the history of the Browns through 1964 is from the author's book, *Return to Glory: The Story of the Cleveland Browns,* published in 1965 after the Browns won their last NFL championship.

BL

CONTENTS

INTRODUCTION

There is a certain madness which afflicts millions of Americans each year. It starts in the waning, sultry days of summer and continues until much of this country is buried under a coat of white. It is called professional football, a game played by men for money. It is a game that combines the elements of speed, sophisticated strategy and violence into an unsurpassed spectacle, a game that is perhaps a microcosm of life in the United States in the 1980s.

Each year more than 13,000,000 persons purchase tickets for the 224 regular season games played in the National Football League, averaging nearly 60,000 per game. It is a far cry from the average of 8,211 fans who paid to see NFL games in 1934, the first year in which attendance records were kept. When pre-season games are included, the attendance total for the average season today approaches 17,000,000.

Tickets are a valuable, hard-to-get commodity in most of the 28 NFL cities, from sun-drenched Anaheim to historic Washington, D. C., and from Seattle to sultry Houston. In thousands of instances, spectators have seats on Sunday afternoon only because they had the foresight years earlier to purchase season tickets to watch their favorite teams perform. There are very few tickets available in most cities for those who have not committed themselves for the season.

But the major audience is far from the playing fields. Millions more see their favorite teams play on television, mainly on Sundays and on Monday nights. All three networks have a piece of the pro football television pie, but they pay dearly for their portions. Each of the 28 professional football teams receives more than $5,000,000 a year for the rights to televise its games.

Pro football had its beginnings in the big cities of the East and the Midwest, but its popularity ultimately spread to every section of America. To the farmer in Iowa, the druggist in Montana, the engineer in Alabama, pro football originally was something read about on the sports pages or heard about on radio. Not until televison came along did this great sports spectacle get carried into every nook and cranny of North America. Before television trained its eye on the game, pro football was essentially a regional game and, with a few exceptions, its players were regional stars.

But once pro football became a first class attraction, television took it everywhere and made it the popular game it is today.

Many men and organizations have had a hand in professional football's success, but one organization can claim a large share of the credit for popularity of the game in America. That organization is the Cleveland Browns. The Cleveland organization was a postwar baby, born with a silver spoon in its mouth. From the day the Cleveland Browns were founded by a far-sighted taxi magnate named Arthur B. McBride, with Paul Brown as its coach and general manager, it was never operated as a hobby. A full-time business, with a full-time staff, it had a half dozen coaches who were hired on a year-round basis, and it scouted college talent on a scale never before practiced in pro football. The Cleveland team enjoyed unparalleled success on the field. When other teams couldn't beat the Browns, they copied them, and all of professional football benefited.

Ultimately, when a dynamic young man from Brooklyn named Art Modell took control of the club, Paul Brown was toppled from the lofty peak he enjoyed for so long. After two years Modell found that life with Paul Brown was intolerable and he fired the architect of the Cleveland Browns. It was a bold move, one of many Modell would make. Modell hired Blanton Collier, a man who had been Paul Brown's long-time friend and aide, and the two made their way back to the top of the football world in two short years. The Browns remained near the peak during the remainder of the 1960s, then began a slow tumble into the land of mediocrity. In those dreary years of the mid-1970s, the team had three losing seasons in four years. Its legion of fans was understandably distraught.

In that time of dark depression for Browns followers, Art Modell made another bold move. While prudence dictated the hiring of a coach with established head man credentials, Modell selected an obscure assistant coach named Sam Rutigliano, whose only head coaching experience had been on the high school level.

In three years, Rutigliano, utilizing much of the talent he inherited, including an underrated quarterback named Brian Sipe, brought the Browns back to respectability in a season that captured the imagination of Cleveland's long-disappointed football fans. It gave a new spirit and reason for being to a city that had been down on its luck for years.

This is the story of the Cleveland Browns from the day the team was founded in a Chicago newspaper office to the Kardiac Kids of today. It is a story unique in the annals of sports.

BL

Cleveland, Ohio
March, 1981

The Kardiac Kids

It was not surprising that most of the men they called the Kardiac Kids were awake and dressed long before the the operator at Stouffer's Cincinnati Towers put in the ordered 8 a.m. wake-up calls for the 45 members of the Cleveland Browns. On this cold, winter day, the Browns were 240 miles from home to do some Christmas shopping for themselves and the reawakened city they represented. Though the "store" wasn't scheduled to open for five more hours, the players were understandably anxious. Sleep was not a high priority item at this time.

On December 21, 1980, Coach Sam Rutigliano and the Cleveland Browns had only one item on their shopping list -- a victory over the Cincinnati Bengals at Riverfront Stadium in the final game of their regular National Football League schedule. With a win would come Cleveland's first American Football Conference Central Division championship in nine years and a ticket to the AFC play-offs, where fame, fortune and a possible Super Bowl appearance lay just down the road.

Without victory, the Browns probably would be left window shopping again -- the Kardiac Kids standing with their noses pressed against the glass like poor youngsters in front of a toy store, coveting wonders that were out of their reach.

Window shopping had become a way of life for the Browns in the 1970s. Their last trip to the promised land of the play-offs had been in 1972, when they won a "wild-card" spot, a sort of second-class passage that is awarded to a handful of teams finishing second in their divisions.

Each year thereafter, they had been left out in the cold, heaping frustration after frustration upon their loyal fans, many of whom remembered an era when a play-off date for the Cleveland Browns was almost as certain as Christmas itself.

Nearly six months earlier, when the Browns assembled for pre-season workouts on an oppressively hot and humid day in July, there was a high probability that when the 1980 season was history the Cleveland Browns would have opened the new decade just the way they had completed the last -- on the outside looking in. A "wild-card" spot in 1980? Perhaps. Champions of the AFC Central Division? Never. It was a matter of pure logic. To get to the top of the division, the Browns would have to leapfrog what generally were considered to be the two best teams in all of professional football -- the four-time Super Bowl Champion Pittsburgh Steelers and the Houston Oilers. The legendary Steelers had captured their second straight Super Bowl and fourth in six years by pasting the Los Angeles Rams, 31-19, in January, 1980. On the way to Super Bowl XIV, they had taken the measure of Houston, 27-13, in a hotly contested AFC championship game.

As a new season approached, the Steelers appeared to be the same old Steelers, proud and powerful and apparently with enough talent to dominate the NFL for another year. If there was to be a challenge, most experts felt it probably would come from Houston, which had acquired play-off hardened quarterback, Ken Stabler, from the Raiders to direct an offense that already boasted Earl Campbell, the NFL's best rusher.

In their second-year under coach Rutigliano in 1979, the Browns had made a game run for a "wild-card" spot in the play-offs, but came up short with a 9-7 record, though it was one of the most exciting seasons in Cleveland history. The outcome of 12 of their 16 games was in doubt until the final minute and three of the contests went into sudden-death overtime. During one home game, a fan looped a banner over a Cleveland Stadium railing labeling the Browns the "Kardiac Kids." It was appropriate and it stuck. When you watched the Browns your heart was usually in your mouth, win or lose, down to the final second of the scoreboard clock.

One of the major reasons for these almost-weekly heart-stoppers was Brian Sipe, the cool Californian who had emerged as one of the league's best quarterbacks. With Sipe, the Browns had an explosive offense that accentuated a cadre of marvelous receivers and the running of Mike Pruitt, who had blossomed into a 1000-yards per season running back. Sipe threw 28 touchdown passes in 1979 to share the NFL title in that department. Unfortunately, he also led in interceptions, having thrown 26. The Browns' offense produced a respectable average of 22.4 points a game, but the defense yielded an average of 22 -- and that was Cleveland's Achilles' heel.

"We've got to stop the bleeding defensively," Rutigliano had declared in a pre-season analysis. "In order to stop the bleeding, we have to basically stop the running game. We haven't done a good job of that in the past."

The job of putting a tourniquet on the defense was handed to Marty Schottenheimer, who had been appointed defensive coordinator early in the year, after Chuck Weber left Cleveland for a similar position with the Baltimore Colts. Schottenheimer, a former All-American linebacker at the University of Pittsburgh, had spent the previous two seasons tutoring linebackers for the Detroit Lions.

Schottenheimer and Rutigliano decided to switch the Browns' basic defense to the "3-4" which utilizes three linemen and four linebackers. Their reasoning was that the Browns had better linebackers than linemen and that defensive alignment would be more effective in stopping the run. The drawback, of course, was that with only three rushing linemen, a sustained pass rush would be very difficult. Pass rushing had been a major problem in 1979 even when the Browns rushed four and five men.

The key to improving the pass rush lay in the improved health of Jerry Sherk, an 11-year pro-veteran who had contracted a deadly staph infection in his left leg in the tenth game of the 1979 season. The one-time all-pro defensive tackle spent five weeks in the Cleveland Clinic as doctors fought to save his leg and life. Following that ordeal, Sherk underwent a rigorous conditioning program to rebuild his legs and overall strength, sapped by the loss of 35 pounds.

Though the Browns were not counting on it, the return of a healthy Sherk obviously would be a critical factor in the team's 1980 fortunes. The Browns had come away from the annual spring college player draft without any new players who could step into a starting role on the defensive line. Their first draft pick, in fact, had been a runner, Charles White, the small but fleet Heisman Trophy winner from the University of Southern California. He had been selected by the Browns in the No. 27 position, having been passed over by 26 other teams. The No. 2 choice for the Browns was Cleveland Crosby, a mountainous defensive end from Arizona who quickly proved to be a disappointment and was cut shortly after the season started.

When the Browns opened their exhibition season in August, the defense wasn't just bleeding, it was hemorrhaging continuously. Life also was drained out of the offense, it seemed, as the team was humiliated in Kansas City, 42-0. At Cleveland Stadium the following week, the gushing had slowed, but the offense was nowhere in sight in a 12-3 loss to the Washington Redskins. Later, in Chicago, the Bears streaked to a 26-8 lead before Sipe, the miracle worker, engineered a 32-31 victory, a typical Kardiac performance that was settled on a 10-yard pass to wide receiver Dave Logan with 1:30 remaining. Sipe tossed five touchdown passes in the victory, but the glory of that feat was dulled by the fact that most of the points were collected against Chicago's second defensive team. There certainly was nothing to cheer about in the exhibition finale as the Browns were drubbed by the Minnesota Vikings, 38-16.

Still, the ever-confident, articulate Rutigliano stood at the podium at the annual Cleveland Touchdown Club kick-off luncheon and predicted the Browns would win a play-off berth.

It was obvious at the dawn of the new season that the Browns needed defensive help, but the fans were somewhat disappointed when the club made an 11th-hour deal with Buffalo for Joe DeLamielleure, a five-time all-pro offensive guard. The price was a couple of future draft choices. The 245-pound, 6'3" star was visibly unhappy at Buffalo, wanted to leave, and had shown his displeasure by boycotting the Bills' training camp. The Browns jumped at the opportunity to get the Buffalo star. "Any time you have a chance to trade for a great player -- and the price is right -- you take him regardless of position," explained Peter Hadhazy, the Browns' Hungarian-born general manager.

The first real test for the 1980 Cleveland Browns came in the season's opener at New England. The Patriots had high hopes for the 1980 campaign. Newcomer Charles White, who had gained 6,245 yards and scored 49 touchdowns for USC, won a spot in the starting offensive line-up, in order to give star running back Gregg Pruitt more time to recover from a severe knee injury which kept him out of much of the 1979 season.

A surprise starter at nose tackle, sandwiched between Jerry Sherk and Lyle Alzado, who had emerged as the spiritual leader of the Cleveland defense, was Henry Bradley, who signed on with the Browns as a free-agent in 1979, but who had been cut in late August of that year. He had spent the next two months driving a truck.

After Sherk was felled by the leg infection, Bradley, 6'2" and 260 pounds from Alcorn State, was re-activated and joined the team for the final six games. Another newcomer to the lineup was Lawrence Johnson, a second-year cornerback from Wisconsin, who substituted for Oliver Davis.

The Browns were simply awful at Foxboro, Massachusetts, where they took a 34-17 shellacking at the hands of the Patriots. It was even worse than the score indicated because the Browns rallied for two fourth quarter TDs after trailing, 34-3. As bad as the outcome of the game was, the fact that Jerry Sherk realized he couldn't cut it and left the game did little to boost the morale of the team.

What bothered a lot of people was the fact that the Browns' next game was to be on Monday Night Football on ABC-TV with a national television audience. Cleveland's image was already bad enough. Further embarrassment was not needed. As it turned out, Houston completely dominated the game in a 16-7 win before 80,243 at Cleveland Stadium. The Oilers had the ball for 77 plays to 41 for the Browns, and controlled it for 42:20 minutes to 17:40 for the home team. Again, it was a costly affair for Cleveland because cornerback Larry Johnson suffered a shoulder injury which put him out of action for the rest of the season.

"I wish I knew the answer," Rutigliano said glumly after the game when reporters pressed him for an explanation of the team's poor showing. The Kardiac Kids plainly needed resuscitation, especially the offense which promised so much but which, so far, had produced so little.

The defense hadn't quite come together, either. Though the team had flirted with the 3-4 defense the previous season, it was having difficulty adjusting to the new alignment. Members of the unit were acting mechanically instead of instinctively, going through the motions as if they were students in a dance studio being taught a new step.

The Browns were now 0-2, with 14 games left to play, including two with Pittsburgh and another with Houston. Past history told the Browns they would have to win at least 10 of those remaining 14 games in order to keep alive the hope for a "wild-card" spot.

Before the Browns took the field at the Stadium to face the Kansas City Chiefs in game No. 3, the soft-spoken Rutigliano had some advice for his players: "Let's open up today the way we did last year. Let's get our fast break in gear and make them feel they have to stop our passing game."

Whatever the Browns agreed to pay Charles White (it was reported to be more than $1,000,000 for six years) the 183-pound Californian earned a good portion of it against the Chiefs. Displaying the verve and dash that made him a unanimous All-American, White gained 159 yards rushing and receiving, and scored the game-winning touchdown on a 31-yard pass from Sipe in the third quarter. Sipe completed 23 of 36 passes for 295 yards in the 20-13 win.

Sipe was in the groove again at Tampa Bay the following week. After missing his first six passes, the boyish-looking quarterback completed 13 in a row, and finished with three touchdown strikes and 318 yards in a 34-27 win which the defense almost squandered. With ten minutes remaining, the Browns had a 31-13 lead. With the clock down to 45 seconds remaining, the Buccaneers had closed the gap to 34-27, and recovered an onside kick. As time expired, the Bucs were left 20 yards short of tying the score and sending the game into overtime.

Tampa Coach John McKay, never at a loss for words, had little praise for the victors. "They aren't that good," he said.

The Browns certainly gave credence to McKay's remarks against Denver the next week. The Broncos, playing without six regulars, parlayed four Fred Steinfort field goals into a 19-16 victory. The pay-off kick, a 19-yard chip shot, broke a 16-all tie with about nine minutes remaining. Denver's only touchdown was a 93-yard gallop in the second quarter by former Ohio State star Randy Gradishar, a linebacker, who knocked down an attempted Sipe pass at the Bronco one, caught a rebound, and went all the way.

In spite of the loss, Cleveland's performance in holding the Broncos without an offensive touchdown was encouraging. For the defense, the best was yet to come for the defense at the Kingdome in Seattle against the Seahawks' sensational quarterback, Jim Zorn. The Browns showed something new defensively, jumping in and out of an 11-man line on numerous occasions. Zorn, under constant pressure, was sacked five times, three by Alzado, as Cleveland cruised to a 27-3 victory. Five previous games produced only eight sacks.

Mike Pruitt had his first 100-yard rushing day of the season with 116 yards in 24 carries while Sipe threw touchdown passes to Charles White and Keith Wright, the little wide receiver who was making a comeback after knee surgery in 1979.

Coach Rutigliano was elated. "That's the best we've played in three years," he gushed. "It's the first time we've put together fine performances by all our units -- offense, defense and the special teams."

With six games played, the Browns had a 3-3 record and, surprisingly enough, were only a game behind an injury-riddled Pittsburgh team that had already lost two games.

There was a problem, though, as Cleveland prepared to host Green Bay at the Stadium. Sipe had suffered a second degree sprain of his left knee in the Seattle victory and was listed as a doubtful starter all week. If Sipe were unable to play, the team would have to call on Paul McDonald, a rookie who had yet to throw a pass in a regular season pro game. McDonald, a 185-pound, 6'2" lefty, was the Browns' fourth-round draft choice after he led the University of Southern California to a national championship and two Rose Bowl victories. The youngster prepared all week to replace Sipe in the lineup.

Sipe, though, was ready when Sunday rolled around, gimpy knee and all. He was superb in another miracle finish. The Browns took a 13-0 lead, but Bart Starr's Packers chipped away and finally took the lead, 21-13, with seven minutes remaining.

It took only 28 seconds for Sipe to cut the margin to one point. First he hit Calvin Hill, the aging former Yale and Dallas Cowboy star, on a pass play that covered 50 yards. He followed with a 19-yard strike to tight end Ozzie Newsome in the end zone. With 16 seconds remaining, Sipe produced more lightning, this time a 46-yard touchdown pass to Dave Logan, to give Cleveland a 26-21 victory. That day Sipe completed 24 out of 39 passes for 391 yards, the second best one-game passing performance in the team's history. He also ran for 33 yards.

The same weekend, when Pittsburgh lost its third game, a 45-34 decision to Oakland, the awakening Browns found themselves in a three-way tie for first place with the Oilers and the Steelers -- but with Coach Noll's defending Super Bowl champions on the horizon the following Sunday.

It was time to find out whether the Browns were really improved or not. As the team began practice on the Wednesday before the game, Charles White was nowhere in sight. He reappeared later and was immediately sent to Sam's office. "I let him talk and he didn't talk long," said Sam. "He said he had made a mistake and that he had no excuse to offer. I proceeded to tell him about the magnitude of missing practice." As a penalty, White was slapped with a stiff fine, reportedly in excess of $500. There was speculation that White had overslept and had been too embarrassed to admit it.

On Sunday, the Browns hosted their old enemy, the limping champions from Pittsburgh. The Steeler injury list had grown to epidemic proportions. Quarterback Terry Bradshaw, super receivers Lynn Swann and John Stallworth and rugged Franco Harris were out of the offensive lineup. Fearless Jack Lambert, the intimidating linebacker, was sidelined from the defense. Imagine the Browns playing without Sipe, Reggie Rucker, Dave Logan and Mike Pruitt!

The Steelers put their fate in the hands of a young man who grew up on Cleveland Browns football, Cliff Stoudt of Oberlin, Ohio, who had starred at nearby Youngstown State University. The 79,095 people at Cleveland Stadium were treated to an exciting aerial circus between the veteran Sipe and the Pittsburgh understudy. Stoudt, who made the fans forget about Terry Bradshaw with a 310-yard passing day, propelled the Steelers to a 26-14 lead early in the fourth quarter. Then Sipe went to work. First he capped a 73-yard drive with a seven yard scoring pass to Greg Pruitt, then he rifled an 18-yard pass to Ozzie Newsome for the go-ahead touchdown. Don Cockroft's extra point made it 27-26. Stoudt wasn't finished. The young quarterback tried to put together one more drive but was stifled when cornerback Ron Bolton intercepted on the Pittsburgh 47 with 1:53 remaining. The Browns had their first victory over the Steelers in seven tries dating back to 1976, and, more importantly, shared the AFC Central lead with Houston with a 5-3 record.

One of the very bright spots on that exhilarating day for the Browns was the work of Greg Pruitt, who caught eight passes for 71 yards. The tough little running back from Oklahoma showed he was coming all the way back from knee surgery. His return to form promised to give the already potent Cleveland passing game another dimension.

But the joy over Pruitt's return was offset by bad news about Jerry Sherk. The injured defensive tackle had been ruled out for the season and there were doubts that he would ever play football again. Enter a young man named Marshall Harris, who replaced Sherk at New England. The 261-pound, 6'6" defensive end from Texas Christian, an eighth-round draft choice by the New York Jets in 1979, walked out of the New York training camp that summer to pursue a career as an art director in a Manhattan advertising agency. In December, he went back, hat in hand, to the Jets and asked for another chance to make the team. He was told bluntly: "We don't take players like you back." Harris was signed by the Browns as a free agent and now was the third starter on the defensive line.

The Browns had a three-game winning streak to carry into the second half of the season and another date on TV's Monday Night Football against the Chicago Bears. A crowd of 83,224 at the Stadium (largest in the NFL for the season) and a national TV audience were left on the edges of their seats until the end by the thrilling play. Once again, the Browns had trouble maintaining a comfortable lead, achieved by Mike Pruitt's 129 yard rushing performance and a 298 yard throwing show by Sipe. Cleveland's 27-7 fourth quarter lead was cut to just six points, 27-21, when Vince Edwards passed to Robin Earl with 45 seconds remaining. The Bears tried an onside kick, but the ball was recovered by Cleveland cornerback Judson Flint. Sipe's statistics for the night put him ahead of two former Cleveland stars of the past in total passing yards. Brian now had 13,534 yards to 13,499 for Otto Graham and 13,361 for Frank Ryan, heroes of earlier generations.

The Browns were splendid in containing Chicago's super star, Walter Payton, limiting the NFL's No. 2 rusher of 1979 to only 30 yards. But what still concerned Rutigliano was the team's inability, once again, to mount a pass rush when it counted. That problem was made worse by the fact that the next opponent was Baltimore, whose quarterback, Bert Jones, was one of the league's slickest.

At Baltimore, the Kardiac Kids repeated their death-defying routine. The Browns had an apparently comfortable 28-13 lead late in the fourth quarter, but the talented Jones engineered two touchdowns in the final 1:27, the last coming on a five-yard pass to Don McCauley with 19 seconds remaining. Steve Mike-Mayer, who had missed an extra point try for the Colts in the second quarter, converted to make it 28-27. Then it was time for the inevitable last-minute onside kick against the Browns.

Mike-Mayer booted the ball softly and it was caught -- and dropped by Thom Darden. Somehow, defensive back Autry Beamon outmuscled a gang of Colts and preserved the victory.

After the game, Rutigliano seemed to echo what everyone else was thinking when he said: "We can't seem to do things the easy way."

If there was one unhappy truth that summed up the Browns' frustrations of the 70s, it was that they had never won a game at Pittsburgh's Three Rivers Stadium, opened at the beginning of the decade. Now they were rolling into Three Rivers with a five-game winning streak and a share of the lead in the AFC Central. This, however, was a different Steeler team from the one the Browns had met three Sundays earlier. Bradshaw, Swann, Harris and Lambert all were back. Only the fleet Stallworth was missing.

It was a classic struggle between the two turnpike rivals. Cleveland took a 13-7 lead at the half. Neither team could mount a score during the third period, but late in the fourth quarter the Steelers began driving. The clock had just nudged under three minutes and the Cleveland defense, which had picked off Terry Bradshaw four times, stopped Pittsburgh one yard short of the goal line.

Cleveland took over within the shadow of the goal posts, but could only muster two yards in three plays. Rather than face the prospect of Johnny Evans punting from the back of the end zone, Sam ordered the back-up quarterback/punter to fall on the ball in the end zone, giving Pittsburgh a safety and two points. This cut Cleveland's margin to 13-9, but Evans had the luxury of a free kick from the 20 yard line, unmolested by rushing Pittsburgh linemen.

Pittsburgh's Theo Bell caught Evans' kick on his own 30 and ripped off an 18-yard return to the 48, with 1:44 remaining. By the time the clock had slid to 17 seconds, Bradshaw had the Steelers on the Cleveland three, setting the stage for one of the most controversial plays of the season. The balding, blonde Bradshaw rolled to the left and passed to Lynn Swann in the left corner of the end zone just before he fell out of bounds. The Cleveland defense was all over the officials, claiming that Pittsburgh's Theo Bell had "picked" or blocked cornerback Ron Bolton by running into him, thus enabling Swann to dash into an open area. The cries for an offensive interference penalty went unheard and Pittsburgh had a 16-13 victory. The Three Rivers jinx was still alive, partly beause Don Cockroft, the 13-year veteran, had missed three field goals.

The Browns packed up their pride and returned to Cleveland to face the Cincinnati Bengals, led by a new coach, Forrest Gregg. He had coached for three years at Cleveland, 1975-1977, and had been unceremoniously fired by Art Modell, paving the way for the hiring of Rutigliano. Gregg subsequently had made it clear he did not think he had been treated fairly in Cleveland and the newspapers were filled with stories about a Gregg "vendetta" against the Browns.

"Unfortunately, I can't play in the game," Gregg said. "I'd be a lot more emotional about it. It wasn't a pleasant experience in Cleveland. All anyone can ask for is another opportunity. I have it here.'' That fresh opportunity had been given Gregg by Paul Brown, who had been fired by Modell 18 years earlier as Cleveland's coach and general manager.

Rutigliano himself stayed out of the controversy. "Frankly," he said, "if you can't say something good about somebody, then don't say anything," he remarked.

The game turned out to be an easy victory; one of the few times in 1980 when Cleveland built up a big lead and didn't blow it. Cincinnati took a 7-0 edge, but Sipe came back with four touchdown passes to pace a 31-7 rout, helped by the fact that the Browns' defense intercepted Bengal quarterback Ken Anderson on two occasions. The icing on the cake was a 31-28 overtime victory by the New York Jets and another Pittsburgh loss. The Browns, at 8-4, were again tied with the Oilers for the AFC Central lead. Their next stop was the Astrodome.

There had been many heroes in the first 12 games of this storybook season, but the Browns found a new one in Houston. No one had heard much about Cleo Miller, the six-year veteran from Arkansas-Pine Bluff who had filled in admirably in 1979 when Gregg Pruitt was knocked out of action. Miller, who had carried only 12 times to date in 1980, knifed over for touchdowns of six and one yard as the Browns took a 14-7 halftime lead. In the third quarter, the 214-pound fullback took off on a brilliant 50-yard run that paved the way for a 25-yard Don Cockroft field goal, giving the Browns a 17-7 lead. The Oilers came back with a 30-yard touchdown pass from Stabler to reliable Dave Casper and the extra point to shave the margin to 17-14. It was nail biting time again.

Stabler, whose specialty in his career with Oakland had been pulling games out of the fire, tried desperately to salvage a win, or at least to tie the game and send it into overtime. For a moment it appeared that the bearded veteran would succeed. But strong safety Clarence Scott intercepted Stabler's last desperate pass at the Cleveland 42 to preserve the 17-14 victory. No one could remember when Cleveland had won a more important game.

Rutigliano was ecstatic about the performance of his defensive unit which twice intercepted Stabler and "limited" Earl Campbell to 106 yards, no small accomplishment. "I really thought we'd need 24 to 30 points to win," Sam said in the postgame uproar of the team dressing room, "but we didn't because the defense keeps getting better and better, like a good wine. From here on we're going to play like hell. I don't see how we'll let anybody stand in our way."

It was now up to the Browns. They had a 9-4 record and a one-game lead with three games remaining. The future was squarely in their own hands. Three straight victories and the impossible dream was theirs.

As the Browns rallied to overcome their early season woes and establish themselves as a real contender in the AFC Central Division, the fires of enthusiasm among Cleveland fans burned more brightly with each succeeding week. But you could not blame Clevelanders if they viewed the spectacle of the Browns making a run for the AFC Central title with cautious optimism. They had been disappointed so many times in the past.

Following the Houston game, the frustration of years was put aside and a new feeling of pride and confidence in the team took over. In the closing minutes of the Browns-Houston telecast, Cleveland TV station WKYC announced the Browns' arrival time at Cleveland Hopkins International Airport. Cleveland's most loyal fans immediately picked up the cue. They knew what to do, where to go, to give expression to their joy.

More than 15,000 screaming fans jammed the airport grounds and terminal that night, creating a monumental traffic jam outside the sprawling facility and stifling conditions within the terminal itself, where the air conditioning system couldn't handle the mass of humanity. Dozens of people collapsed from heat exhaustion and had to be treated at a makeshift emergency room. Crowds battered police barricades and flooded the South Concourse, where the Browns' plane was scheduled to arrive. No one could remember such a civic outpouring for any Cleveland sports team in recent history.

In their exuberance, the fans did more than $10,000 damage to the airport. "This is the last terminal arrival for the Browns this year," warned Airport Director George Doughty. "As far as I'm concerned, they can schedule arrivals some place other than the airport."

The enthusiasm was marvelous, but the Browns still had three more football games left to play, including an impending Stadium clash with the New York Jets, the same 3-10 Jets who had upset the Oilers in an overtime game earlier that autumn.

The Jets game was another heart-stopper. Once again the Browns were unable to hold onto a lead. A 10-0 third quarter margin suddenly became a 14-10 New York bulge when Jet quarterback Richard Todd passed five yards to Mickey Shuler midway in the fourth quarter. It took Brian Sipe six plays to move the Browns back on top for good. The key play was a 45-yard bomb to Reggie Rucker, which set up a five-yard scoring pass to Greg Pruitt, who finished the game with 10 catches, the most receptions in a game by a Browns receiver since 1952. Cockroft's extra point made the margin, 17-14. Sipe had a record 30 completions for 340 yards on a day when the Browns muffed several scoring opportunities.

Never before had Cleveland fans been treated to a more graphic illustration of the intensity and dedication of defensive end Lyle Alzado than they were given in the New York game. In the second quarter, the bearded graduate of Yankton College pulled a hamstring muscle and limped to the sidelines. Team doctors warned him that if he played any more against the Jets he risked aggravating the injury and missing the rest of the season. Nevertheless, early in the fourth quarter, when the Jets were moving toward the touchdown that would put them ahead, Alzado sneaked back onto the field. "At first Marty Schottenheimer grabbed me and pulled me back," Alzado said later with a grin. "He wanted to keep me out. But that's a big sideline. I went down to the other end of the bench when Marty had his back turned and I went in and sent Elvis Franks out." Alzado remained in during most of the fourth quarter because, as he said, "I wanted to fire 'em up."

There were two games to play and the 10-3 Browns needed a victory at Minnesota or a loss by Houston at Green Bay to clinch their first play-off berth since 1972. They got neither. In 14 horrifying seconds at Bloomington, Minnesota, what appeared to be a sure play-off spot was torn from Cleveland's grasp. Midway through the fourth quarter, Mike Pruitt culminated a 16-play, 83-yard drive with a five yard run into the end zone and Don Cockroft's perfect placement gave the Browns a 23-9 lead. Two minutes and 15 seconds later, the Vikings closed the gap to 23-15 on a Tommy Kramer to Sammy White pass.

With 2:18 remaining and the Browns trying to run out the clock, Sipe faded back on a second and nine play from the Cleveland 41, and threw the ball right into the arms of Minnesota's Bobby Bryant at the 44. The Viking defender returned it to the 47. Five plays later, Kramer tossed a 12-yard scoring pass to Ahmad Rashad and Rick Danmeier's point after shaved Cleveland's lead to one point with 1:35 left to play.

Cleveland tried unsuccessfully to play out the clock once again, but with 14 seconds remaining a Johnny Evans punt gave the Vikes the ball at their own 20. There was time for one play, maybe two and 80 yards to go. Kramer passed to Joe Senser who lateraled to Ted Brown and the Vikings somehow managed to get out of bounds at the Cleveland 46, a gain of 34 yards. The clock showed four seconds remaining. Kramer lined up receivers Rashad, Terry LeCount and Sammy White on the right side, sent them streaking, and fired the ball high and far into the right corner, hoping for a catch, a volley ball tip, interference -- anything. It was the consummate prayer shot.

The Browns defenders were on the spot. Thom Darden jumped and batted the ball down. Unmercifully, it landed in Rashad's left hand for a miracle catch as time ran out. Danmeier's extra point was academic. The Vikings had scored 19 points in the fourth quarter to win, 28-23. "I should have intercepted the ball," Darden said of the Alley-Oop pass. "I got my hands on it. The ball hit my left hand and I guess it ricocheted off and the next thing I knew Rashad had it."

In the stunned Cleveland dressing room, Art Modell cornered Brian Sipe and said "great game." Sipe responded coolly, "Next week, Art. That's the great thing about this. Next week this will be forgotten."

In spite of the heart-breaking loss, more than 1,000 fans showed up to greet the Browns when they returned from Minneapolis. This time, the team's aircraft parked next to the old Army Tank Plant, well away from the main terminal area.

Fifteen weeks of competition all boiled down to one last game. The Browns and Houston were tied for the lead in the AFC Central and, unbelievably, in this final week of the season, not one team had clinched an AFC title, not one "wild-card" spot had been settled. The AFC East was still up for grabs between Buffalo (10-5) and New England (9-6) and San Diego and Oakland were tied at 10-5 in the West. Even Pittsburgh, with a 9-6 record, had a slim, slim chance for a play-off berth and an opportunity to defend its Super Bowl title.

The season's action boiled down to this: A victory at Cincinnati would give the Browns the title in the AFC Central, regardless of what Houston did in its finale against Minnesota. The victory would leave Cleveland with an 8-4 record against AFC teams, while the best Houston could do was 7-5. If both teams lost -- Houston against Minnesota, a National Football Conference foe -- both would be tied 7-5 in AFC play, but the Oilers would be Central champions because they would have a better record in the AFC -- Houston 4-2 vs. Cleveland's 3-3. The only other hope for a "wild-card" spot for the Browns rested in a New Orleans upset of New England and that was extremely remote. The Saints had won only one of 15 games.

Ernest Hemingway couldn't have written a better scenario for this last chapter of the regular season. It was not forgotten by anyone who followed the fortunes of the Browns that they had lost the last game of the previous two seasons at Cincinnati, 48-12, in 1978, and 16-12, in 1979. And now, Forrest Gregg and Paul Brown, two men dismissed by Art Modell, had the richest of opportunities for revenge -- right on their own turf. Even without that emotional component, the Bengals were to be feared, especially as they had already won twice as many games in 1980 as in 1979, and were riding a three-game winning streak.

Gregg toyed with understatement in an interview with veteran *Plain Dealer* writer and columnist Chuck Heaton when asked about the significance of the fact that both he and his boss had been axed by Modell. "Every game is important and this one is no different because it's the Browns," Gregg told Heaton. "Sure, we want to win. That would make it four straight and provide something that would carry over to next season. I know the Browns will come in here highly motivated. They will be a firey team desperately wanting to win. Our team has no place to go but home."

On Saturday, December 20, the Browns held their final workout at Baldwin-Wallace College in Berea, lunched and reported to Cleveland Hopkins International Airport for Delta Flight 845 to Cincinnati. At about 3 that afternoon they checked into their Cincinnati hotel to the accompaniment of cheers by nearly 100 fans who had camped at the hotel awaiting their arrival. One Browns fan had a portable tape player that was blaring out a parody rendition of "The Twelve Days of Christmas" that featured the Cleveland Browns instead of "a partridge in a pear tree." The song had been selling like hotcakes in Cleveland. With the exception of a brief 15-minute team meeting at 6 p.m., the players were then turned loose on their own, free to dine anywhere on the $16 provided by the club, but with instructions to be in their rooms by 11 p.m bed check. In the meantime, there was revelry in Cincinnati's bars and restaurants. Anticipating a return to glory, thousands of Cleveland fans had made the trip to the Queen City and were whooping it up.

Sunday dawned bitterly cold but clear. At the appointed 8 a.m. wake-up hour, several players already were straggling into Bronze Room A on the second floor of the South Tower for a pre-game taping by trainer Leo Murphy and assistant Bill Tessendorf. Players removed shoes and socks, hoisted themselves on eight foot tables and sat patiently while their ankles were wrapped. Many, especially those with cowboy boots, deferred the operations until they reached the stadium, because it was difficult to get the boots back on over their taped ankles.

As is traditional on Browns' road trips, the players had their choice of Catholic or ecumenical services. They had plenty for which to pray.

At 9 a.m., in the same room where the taping had occurred, the Browns gathered for their traditional pre-road game meal, a buffet featuring such usual breakfast favorites as spaghetti, white fish, strip steaks, scrambled eggs, bacon, pancakes, dry cereals, baked potatoes and buttered or dry toast. A lot of the players ate spaghetti. Lyle Alzado, the hulking defensive star, wolfed down a small portion of scrambled eggs and was out of the hotel a few minutes after the meal started. He got into a cab with Leo Murphy, Bill Tessendorf and Dr. Leonard Greenbaum, the team's osteopathic physician, and was on the way to Riverfront Stadium. Alzado always likes to get to the game site early so that he can begin whipping himself into an emotional frenzy.

The Browns had scheduled two busses to make the 10-minute trip to Riverfront, one at 10 a.m. and the other at 11:15. Most of the coaches and many of the players, including Brian Sipe, Greg Pruitt, Reggie Rucker, Calvin Hill, Cleo Miller, Dave Logan and Clay Matthews, were on the first bus to depart for the field.

At Riverfront Stadium, on the banks of the Ohio River, Sipe left the bus, went to the dressing room, dropped off a shoulder bag and headed for the field. Dressed in street clothes, the Cleveland quarterback began a pre-game ritual -- walking the field. Even though Riverfront has artificial turf, he checked the footing at several points on the field, the wind conditions, sunny and shady areas and carefully noticed the location of the 30-second clock. Satisfied that he had done his homework, Sipe returned to the dressing room to join his teammates.

Despite the importance of the game, there seemed to be an air of confidence in the locker room as the Browns dressed for game No. 16. For the players this was their Super Bowl. Nothing else mattered. The Browns hustled onto the field for their pre-game warm-ups and were greeted by a heart-warming sight, a sea of brown and orange, and cheers from their faithful followers. They were not alone. Then they returned to the locker room for some words from Sam. He was not a classic locker room orator, preferring instead to talk to his players in almost a fatherly manner. "Look," he said softly, "there are 800,000,000 Chinese who don't give a damn if we win or lose." He urged them to "hang loose" and to play with "controlled intensity."

"We're a team with hope," Rutigliano stressed. "Cincinnati is a team that's going home for the winter." The situation favored a team with hope. "When you lose, you find a way to lose," he said. "And when you win, you find a way to win."

He reminded them of the disaster in Minnesota the previous week and recalled reading books by members of the Kennedy family, especially Rose Kennedy who had lost two sons to assassins' bullets.

"The tragedy itself was difficult," Rutigliano said. "But the way in which you react after the tragedy is far more important."

Though he was not trying to compare the loss of a football game to the Kennedy tragedies, the message was clear: Forget about what happened in Minnesota and face the future. That future was upon them.

As Don Cockroft prepared to kick off for the Browns, the skies were sunny, the temperature was 15 degrees and the wind was blowing a moderate 11 miles per hour. Cockroft approached the ball and lofted a high kick that was taken well short of the goal line and returned to the Bengal 37. On the first play from scrimmage, second year quarterback Jack Thompson from Washington State, substituting for injured veteran Ken Anderson, handed off to Pete Johnson, a muscular 260-pound former Ohio State fullback. Johnson had missed five games with injuries and the Bengals had lost them all. Now back in good health he was on a tear and had racked up four straight 100-yard plus games. On the first play from scrimmage Johnson barreled ahead for seven yards. The Browns stopped him with a one yard gain on the next play, but a face mask penalty gave Cincinnati a first down at midfield. A four-yard burst by Johnson and an incomplete pass set up a third and six at the Cleveland 46. On the next play, Thompson fired a pass over the middle to Pat McInally, the Bengals' wide receiver and punter. McInally made a leaping catch and simultaneously Thom Darden hit him in an attempt to strip him of the ball. The four-year veteran from Harvard dropped the ball like a lead sinker and fell backwards unconscious to the artificial turf. For ten minutes the 210-pound, 6'6" Bengal lay prone on the green carpet while doctors and trainers worked to revive him. He was finally removed from the field on a stretcher, suffering what appeared to be a severe neck injury. Darden was socked with a 15-yard personal foul penalty which gave the ball to Cincinnati on the Cleveland 31. However, the best Cincinnati could do was a 42-yard field goal by Jim Breech. (Darden later claimed the terrifying blow was unintentional, but after reviewing films of the hit, NFL officials socked the veteran free safety with a $1,000 fine for what was described as an "unnecessarily rough" blow.)

The Bengals, angered by the injury to McInally, continued to play with great intensity and the first quarter ended with Cincinnati leading 3-0. Early in the second period, after the Bengals drove 76 yards for a touchdown to open up a 10-0 margin, there were no smiles on the Cleveland sideline.

After the Cincinnati kick-off, Sipe uncranked his talented throwing arm and culminated a 66 yard drive with a 42-yard scoring pass to 33-year-old Reggie Rucker, who made a finger tip catch at the 15 and ran into the end zone. Cockroft's extra point made it 10-7 with 7:06 left in the half. The Bengals, unable to generate anything offensively in the next series of downs, sent in a punter. Who? None other than McInally, who apparently made a miraculous recovery. The injury turned out to be stretched neck muscles. After McInally was roughed by Oliver Davis on the punt, the

Bengals were given an automatic first down which they failed to take full advantage of.

With 34 seconds remaining in the half, the Browns got a big break. Charlie Hall recovered a fumbled Cleveland punt on the Bengals nine. Sipe missed on three straight passes and Sam sent in Cockroft to kick a 26-yard field goal. The cross-state rivals went to the dressing room at half-time tied 10-10.

A 39-yard kick-off return by little Dino Hall gave the Browns excellent field position at the Cincinnati 47 to start the second half. On the second play of the period Sipe threw a pass to the outside and Ray Griffin, former Ohio State defender and brother of two-time Heisman Trophy winner, Archie (also with Cincinnati), intercepted and ran unmolested 52 yards into the end zone. Breech's extra point put Cincinnati in front again, 17-10.

On the fifth play of a drive that started on the Cleveland 31, Sipe hit substitute wide receiver Ricky Feacher with a 35-yard touchdown strike. Cockroft converted and it was 17-all. Two plays after the kick-off, the Browns got another break as Ron Bolton made his sixth interception of the season and 33rd in his career. Feacher, a 5'10'' speedster from Mississippi Valley, was a hero once again, making an uncanny catch on a 34-yard pitch from Sipe, to put the Browns out in front for the first time. Cockroft's conversion made it 24-17.

With 14 seconds left in the third quarter, Thompson and McInally combined on a sensational 59-yard touchdown pass and it suddenly was 24-all. The game was still up for grabs. With just 15 minutes left to play, an entire season was in the balance for the Browns.

As the two teams parried offensive thrusts in the final quarter, it became obvious that the Kardiac Kids needed another miracle. New England had come from behind to beat New Orleans and the Browns' ticket to the play-offs could be purchased only in Cincinnati. McInally, the hero moments earlier, provided the opportunity when he lofted a 14-yard punt that drifted out of bounds at the Cleveland 45 with 6:04 remaining. Sipe consumed more than 4½ minutes driving the Browns to the Cincinnati five where the touchdown drive sputtered. Don Cockroft was called in to attempt what probably was the most important field goal of his career and he responded with a perfect 22-yard shot that gave the Browns a 27-24 lead with 1:29 remaining.

It still was not over. Despite an injury that had kept him out of the game for 58½ minutes, Forrest Gregg inserted Ken Anderson for the final series after the Bengals had returned the kick-off to their own 32. With third and seven on their own 35, Anderson, a nine-year veteran, and rookie wide receiver Steve Krieder combined for a 32-yard pass play that gave Cincinnati a first down at the Cleveland 43. Anderson tossed nine yards to Dan Ross at the Cleveland 34, and then hastily threw the ball out of bounds on the next play to stop the clock with four seconds remaining. On the next play, Anderson passed 20 yards to Krieder who was nailed by Ron Bolton about ten yards inside the sideline. Bolton held Krieder down as time ran out. The Browns were champions of the AFC Central and in the play-offs for the first time in eight years.

In an enclosed box high above the artificial turf, Art Modell was visibly ecstatic. In the Browns locker room, Sam Rutigliano, the Brooklyn native who had made good, knelt with his players in prayer. As the players got to their feet, one of the Browns yelled, "For all the good guys -- thank you."

Sam Rutigliano, who never has trouble finding a word to say, called it his most fulfilling season as a coach. And then in what surely was the understatement of the day added: "Our guys gave it all they had all season, and won in spite of the coaching!"

Brian Sipe, who completed 24 of 44 passes for 308 yards and three touchdowns, said the turning point in the game was Ray Griffin's 52-yard touchdown on one of Sipe's two interceptions of the day. "I got mad when that happened," he said. "I think we all got mad. After Griffin ran it back, I felt more aggressive than I had at anytime in the game, and I was determined that they wouldn't beat us."

The Browns, coaches, officials and the media piled into three buses for the quick trip across the Ohio River to the Greater Cincinnati Airport, which actually is in Kentucky. Once airborne, the Delta crew broke out the champagne and there was a noisy victory celebration during the 40 minute flight to Cleveland. Art Modell, who had been maligned for years because of the Browns' inability to make the play-offs, toasted his players on the public address system. Brian Sipe walked the length of the plane and shook hands with each of his teammates.

As the plane approached Cleveland Hopkins Airport, the players decided on the order of exit upon their arrival at the tank plant, where a long welcoming platform had been put in place. Rutigliano, the architect of Cleveland's best won-loss record in more than a decade, would be first, then the assistant coaches and finally, the players. And that's the way it was as more than 15,000 fans cheered the Cleveland Browns for their most important victory in 16 years -- for an incredible season. Sipe, dressed in corduroy pants, a sweater and open jacket, told screaming fans: "We won this one for you, Cleveland."

And in the din, Mayor George Voinovich greeted the players and shouted: "This is the best thing that's happened to the city since I've been mayor, next to getting out of default." Then he paused and added, "But, maybe this is more important."

He was right. For a once beleagured city, it was.

2

"Red Right 88"

The basement of the sprawling home in Waite Hill east of Cleveland was an unlikely place for a morning at the movies. On a cold December day in 1977 four men were huddled around a portable projector watching game films of the Cleveland Browns. The host was Art Modell and with him were Peter Hadhazy and Mike Nixon, chief of college scouting for the club. The fourth man was 45-year old Sam Rutigliano, who was eagerly seeking his first coaching job in pro football.

This was a test for Sam. Modell was already becoming impressed with Rutigliano as a man and a personality, but wanted to find out how much the candidate really knew about football and how he rated the Cleveland talent. He had invited Nixon to attend to make an appraisal of Rutigliano's football mind. Nixon, an old hand at the game, was well qualified. He had previously been head coach of the Pittsburgh Steelers and the Washington Redskins. The four men spent more than two hours in the darkened basement looking at the films of the team's performances under Forrest Gregg. Sam told Modell, Hadhazy and Nixon that he was impressed with the talent he had seen on the small screen, and noted that the Browns had the nucleus of personnel to become a winning team. The Cleveland Browns did not have to be rebuilt from the ground up, he said.

Rutigliano had done his homework before coming to Cleveland. He knew that there were some who said that Brian Sipe did not have a strong enough arm to be a top NFL quarterback; that his passes sometimes fluttered or wobbled and lacked zip. The would-be coach watched Sipe carefully on the screen, studying his every move. He had been around long enough to know that the key to getting into and winning the Super Bowl was having the right quarterback as the Green Bay Packers with Bart Starr, the New York Jets with Joe Namath, the Dallas Cowboys with Roger Staubach and the Pittsburgh Steelers with Terry Bradshaw proved.

Recalling that morning in Modell's basement, Rutigliano said: "I thought people underestimated what ingredients it takes as you measure the throwing ability of a quarterback. Baseball is a great example of what I'm talking about. Somebody is always measuring the speed of pitches. But there are many pitchers who haven't been able to break a pane of glass but are great in the major leagues. And there are a bunch of guys who can throw a ball through a brick wall who are selling insurance."

Rutigliano wasn't worried about the thrust of Sipe's passes because he noticed some other things. The films showed him that Sipe very rarely missed open receivers, never turned his shoulders, and never moved his feet.

"If you look at a quarterback in the pocket, if he squares his shoulders parallel to the line of scrimmage, he's really looking to get out," Sam explained. "He's like looking to get out of a house that's on fire. He's looking for escape routes."

He saw that Sipe had great concentration in the pocket. "It's a very, very rare quality," Rutigliano said. "Brian moved around in the pocket but only so that he could see his receivers. He didn't have 'nervous feet'. When a quarterback has 'nervous feet' it usually means he's nervous from the neck up. If a quarterback has great concentration and courage and lets the ball go at the last possible second, it means he gives the receivers and their patterns a chance to develop. Most quarterbacks want to get rid of the ball faster. I saw in the films that Brian didn't -- that he kept the ball until the last possible second and took some awful shots."

It was Rutigliano's judgment after watching the films on that frosty morning that Brian Sipe had enough talent to carry Cleveland to the Super Bowl eventually. With proper coaching, the right supporting cast, nurturing and an an offense designed to maximize Sipe's talents, the young quarterback from San Diego could become one of the best.

Rutigliano, then an assistant to Hank Stram at New Orleans, told Modell, Hadhazy and Nixon that if hired, he would design an offense tailored to Brian Sipe the quarterback -- not install an attack of his own choosing and tell Sipe to run with it.

Sam Rutigliano, who grew up in the streets of Brooklyn, knew a meal ticket when he saw one, even if only on film.

When he got the job a few days later, Rutigliano called Sipe in San Diego and told him, "You're my quarterback."

Sipe, whose ride to the Browns' No. 1 quarterbacking slot had involved some strange twists, took Rutigliano's call with a grain of salt. He remembered thinking, "Well you've got to be a little bit of a politician to be head coach. He was probably trying to tell me exactly what I wanted to hear, but I could expect something less than that. I was frankly a little bit surprised when I got to know Sam a little bit better and reported to his camp and found out that, in fact, he was dead serious."

You could not blame Brian Sipe if he expected some disappointment. It had happened before, especially on the day in 1972 he was drafted into professional football. A three sport star (baseball, football and basketball) at a San Diego-area high school, Brian went to San Diego State and played under coach Don Coryell, later head mentor of the San Diego Chargers. Brian, thriving on Coryell's pro-type offensive which accentuated the passing game, set 11 school passing records and was the NCAA passing champ in 1971.

It was obvious that Sipe had some physical deficiencies. He was

Writers' Association and the *Sporting News*. But the big question now was how far Brian Sipe's considerable talents could carry the Cleveland Browns on the Road to Super Bowl XV.

The Browns had two weeks to prepare for their first play-off game, but it would be a week before they knew the identity of their opponent. On the AFC side, Buffalo had won the Eastern Divison crown with an 11-5 record, while San Diego was the winner in the Western Division with the same mark. The "wild card" teams were Houston and Oakland, second place finishers in the Central and Western, respectively. Both were 11-5.

Under the somewhat complicated play-off system, Houston and Oakland were matched in the first game. If Houston beat Oakland, Cleveland's opponent would be Buffalo, because play-off rules dictate that teams in the same division could not be matched against each other at that stage of the competition. An Oakland win over the Oilers would produce a Cleveland-Oakland matchup.

At any rate, the game would be played in Cleveland, because the Browns were division champs. Cleveland was in an emotional tizzy for two weeks. The Browns 47,000 season ticket holders had the first lock on seats for the game, leaving only about 20,000 other tickets available to the public. Those went on sale on December 23 for the game to be played on Sunday, January 4. They were swallowed up in two hours at the Cleveland Stadium and Ticketron outlets. Some playoff-hungry fans camped at the Stadium all night long to be at the head of the line when the windows opened at 10 a.m.

The town which had been battered, bruised and ridiculed, was on an emotional high. For many years Cleveland had suffered through political confrontations and upheavals as well as periods of racial tension. Its school system was literally bankrupt and emotions were torn by forced busing. Industry was fleeing to greener and warmer pastures. Cleveland had endured two years of Mayor Dennis Kucinich and an abrasive city administration, during which time the city had defaulted on millions of dollars in loans from major Cleveland banks, the first time that anyone could remember when a big city wasn't able to meet its financial obligations. The city of Cleveland's population was eroding rapidly. Once the nation's sixth largest city, Cleveland was now near the bottom of the second ten, and some folks joked that if the population drain continued, the Forest City might just become a ghost town.

Under its new mayor, George Voinovich, the city had come out of default, but the financial situation still remained critical. The news about the end of default was greeted with a general "ho hum" by the people of Cleveland and the surrounding suburbs.

Looking at other aspects of the Cleveland sports picture, the Indians baseball teams had been wallowing in mediocrity for so long that few could remember when they last were contenders for the American League pennant. And the Cleveland Cavaliers basketball team, which had moved out to a no man's land called Richfield, between Akron and Cleveland, was fast becoming the laughing stock of the National Basketball Association. In a decade of competition, they had made the play-offs only once and now seemed farther away than ever.

What Cleveland needed desperately was a rallying point, a new sense of identity. The Browns' rush to the AFC Central Division title, and the gambling, exciting, heroic way in which they had done it, provided that badly needed spark and, most importantly, a sense of pride.

Art Modell was certainly pleased with the artistic performance of the Browns. The divisional championship was vindication for the monumental chance he took in signing Sam Rutigliano. "My biggest reward, though, is what the Browns have done for the community," he said unabashedly. "That is far and away my greatest source of satisfaction, and that of the organization."

Expressions of the public euphoria were everywhere. "Go Browns!" signs cropped up in retail establishments all over town. The East Ohio Gas Company, which occupies most of a building on the corner of East Ninth and Superior, got into a hassle with its landlord when it put a huge "Go Browns" sign in the windows. After a public outcry the landlord finally rescinded his order to remove the sign.

In the three Christmas shopping days after the victory in Cincinnati, retailers were besieged by buyers for everything identified with the Cleveland Browns -- mugs, sweater, sweatshirts, Kardiac Kids bricks, huge styrofoam fingers that pointed to the Browns as "No. 1," hats, jackets, pennants, ponchos, towels. Sales were measured in millions of dollars. Players were in great demand to make personal appearances and the supply and demand situation pushed up their fees. Most of the regulars were demanding as much as $750 to $1,000 for an appearance. Sipe was offered as much as $3,000, but turned down all requests.

Late on Sunday afternoon, December 28th, most eyes in Greater Cleveland were focused on the tube as Oakland and Houston battled in the "wild card" game. The Raiders were devastating as they virtually shut down Earl Campbell and the Oilers, 27-7. Oiler Coach Bum Phillips called Oakland's performance the finest he had seen in the NFL in a decade. The mystery of whom the Browns would play on January 4 was over. It would be the Oakland Raiders, a surprise team like the Browns. In pre-season prognostications, the Raiders, coached by Tom Flores, had been picked to finish last in the Western Division, a notch above the Browns, who were figured to be third in their division.

Oakland had been one of the most consistent teams in football during the 1970s. They were in the play-offs seven out of ten seasons and won the Super Bowl in 1976. They had missed out in 1978 and 1979, and were not expected to make it in 1980. During the off-season they had made the trade with Houston which sent Ken Stabler to the Oilers for Dan Pastorini. Oakland's play-off hopes were seemingly dashed in early October when Pastorini fractured his leg. The quarterbacking duties fell to Jim Plunkett, who had been resurrected by Flores after not having lived up to expectations at New England and San Francisco. Plunkett, a Heisman Trophy winner at Stanford in 1970, had thrown only 15 passes for the Raiders in 1978 and 1979. Though he had a strong arm, Plunkett had frequently been erratic in the past. He was nothing short of sensational after replacing Pastorini, though, and was primarily responsible for bringing the Raiders into the play-off picture.

Oakland also had some superb supporting talent in people like running backs Mark Van Eeghen and Kenny King and receivers Raymond Chester and Cliff Branch. They also had another super offensive threat in punter Ray Guy, who had a booming 43.6 yards per kick average, third-best in the NFL. (On the other hand, Johnny Evans, Cleveland's punter, had one of the worst averages among the regulars at 38.6 yards.) The Raiders also had a solid defense led by left cornerback Lester Hayes, who had topped the league with 13 interceptions during the regular season, and super linebacker, Ted Hendricks.

Cleveland's winter weather was about as bad as it could have been during the week preceding the showdown between the Browns and the Raiders. Heavy snows buried the tarpaulin covering the field and the turf was frozen solid. At midweek, snowplows equipped with rubber blades cleared the snow. Huge kerosene blowers were placed under the edges of the tarp and around the clock hot air was pumped in to thaw the field. The Browns worked out in the cold all week, but the Raiders took their time getting to Cleveland -- and who could blame them? The Raiders arrived late Friday on a chartered 747, just slipping in under the NFL's mandatory rule that visiting teams must be at the site at least 36 hours before game time.

Sunday morning dawned bitterly cold. The temperature hovered near zero. Those with tickets had a choice. They could brave the elements or they could stay home and watch the game on television because it was a sell-out and the traditional blackout had been lifted. Only a few thousand decided to rough it in their family rooms. The rest, more than 77,000 persons, trundled off to Cleveland Stadium in the warmest wear they could find. Situated on the edge of Lake Erie, the Stadium is not a place for the fainthearted on wintery days, when lake winds lash in and swirl around the giant horseshoe. As they headed for the stadium on the streets of downtown Cleveland, the street merchants were out in force, selling Browns paraphernalia and souvenirs -- t-shirts, signs, woolen hats, etc. Despite the devastating cold, the entire scene had a carnival-like atmosphere.

Inside the stadium, the field looked like an island surrounded by snow and tarps strewn around at random. Hundreds of hand-made signs were hung over the upper and lower deck railings: "On to the Siper Bowl." "Believe." "Nobody but Cleveland."

Heated benches for the players had been trucked in from Philadelphia overnight after they had been used the day before in the Philadelphia-Minnesota NFC showdown which the Eagles had won. The temperature at game time was one degree with a 35 below zero wind chill factor. The wind was blowing at 16 mph from the northwest. It was not a day fit for man or beast or football.

Cockroft kicked off for the Browns and Oakland took over on its own 31, but gained only a yard in three tries. Guy then turned it over to Cleveland on a 41-yard punt. It was obvious that players on both sides were having trouble with their footing on the slippery turf. The Browns picked up only five yards on their first series and Evans punted it back, a 36-yard kick. On the third play of the next Oakland series, Ron Bolton intercepted a Plunkett pass intended for Bob Chandler on the Cleveland 27. Mike Pruitt lugged the ball on three straight carries, giving Cleveland the initial first down of the game at its own 38, but the offense fizzled and Evans was forced to punt again. His kick was short and wobbly, but it bounced right, rolling end-over-end down the field, and settled on the Raider 11.

Once again, the Raiders could not muster a first down and Guy punted one 49 yards. Dino Hall fielded the ball at the Cleveland 37 and returned to the 48, giving the Browns excellent field position. Sipe tried three straight passes and the third was picked off by Lester Hayes who brought it to the Raider 36. The Cleveland defense held and once again the Raiders kicked it away.

The two teams exchanged kicks after listless offensive efforts on the slick, frozen field and with less than two minutes remaining in the first quarter the Browns had the ball on their own 40. In three plays, Sipe had the ball on the Raider 29. As the quarter ended he caught Rucker in the end zone with a perfect pass. Rucker had it in his hands and dropped it. At the end of the first 15 minutes, the two teams were deadlocked at zero and Brian Sipe primed to strike again. Cleveland's defense had been near-perfect in the first quarter. The Raiders had been limited to 15 yards and no first downs.

Sipe could not penetrate the Oakland goal line in two more passes and Cockroft was called upon to do his thing. His 47-yard attempt was short. Cockroft had another chance to redeem himself less than two minutes later, when Sipe couldn't generate a touchdown after Plunkett was sacked and fumbled. Marshall Harris recovered the ball on the Raider 23. When the Browns stalled on the Raider 12, Cockroft tried again unsuccessfully from the 27.

Midway in the second quarter, the Raiders were still without a first down. On a third and four situation on the Oakland 32, Plunkett fired to Chandler, but Bolton stepped in front of the wide receiver, grabbed the ball at the Raider 42 and ran all the way for a touchdown. Middle linebacker Ted Hendricks blocked Cockroft's extra point try, but the fans were delirious with the Browns' 6-0 lead.

The Raiders got the ball with 6:01 remaining in the half and Plunkett went to work. After a pair of incomplete passes, the recycled quarterback finally connected with Kenny King on a 15-yard aerial and the Raiders had a first down on the Cleveland 49. It was the first time the Raiders were in Cleveland territory. By the time the clock had moved near the one-minute mark, the Raiders were on the Cleveland 28. On third and 13, Plunkett hit Chester with a 26-yard completion and the Raiders had the ball on the

Cleveland two. Mark Van Eeghen smashed into the left side of the line, fumbled, recovered the ball, and was credited with a one-yard gain. Plunkett tried to pass to tight end Derrick Ramsey, but the ball went awry. Finally, the gritty Van Eeghen lunged over right tackle for the score. Chris Bahr kicked the extra point and with 22 seconds remaining in the half the Raiders' only offense of the half had produced a 7-6 lead. Cleveland's vaunted offense had come up with no points.

Rookie Charles White streaked 28 yards with the second half kickoff to give the Browns decent field position at their own 40. In three and a half minutes the Browns moved the ball to the Oakland 12, where once again they couldn't punch it across. After missing two field goals at the open end of the stadium, Cockroft found the range at the closed end with a 30-yard kick. Cleveland was back on top, 9-6. The Browns blew another golden scoring opportunity when they drove from their own 36 to the Oakland 18. This time rookie Paul McDonald fumbled the snap on a field goal try, tried to run with the ball and was thrown for an 11-yard loss.

For the second time in the quarter, the Raiders were unable to generate anything resembling a first down and Guy punted away to Dino Hall. The little guy returned the ball 17 yards to the Oakland 44. A 21-yard pass to Logan and an interference call on the Raiders' Dwayne O'Steen gave Cleveland a first down on the Oakland 9. Greg Pruitt swept the right side for a yard. Sipe was sacked, fumbled, and the ball was recovered by Joe Delammielleure on the Raider 12. Sipe's pass to Logan in the end zone was no good and once again it was time for a field goal try. With 2:40 remaining in the period, Cockroft kicked his second field goal, a 29-yard shot, to give the Browns a 12-7 margin which was the score when the period ended.

As it had done at the end of the second quarter, the Oakland offense suddenly came to life. And in a drive which started on their own 20 on the last play of the third quarter and consumed nearly six minutes, the Raiders marched down the field. The tough running of King and Van Eeghen was masterfully combined with the passing of Plunkett, who completed passes of 19 yards to Cliff Branch and 27 yards to Chester. The Raiders had a first down and goal to go at the Cleveland three. Plunkett called on the durable Van Eeghen. He slugged ahead for two yards on the first try, then inched ahead to the one-foot line on the next. Finally, on third down he rolled over the goal line to put the Raiders out in front. Chris Bahr's conversion made it 14-12.

With the clock showing 4:39 remaining, the Browns took over the ball on their own 28, after a short Guy punt. On the first play, Sipe was forced to scramble and fumbled and Oakland's Otis McKinney recovered at the Cleveland 25. There was a stunned silence in the beige horseshoe on the lake. The Raiders called on Van Eeghen once again. One yard to the 24, eight yards to the 16, another half-yard to the 15½. Now it was fourth down and a half-yard to go for a first down. Coach Tom Flores decided against going for what would be a 32-yard field goal, and instead called for another Van Eeghen smash.

The 225-pound, 6'2'' back hurled into the right side of the Cleveland line. It did not give an inch. The Browns had the ball. They were alive, 85 yards from their own goal line. The clock showed 2:22 remaining. There was plenty of time for another miracle finish, a patented Kardiac Kids charge that would swipe victory from the Raiders in the final seconds.

On first down, Sipe's pass to Rucker was too long. On second down, Sipe slipped on the slick turf but managed to connect with Newsome on the left side for a 29-yard completion. The official signaled the the the two-minute warning and the Browns were on their own 45. The fans were on their feet yelling "Go, Go, Go."

Brian's pass to Greg Pruitt was incomplete and then the Browns quarterback lost a yard on a broken play. On a third down and 11 play, Dwayne O'Steen was called for interference on Reggie Rucker and Cleveland had a first down on the Oakland 49. Sipe then fired to Greg Pruitt down the left side, the little running back caught it and dashed out of bounds at the Oakland 28. The clock showed 1:12 remaining. After an incomplete pass, Sipe handed off to Mike Pruitt and the former Purdue star exploded up the middle for a 14-yard gain, and a first down on the Oakland 14. Pruitt went up the middle again for another yard. The Browns called time out with little more than a half-minute remaining. Rutigliano huddled with Sipe and Jim Shofner on the sidelines. If the Browns failed to gain anything in the next two downs, they could still win with a field goal. But a field goal was no sure thing, even at that distance. Don Cockroft had kicked only 18 of 32 field goals during the season, and had already missed two on the frozen turf at the open end of the Stadium. He had also been affected by knee and sciatic nerve problems since early in the season and this obviously had affected his kicking. Sipe thought the Browns would run the ball for the next two plays and was shocked when Rutigliano, who had been criticized for gambling too frequently when the situation did not dictate, called "Red Right 88," a pass play. Sam also told Sipe: "If you get in trouble and the receivers are covered, throw the ball into Lake Erie." Sipe questioned the call initially, but then agreed with the strategy to try one pass, run on the next down and attempt the field goal. On the "Red Right 88" play, Dave Logan, on the left, was the intended receiver. He was to run under the coverage into the right corner while Ozzie Newsome and Reggie Rucker were to cross over.

Sipe returned to the field, took the snap and faded back quickly. He did not want to get sacked, taking the Browns out of field goal range. Logan cut toward the right corner, but weak safety Burgess Owens was there with him. Sipe opted to throw to Newsome who was cutting over the middle to the left side of the end zone. In the meantime, Owens had cut free of Logan, leaving him wide open, and moved in front of Newsome along with strong safety Mike Davis. Sipe's pass arched slightly behind Newsome. Davis lunged for the ball and intercepted with 49 seconds remaining. The Browns had run out of miracles. The Kardiac Kids were dead for this season.

Gambling Sam had rolled the dice for six and crapped. You could hear the collective groans of the Cleveland fans all the way to Oakland, California. The Cleveland Stadium turned into a giant, frigid mausoleum and most of the fans left their seats and headed for the exits.

Sipe, who was knocked to the turf as he unloaded the ball, did not see the end of the play. He heard the fans and knew the season was over. As he walked dejectedly to the sideline, he was greeted by Rutigliano. "I love you," Sam said reassuringly. "I love you." The Raiders ran out the clock to preserve the 14-12 victory, the first stop on the road to the Super Bowl, a 27-10 win over Philadelphia and the World Championship.

Rutigliano, a compulsive gambler on the sidelines, had no apology for the call. "We felt the field goal was no gut cinch," he said in the dressing room. "It was our plan to throw on second down, then run the ball on third down and if we didn't get it into the end zone by then, go for the field goal. The play we called was a play that has been successful in the past. Unfortunately, it was an errant throw. But I'd rather put my money on Sipe's arm than take a chance on a field goal."

Sipe admitted in the locker room that he had questioned the call. "But we've done so well playing that kind of offense. I thought we would run the ball, the staff was adamant it was the right play."

Oakland's Plunkett had perhaps the most thoughtful explanation for the decision by the Browns. "I believe the wind is the reason they didn't run the ball into position for a field goal try," he said. "It was tough at that end of the field and they had those problems earlier. Remember, all the points except for the Cleveland touchdown on the interception were scored at the closed end of the field."

Strangely enough, there were no tears in the Cleveland locker room. Perhaps Brian Sipe summed it up best: "I am not going to sing the blues because we lost," he said. "We lost, but it was too great a year to be singing the blues. We did things dramatically all season, and I guess it is only fitting that we lose in a dramatic fashion."

"I am not going to let this get me down, or the team," he continued, surrounded by hordes of writers. "We've played a lot of good football. We won the AFC Central after nobody gave us a chance, and we played it right down to the wire. I'm disappointed, but I am going home to San Diego and be damned happy with what we accomplished."

"But the important thing," said Sipe, who completed only 13 of 40 passes to his frozen receivers for 182 yards and had three interceptions, "is that we had a dream -- and we almost made it come true."

There had been many more productive seasons in the 34-year history of the Cleveland Browns, but considering the fact that the Browns had been out of the play-offs for so long, there certainly had never been a more satisfying season.

3

Mickey and Paul

Unlike most National Football League teams, which are steeped in a tradition which dates from the days when professional football generally was looked upon with jaundiced eyes, the Cleveland Browns are a product of the post-World War II era. As the Browns went to training camp at Hiram, Ohio, in the summer of 1980, they were preparing for only their thirty-fourth season in professional football. The New York Giants, the Green Bay Packers and the Chicago Bears were much older.

The birth of the Cleveland Browns can be traced to a day early in September, 1940, when an 18-year-old Cleveland youngster named Arthur McBride, Jr., enrolled at the University of Notre Dame. Young Arthur was the son of Arthur McBride, Sr., known to almost everyone in Cleveland as "Mickey."

McBride, short and stocky, was a hard-nosed, wealthy businessman in his fifties, who had vast real estate holdings in Chicago, Cleveland and Florida. He owned taxicab companies in Cleveland, Akron and Canton, a radio station, a printing company and a race wire syndicate.

Arthur McBride had made it to the top the hard way. At the age of six, he was selling newspapers in Chicago. By the time he was 23, he was a two-fisted newspaper circulation executive earning $10,000 a year. In 1913, McBride moved to Cleveland as circulation director of the *Cleveland News,* where he remained until 1931, when he went into business for himself. In his own business, everything he touched seemed to turn into gold.

McBride had an overpowering knack for making money, and he had no time for such Saturday and Sunday nonsense as watching football games. Until 1940, he had never seen a game. The only thing he knew about it was that thousands of people went crazy every weekend watching 22 men maul one another.

However, all this changed one weekend during his son's years at Notre Dame. Mickey was persuaded to journey to South Bend to watch the Fighting Irish trample a helpless opponent. After the game he hopped in his car and hurried back to Cleveland so he could watch the Cleveland Rams in their National Football League game the next day. Mickey became a fan that weekend. From then on, he followed the Fighting Irish all over the country and usually saw the Rams' games on Sunday.

Professional football was still a relatively young enterprise when McBride was developing his insatiable football appetite. Those were the days when the Rams played at a Cleveland high-school stadium and found many of the field's 10,000 seats unoccupied at their Sunday afternoon games. The Rams had been a losing venture, both artistically and financially, ever since the team was founded in 1937 by Cleveland attorney Homer Marshman and a group of businessmen. In their first four seasons, the Rams won 14, lost 28 and tied 2. In June, 1941, Marshman and his associates sold the franchise to Daniel F. Reeves and Frederick Levy, Jr. The team continued to fail miserably on the field and at the gate, winning 7 and losing 16 in their first two seasons under the new owners.

The fact that the Rams and other National Football League teams continually finished in the red did not deter McBride, who had a record of success in virtually every business venture he touched. Mickey was convinced that a sound team and proper promotion could transform Cleveland into a good football city. In 1942, McBride offered to buy the Rams from Reeves, who had also acquired Levy's holdings. But Reeves refused to sell.

Two years later, McBride got his chance. Arch Ward, the promotional-minded *Chicago Tribune* sports editor, began to talk about a new professional football league, to be known as the All-America Conference. Ward, who had operated the annual College All-Star game for the *Chicago Tribune,* was convinced that the time had come to establish a second major league in pro football. He envisioned a situation in which the National Football League and the All-America Conference would operate much like the American and National Leagues did in baseball. Each season would be climaxed by a championship game between the winners in the two circuits.

McBride heard about Ward's idea and held several discussions with him. He finally agreed to put his sizable bankroll behind a team in Cleveland. "I'll go in," the soft-spoken McBride told Ward, "but I've got to have the best coach and the best players in the country. I've got to have the best promotion, too."

Ward, McBride and five other prospective club owners held a secret meeting at a St. Louis hotel on June 4, 1944, and thrashed out plans for the new league. Formal announcement of the formation of the new league was made in Chicago on September 3, 1944, and the Cleveland franchise was awarded to McBride. The news was given only minor attention in Cleveland newspapers, and no one really got excited. After all, the All-America Conference was a paper league and no one knew when it would begin operation. Besides, most Clevelanders were too preoccupied with the progress of World War II to be worried about a new professional football team.

McBride returned to Cleveland after the club owners' meeting in Chicago and set out to find his coach. He walked into the sports department of the *Cleveland Plain Dealer* one night and asked John Dietrich, the veteran and respected football writer for the morning paper, a simple question: "Who is the best football coach in the country?"

Dietrich didn't even stop to think. "Paul Brown," he answered, and proceeded to give McBride a briefing on Brown's meteoric rise in the coaching profession. He explained Brown's extraordinary success at Massillon (Ohio) High School, his jump from there to Ohio State University and then to coach of the wartime team of the Great Lakes Naval Training Station, near Chicago.

Mickey next sought Arch Ward's advice on Brown and the conversation helped to cement his chances of signing the young coaching genius. Ward had developed a close friendship with Brown during Paul's three years in the Big Ten as Ohio State's head man. He was an ideal middleman in the negotiations. Brown, who was on a leave of absence from Ohio State, was serving as a Navy lieutenant, and was stationed at the Great Lakes Naval Training Station.

Having won the national collegiate football championship in his second year at Ohio State, Brown already was a big name in coaching circles. Ward was well aware of the prestige Brown's name would give the new league. He contacted Brown and relayed McBride's proposition. No coach had ever before been offered so lucrative a deal. McBride promised Brown $1,000 a month until the end of the war -- and no one knew at that time when it would end -- and $20,000 a season, plus 15 per cent of the profits once Brown came aboard full time.

Brown listened attentively, then arranged to meet McBride. He asked McBride two significant questions: Was he really wealthy, and was he willing to spend his money to create a winning team? McBride assured Brown that he had plenty of money and was willing to spend it. Brown still was hesitant.

"He kept talking about his loyalty to some 'saint,'" McBride recalled. "It turned out to be Lynn St. John, the Ohio State athletic director. He also was telling me about his status as a professor at Ohio State and his tenure. I finally asked him if he had ever heard of the Cleveland Trust Bank and when he said 'yes,' I asked him if he could cash in his titles for money. That seemed to be the clincher."

It took three weeks of talking, but the 36-year-old, prematurely bald Brown finally signed a five-year contract in Ward's office at the *Chicago Tribune,* with the newspaper's attorneys present.

Unlike the announcement that Cleveland would have a team in the new All-America Conference, the news of Brown's signing as coach and general manager attracted wide attention. The *Cleveland Plain Dealer* carried the story on page one. John Dietrich, who had recommended Brown, wrote: "In the most astonishing football story in many years, Lt. Paul E. Brown, the Massillon boy who skyrocketed to fame as coach at Ohio State and Great Lakes, yesterday signed a five-year contract as coach and general manager of the new Cleveland professional team in the All-America Conference." And, in the *Cleveland Press,* veteran football writer Jack Clowser quoted Brown as saying, "You know me. I'll try to build a football dynasty in Cleveland."

Off the field, Paul Brown looked like a highly successful businessman, impeccably attired in conservative clothes. In a social gathering he could be warm and friendly, even downright charming. He even had an affinity for playing practical jokes. But once he donned the brown slacks, white T-shirt, football cleats and dark baseball cap which became the Brown practice session trademark, all of the warmth and charm disappeared. He was all business -- the master of the show. He was lean and hard, an appearance he kept by participating in calisthenic drills with his players. Brown was coldly efficient. He carried a long psychological needle and wasn't afraid to use it at the right time to get the most out of his players. Very often, Brown's needling at the expense of a player or players would produce laughs among his players. It was just one of his psychological tricks to keep the squad "loose."

There were many who had considered Brown's decision to leave the relative security of Ohio State University to coach the new Cleveland team as the most daring kind of move. But Brown had grown accustomed to facing tremendous odds all his football life, and somehow always had managed to wind up on top. He weighed only 100 pounds when he first reported to coach Dave Stewart as a candidate for the Massillon team in the middle 1920s. By the time he was a junior, he had grown into a 130-pounder. He quarterbacked the Tigers during his last two years in high school.

"He was like a banty rooster," Stewart recalled, "full of authority and self-confidence. When he was my quarterback, his voice rang with inspiration as he called the plays. The kids believed in him and he ran them like a Napoleon. He began to run my business, too, when he was a senior and insisted on making decisions on the substitutions."

After graduation from Massillon, Brown enrolled at Ohio Sate, but soon realized that 135 pounds wasn't heavy enough for Big Ten football. He transferred to Miami University of Oxford, Ohio, where he became a better-than-average runner and passer.

Brown's coaching career began in 1930 at Maryland's Severn Prep, a Naval Academy preparatory school. In two years, his teams rolled up a record of 16 wins, one loss and a tie. Planning on a law career, Brown attended law school for a year and a half while coaching at Severn. However, in 1932 he returned to Massillon High as head football and basketball coach and plans for the new career evaporated. The Tigers were in the athletic doldrums, but Brown rolled up his sleeves and went to work.

It was at Massillon that Brown began to demonstrate the qualities that were later to establish his reputation as football's greatest organizer. Instead of stressing immediate gridiron victories, he inaugurated a program aimed at producing a long-range policy for future success. He organized and coordinated efforts of coaches in Massillon High School with the football programs in Massillon's junior high schools. He mapped and directed the entire setup, stressing attention to fundamentals at all times.

Even so, Brown twice almost lost his job. In his first season, he inherited one member of his predecessor's coaching staff as an assistant. The coach also was a part-time farmer and left school early each afternoon to go home and handle some of the farm chores. Each afternoon, his arrival at practice became later. About halfway through the season, the assistant coach pulled up to the practice field mid-way through an afternoon session. The fenders of his car were loaded with sacks of grain. The assistant walked onto the practice field in rubber boots. Brown walked up to the aide and calmly but tersely told him in no uncertain terms that it would be unnecessary for him to report for further duty.

Summoned to the superintendent's office when he arrived at school the next morning, Brown admitted that he had sacked the assistant and said, "Everyone on my staff must be dedicated to his job. This one isn't. If you interpret my action yesterday of requesting him not to show up any more as firing him, I did."

"Suppose I told you that you were fired?" the superintendent asked.

"That's your privilege, sir," answered the 24-year-old Brown, "but I wouldn't do it if I were you."

Brown weathered the storm and finished the season with a 6-3 record. His next team won eight and lost two, and his third won all but one of ten games.

By all odds, he was a successful coach. Still, some of the Massillon wolves were out for his scalp. His team made the error of losing three straight games to neighboring Canton McKinley -- and in Massillon, that was a cardinal sin. But Brown turned his critics into believers. In the next six years, he never again lost to McKinley. In the next six seasons, his team played 60 games, winning 58, losing one and tying one.

When Brown arrived at Massillon, the school had a stadium with a capacity of 5,000. During Brown's tenure, the school built a new stadium seating 21,000. Eight home games in the 1940 season drew 161,000 people, more than any college team in the state, with the exception of Ohio State, had drawn.

The Brown success story at Massillon spread across the country, and Massillon became known as the capital of high-school football in the nation. Opponents of Massillon had to work harder just to stay on the same field, with the result that the entire level of high-school football played among the big independent schools in the state improved. The battles between Massillon and Canton McKinley drew nationwide attention. Graduates of Paul Brown's school of football at Massillon began showing up on the rosters of colleges throughout the state and across the country.

As the Massillon Tigers rolled up one state championship after another, Brown began receiving offers from small colleges throughout the state. He wasn't interested. He had only one goal in mind at that time: to be head football coach at Ohio State University.

During his coaching career at Massillon, Brown spent some summers working toward his master's degree at Ohio State. One summer evening, Brown and his wife, Katy, strolled around the campus. They walked into the university's huge stadium with its 80,882 seats. "Someday I'm going to be football coach here," he confided.

Brown got his long-awaited chance to take over the helm of Ohio State Football in 1941, when Francis Schmidt left as head coach. Brown didn't have to do much lobbying for the job. Almost everyone else did it for him. The Ohio State Athletic Committee was swamped with letters demanding that Paul Brown be hired. Governor John Bricker and OSU President Howard Bevis were bombarded with letters. The Ohio High School Football Coaches Association campaigned on Brown's behalf, and newspapers carried editorials supporting him.

Paul got the job. In his first season, he guided the Buckeyes to a record of six wins, one loss and a tie. In 1942, OSU won nine of ten games and was crowned the national collegiate champion. Calls to military service wrecked Ohio State's 1943 team, and Brown had his first losing campaign.

Not long after that Brown found himself in the service, assigned to the Great Lakes Naval Training Station and working as football coach and athletic officer. It was while he was leading the 1944 Great Lakes team to a record of nine wins, two losses and a tie that the All-America Conference was formed and he agreed to direct one of its key franchises. Brown's big job was finding people to man the coaching and playing ranks for the new organization. He knew the kind of men he wanted and went after them with relentless pursuit. Paul Brown's careful selection of his associates was to pay unprecedented dividends for more than a decade. With his characteristic determination and enthusiasm he plunged head-long into the huge organizational task of getting McBride's venture under way.

4

The Maestro from Waukegan

While Paul Brown was establishing himself as a coaching wizard at Massillon High school and Ohio State University, a dark-haired young man from Waukegan, Illinois, was proving himself to be an athlete of unusual ability. He was Otto Graham, Jr., whose father was music instructor at Waukegan High School and whose mother taught the same subject in a rural Illinois school system. Otto could play the French horn, the piano, the violin and the cornet well, but it was his athletic accomplishments that made him the darling of Waukegan. He earned a batch of letters in basketball, football and track. In basketball, he set a new scoring record in the Chicago Suburban League and became the first Waukegan boy ever to win a place on the Illinois All-State first team. In football, he was good enough at halfback to win a third-team berth on the All-State team.

Waukegan, like most Illinois towns, was basketball mad. Players on the basketball teams were full-fledged community heroes. Gyms were packed for every game. In comparison, there usually were plenty of vacant seats at football games.

Despite the fact that Graham was being hailed as "the greatest [Illinois] high school basketball player since Lou Boudreau roamed the hardwood for Thornton Township," there was no great collegiate clamor for his services. And those who did want him were primarily interested in his basketball talents. "I had a couple of offers to go to college," Graham recalled years later. "No Cadillacs, though. Just a plain tuition scholarship. For Basketball, of course." He chose Northwestern and entered in February, 1939.

The amazing part of the Otto Graham story is the fact that he wasn't even invited out for the football team in his freshman year. But Otto was a basketball player through and through, and this didn't bother him. During the fall of 1939, he contented himself with playing intramural football. "We had four or five All-Staters on our intramural team and we had a lot of fun," he said. Through the grapevine, word reached the Northwestern football coaching staff that there was a freshman playing in the intramural league who could really toss the football. The coaches took in some of the games and Graham was invited to try out for the team.

Graham performed well in spring practice in 1940, but tore a ligament in his knee. When it still bothered him that fall, he was advised to have an operation and drop out of school to save a year of playing eligibility. He agreed.

He came back in 1941 and played tailback, as understudy to the nationally famous Bill DeCorrevant. In 1942, he was understudy to no one. He was great, displaying maturity, poise and a priceless gift for football strategy. He was rated as one of the greatest passers in college football. But despite his individual brilliance, Northwestern finished the 1942 season with a record of one win and nine defeats. "The best team ever to finish last in the Big Ten," noted one columnist.

In 1943, Graham pulled his team up from last place to second in the Big Ten. He was phenomenal as a passer, dangerous as a runner, strong on defense and a powerful kicker. Northwestern finished with an 8-2 record, and Otto Graham was named All-American. He was also awarded the *Chicago Tribune* Trophy as the most valuable player in the Western Conference. In three seasons at Northwestern, Graham completed 157 of 321 passes for 2,162 yards, a conference record at the time.

Graham was the scourge of the Big Ten in basketball and also earned his spurs as a baseball player. He picked up eight letters at Northwestern -- three in football, three in basketball and two in baseball.

Graham turned from his great 1943 football campaign to the hardwood and had some of his finest basketball moments. But he decided to pass up the second half of the 1943-44 cage season and graduate early so that he could enter the Navy V-12 flying program.

Before his graduation, Northwestern honored him at a special pre-game basketball game. Typical of the plaudits heaped on Graham that evening were the comments written for the occasion by Kenneth S. (Tug) Wilson, Western Conference football commissioner:

"I have been in the coaching business for longer than you have been alive, and it has been my pleasure to know many fine, outstanding young men. As I sit here thinking about that group, there are many who stand out by their actions on the playing field and their conduct off it. Occasionally, there is an individual who, by his sheer ability and personality, stands head and shoulders above all the rest. That, in my book, is Otto Graham."

His college career ended, Graham headed for the University of North Carolina at Chapel Hill and the Navy V-12 program. Shortly after his arrival, he received a letter from Gus Dorais, coach of the Detroit Lions of the National Football League. There was nothing really urgent about it. It merely notified Graham that he had been chosen by the Lions in the annual player draft. "This draft rule means that if you have any desire to play football in the National League, it would have to be with the Detroit Lions," Dorais wrote. A few years later, Graham was to recall, "Nobody ever mentioned salary or anything like that. I was their property so they weren't worrying about me."

Graham put his football talents to work for the North Carolina Pre-Flight team in the fall of 1944 as a fullback and later as a T-quarterback. It was his first experience behind the center in the T-attack and he performed well.

Meanwhile, Paul Brown already was thinking about his postwar pro football team. After watching Graham work with the North Carolina team, Brown knew he was the man he wanted for his quarterback. Unlike the Detroit Lions, who were content to take Otto for granted, Brown went after the talented Graham, who had been described as "the greatest thing to come out of Waukegan since Jack Benny." Brown offered Graham $250 a month through the rest of the war if he would sign with the still-nameless Cleveland entry in the All-America Conference. Graham liked the money and signed.

Soon after Brown's appointment to the Cleveland job, owner Mickey McBride arranged for Paul to spend a weekend in the city and to attend a football luncheon. Newspapermen from all over the state were invited. Thomas A. Burke, then mayor of Cleveland, was present, as were other city officials, representatives of the Chamber of Commerece, the Advertising Club and many of the state's high-school and college coaches.

"Cleveland is basically a good sports city," Brown told his listeners. "The fans want the best and they come out for the best. But the possibilities in pro football never have been scratched below the surface. I realize it will take more than a year or two to build, but we're not going to waste any time. It will be a tough go, but that's the way I like it."

Then he turned to McBride and said, "And, Arthur, we'll build a winner and make it go here if it takes every cent you've got!"

McBride smiled. He knew he had picked the right man for the job.

World War II was still raging and the end was not yet in sight. There was no assurance when the All-America Conference would start operating, but the Browns were in business. Before Paul Brown left Cleveland that weekend, temporary offices were set up in the Leader Building, and Brown announced he had signed two assistant coaches and his first player. That player, of course, was Otto Graham.

"The first player of any importance on any team is the quarterback," Brown said. "He must be an artist throwing the ball; a particular kind of boy, a quick thinker, a finesse man."

There were those who raised eyebrows at the signing of Graham as a quarterback. His experience had been mainly as a tailback, even though he had been a great college passer. It usually takes several seasons to develop an accomplished T-quarterback. Of Graham, Brown was to say later, "He represented that exceptional throwing you have to have in pro football. But much more than that, I had gotten to know him as a man when he was at Glenview, Illinois, Naval Air Station and I was at nearby Great Lakes. I got to like his personality. He had the basic requirements of a T-quarterback -- poise, slick ball handling as demonstrated by his basketball and, above that, distinct qualities of leadership. We never were afraid that he wouldn't be able to adapt himself to the 'T'."

The first two assistant coaches signed by Brown were Johnny Brickels, an old friend and high-school coaching rival from New Philadelphia, Ohio, and Bob Voigts, another former Northwestern star who had been one of Brown's assistants at Great Lakes. Voigts was somewhere on sea duty with the Navy, but the personable and likeable Brickels, then head basketball coach at the University of West Virginia, was immediately available and moved to Cleveland to set up the offices.

Under directions from Brown at Great Lakes, Brickels toured the country signing players. The Browns opened a wide gap over their All-America Conference rivals in the talent hunt.

In his nine years at Massillon High, three at Ohio State and two at Great Lakes, Brown had developed an intimate knowledge of three groups of football players -- those at Massillon, those at Ohio State and those at Great Lakes -- and of the players who had opposed all three teams. From those groups he built the foundation for his first team. In addition to Graham there were Mac Speedie, Dante Lavelli, Edgar "Special Delivery" Jones, Don Greenwood, Lou Rymkus, Eddie Ulinski, Lou Saban, Tommy Colella, John Yonakor, Cliff Lewis and Lin Houston.

Brown would have no part of any recruiting covenant, written or verbal. There was some talk about a "no raiding" agreement with the National Football League. He wanted none of it. A so-called gentleman's agreement aimed at barring blacks from the new league also ultimately fell on his deaf ears. Nor would Brown keep away from players in service who had remaining college eligibility. This policy resulted in a break with Ohio State University which never healed.

Lou Groza had been one of Ohio's most renowned high-school athletes at Martins Ferry, a small manufacturing town on the Ohio River, about 60 miles southwest of Pittsburgh. He was one of four sons of "Big Spot" Groza, a well-known gentleman in the small community.

Always a good-sized youngster, dark-haired Lou started playing touch football with his older brothers Frank and John and younger brother Alex on Avondale Street in front of the Groza home. Brother Frank was his first place-kicking coach. Since there were no ready-made goal posts near-by, telephone wires strung over one end of Mill Field near the Groza home made an easy target for the youngster. With plenty of practice and coaching from Frank, Lou became an accomplished kicker.

As had brothers John and Frank before him, Lou made the Martins Ferry football team and soon became one of its outstanding stars. Big, strong and agile, Lou also turned into an outstanding basketball player, leading Martins Ferry to the state championship in his senior year. At 17, he was an outstanding college prospect. He had won a total of 10 letters in basketball, football and baseball and captained all three teams in his senior year. College recruiters descended on Martins Ferry by the dozen, promising anything to get the nod from the all-around athlete.

Paul Brown, then at Ohio State, sent Gomer Jones, an assistant at OSU, to Martins Ferry to talk with Groza. Jones had been one of Groza's coaches during his athletic career at Martins Ferry. Jones told Groza that in addition to an opportunity to play big-time football, he would also get an excellent education at Columbus, Ohio. Groza, who had been a good student in high school, thought the Jones sales talk made sense and accepted a full scholarship and a job that paid $50 a month. "It wasn't the fanciest offer, but it was reasonable," he recalls.

Groza enrolled at Ohio State in the fall of 1942, but his college career was short-lived. He played on the Buckeye freshman team, which went undefeated in an abbreviated three-game schedule. Then he went into the Army.

Groza never played a varsity game for the Buckeyes, but Brown, remembering his tremendous place-kicking as a college freshman, went after him. As Groza went through his military career, he kept hearing from Brown. "It was a helluva thing," said one of Lou's Army buddies. "Brown kept sending him equipment and letters and we kept chasing Lou's kicks."

Dante Lavelli had played on Brown's national championship team at Ohio State in 1942, then entered the service. Brown contacted him, too, notwithstanding Lavelli's two years of remaining college eligibility.

When the news broke that Brown was seeking the services of Groza and Lavelli, open warfare erupted between Brown and Ohio State University. "When Paul Brown starts going after boys like that, he's in for a fight," declared Lynn W. St. John, the Ohio State athletic director. "We're all determined that if that's the way Brown wants to play the game, then we're ready for the biggest knock-down-and-drag-out fight to protect our own interests that you ever saw. We definitely are not going to stand by and see these boys go into pro football while they still have seasons of college eligibility left and want to come back and play them."

Brown shot back that he was just trying to find out what the two players wanted to do after the war, and that he was not violating the rule that a pro club shall not sign a player before his college class graduates. Brown further pointed out that the All-America Conference did not expect to start operations until the fall of 1946 and, by that time, both Groza's and Lavelli's college classes would have graduated.

"A good-paying job with a professional football team has helped many young men to complete their education as lawyers, doctors, dentists and engineers," Brown was quoted. "I repeat, we're not trying to snatch athletes who want to return to college. However, we're going to run our business aggressively -- that means to win -- and if a boy, or his parents, comes to us and says he would rather play pro football, that's another thing."

McBride sat on the side lines during the fracas. "I'm not familiar with the details," he said. "I'm just the fellow who's putting up the money for the club."

Brown signed both Groza and Lavelli over the cries of the anguished Ohio State officials. And to complete his coaching staff, Brown next contacted Fritz Heisler, who had been a 135-pound end on one of his first Massillon High teams. After completing high school, Heisler enrolled at Miami (Ohio) University, where he was an outstanding guard. Upon graduation from college, he returned to Massillon as one of Brown's assistant coaches. When Brown moved to Ohio State, Heisler went along as freshman coach. It was logical then, that Brown should add Fritz to his Cleveland staff. At Great Lakes, Brown had become acquainted with Blanton Collier, a high-school coach from Paris, Kentucky, who demonstrated a remarkable knowledge of technical football. Collier was named backfield and defensive coach. To complete his staff with a coach of professional experience, Brown hired Red Conkright, who had been a star with the Cleveland Rams and later the team's end coach.

Brickels continued the relentless search for talent. Players were given bonuses for signing and many were put on the payroll for nominal amounts, pending completion of their military service. Expenses began to mount, and McBride was fully aware that Brown meant business when he said the football team might cost McBride every cent he had. However, only once was he known to have questioned Brown's seemingly total disregard for his fat bank account. "Tell me," he said to Brown in a long-distance call to Great Lakes while looking over the names of Paul's five assistants, "do we need all these 'second coaches'?"

Paul Brown insisted that he did. He was building the biggest and most effective coaching staff in the history of pro football. It cost money, but it was one of many Brown innovations that was to become standard operating procedure in the game before many years passed.

5

All Alone in Cleveland

On paper, the Cleveland entry in the All-America Conference was taking shape. McBride had a coaching staff and a number of players under contract, and his bank account showed a sizable dent. He still had a few major problems, however. He needed a name for the new team and he still had to contend with the Cleveland Rams, who had been doing business at the same old stand for years. McBride had to challenge them for recognition.

To solve the first problem, McBride began spending some money on his own. He decided to let the fans pick a name for the new club and ran newspaper advertisements announcing a special contest. "Cleveland's great new team in the All-America Football Conference, to be coached by Paul Brown as soon as he is released by the Navy, needs a name," the ads proclaimed. "You can pick the name and win yourself a $1,000 War Bond doing it."

The entries rolled in. A Navy man, John J. Hartnett of Lawrence, Massachusetts, stationed in the Field Branch of the Bureau of Supplies and Accounts in Cleveland, was the winner. He was one of 36 entrants who picked the name "Panthers." The contest judges awarded the first prize to Hartnett on the basis of a 49-word letter accompanying his suggestion. The others who picked "Panthers" were given season passes for the first year.

A few weeks after the contest was settled, a man named George Jones arrived on the scene to remind McBride that in the 1920s he, Jones, had owned the Cleveland Panthers, a semi-pro team which played in northern Ohio. McBride could easily have handled the problem of the prior claim, but Paul Brown vetoed the name "Panthers." "I won't start out with anything associated with our enterprise that smacks of a failure," Brown told McBride. "That old Panther team failed. I want no part of that name."

A great majority of the contest entrants had suggested the team be called the "Browns" in recognition of its head coach. Paul Brown had turned down the suggestion, but after the "Panther" incident he relented and became the only man in pro football to have a team named after him. A second $1,000 War Bond was awarded to William S. Thompson of Euclid, Ohio, for the suggestion and the best accompanying statement.

Next McBride undertook an advertising campaign to make the Cleveland Browns a household word throughout northern Ohio. The Browns were advertised on billboards. Newspaper advertisements proclaimed the beginning of the sale of season tickets. The backs of McBride's taxicabs also carried season-ticket notices. A staff of 20 girls was hired for a season-ticket telephone campaign, and ticket agencies were established throughout Ohio.

During it all, the Rams remained. They went into the 1945 campaign with a brillant young quarterback named Bob Waterfield, won nine of ten games and captured their first Western Conference championship in the National Football League. Before a small, half-frozen assemblage of 32,178 fans in Cleveland Stadium, they defeated the Washington Redskins, 15-14, in the world championship game. But despite an artistically successful season, the Rams' books were covered with red ink. In four home games, the Rams had played to only 73,000 spectators.

Shortly after the Rams-Redskins championship game, James E. Doyle, the popular *Plain Dealer* sports columnist, observed: "The Cleveland Browns, who have never played a football game, already are receiving more publicity than the Cleveland Rams, who've just won this world football championship."

Rams' owner Dan Reeves, who had suffered through four losing seasons, was not unaware of this tremendous publicity build-up and what the future might bring when the Browns finally played a football game. At the National Football League meeting early in 1946, Reeves asked permission of his fellow owners to move to Los Angeles. They balked, claiming that it was unfeasible to travel across country to play on the West Coast. Reeves offered Texas as an alternate spot, but the owners put up the same argument. The Rams' owner, who later admitted that he originally bought the team in 1941 with the ultimate aim of moving out of Cleveland, threw a bomb at his fellow magnates: Either he be allowed to switch his franchise, or he would quit the game. The other owners reluctantly gave in. In mid-January, 1946, Dan Reeves announced he was pulling the Rams out of Cleveland and taking them to Los Angeles, leaving the Browns in command of the rich Ohio market. The move eliminated any chance of a head-to-head combat with the Browns for the pro-football dollar, but the two teams were to have a battle of another sort.

Paul Brown was released from the Navy on March 2, 1946, and immediately announced that he had signed two members of the Rams' championship backfield -- Tom Colella and Don Greenwood. He later persuaded center Mike Scarry and tackle Chet Adams to leave the Rams in favor of staying in Cleveland. So long as the Rams had planned to stay in Cleveland, Brown had made it clear he would not attempt to raid the roster. When they became the Los Angeles Rams, it was another story.

Dan Reeves was incensed and slapped a lawsuit against the Browns, challenging the new team's right to the services of Chet Adams, who had played for the Rams in 1940, 1941 and 1942. Adams had signed a contract with both the Rams and the Browns. In a hearing before Federal Judge Emerich B. Freed in Cleveland, the Rams claimed that Adams was invaluable and could not be replaced. They contended that because he had signed a Rams' contract, he should not be allowed to play with the Browns. Adams and the Browns contended that although he had signed with the Cleveland Rams, his contract was not binding when the franchise was shifted to Los Angeles. The big tackle made it clear during the legal squabble that he would never play in Los Angeles. Reeves knew this, but said he was persisting in the suit because of the principle involved. Judge Freed dashed the Rams' hopes when he ruled that Adams, indeed, had signed a contract with the *Cleveland* Rams but that with the club on the West Coast, that contract was invalid. Adams won the right to play for the Cleveland Browns.

In addition to the four Rams, Paul Brown lined up several other pro veterans, which gave him a nucleus of experienced players around which to build his first team. These included Lou Rymkus, who had played with Washington in its 1942 championship year; Edgar Jones and Jim Daniell, ex-Chicago Bears; Bud Schwenk of the Chicago Cardinals; and Gaylon Smith, another ex-Ram.

Ohio State University had no recourse in the courts because of Brown's alleged raiding of brilliant young talent and his decision to bolt the university, but it mounted a war of words. Obviously disturbed by Brown's resignation to take the professional job, Athletic Director Lynn W. St. John sent a letter to an Ohio State alumnus, which was reprinted in the Ohio State alumni monthly magazine. Si Burick, sports editor of the *Dayton Daily News,* called it "five pages of the bitterest verbal vitriol ever directed at an individual in sports."

"In it, he berates Brown for leaving Ohio State to take a job calling for a much higher salary. Since when has professional football become a disgraceful enterprise? It is a growing sport that needs neither apology nor apologists," Burick commented. "Since when is it a crime to accept a job that offers more money? The issue appears to be a monument to paradox. St. John apparently finds Brown to be a person of vicious character. Yet he admits a financial inducement was made to get him to stay at Ohio State. If Brown is all St. John says he is, isn't this disgustingly inconsistent?"

With controversy swirling around his head, Brown set a hectic pace following his release from the Navy. He was constantly on the move in promotional activities, visiting key cities throughout the state, making speeches and holding press conferences to build interest in the new football team.

Finally, Brown, his staff and players headed for training camp at Bowling Green State University in northwestern Ohio on July 26, 1946. The *Cleveland Press* marked the occasion with a huge picture of Brown with an armful of footballs. The caption on the picture read: "Hey Elmer, Now They've Got a Ball." This was in reply to an acid comment made by

Elmer Layden, then commissioner of the National Football League, when he was asked about the new All-American Conference.

"What new league? Let them go get a football first, and then play a game."

It was a remark he later wished he had never uttered.

6

Some Amateur Team

"We will be the most amateur team in professional sports. I don't want fellows who are strictly professional. I don't want you to think of the money you'll be making; rather I want you to think of the game first and the money second." Thus Paul Brown, lean, handsome and superbly conditioned, began his opening remarks before 49 football candidates at Bowling Green. His language was crisp. He was like a military commander addressing his troops.

"I don't plan to coach this team a bit differently than I did in any of my previous coaching jobs. We'll start with fundamentals and if we have an All-American tackle here whose stance we dislike, we'll take him aside and retrain him.

"It's going to be a tough team to make because we want players with zip and go and love for the game, but just the same we're going to have fun with the thing.

"We've got money invested in you, and on paper it looks as if we would have a good team. But we won't be able to use you if you've lost the fire you had when you were in college.

"We're starting from scratch, and I want you to think in terms of being the best. We'll settle for nothing less than a winner. We want to be the best. When you think of baseball, you immediately think of the New York Yankees. When you think of golf, Bobby Jones comes to mind. When you think of boxing, it's Joe Louis. One of these days when people think of football, I want them to think of the Cleveland Browns."

It was an eye-opening little speech. But from that moment on, Paul Brown commanded the respect of his squad, which included many service-hardened veterans and recruits from other professional teams. Any who thought Brown was speaking just to hear himself talk soon were to find out that he meant every word he said.

First, Brown demanded that his players measure up to certain standards in appearance, even when they were out of football uniform. He insisted that they wear clean T-shirts in camp and ties and jackets when they appeared in public. He had no use for a player who didn't project the image of a gentleman. There is no better illustration of this than an incident which occurred during those first days in Bowling Green. A rookie lineman with a fine college record knocked on the door of Brown's room. "You Brown?" the player asked. Brown was stunned at the sight of the disheveled player at the door. He quickly surveyed the player's dirty slacks and unshaven face, then retorted in his typically cutting way, "Oh, yes. I'm sorry, but there's been a mistake. The business manager will see that you get transportation home."

The Cleveland coach was well pleased with the general physical condition of the squad, especially those players who had recently been released from service.

"Gee, some of these guys are in great shape," he remarked.

"Some of them aren't, too," quipped Jim Daniell, the ex-All-American from Ohio State.

The Bowling Green State University campus provided a perfect backdrop for the Browns' first training camp. It gave the players a college-type atmosphere in which to labor. The charming buildings, lush green lawns and hundreds of shade trees provided a stark contrast for those players who had recently roamed the battlefields in Europe and the Pacific. The university is located in the town of Bowling Green, just south of Toledo and about 120 miles west of Cleveland. At the time the Browns convened their camp, the only students on campus were those engaged in summer school activities.

The team and coaches stayed in a sorority house, which had the advantage of keeping the players in a tightly knit easily controlled group. Meals were served in the sorority house and the Falcon's Nest, a rustic, rambling, collegiate juke-box hangout in the center of the campus.

The Browns utilized the school's athletic department facilities for changing clothes and for holding meetings and practice sessions. Those who suffered bumps and bruises during those first few days didn't have to go far for treatment. The campus hospital was next door to the football practice field. All in all, it was an ideal setup.

Football under Brown was like nothing any of the players had experienced before. They kept notebooks of plays and maneuvers and took regular examinations and quizzes to determine how much they had absorbed. They were drilled to perfection on fundamentals. Each man had specific moves on every play, and he was expected to know not only his own assignment, but those of everyone else on the team as well. It was a time for seriousness. Every man worked all of the time, and no one wandered away from the team room or from practice without permission of the coaches. Brown made every minute count. Those players who found Brown's regimen too much for them soon found themselves out of a job with the Cleveland team.

Six of the Browns' key players, including the talented Graham around whom Brown planned to build his offense, missed the first few weeks of practice because of duty with the College All-Star team. Vince Banonis and Ted Fritsch, a pair of seasoned National League veterans, reconsidered and made last-minute decisions to return to their NFL teams. Banonis, property of the Detroit Lions, had never reported to the Browns.

Fritsch, a Green Bay fullback, had shown up at camp but left after a few days to rejoin the Packers. Brown appeared unconcerned. He was counting on Gene Fekete, an outstanding member of the national championship team at Ohio State in 1942, to play fullback. But Fekete suffered a bad knee injury at the All-Star camp which dimmed his football future.

The head coach, however, already was prepared and made a bold move. While the All-America Conference had no written rule that black players should be excluded from rosters, it was significant that none was listed on any of the rosters when the teams entered training camp. But on one of those early days in camp, a big, 235-pound black reported to the Bowling Green training camp. He was Marion Motley, a great fullback on Brown's last Great Lakes team, the boy who had ripped apart a highly favored Notre Dame team, 39-7, in the final game of the 1945 season. From the day Motley arrived there was no question as to who would play fullback for the Cleveland Browns. With Motley came Bill Willis, an All-American tackle under Brown at Ohio State. They were the only black players in the All-America Conference that first season, but their rise to stardom under Paul Brown opened the way for others of their race to excel in the professional sport.

The camp was not without other problems. Bud Schwenk, a quarterback whose professional experience had been with the Chicago Cardinals, was hobbling on a bad knee. So was Fred (Dippy) Evans, an outstanding halfback candidate from Notre Dame. Bob Steuber, whom Brown rated highly as a halfback, spent most of his time in the college infirmary with a leg infection that refused to respond to treatment. Center Mike Scarry, who came from the Rams, suffered a severed Achilles' tendon.

After three weeks of practice, the team finally staged an intrasquad game in Toledo that was so bad Brown himself described it as "undoubtedly the raggedest exhibition of football possible outside of a grade school." Though the game was a little unnerving for Brown, he never let up and pursued the problems with his customary perserverance.

Despite the long hours of hard work, player meetings and staff sessions, there were some moments of relaxation and a time for levity off the playing field. Cliff Lewis, the former Lakewood, Ohio, High School star and ex-Duke quarterback, was one of the wittiest players in camp. He told the seven-year-old daughter of one of the reporters covering the camp that Chet Adams could down 16 containers of milk at one meal. The youngster, a camp visitor, was skeptical and pressed for a demonstration. He drank the milk and ate his meal, too.

One of the guard candidates was 195-pound George Cheroke from Ohio State. He was a physical culture enthusiast with bulging muscles which he developed by lifting bar bells. He had a set in camp and worked out daily. Frank Gatski, a powerfully built 240-pound rookie center from the hills of West Virginia, had never seen bar bells. Gatski asked Cheroke what he did with them.

"You lift them," Cheroke answered.

Gatski leaned down with his right hand and easily lifted a bar. "You mean like this?" he asked. Cheroke gaped in amazement and the rest of the players broke into uncontrolled laughter.

Five weeks after camp opened, the Browns played their first game, an exhibition contest with the Brooklyn Dodgers in the Akron, Ohio, Rubber Bowl. A standing-room crowd of 35,964, a record for the Bowl, witnessed the dress rehearsal.

The Dodgers were coached by Mal Stevens, who had installed what he called an "A to Z" formation. In the first quarter of the game, quarterback Glenn Dobbs and Joe Davis combined on a scoring pass and Jim McCarthy booted the extra point to put the Dodgers out in front, 7-0. A Browns fumble paved the way for another Brooklyn tally and the Paul Brown boys found themselves down by 13 points.

In the second quarter, Cliff Lewis capped a drive with a seven-yard scoring pass to Fred "Dippy" Evans for the Browns' first touchdown in competition. Lou Groza booted the first of five extra points and the Cleveland club went to the dressing room at halftime trailing, 13-7.

Two Graham touchdown passes and a pair of Brooklyn miscues enabled the Browns to surge ahead in the second half. First John Rokisky picked up a Brooklyn fumble and dashed 55 yards for a touchdown. Then Graham, who had led the College All-Stars to a 16-0 victory over the Los Angeles Rams and had been in camp only about a week, climaxed a 75-yard drive with a two-yard flip to Speedie.

Evans, who had scored the Browns' first touchdown, brought the crowd to its feet in the fourth quarter when he snagged one of Dobbs' passes and turned it into an 83-yard touchdown. Then Graham wrapped it up for the Browns with a two-yard pitch to George Young. The Browns wound up with a 35-20 win over the Dodgers.

That same night, the Browns unveiled another treat for the fans, the Musical Majorettes, a snappy group of young ladies attired in short skirts who entertained at halftime. "These girls are all musicians," said George "Red" Bird, the director of the Browns' own band. "This isn't an organization of drum majorettes." The young ladies drew lusty applause from the sellout crowd.

The following Friday night, almost two years from the day the All-America Conference was organized at a meeting in Chicago, the Browns played their first regularly scheduled game in the new league against the Miami Seahawks.

By this time, Paul Brown had whittled the squad down to 33 players, including seven former Ohio State University gridders. The centers were Mike Scarry (Waynesburg College), Frank Gatski (Marshall College) and Mel Maceau (Marquette University). Bill Willis, Lindell Houston and George Cheroke (all of Ohio State), Ed Ulinski (Marshall College) and Bob Kolesar (University of Michigan) were the guards who had survived the cut.

Lou Groza and Jim Daniell (both of Ohio State) and Lou Rymkus (Notre Dame), Ernie Blanda (Tulane) and Chet Adams (Ohio University) made up the tackle corps. Brown had selected seven ends, John Yonakor

(Notre Dame), George Young (University of Georgia), John Rokisky (Duquesne Univerty), John Harrington (Marquette University), Dante Lavelli (Ohio State), Mac Speedie (University of Utah) and Alton Coppage (University of Oklahoma).

Otto Graham (Northwestern University), Cliff Lewis (Duke University) and Lou Saban (Indiana University) survived at quarterback, and Gene Fekete (Ohio State), Gaylon Smith (Southwestern University) and Marion Motley (University of Nevada) landed fullback spots. The seven-man halfback corps included Bill Lund (Case Tech), Ray Terrill (University of Mississippi), Don Greenwood (Illinois University), Bob Steuber (University of Missouri), Edgar Jones (University of Pittsburgh), Tom Colella (Canisius College) and Fred "Dippy" Evans (Notre Dame).

The day before the game, Harvey Hester, owner of the Miami team, reviewed the Browns' roster and commented to the Cleveland coach, "Boy, I feel sorry for you in this league. You don't have enough Southern boys on your team." Hester apparently felt that teams in the league which stocked up heavily on players from southern colleges had an advantage over a team like the Browns, which had only four boys from Deep South schools on its roster. He was in for a rude awakening.

Meanwhile, Mickey McBride's promotion campaign had paid off. A crowd of 60,135 -- nearly as many fans as had seen the Rams in their entire home schedule in Cleveland the year before -- were on hand for the debut. They weren't disappointed.

Because of his showing in the Brooklyn exhibition, Cliff Lewis drew the starting quarterback assignment. The game was just minutes old when Lewis floated a pass to Mac Speedie for the league's historic first touchdown. The Browns scored four more touchdowns, and Lou Groza launched a career that was to establish him as one of the greatest placekickers of all time. Using a 72-inch tape with a crosspiece at the end devised by the ball holder, Don Greenwood, the powerfully built young man from Martins Ferry booted three field goals.

The Browns' defense was superb and Cleveland walked off the field at the end of 60 minutes of football with a 44-0 victory over Miami. No one in Cleveland Stadium that night could help but be impressed with what he saw.

The Browns were good -- too good.

7

An All-America Flop

Paul Brown's first season as a professional coach was just getting started when he earned for himself a trademark that was to remain with him through most of his professional career. After getting a look at the Browns' awesome offense, rival coaches and sports writers began calling Brown a "pass and trap" coach. The description stuck.

It really began in the Browns' second game of the season against the Chicago Rockets at Soldier Field, where Marion Motley, the muscular ex-Canton McKinley High School and ex-University of Nevada fullback, first demonstrated he was on his way to becoming one of pro football's most fearsome runners. Despite his size, the 230-pound Motley had a lightning take-off and ran like a sprinter. In his Navy days at Great Lakes, Motley could stay a step or two ahead of Grover Klemmer, then the world record-holder in the 440-yard dash, at distances up to 75 yards. Brown wanted to make maximum use of Motley's speed and power, and he advised the fullback not to get fancy once he passed the line of scrimmage. "Just run right at them and over them," Brown advised.

Motley tried the technique against the Rockets. On the trap play, Otto Graham would take the snap from center, spin and fade back as if he were preparing to pass. Motley would stay in position, take the hand-off from Graham and then, with his tremendous starting ability, blast through the hole created by the trapped defensive lineman. Early in the game, Motley took off and was met head-on by Elroy Hirsch, destined to become a pass-catching star with the Rams but then a Chicago halfback and safety man. Motley ran right over him and was off on a long touchdown run, a decisive one in the Browns' second straight victory, 20-7.

The Browns followed up their Chicago victory with triumphs over Buffalo, 28-0; New York, 24-7 and 7-0; and Brooklyn 26-7.

Cleveland had six straight victories when the team played host to the Los Angeles Dons. Football fever had really hit the town, and 71,134 fans showed up as Motley sprinted for two long touchdown runs in a 31-14 victory.

The passing of Graham and the running of Motley were the talk of the league. The Browns had been so convincing that the belief grew that they were too good for the All-America Conference, and that their superiority would ruin the league. Graham, helped by his swift ends Lavelli and Speedie, was hitting on his passes regularly. Using new pass patterns developed by Brown and his aides, Graham and his receivers were hard to stop. Graham tossed passes that floated through the air, and Speedie and Lavelli could take them on their fingertips on the dead run without breaking stride. Motley's trap running was a constant threat.

One of the Browns' most effective offensive weapons was the side-line pass, which later was adopted by virtually every team in football. The Cleveland version was whipped up in a 1946 practice session. "The pet pro pattern then was the Z-out, where the receiver zee'd and went deep," Speedie recalls. "In practice our defense men knew all the signs. When I made my first move, they immediately retreated deep to the final cut zone. We had to change things in order to have a good workout. I came back to the huddle one time and said, 'Otto, let's cut the pattern short just before the last break and you hit me at the side line.' We tried it some and Coach Brown put it into the offense. I guess that's where the side line pass was born." It was fine for short yardage.

The Browns looked great, but after seven straight victories they proved they weren't invincible. Another crowd of 70,000 was on hand at Cleveland Stadium for the game with San Francisco, but this time they watched the Frankie Albert-Alyn Beals passing combination carve the Browns apart. The 49ers won, 34-20.

It was, however, a significant day. The primary victim of the Albert-Beals artistry was a fine Cleveland running halfback, Edgar Jones. The fact that Jones had some weaknesses as a defender set Brown to thinking in terms of separate offensive and defensive units. The rules then stipulated that only one player could be substituted when the clock was running, and, while Brown did take advantage of this to get as many "specialists" on the field as possible, most of the players, including Graham and Motley, played on both offense and defense.

The following week, the Browns headed for their first West Coast game, with the Los Angeles Dons. A pair of fourth-quarter mishaps cost the Browns another victory. Tommy Colella failed to get off a punt and the Dons scored a touchdown. Then Ray Terrell fumbled and the Dons won the game on a field goal in the closing seconds, 17-16.

Pressed for time because the team was flying to San Francisco immediately after the game, the reporters covering the contest for the Cleveland papers abandoned the customary post-game visit to the dressing room to interview the coach and players. "I know what Paul will say," suggested one of the journalists. " 'We stunk out the joint'!"

However, Brown departed from the obvious and instead applied a touch of psychology. When the bus pulled up at the airport, he kept the doors closed for a moment and said, "I thought we played a good football game today and were beaten by the breaks of the game. But I don't want anybody to talk about it. Let's not talk about anybody. We coaches probably made some mistakes, too. It's all part of the business. Now let's all keep our heads up. Next week, the chips are down."

The Browns were crippled when they faced the 49ers. They played most of the way with substitute halfbacks Bill Lund an Ray Terrell. Gaylon Smith was at fullback. Lund and Smith turned in heroic performances, and the Browns regained the winning touch with a 14-7 victory.

Two weeks later, Cleveland clinched its first division championship with a 42-17 victory over Buffalo, then hit a high point in the season by rolling up 66 points against Brooklyn. The total still stands as a team scoring record.

The Browns were so far in front in this one that the players wanted Lou Saban to have a shot at scoring. Throughout the season, Saban, a big star at Indiana when that team had won its last Big Ten championship in the early 1940s, always was the first man substituted when the Browns lost the ball. He moved in as a right linebacker. Late in the game, with Cleveland in possession on the Brooklyn one-yard line, Saban's teammates pleaded with Brown to put Lou in on offense and let him carry the ball. Brown was agreeable, but Saban refused. "That's an insult," he quipped, "asking me to score from thé one-yard line. If you want me to get a touchdown, give me the ball when we are on the 50-yard line."

As the Browns readied themselves for the title game against the New York Yankees, Paul Brown shocked the team and the community by taking the severest disciplinary action in all his years in football. Jim Daniell, tackle and team captain, end Mac Speedie and tackle Lou Rymkus were engaged in an argument early one morning with Cleveland Police Sgt. Joseph Strauss and Patrolman Tom Osborn at East 81st Street and Euclid Avenue. Daniell was taken to the Central Police Station and charged with intoxication, while Speedie and Rymkus were charged with disorderly conduct. That afternoon, the trio showed up at the Browns' League Park practice field. Speedie and Rymkus were allowed to practice, but Brown told Daniell tersely that he was no longer a member of the team. "We run the team on a certain basis and it's up to the players to observe the rules or take the consequences," snapped Brown, who reluctantly allowed his players to smoke but had an embargo on drinking during the season. "Daniell is not being made an example," Brown continued. "He's simply getting what's coming to him."

Daniell was later cleared of the intoxication charges but was never reinstated by Brown. The coach later gave the Chicago Rockets the player rights to the erstwhile captain, but Daniell never played in another game. Instead, he elected to enter his family's steel business, where he ultimately became a wealthy executive.

It wasn't the first time in his career that Paul Brown had shown he meant business when he set the rules. At Ohio State in 1941, Brown fired a star end for straying from the path set by the coach.

While the Daniell incident left Brown short of tackles before a crucial game, it served as basis for discipline for years to come. Brown's action was an object lesson to future players.

In the championship game at Cleveland, the Browns maintained the momentum they had built up after their two straight losses to San Francisco and Los Angeles. Edgar Jones' diving catch of a low pass put Cleveland in position for Otto Graham to throw a touchdown pass to Lavelli late in the game to give the Browns a 14-9 victory over the Yankees for their first championship.

It was a gratifying triumph for the Browns. After Cleveland's first victory over the Yankees, early in the season, Ray Flaherty, the New York coach, had lashed his team for a poor performance. "You lost to a team from Podunk with a high-school coach," he told his players. Brown never forgot it, and never would pronounce Ray's name correctly. It always came out "Flattery."

A spectator at the first title game was Adam Walsh, who had coached the champion Cleveland Rams in 1945. "An interesting team," Walsh was quoted as saying, "but not good enough for the National League." Future events were to prove his judgment rather shortsighted.

All in all, it was a brilliant season, with the Browns winning 13 of 15 games, counting the championship, and racking up a spectacular attendance of 399,962 in seven regular season home games.

The Browns' success in the inaugural year helped Bob Voigts land the head coaching job at his alma mater, Northwestern University. Brown replaced him with Bill Edwards, a long-time Massillon friend who had coached at Western Reserve University and with the Detroit Lions. Red Conkright, another assistant, resigned and took a job with the Buffalo Bills. Dick Gallagher, later to become the general manager of the champion Buffalo Bills in the American Football League, took over as end coach of the Browns.

Typically, Brown started the 1947 training season by sounding a warning. Only 26 players from the championship squad returned for a second season and heard his message: "As of this moment, we no longer are the champions. The romance is over insofar as our achievements of a year ago are concerned. Right now, we start to do it all over again."

With the team player limit established at 35, there was room for nine rookies, and some bright new stars crashed the roster. One of these was Horace Gillom, whom Brown had coached in both football and basketball at Massillon High School. Brown, who had called Gillom the greatest all-around high-school athlete he ever had seen, showed no reserve in describing his new player to newspaper reporters prior to the first practice session that year. "Horace has suction cups on the ends of his arms, and he just sucks the ball in," Brown said.

Everyone was anxious to take a look at Gillom, who had dropped out of the University of Nevada to sign a pro contract. The year's first pass was directed to Gillom. Graham was on the target but Gillom dropped the ball. The silence was devastating. Gillom never really made it big as an end. He had too much competition from Speedie and Lavelli. But he made his mark with his booming punts, and still holds the record for the longest Brownie boot, an 80-yarder.

Brown again invaded Ohio State and came up with Tony Adamle and Bob Gaudio, a pair of native Clevelanders. Adamle, a fullback, was loaded with enthusiasm. In the face of competing with the rugged Motley, Adamle calmly stated that he expected to win a regular job. He did, a year later, when complete offensive and defensive units were installed for the first time. He didn't make it as a fullback, but as a linebacker. It was Adamle's determination that earned him the captaincy of the team in later years. After retiring from pro football in 1951, he entered medical school and became a practicing physician in Kent, Ohio, near Cleveland.

Gaudio, too, created quite a stir upon his arrival at the Bowling Green training camp, but in a different way. Bob pulled up in an expensive convertible. A bar from window to window in the rear seat was loaded with sport coats and suits. Bob came from a wealthy family in Cleveland and played pro football for sheer enjoyment. Gaudio took quite a ribbing from his teammates and the ever needling Brown, who quipped, "You'll notice that Otto Graham drives a Plymouth and Gaudio drives a Cadillac. That's why Graham plays quarterback and Gaudio plays guard."

Early in the training season, Brown swung his first major player deal sending five players to the Baltimore Colts in exhange for Weldon Humble, an All-American guard from Rice Institute. Baltimore had inherited the Miami franchise at the end of the first season.

The Browns opened their 1947 season at home to a crowd of 63,263, signaling another prosperous year at the gate. Cleveland blasted the Buffalo Bills, 30-14. Four weeks later the team again clashed with the New York Yankees. It was a World Series Sunday, but a crowd of 80,067 watched the Browns beat the New Yorkers for the fourth time in a row in a 26-17 thriller. A week later, Los Angeles took advantage of a pair of costly Cleveland fumbles and won, 13-10. The next Sunday afternoon, October 19, 1947, Groza's field goal gave the Browns a 31-28 victory over Chicago to launch an amazing Cleveland unbeaten streak which stretched through 29 games.

The Browns were not without some anxious moments, however, through the remainder of the 1947 season. Buffalo, quarterbacked by George Ratterman, the ex-Notre Dame star, gave the Browns a fierce struggle for more than half a game, but the contest was broken up by one of the most sensational plays in Cleveland history. With the Browns ahead, 14-7, Buffalo hammered into scoring position, but was held on the one-yard line. Cleveland took over. Graham, then calling most of his own plays, went into the huddle and said he always wanted to throw a pass from deep in the end zone. He called for a pass to Speedie.

"Too dangerous," one of his teammates warned. "What if you can't get the pass off?"

"I'll throw the ball away," Graham replied. "I'll throw it up in the stands. Then let them penalize us half the distance to the goal line."

The Browns lined up and Graham took the ball and dropped back. He looped a little pass to Speedie, who was still in the end zone. Speedie slipped away from the shocked Buffalo defenders and ran all the way for a touchdown. It went into the record books as a 99-yard touchdown pass and the Browns emerged with a 28-7 victory.

The next week against Brooklyn, a pair of missed conversions by a place kicker named Phil Martinovich, while the Browns missed one of their own, preserved a 13-12 victory, but the real hair-raiser was still to come.

With three games still remaining in the 1947 season, the Browns already had clinched their second straight division title. They were a little complacent when they arrived in New York to meet the Yankees. The Yankees were aroused after the humiliation of four straight losses to Cleveland and were eager for a big killing. It looked for a while as if they were going to get it.

There were 70,060 persons crowded into Yankee Stadium, the biggest throng to see a professional football game in New York since 70,000 packed the Polo Grounds on December 6, 1925, to watch Red Grange, fresh out of Illinois, in action.

The fans howled with delight as the Yankees scored the first four times they had the ball, twice in the first quarter and twice in the second. Orban (Spec) Sanders scored three times on runs of one foot, three yards and 27 yards, and Claude (Buddy) Young, the ex-Illinois flash, tallied from the five to propel the Yanks into a 28-0 lead. With less than five minutes remaining in the first half, Graham finally aroused the Browns from their lethargic state. He fired a 34-yard touchdown pass to halfback Bill Boedecker, and the Clevelanders were on the scoreboard for the first time. As the Yanks went to the dressing room with a 28-7 lead at halftime, they received a tremendous ovation from the crowd.

New York showed little sign of cooling off after the half, driving down the field until they had a first down on the Cleveland one. About this time, Jim Schlemmer, the colorful sports writer who was covering the game for the *Akron Beacon-Journal,* packed up his notes and left the press box. "This one is all over and I don't want to miss my six o'clock flight home," he said wryly.

Eddie Prokop, a Cleveland boy playing halfback for the Yankees, was given the chance to score the touchdown that could put the game out of reach of the Browns. Four times Prokop hammered at the goal line and four times the determined defense thwarted his efforts. The brilliant goal-line stand provided the spark for one of the most stirring comebacks in the Browns' history.

Cleveland took over on the one-foot line and Graham faded back to pass in the end zone. He and Mac Speedie, the lanky ex-Utah end, made connections on an 82-yard play. Mickey Mayne plunged to the 12-yard line of the Yanks, and then Graham calmly lofted a 12-yard touchdown pass to Motley. The Browns had narrowed the margin to 14 points.

Three minutes later, following two long completions, Motley rambled over from the 10 and the Browns were back in the ball game. Finally, late in the fourth quarter, Jim Dewar raced over from the five-yard line to cap a 90-yard, 14-play drive that was punctuated by the fine running of Motley and the accurate passing of Graham.

Lou Groza had been on the bench all day with an injury and Lou Saban, his replacement, had already booted three extra points. On the fourth and crucial kick, the ball slithered off the side of Saban's foot, but just managed to cross the bar for a 28-28 tie. "It's the first time I ever saw a spiral kicked from placement," Paul Brown kidded Saban in the dressing room.

At game's end, the Yankees had driven to the Browns' 36 but time ran out before they could kick a field goal. As they left the field, the fans, who had cheered them wildly at the half, stood and booed.

Meanwhile, Schlemmer had found the Manhattan traffic extremely heavy and eventually missed his plane. But, more important, he missed the great comeback, and some of his colleagues never have allowed him to forget it.

Despite the tie, the Yankees finished two and one-half games ahead of Buffalo in the Eastern race and the Browns and the Yankees again met for the championship, this time in New York. It was a cold December day, but 61,879 showed up to watch the two teams play on an icy field. The footing bothered everyone except Motley, who blistered the Yanks with his brilliant running. The Browns' defense held the Yankees without a touchdown and Cleveland racked up its second AAC championship, 14-3.

The Browns finished the season with another great year at the gate, drawing 392,760 for seven home games. Graham completed 163 of his 269 passes, yielding a net gain of 2,753 yards and a .606 percentage, and tossed for 25 touchdowns. He was honored as the most valuable player in the league. Motley, who rambled for 889 yards on the ground, ends Speedie and Lavelli, tackle Lou Rymkus, guard Bill Willis and Graham were named to the All-Conference team. In two years in the All-America Conference, the Browns had rolled to 24 wins, three losses and a tie, but the best was yet to come.

The 1948 Browns swept through their 14-game schedule unbeaten and untied, and hammered the Buffalo Bills, 49-7, for their third straight championship. This was the first professional football team to go through a season with a perfect record, and on the strength of that unbeaten campaign Paul Brown called the 1948 group his greatest team. "They earn this distinction because they didn't lose a game," he said. "Until another team does it, I've got to call this team the best."

It was an interesting and exciting year. Brown made a couple of the best trades of all his years of professional football. He held the draft rights to Bob Chappius, the All-American halfback from the University of Michigan and a big name in Mid-western football. But he traded Chappius to the Brooklyn Dodgers for a six-foot, four-inch halfback named Dub Jones. He remembered Jones for the spectacular defensive day he had against the Browns in 1947 and wanted him to bolster his defensive backfield. As usual, the second-guessers were busy after Brown made the deal, but he was unperturbed. "We've got Otto Graham and the most we could expect from Chappius would be as a second-string quarterback," Brown commented. "We're getting a player we need." Chappius was never a star in Brooklyn, but Jones made it big in Cleveland, not as a defensive back, but as a standout on offense.

Another big addition to the squad that year was Forrest (Chubby) Grigg, an immense tackle who had been in the league two years, one with Buffalo and one with Chicago. When Speedie, who had played opposite Grigg in four games in those two years heard about the trade, he telephoned Paul Brown and commented, "A great player, Paul. He doesn't tackle anyone, he just absorbs them."

Grigg had played at about 330 pounds with Buffalo and Chicago. Ordinarily, Brown wouldn't have taken a second look at a player of this size. He wanted his players "lean and hungry." But now he was beginning to realize the importance of weight in professional football. Still, Brown thought a streamlined Grigg would be more effective, and when he signed Chubby to a contract he inserted a clause providing a $500 bonus if the huge tackle reported to camp weighing no more than 280 pounds. Several weeks before reporting to training camp, Grigg began training diligently and went on a strict diet. He made the trip from his Texas home to Bowling Green by car and didn't eat a single meal along the way.

The big moment came when he arrived at camp. He walked confidently to the scale in the Bowling Green athletic office. Chubby stepped on the scale and the indicator shot to 250 pounds and stopped. Wally Bock, then the Browns' trainer, stood puzzled for a moment. He knew that a man of Grigg's bulk weighed more than 250 pounds. A little investigation revealed that the athletic department scale was broken. Bock and Morrie Kono, the equipment manager, called time out, hired a truck and moved in a new scale. Chubby tried again. This time, the indicator stopped at 275½, and Grigg happily collected $500. He also won a starting job as a defensive tackle and was an important member of the team for the next four seasons.

The Browns also acquired Alex Agase in the same trade that brought Grigg to Cleveland. Agase had been a star at Purdue as a naval trainee during the war years and later had achieved All-American recognition at Illinois. He had played two seasons with the Chicago Hornets.

Agase turned out to be a perfect example of what Brown meant when he said that a player would be taught his way of doing things, his All-American reputation notwithstanding. Brown's guard coach Fritz Heisler was displeased with some of Agase's techniques and launched a retraining course. Agase resented the instruction at first, nearly touching off open warfare during practice one afternoon. but he finally agreed with Heisler.

One player who was not entirely happy with his lot during the 1946 and 1947 seasons was Groza. "I'm a kicker," he said. "I want to be a football player." Groza worked hard in practice trying to make up for the college experience he lacked. Just before the start of the 1948 season, Brown approached Groza and told him, "You'll play left tackle on offense." Groza ultimately became one of the game's finest tackles.

Lavelli suffered a broken leg in an exhibition game against Baltimore and was out for half the season, but the Browns still managed to escape defeat. They had a close call in the opener against Los Angeles, which attracted more then 60,000 fans for the third straight year, but managed to outlast the Dons, 19-14.

They played the Baltimore Colts in ankle-deep mud and escaped with a 14-0 victory. An attendance record of 82,769 was set in the game with San Francisco, a mark that was to stand for 12 years. The 49ers game, a tightly fought contest all the way, was won by the Browns, 14-7, and it was in this battle that it became apparent that the Browns could be a power in any league, despite the opinion held by many old-line National Leaguers.

A member of the 49ers in 1948 was Riley Matheson, who had played several years of National League football with the Rams. Matheson recognized that the Browns were a solid football team, one capable of beating any opponent, but he tempered his comment by saying they might not do it so consistently in the older, more established National Football League.

The Browns hit their high point of the 1948 season after the 49ers victory. Their schedule called for them to play three games in eight days. They took a big lead in the first half at New York and whipped the Yankees 34-21, to frustrate the New Yorkers for the eighth straight time. They had a Thanksgiving Day date in Los Angeles and defeated the Dons, 31-14. The victory was marred by Graham's injury to his left knee. He was a doubtful starter for the San Francisco game three days later.

The team flew to San Francisco following the Los Angeles game. Accommodations for the three-day stay had been arranged at the Sonoma Mission Inn, 40 miles north of the city. Arrangements were made for the players to take a dip in the sulphur water at Boyes Springs to ease their bumps and bruises, but the swim didn't help Graham. His knee stiffened and he couldn't practice. He spent two days in his hotel room under treatment by trainer Bock.

Drama surrounded the game. The 49ers, who had come close but didn't quite make the title games in 1946 and 1947, had a fine team. They had a record of 11 victories and one defeat when the Browns rolled into town with a perfect record in 12 games. If the 49ers won, it would throw the race into a tie and bring about a play-off in Cleveland, providing both teams triumphed in their final games a week later. A victory over San Francisco would clinch a third consecutive divisional crown for the Browns. Graham was the key man. No one expected him to play and, for the first time in their history, the Browns were rated underdogs. Some observers took the view that the Browns would ease up and force a play-off to attract another big crowd in Cleveland.

On Sunday morning Graham hobbled out of the hotel to the team bus leaving for Kezar Stadium. Brown had instructed his great star not to dress for the game, but Graham wasn't listening. He asked Bock to tape the injured knee tightly because he wanted to test it in the pre-game workout. After the workout, he returned to the dressing room and told Brown he couldn't play, but he kept on his uniform and took a place on the bench.

The Browns lost the coin toss and the 49ers elected to receive. Forrest Hall returned the kickoff, but fumbled. The Browns recovered. Graham hopped up and dashed onto the field with the offensive unit. On the first play, he dramatically threw a 28-yard touchdown pass to Lavelli. Groza kicked the extra point and the Browns had a 7-0 lead.

Graham forgot about his injured leg and so, apparently, did Paul Brown. In the third period, deep in their own territory, the Browns had a fourth down and one yard to go. Brown sent in a play calling for a quarterback sneak. Graham, lacking his customary drive, tried and failed, and the 49ers took over. They quickly moved to a touchdown to take a 21-10 lead.

Cleveland made another rousing comeback and finally won the game on a touchdown pass from Graham to Edgar Jones, who caught the ball going at full speed under the goal posts. It put the Browns into a 31-28 lead, which they protected by controlling the ball the last seven minutes of play. The Browns were champions of the division again.

Meanwhile, Buffalo had finished its regular season in a tie with Baltimore for the Eastern championship. The Bills beat the Colts in the play-off game, 28-17, but were no match for the Brown in the title clash. Motley rolled for three touchdowns as the Browns plastered the Bills, 49-7.

Graham again won most valuable player honors, but this time he shared the distinction with Frankie Albert, the plucky quarterback of the 49ers.

Unrest began enveloping all professional football at the end of the 1948 season. Expenses were soaring out of proportion to attendance. Players' salaries rocketed as the rival leagues bid for the top college stars in the annual player draft. Unlike the American Football League, which was to come along more than a decade later to challenge the NFL, the All-America Conference owners had no plush television contracts pouring millions into bank accounts. Losses mounted steadily and most teams were bathed in red ink. Attendance slumped. Cleveland's seven-game figure was down to 318,619, compared with 392,760 the previous year. The Browns' complete domination of the All-America Conference didn't help the attendance situation in other league cities. Cleveland made a modest profit, and Arthur McBride, still bound to see the AAC succeed, gave financial assistance to some of his colleagues.

Meanwhile, Paul Brown was beginning to show some concern about the costly football war, and was entertaining thoughts of returning to the quiet surroundings of a college campus. But after giving it some deep thought, he decided to stay with the sinking AAC ship. "The Browns were doing all right, but I didn't have the stomach for making excuses for the rest of the league," he said later. On January 1, 1949, Brown put an end to speculation that he might return to the campus by signing a seven-year contract with the Browns. "I've decided to stick with it. I'm going the route," he said.

Hope for a peaceful settlement between the two leagues heightened later in January when the AAC and the NFL arranged simultaneous meetings at adjacent hotels in Chicago. Several days were spent in merger talks, but the peace move collapsed when the NFL wanted only the Cleveland and San Francisco franchises in its circuit. At one point in the discussions, the late Anthony J. Morabito, colorful owner of the San Francisco team, turned to McBride and said, "Look, Mickey, let's you and I forget the rest of these fellows and take our teams on a barnstorming tour around the country. We'll play in a different city every week."

The Browns-49ers rivalry was the hottest in pro football. In six games in three years, the teams had played before 384,987 for an average of 64,164 per game. But McBride laughed off Morabito's comment and rebelled at the suggestion that six of the All-America Conference teams throw in the sponge, clearing the way for his own team and the 49ers to join the NFL. He refused to ditch his friends, among them owners Ben Lindheimer of the Dons and Jim Breuil of the Bills. He stormed out of one of the meetings and said the AAC would try it for another year. "I'll not throw anybody to the vultures," he promised.

The All-America Conference did operate another season, as a seven-team league, but the handwriting was clearly on the wall. The Brooklyn and New York franchises were merged and became known as the Yanks. Still, everyone wanted peace, and informal talks continued as several owners in both leagues stated flatly they'd have to give up unless a settlement came.

As usual, the Browns dominated the AAC in 1949. Only six new players were able to make the team. Cleveland started the season at Buffalo and trailed 28-7, with only 12 minutes to play. Another whirlwind finish produced a 28-28 tie. The game was typical of the Browns' play throughout the early part of the season. Surfeited with the success that comes with a long string of victories, with pulling out victories or ties in games that seemingly were lost, the players became "full of themselves," as Paul Brown put it.

After a string of 29 games without a defeat, the Browns ran into a buzz saw in San Francisco. On October 9, 1949, the deft left arm of Frankie Albert and the jarring runs of the fullback Joe Perry combined to dismantle Cleveland. The 49ers waltzed to a 35-14 lead just before the half ended, but the confident Browns weren't worried. They thought it was only a matter of time until they would catch up.

"Don't worry, we'll get going, Coach," Edgar Jones told Brown when the 49ers spread their lead to 21 points. But the 49ers hammered the Browns into helplessness, 56-28. It was the largest point total scored against the Browns in their brief history.

As the big clock on the scoreboard was beginning its last revolution, a policeman walked up behind the Cleveland bench and shouted to Paul Brown, who was suffering along the side lines, "Hey, Coach, what are you going to do now?"

"We couldn't go on forever," he said. "The end had to come sometime, and as long as it did, I'm glad it was against San Francisco." He had a high regard for Morabito and for Buck Shaw, the 49ers coach.

Immediately after the game Cleveland headed for Los Angeles and a date with the Dons, and Brown's delayed reaction began setting in on the short airplane ride south. He herded the players together upon arrival at the Green Hotel in Pasadena and lashed them for their complacency, ending the lecture with a threat to break up the team unless the players started performing up to their ability.

Five days later, in a complete reversal of form, the Browns routed the Los Angeles Dons in a night game, 61-14. Edgar Jones suffered a broken collarbone in the game. "Edgar was only a decoy on the play, but he went out of his way to find someone to block," Brown commented. Jones' superlative effort was typical of the performances by all the Browns that night. Graham threw six touchdown passes, still a team record for one game, and Lavelli snagged five of them, a mark that still stands.

Brown's blast at his team after the San Francisco debacle prompted *Collier's* magazine to carry an editorial headlined, "Aw, C'mon, Coach, It Ain't That Bad." In it, Brown was chided for the importance he placed on winning.

Brown defended his stand. "It wasn't the fact that we lost, but the way we looked in losing," he explained. "I knew we had a good football team, but didn't look the part. The players are paid well to do a job for me, and all I want is for them to perform to the maximum of their ability."

The Browns next met the 49ers in Cleveland and avenged the humiliating loss. They won 30-28, and went unbeaten for the rest of the season.

With only seven teams in the League, the four top teams engaged in a round-robin play-off at the end of the regular campaign. The Browns finished on top and met and defeated fourth-place Buffalo, 31-21, in the semifinal play-off. San Francisco whipped the Brooklyn-New York team, and the old rivals clashed a third time that season -- this time for the title.

Two days before the game, the long-awaited news of the end of the football war was announced. The merger of the All-America Conference and the National Football League took the edge off the championship contest. Although 72,180 spectators had watched the rivals in their game at Cleveland six weeks earlier, only 22,550 were on hand for the last rites of the AAC. The Browns, once more a methodical football machine, beat the 49ers, 21-7, for their fourth straight championship.

The Browns finished their All-America Conference history with 52 victories, four defeats and three ties, including championship games. They were the only champion the AAC ever knew, and their domination undoubtedly hastened the demise of the league for which Arch Ward had such fond hopes when he publicly announced its organization in September, 1944. The total command taken by the Browns, combined with the high cost of acquiring talent, dwindling attendance and mounting travel expenses all played a major part in the demise of the AAC.

As events were ultimately to prove, Arch Ward and the founders of the AAC were about 15 years too early in their bid to challenge the NFL as a major league. The economy just wasn't ready to support two major football leagues.

Now, with the AAC dead and buried, the major question was whether Paul Brown and his superb football machine were ready for the National Football League.

8

The Best Was Yet to Come

Soft-spoken Mickey McBride, a man of intense pride, bolted out of the National League reorganization meeting in Philadelphia in January, 1950, and confided to friends that he was going to pay off Paul Brown and get out of football. "They made a deal and now they don't want to go through with it," he roared.

In the merger agreement between the two leagues, Cleveland, San Francisco and Baltimore were the only All-America Conference teams that were allowed to continue. Some deals were made, and one of them specified that the Browns were to acquire the rights to six Buffalo players. Jim Breuil, Buffalo's owner, disbanded the franchise and bought into the Browns. Since the league wanted a strong team in New York, the Giants were allowed to take six players from the disbanding New York Yankees. The Giants selected six defensive specialists and there was no disagreement on this transaction.

McBride finally cooled off after his tirade and returned to the meeting room, and the deal was finally closed. Instead of six players, the Browns got three of the Bills -- halfback Rex Bumgardner, guard Abe Gibron and tackle John Kissell. McBride was never completely satisfied, but went along with the decision.

There were other squabbles. There was the question of east-west alignment, and the matter of what to do with players already drafted by both leagues. Both the Browns and the Detroit Lions, for example, held the draft rights to Doak Walker, the Southern Methodist All-American halfback. NFL Commissioner Bert Bell had ruled that these problems should be settled by the teams involved. They should either make a trade or flip a coin, he said. The Browns and the Lions made a deal in which Paul Brown agreed to relinquish his claim on Walker in exchange for the Lions' first draft choice.

Brown talked trades with others among his new competitors. One of these discussions was with Ted Collins, the flashy owner of the NFL's New York Bulldogs and songstress Kate Smith's manager. Paul already had established his shrewdness in the player trades, and Jack White, assistant Bulldog coach and now a member of the New York Yankees baseball organization, cautioned the crafty Collins, "Better not make a deal with him. Paul will end up with your Kate Smith."

In the drafting of players from the pool of those left without a connection when the Los Angeles Dons, Buffalo Bills, Chicago Hornets and New York-Brooklyn disbanded, the Browns got halfback Ken Carpenter and end Jim Martin. They also landed tackle John Sandusky and halfbacks Ken Gorgel and Don Phelps.

Three key members of the 1949 squad retired, and the Browns were in need of help. Linebacker Lou Saban and guard Eddie Ulinski quit to enter coaching careers, and Edgar Jones left to go into the steel business in Pittsburgh. Brown also lost another of his assistants to college coaching when Dick Gallagher took over as head man at Santa Clara.

However, the hard core of the team which had carried the Browns to four straight AAC championships remained. Brown often was quoted as saying that the success of the pass-and-trap offense depended upon the strength in the "Big T." This is how he referred to fancy, pass-catching ends, a big and powerful center and a talented quarterback and fullback. Speedie, left end; Lavelli, right end; Frank Gatski, center; Graham, quarterback; and Motley, fullback, were still in their prime. Cleveland also still had its amazing field-goal kicker, Lou (The Toe) Groza. It may have been just a coincidence, but at the NFL rules meeting prior to the opening of the season, the guide tape, developed by Groza and Don Greenwood, his original holder, was ruled illegal.

Many of the veteran National Leaguers still were unimpressed with the Browns, despite the team's tremendous four-year record and its individual stars. Many did not hesitate to voice the opinion that the Browns would soon find out what it was like to play in a "real" professional league.

One incident which illustrated the animosity between the Browns and the old NFL teams came in January, 1950, when Graham was at the Washington Touchdown Club to receive an award as the outstanding 1949 player in the defunct All-America Conference. George Preston Marshall, the outspoken owner of the Washington Redskins and one-time laundryman, presented a similar award to Steve Van Buren of the Eagles for his NFL performance that season. During the presentation, Marshall jokingly remarked that Van Buren had driven Jimmy Conzelman, the former coach of the Chicago Cardinals, right out of pro football and back into private business. Conzelman had quit after the Eagles beat the Cardinals in the 1949 NFL title game. Then O. O. Kessing, commissioner of the AAC, rose to make the presentation to Graham. He noted that it was unusual for the head of a defunct league to be invited to such an affair.

Graham couldn't contain himself. "The AAC isn't defunct," he said with a broad smile on his face. "We simply absorbed the National League.

"Speaking of what happened to Mr. Conzelman," Otto continued, "maybe Mr. Marshall had better buy back a piece of that laundry business if we play the Redskins next year."

Marshall, never one to back off from a verbal duel, shot to his feet.

"You probably won't even have a job next year. Maybe you'd like to drive one of those laundry trucks," he retorted.

Graham got in one more verbal swipe when he said firmly, "Mr. Marshall has caused many men to lose millions of dollars through his stubbornness during the so-called football war."

Speculation on Cleveland's future in the NFL provoked some heated arguments between January and July, when the Browns went to training camp at Bowling Green.

"We've established quite a reputation in four years of All-America Conference competition," Brown said as he began a forceful opening-day speech. "But we've been taunted and kidded about playing in an inferior league. It has been said the worst team in the National League the last four years could beat the best in the All-America Conference.

"We have not only this year at stake, but four years of achievement. I'm asking you to dedicate yourselves more than ever before to preserve the reputation you've made.

"It won't be easy. Because we're new to the league, things may be a little rough at times. But remember, the worst thing you ever can do to an opponent is to put the most points up on the scoreboard. They understand that more than anything else."

The first direct contact with the National League came three weeks after training camp opened. Facing the Browns in an exhibition contest at the Glass Bowl in Toledo, Ohio, the Green Bay Packers received the opening kickoff and moved straight down the field for a touchdown.

"When I saw that happen," Brown confessed later, "I did wonder myself if perhaps we were in the wrong league."

Cleveland took the next kickoff and had the score tied in two plays. Two passes by Graham, the second a long-distance job to Dub Jones, got the tying touchdown. The Browns eventually won 38-7.

Paul Brown's charges went through a five-game exhibition schedule without a blemish. After they edged the powerful Chicago Bears, 27-23, some of the doubters began to be believers. But one of the few National Leaguers still unconvinced was Earl (Greasy) Neale, coach of the Philadelphia Eagles. While the Browns were dominating the AAC, the Eagles had won three straight Eastern Conference championships in the NFL and had conquered the Chicago Cardinals and the Los Angeles Rams in the title play-offs in 1948 and 1949.

Appropriately, the regular schedule matched the two champions in the NFL opener for 1950. To be played in Philadelphia, the game was sponsored by the *Philadelphia Inquirer*. The newspaper sent an observing reporter to cover the Browns' camp. He was likable Mort Berry, who later became publicity director of baseball's Philadelphia Phillies. Berry was quickly impressed, and his daily dispatches warned Philadelphia fans of the Browns' prowess. It was more than a publicity build-up for the game. Berry was sincere.

Neale steadfastly maintained supreme faith in his team, especially his defensive unit. He even boasted that he hadn't bothered to scout the Browns. "They are just a basketball team. All they can do is throw the ball," Neale said.

The Philadelphia coach was convinced that his linebackers could handle the Cleveland passing attack. This was the heart of his defense. Eagle linebackers planted themselves in front of the offensive ends and held them up as they attempted to break downfield for a pass, a legal maneuver if it were to take place before the ball is in the air.

The Browns approached their opener thoroughly prepared. They had been aiming for the Eagles throughout the exhibition season and Speedie and Lavelli were well grounded in the defense techniques of the alert Philadelphia linebackers. The two Cleveland ends were quick, agile and smart, and were ready for the big test.

Paul Brown, a master psychologist who didn't believe in fiery oration or locker-room pep talks, applied the long needle to his defensive unit during the team's pre-game meal at the Warwick Hotel. "Just think," he said, "tonight you fellows will have a chance to touch the great Steven Van Buren."

A crowd of 85,000 was on hand at Philadelphia's Municipal Stadium for the game. Most of the partisan fans had come fully expecting to see the Eagles destroy the Browns.

Cleveland kicked off, held for downs and the Eagles punted. Don "Dopey" Phelps fielded the ball and took off. The Browns' deadly blocking dropped the Eagles along the way, allowing Phelps to go into the end zone standing up. A clipping penalty nullified the score. The Browns punted, but the Eagles failed to score and once more were forced to kick. Phelps, again taking off on a long-distance return, was stopped short of a touchdown this time. But an official's flag signaled another penalty against the Browns. Philadelphia finally got on the scoreboard first, when Cliff Patton booted a 15-yard field goal from a difficult angle.

The Browns took the subsequent kickoff and began to move down the field. The Eagle line was tough and experienced, and the going was rugged. Graham mixed up his plays. He failed to complete his first three passes and the Philly fans began to hoot. But Graham was cool, and the riding didn't faze him. Suddenly, he faded back, danced away from Philadelphia linemen and lobbed a pass straight down the field to Dub Jones, 34 yards away. Jones grabbed the ball on the 25-yard line and went the rest of the way into the end zone. Groza kicked the extra point and the Browns were ahead, 7-3.

In the second quarter, the Browns demonstrated their defensive prowess when they stopped two fierce Philadelphia drives, one of them on the two-yard line. Then the Browns started a drive on their own 29-yard line. Graham methodically moved them to the Philadelphia 26, where he retreated into his protection pocket and coolly hit Lavelli under the crossbars for his second touchdown pass. Groza's extra point made the score 14-3.

Early in the third period, four straight completions by Graham moved the ball 67 yards to the Philadelphia 13. Graham missed connections on a pass, but tried again. He was hit solidly by Norm Wiley of the Eagles, but bounded away and again found Speedie in the end zone. Groza kicked the extra point and the Browns were comfortably ahead 21-3.

The Philadelphia fans, who for years had been fed with the story that the AAC was a minor league, couldn't believe what they were seeing. It was a great offensive and defensive effort, and the Browns walked off the field at the game's end with a 35-10 victory.

Greasy Neale, in a state of shock, said, "Jeez, they got a lot of guns."

Perhaps the most glowing tribute paid the Browns came from the Eagles' Pete Pihos, one of the National League's all-time great ends, who was met by his wife outside the dressing-room after the game.

"What happened honey?" his wife inquired.

"I guess we finally met up with a team from the big league," Pete answered.

Commissioner Bell told Paul Brown that "the Browns were as good a football team as I've ever seen."

Brown, inwardly happy about the outcome, maintained his usual poise in the post-mortems. "We won't gloat about this," he said. "We have a long season ahead of us." He was right.

The Browns easily won their second game, against Baltimore, 31-0. Then they prepared to open their home schedule against one of the National League's old-line powers, the New York Giants. Despite the fact that this was the Browns' first home effort against a National Football League team, only 37,467 fans showed up for the contest.

Steve Owen, the Giant coach, and the late Jack Lavelle, his chief scout, had watched the Browns whip the Eagles and brewed up a special defense aimed at stopping Graham's passing. In what they called an "umbrella defense," the Giants played a 6-1-2-2 defense and had their ends drop off for pass coverage instead of having them rush the passer. This gave the Giants seven men to cover the Browns' swift and tricky pass catchers. The defense baffled the Browns.

Midway in the first quarter, the Giants drove 52 yards in seven plays and fullback Eddie Price blasted over from the two for the touchdown. The extra point try was no good, but the Giants had six points on the scoreboard and that was all the scoring for the day.

Graham failed to complete a pass in the first half, but Brown made some adjustments at intermission, and Otto eventually connected on 12, right into the "umbrella." Yet the Browns threatened to score only once, reaching the New York 10-yard line. Here the trap play was called on second down. Motley ran into Graham, knocking the ball from his hands. The Giants recovered to kill the threat.

It was significant that three of the players in the New York defensive backfield were Otto Schnellbacher, Harmon Rowe and Tom Landry, all members of the New York Yankees of the All-America Conference in its final year who had been awarded to the Giants in the merger agreement.

Cleveland's defense was great, but New York's was just a little better. The final score was 6-0. It was the first time in 62 games that the Browns had failed to score. Only three times had they been held to one touchdown in a game.

It was touch and go the rest of the season for the Browns. They beat the Pittsburgh Steelers, 30-17, and the Chicago Cardinals, 34-24, on consecutive Sundays.

The victory over the Cardinals was costly for the Browns. They lost Lennie Ford, the big, bruising defensive end, for the rest of the regular season. Ford had played both ways with the Los Angeles Dons, but with the Browns he was restricted to defense. Strong, agile and fearless, he was the nemesis of enemy quarterbacks. He was playing a great game against the Cardinals. In the third period, the Cardinals ran a wide play around Ford's end. Ford was blocked and dropped to the ground as the official's flag went down. He was ejected from the game for committing a personal foul. But it was Ford who had been clobbered. He suffered a broken jaw and took his nourishment through straws for the next several weeks.

After the Chicago game, the Browns invaded New York for a return game with the Giants at the Polo Grounds. Again, the Giants' defense was tough. Groza got two field goals, but the Browns' only touchdown was a gift, set up when a Giant backfield man failed to cover a kickoff and Ken Carpenter fell on the ball inside the five-yard line. Graham took it over for the score. Again, New York won the second meeting, 17-13.

That night, en route to Cleveland, Brown told reporters he was sure his team was past its peak. "This team is over the hill," he said, obviously trying to needle his players.

However, before the Browns reported for their first practice session of the week, on Wednesday morning, Brown began preparing himself and the team for another pass at first place. "We're still taking the position we have a chance," he said. "The season is only half over and there are six games to play, both for us and the Giants."

Motley came ripping back the next Sunday, gaining 178 yards rushing, as the Browns hammered Pittsburgh, 45-7. They were hard-pressed to get by the Cardinals a week later. After scoring on the first offensive play of the game on a Graham-to-Jones pass, Cleveland had to settle on a field goal by Groza for a 10-7 decision.

San Francisco was experiencing difficulty in its first National League season and was handled easily by Cleveland, 34-14. The Browns weren't out of contention by a long shot.

George Preston Marshall's Washington Redskins were the Eastern Conference's weakest team, but no one could have convinced the Browns they weren't a title contender. In their Cleveland visit, the Redskins held a 14-13 lead going into the final minutes of the game, when Graham picked out his receivers flawlessly and directed a touchdown drive that gave the Browns a 20-14 win.

Then the Philadelphia Eagles moved in for a game in the rain and mud at Cleveland Stadium. The Browns got a quick 7-0 lead when Warren Lahr intercepted a pass and returned it for a touchdown. They got six more points on two Groza field goals and won, 13-7. Amazing as it may sound, the Browns didn't throw a pass all afternoon. Brown wanted to give the lie to Greasy Neale's slur that Cleveland was "just a basketball team," and he did. "It was a silly grandstand play," Brown said after the game, "but I wanted to prove we could win the hard way."

The Browns and the Giants came down to the final game of the season tied for first place. Each had a 9-2 record as the Browns invaded Washington and the Giants entertained Philadelphia.

Graham was a leader, a level-headed athlete who never snapped at his teammates and always was ready to assume responsibility and shoulder the blame when damaging errors occurred in offensive performances. Perhaps the only time in his career with the Browns that Otto violently expressed himself over the actions of a teammate came in the Washington game. With the Browns trailing, Motley carried the ball on the last play of the first half and was pushed around by the Redskins' Gene Pepper as he went out of bounds. Motley punched back and was thrown out of the game. On the way to the dressing room, Graham bawled him out. He knew what Motley meant to the team and how much he would be needed in the second half.

Rookie Emerson Cole of Toledo University was teriffic as Motley's substitite in the second half of the game. Graham did some magnificent passing in a near-blinding snowstorm, and the Browns won 45-21.

The Giants got by the Eagles in a defensive thriller, 9-7. Cleveland and New York met for the third time in a play-off for the Conference title the following Sunday in Cleveland.

It was bitter cold the day of the game. The temperature hovered at about 10 degrees and the wind off Lake Erie made things mighty uncomfortable for the 33,054 fans assembled for the contest. The field was icy, and most of the players wore basketball shoes instead of football cleats. Groza wore a basketall shoe on his left foot and a football shoe (minus cleats) on his right, giving him a hard toe for his place kicking.

It was a monumental defensive struggle, just as the two regular season games had been. Groza gave the Browns a 3-0 lead with a field goal in the first half, and the Browns tenaciously held onto the slim margin until midway in the final period. Then disaster almost struck. The Browns lost defensive left end George Young and left linebacker Tony Adamle through injuries. The Giants began pecking away successfully from Steve Owen's A-formation.

Finally, a swift Giant halfback named Charlie (Choo Choo) Roberts broke into the clear and was headed for a touchdown. Bill Willis, a 215-pound middle guard on defense, saved the day. Willis, who had been a sprinter in high school and college, turned on the speed and hauled Roberts down from behind on the Browns' four-yard line. Cleveland's defense held for three downs, and the Giants had to settle for a field goal that tied the score, 3-3.

Time was running out, but there was enough of the game left for the Browns to move into position for another field goal. A close analysis of the Giants' defense indicated to Brown that the quarterback draw play would work. Brown, who was reluctant to let Graham run unless he could find no receiver open, turned him loose in the closing minutes of the struggle. Graham ran and the Browns moved into position for another field goal by Groza. A last-second safety gave the Browns an 8-3 victory, which put them into the world title game in their first season as a National League team.

. Cleveland's foe for the championship game was none other than the Los Angeles (nee Cleveland) Rams, who had fled Cleveland prior to the opening of the Browns' first season. The Rams earned their title game bid by defeating the Chicago Bears in a play-off for the Western Conference crown. The core of the Rams' strength was made up of the same players who had given Cleveland its first NFL championship in 1945, the year before the franchise moved to the West Coast.

It was another frigid day in the Cleveland Stadium "icebox," and only 29,751 watched the battle between the two Cleveland teams, the old and the new. Again the game was played on a frozen field.

The big man in the Los Angeles backfield still was the popular Bob Waterfield, a great quarterback who had passed the Rams to the championship as a rookie in 1945.

Cleveland kicked off and the Rams returned the ball to their own 13-yard line. On the first offensive play of the game, Waterfield faded back and tossed to the legendary "Mr. Outside," Glen Davis, who caught the ball near the side lines at the 45 and ran untouched into the end zone. Waterfield booted the extra point and the Rams had a stunning 7-0 lead.

Six plays later, Graham, who completed three passes and contributed a 21-yard run, pitched to Dub Jones for a touchdown. Groza converted and it was a new game.

Before the first quarter ended, the Rams were out in front again. A 44-yard pass from Waterfield to a brilliant end, Tom Fears, put the ball in position for Dick Hoerner to blast into the end zone. A Waterfield kick made it 14-7.

Early in the second period, Graham rallied his forces and engineered an eight-play drive capped by a touchdown pass to Lavelli. In the conversion attempt, the pass was high. Tommy James, holding the ball for Groza, couldn't set it down in time. Instead, he got up and ran a few yards to his right and tossed a pass to Tony Adamle in the end zone. Adamle dropped the ball, setting the stage for an unbelievable finish.

Cleveland charged into the lead early in the second half, moving 77 yards for a touchdown. Graham tossed his third touchdown pass, a lob to Lavelli, and Groza again converted to make it 20-14.

But the Rams weren't ready to roll over and play dead. Waterfield uncorked three passes to put the ball on the Cleveland 17. Hoerner took over and pounded away at the Cleveland line until he battered over the goal line from the one. Waterfield's kick made it 21-20.

"All right," Graham said to his teammates. "They've got us by one point. We'll get it back."

The Browns had the ball on their own 20 and were attempting to generate a drive. Motley took a pitchout from Graham and spun around right end for eight yards. Then he was cornered and started to run back toward his own goal line in search of running room. Alert Los Angeles defenders finally pulled him down on the Browns' 14 and forced a fumble. Larry Brink of the Rams picked up the stray pigskin and ran into the end zone. Waterfield's boot was perfect and the Rams had a cozy 28-20 lead.

As the clock ticked on, Warren Lahr's interception of a Waterfield pass on the Cleveland 35 brought hope to the Browns and set the stage for their fantastic comeback. Graham and Lavelli teamed up for five straight completions to move the ball to the Los Angeles 43. On fourth down, with one to go, Graham carried to the 40.

The fans picked up the tempo. "Go, go, go," they shouted.

Graham was great in the clutch and finally capped the long drive with his fourth touchdown pass, a flip to Rex Bumgardner who made a circus catch. Groza kicked the extra point, and the only thing separating the two teams was the missed conversion in the first half. The Rams led, 28-27.

The Browns had something going again, but when Graham fumbled on the Rams' 24, there were three minutes left on the scoreboard clock. Graham, disgusted with himself, ran dejectedly off the field. Brown gave him a pat on the back. "Don't worry about it. We're going to win," he said.

"Now Paul was not in the habit of dishing out compliments to a player when he made a mistake," Graham later recalled. "But that particular time he made me feel like a man again.

"I certainly didn't have his confidence that we could pull it out. I didn't even think we could get the ball back again. All the Rams needed was a first down and we'd be out of it. But they didn't get it and, somehow, Paul Brown knew they wouldn't."

The Rams stalled in the huddle and ran the ball into the line in an attempt to run out the clock. But the Browns' defense was superb, and the Rams were forced to punt. Cliff Lewis took the punt and ran it out of bounds on the Cleveland 32. The clock showed 1:50 remaining.

On the first down, Graham faded back but couldn't find a receiver open. He ran the ball 14 yards for a first down. Cool almost to disdain, he passed to Baumgardner for 13 yards and then to Jones for 16 more. He passed again and this time found Baumgardner for 12 yards and a first down on the Ram 11-yard line.

Graham called his own play. He ran the ball directly to his right to get it in front of the goal posts. Then he waved to the bench, and in came the field-goal unit. All the Browns needed to win it was a three-pointer by Groza. James knelt at the 16 and brushed the turf. Hal Herring centered the ball. James carefully set it down. Groza, two and one-half steps behind James, took a short stride with his right foot and a longer one with his left. He kicked the ball between the uprights.

The Browns were champions of the world, 30-28.

When the bedlam finally subsided in the locker room, one football writer asked the obvious of the muscular Groza: "Were you nervous?"

"I don't get nervous when I kick," Groza answered. "I was just going over the things in my mind, reminding myself to remember fundamentals."

Joe Page, a great new Yankee relief pitcher, who had been in some tough scrapes himself, was standing near Groza in the clubhouse. "Like hell," Page said. "I get nervous in a spot like that and so do you. Don't tell me you weren't worried about missing. I know what was going through your mind."

"All I let myself think about," Groza retorted seriously, "were the fundamentals I was going to have to go through. Maybe I hear the crowd when I'm playing tackle, but I don't hear anything when I'm getting ready to kick."

It was a great day for Groza and an equally brilliant one for Graham. He connected on 22 of 32 passes, threw for four touchdowns and had one pass intercepted. Waterfield completed 18 of 32 passes and had four intercepted.

Each of the winning Browns received $1,113.

In summing up the season, Paul Brown commented, "When we went to training camp at the beginning of the season, I knew we had a dedicated group of young men -- young men determined to preserve what we all considered four years of achievement."

9

Second Thoughts

About the time that Paul Brown opened the curtain on the "Biggest Show in Football," a blond burr-head breezed in from Milwaukee with all the subtlety of an atomic bomb. Bill Veeck was his name, and he announced to one and all that he was now the proud owner of the Cleveland Indians. Within a few months during the summer of 1946, Willie Veeck had set Cleveland on its ear. With fireworks, orchids to the ladies, personal salesmanship and promotional gimmicks of all kinds, Veeck had captivated the populace. By the end of the baseball season, the Indians had drawn more than a million fans for the first time in their history.

By 1948, Veeck had put together a ball club to go with his promotional activities, and the Indians won the American League pennant, beat the Boston Braves in the World Series and drew an unbelievable 2,620,627 fans for the season. Veeck stayed around for another season and then peddled his interest in the Cleveland franchise. But for four years he had pushed into the background everything else connected with sports in Cleveland, including Paul Brown. The Browns, with their tremendous success on the playing field, were big news, to be sure. But Bill Veeck was the king, and Paul Brown never was quite able to swallow it. At Massillon, Brown had been Mr. Big. At Ohio State University in football-mad Columbus, he was No. 1. But in Cleveland, those four years, he was the No. 2 man, perhaps even No. 3 in 1948, behind the free-spending Veeck and Lou Boudreau, the Indians' heroic manager-shortstop. Boudreau, the one-time Illinois cage star, reached the peak of his popularity in 1948, when he led the Indians to victory over the Boston Braves in the World Series.

The relegation to second best, plus the problems of the All-America Conference and a lessening of fan interest in the Browns, contributed to Brown's uncertainty about his future in pro football. As a result, rumors occasionally cropped up that he was contemplating a move back to the college ranks. Most of the gossip linked him with Ohio State University. Brown came to grips with his conscience in 1949, when he signed a long-term pact with Mickey McBride covering the next seven seasons. For all intents and purposes, it appeared that Paul Brown was in Cleveland to stay. The money was good and he was the boss, with only McBride to report to when he, Brown, felt it was necessary.

The Browns' sensational showing in their first year in the National Football League had made Paul Brown look like a full-fledged genius, but he still had his doubts about professional football.

Veeck had taken his capital gain and was looking for another baseball property. He no longer was a problem.

The thing that frustrated Brown most was the attendance figures at the Cleveland home games. The Browns were playing in the "big league," but attendance for six home games in 1950 was only 200,319, just about half of what it had been when the Browns began playing a seven-game schedule back in 1946. Too, it was up only 11,000 above the six-game attendance figures for the 1949 season when the Browns were playing in a league which was gasping for breath. Though it was mighty cold, a total of 62,805 had showed up for the tight play-off game with the Giants and the thrilling championsip game with the Rams. While others may have overlooked the dwindling attendance in the light of the Browns' artistic success on the playing field, Paul Brown apparently gave the problem a great deal of thought as 1951 rolled around.

There was also the fact that Arthur B. McBride, the Browns' freewheeling owner, had been subjected to a rough grilling in Cleveland before the U.S. Senate's roving Kefauver Committee, which staged a highly publicized and nationally televised investigation of nationwide gambling. McBride admitted before the Committee that he was the principal owner of a race wire syndicate which supplied clients the results of horse races around the country.

All of these things apparently were weighing on Paul Brown's complex mind. Few people would have guessed that Brown would even consider another job after having forced other members of the National Football League to eat crow. Yet less than three weeks after Cleveland had edged the Rams to become the football champions of the world, Cleveland fans -- still basking in the glow of the heart-pounding triumph -- were shocked to read newspaper reports suggesting the possibility of Brown's return to college coaching.

The first accounts quoted Athletic Director Willis O. Hunter of the University of Southern California as saying that he had talked with Brown and had offered the Cleveland coach the head football coaching job with the Trojans. A few days later, Hunter explained that Brown had eliminated himself from consideration in Los Angeles, saying he "just couldn't afford to take the job at USC," where -- like all colleges -- they don't give the coach a share of the profits, which Brown was getting from the professional Browns.

In the meantime, Wesley Fesler had resigned as Ohio State coach, giving as his reason the tremendous pressures under which a coach labors at Columbus. Adding insult to injury, Fesler promptly took a coaching job at the University of Minnesota.

Buoyed by the announcement that Brown had at least been interested enough in the Trojan post to talk with Hunter, factions within the Ohio State University Alumni Associaton as well as the student body launched a

"Bring Back Brown" campaign. Meanwhile, OSU began the tedious process of screening candidates for the vacant coaching post.

In mid-January, after Brown had returned to Cleveland from the NFL meetings in Chicago, OSU Athletic Director Dick Larkins yielded to Alumni pressure and invited Brown to Columbus to meet with the screening committee. When the committee's invitation was made public, Brown was noncommittal about the possibility of his returning to Ohio State. He had insisted all along that he was interested in remaining with the Browns.

Larkins was asked flatly whether Ohio State planned to offer the job to Brown at the screening session and he replied tartly, "No sir, as a matter of fact we may not even consider him for the job."

Rumors were rampant along High Street in Columbus that those interested in Brown's return had raised a large fund (estimated at between $50,000 and $100,000) to offer Brown if he would come to Ohio State. The money was to be in addition to a $15,000 annual salary.

Most surprised of all by the commotion over Brown's possible return to OSU was the man who was paying Brown's salary at Cleveland, Arthur B. McBride, who remarked, "Paul has never said a word to me that he is thinking of a change. He is a gentleman and an honorable fellow and I think that if he had a change in mind he would mention it to me."

Brown scheduled his Columbus visit for Saturday, January 27, when he would be en route to Florida for his annual vacation. To show their esteem for football's most successful coach, students and alumni planned a giant rally in front of the Faculty Club, where Brown was scheduled to have dinner with members of the Athletic Board. Notices were posted on bulletin boards of the campus buildings exhorting students to "Welcome Back Brown." A word-of-mouth campaign also was launched. Throughout the campus, students urged friends to show up at the rally.

As the meeting hour approached, Earl Flora, sports editor of the *Ohio State Journal,* warned in print: "Brown will be treading on enemy territory the minute he steps foot on the Ohio State University property. Whether you like to hear it or not, he is heartily and even vehemently disliked by an overwhelming majority of the faculty and Athletic Department members."

When Brown arrived at the Faculty Club, a crowd estimated at 1,500 began chanting, "We want Brown." A four-piece band added to the din. The lone dissenting note was evident on an automobile carrying a dummy dressed in OSU's scarlet and gray colors. The car bore placards which proclaimed: "There's no place like home. Cleveland wants you. Go back." It was learned later that the auto was driven by Clevelanders who wanted Brown to remain with the pro team.

Brown moved silently through the cheering, back-slapping crowd, halted on the Faculty Club steps, turned to the crowd and, with a faint smile, lifted his hat. Then he disappeared behind the doors.

Brown, who before the visit had been described as more curious than interested, huddled with the Board for more than four hours. As he emerged from the meeting, the Cleveland coach paused on the steps of the Faculty

Club to announce: "All I can say is that I have been screened, as have a number of other candidates. I'm glad I accepted the invitation. It has been a pleasant experience. I've always considered Columbus the best football town in the country. The period of my life when I coached here was a very, very happy one." The Athletic Board issued a terse "no comment."

Meanwhile, word of what had taken place during the meeting began to leak out. Alvin Silverman, writing in the *Cleveland Plain Dealer,* said that Brown had shocked members of the Board when he told them at the outset of the meeting, "Gentlemen, I am anxious to leave pro football." Most of the Board members, it was pointed out, had believed Brown was making the visit simply as a grandstand play.

Larkins was reported to have said that the controversy over Brown was damaging to the university. The fear was expressed, it was said, that a $15,000 salary would cause dissension among the faculty, since full-time OSU professors were making only approximately $9,000 a year at the time. Some members of the Athletic Board were said to feel that Brown was the greatest coach who ever lived, but that if he were hired, Larkins would have to be relieved of his athletic directorship, a move certain to provoke another controversy. Brown was reported to have remarked that he would come back to OSU only on his own terms.

From Florida, Brown responded that he did not ask for the job, that it was not offered to him, that there was no discussion of terms, salary and staff or other relative matters during the long meeting in Columbus. During a round of golf with Franklin Lewis, sports editor of the *Cleveland Press,* Brown said, "I wasn't applying for a job and they weren't interviewing me for a job. No one seemed to have a definite starting point. My name had been mentioned so frequently that I saw no harm in going down there. After all, I never mentioned a word to anyone about Ohio State. Everyone else did the talking in recent months.

"They still charge me with taking Lou Groza and Dante Lavelli away from the OSU team, but I observed the rule. Either the boy or his class must have been graduated before we could sign him. I made sure that Groza and Lavelli, who came to play for me after the war, went back to OSU to get their degrees. So you see, I didn't take anything away from the university itself. I'd do the same thing all over again. I was operating only according to the rules." While Brown golfed, the controversy continued to rage.

Gordon Cobbledick, veteran sports editor of the *Cleveland Plain Dealer,* speculated as to why Brown might want to return to the college ranks. "Pride figures largely in many of Brown's actions," Cobbledick wrote. "Pride could have inspired a wish to prove himself big enough to lick what perhaps is the toughest coaching situation in the country. Pride could have urged him to wade into a nest of bitter enemies and show the world that he was bigger than any of them."

The Athletic Board finally got around to making a recommendation. It was Wayne (Woody) Hayes, the successful Miami (Ohio) University coach. One group of students, angered at the selection of Hayes, petitioned for the removal of Larkins as athletic director "for personally being opposed to Paul Brown as football coach." Other students sent telegrams to Hayes, asking that he withdraw his name from consideration. Even Ohio Governor Frank J. Lausche was asked by the students and alumni to intervene.

One influential newspaper predicted that Larkins would resign if the job went to Paul Brown, and there were reports circulating that Larkins had prepared his resignation, to be submitted in the event that the Board of Trustees selected Brown. Of the report, Larkins said, "I cannot say the report is true, and I can't say that it isn't. What will happen when a coach is finally appointed is another matter."

The week between the recommendation of the Athletic Board and the Saturday meeting of the Board of Trustees was fraught with turmoil, to say the least. When the trustees assembled to consider the coaching situation, only four of the seven members were present. After some deliberation, in which they were reportedly deadlocked over whether to name Brown or Hayes, the matter was delayed a day or so so that additional members could be summoned. The second session was set for 4 p.m. Sunday, and it was hoped that U.S. Senator John Bricker and industrialist Charles Ketering, two of the three trustees absent from the first meeting, would be on hand. The seventh trustee was on vacation.

Meanwhile, a report of the National Broadcasting Company's radio network stated flatly that Paul Brown would return to Ohio State, barring a last-minute switch.

When the meeting time rolled around, only five of the six trustees scheduled to attend the meeting were in Columbus. The sixth, Senator Bricker, was en route from Arizona and bad weather had delayed his plane. The Senator, who was known to be strongly opposed to bringing Brown back to Ohio State, arrived almost three hours late. Shortly before 7 p.m., the powerful white-haired Republican lawmaker entered the room. An hour and a half after Bricker's arrival, OSU President Howard Bevis emerged from the conference room and announced that Hayes had been selected at a salary of $12,500.

"When I got into the room, the other trustees asked me how I felt about the situation," Bricker recalled years later. "I said I was going along with the recommendation of the screening committee and the Athletic Board." To do otherwise, Bricker reasoned, would destroy confidence in the Athletic Board and university officials. "Then we took a vote and it was unanimous for Woody Hayes," he said.

Hayes took over one of the toughest coaching jobs in the country and held it until 1979, posting one of the finest records in collegiate football.

And Paul Brown, who never really said publicly he wanted the job in the first place, remained with the Cleveland Browns to continue writing his incredible success story.

10

You Can't Win Them All

An attribute Paul Brown saw in young Otto Graham when he picked him to be the quarterback of the fledgling Browns was Otto's "distinctive qualities of leadership." Graham was a natural-born leader, and, during the years of the All-America Conference, Brown had entrusted him with the job of selecting most of the plays once the game was under way. "In the AAC," Graham later recalled, "I doubt that he [Brown] called six, seven or eight plays a game."

But as Cleveland moved into the National Football League, Paul Brown more and more became the twelfth man in the huddle. He did it by alternating two guards as "messengers" to bring play instructions from the "quarterback" on the side lines. By the time the Browns had been in the NFL a few years, Brown was calling virtually every play.

It was not that Brown had lost confidence in Graham. It was just his growing belief that the quarterback had enough responsibility on the field without having to worry about the selection of plays.

"I respect his opinion, but I disagree with him 100 per cent," Graham once said in a first-person story in *Sport* magazine. "His theory," continued Graham, "is this: A player comes out of the game and gives him information. Then he has coaches sitting up there over the 50-yard line with a phone connected to the bench and they're calling down information, too. He says he coordinates all our thinking, then sends in the plays. That's fine, except in actual practice it seldom works. By the time the coaches call down and all the details are hashed out, two or three plays may have gone by.

"I believe these fellows playing pro ball are actually playing coaches," asserted Graham. "They're pros. They know a lot better than anyone else what they can do at a given moment. Lou Groza, for instance, might come back in the huddle and tell me that the opposing tackle was charging too hard and could be trapped.

"I want to call a play right there and then to take advantage of the situation. There were times when I ignored Paul's calls. When my plans worked, he didn't say much. When they didn't he let me know about it."

More frequent use of his own play-calling during games was one of the few changes Brown made in his coaching technique as Cleveland took its place in the National Football League. He continued the regimented summer practice sessions and made highly touted All-American stars go through all fundamentals. If they didn't adjust to the Brown system, they soon found themselves with another club.

As he had done in the All-America Conference, Brown kept his players in the classroom almost as much as they were on the practice field. He felt that a good exercise with a pencil and paper was as important in learning plays and assignments as running through the plays in practice. When it came to copying play after play in a notebook and the endless quizzes and examinations, the veterans, including Graham, were treated the same as the youngster who was going through the experience for the first time.

The Browns may not have liked the hours during the summer practice sessions, but they found life a little more pleasant once the regular season rolled around. At Massillon, Ohio State and Great Lakes, Brown had never scrimmaged his team once the regular season started, and he carried this practice into the pro ranks.

Paul didn't believe in long practice sessons, either. During the championship season, the squad was off on Mondays and Tuesdays. Workouts were limited to sessions of about two hours on Wednesdays, Thursdays and Fridays, and about 20 minutes -- just enough to raise a sweat -- the day before a game. The team reported each working day at 9:30 a.m. and devoted the morning hours to classroom work, discussing offensive and defensive plans for the coming game and viewing game films. Brown made a production of every game.

One football classic that had escaped Paul Brown in his distinguished career was the annual benefit game between the NFL champions and the College All-Stars in Chicago's mammoth Soldier Field. As champions in 1950, the Browns qualified to represent the league in the 1951 game. It didn't count in the standings, but Brown began pointing his team for the game in the most meticulous way.

One of the coach's strictest regulations was that the team practice at a specified time each day, sunshine, rain or snow. A heavy rainstorm hit the Bowling Green training site one day during the week of the All-Star game, and not a fan was present to view the workout. But on a main highway that bordered the practice field, Brown spotted a car with an out-of-state license plate. Suspicious that Herman Hickman, the portly coach of the All-Stars might have sent a spy, Brown summoned assistant trainer Morrie Kono and asked him to investigate. Who else would watch the workout on a day like this if they didn't have a special reason? Kono trotted to the parked automobile and found a motionless occupant. "Looks like an exhausted salesman," Kono reported to the coach. "The guy is sound asleep."

Whatever fears Brown had about the strength of the All-Stars were unwarranted. Cleveland romped to an easy 33-0 victory.

Brown stood pat on his squad in 1951. Only five changes were made in personnel. One of the new additions was Bob Gaudio, who came out of retirement. The most significant new man was Harry (Chick) Jagade, who had played for the Baltimore Colts in the All-America Conference. He was signed as a free agent after sitting out the 1950 season with a broken foot. There didn't seem to be any place on the team for Jagade when he reported, but he was tough and aggressive and made the team, eventually succeeding Motley as the Browns' fullback.

The Browns won four of their five exhibition contests in 1951, including the victory over the All-Stars, and headed into the regular season against their old and bitter rivals from AAC days, the San Francisco 49ers. It was a costly afternoon for Cleveland in more ways than one. The Browns lost the game 24-10, and several players were injured. Tony Adamle, the team captain and a superb linebacker, was carried from the field with what was thought to be a severely sprained ankle.

The second game was with the Rams at Los Angeles, and the Browns were quartered at the Green Hotel in Pasadena the week of the contest. Coach Joe Stydahar of the Rams and his staff had scouted the Browns at San Francisco and witnessed the rash of injuries.

Adamle was absent from practice all week. He took his only exercise by limbering up the injured ankle in walks up and down the long corridors of the hotel. The onetime Cleveland high-school star proved a real inspiration to his teammates when he trotted out to his customary position at left linebacker with the defense at game time on Sunday.

The Browns rebounded from their opening loss with an easy 38-23 victory over the Rams. The game was marked by a rash of penalties against the visiting Cleveland team. Things got so bad that even the Los Angeles fans booed the officials.

It was later revealed that Adamle, a great competitor who turned in a key interception that led to one touchdown, had played the game with a chip fracture in his ankle.

Everyone knew about Cleveland's potent offense, but it was the defense that walked off with many of the kudos in the 1951 season. The defensive unit was perhaps the best in the Browns' history. It included two of the most ferocious men ever to play defensive end, George Young and Lenny Ford. John Kissell and Derrell Palmer were the regular tackles, and Bill Willis played guard. Bob Oristaglio worked part time at end, and Forrest (Chubby) Grigg saw service at tackle. For linebackers, Brown had Adamle on the left side, Alex Agase in the middle and Hal Herring on the right side. Tommy Thompson, who later was to become a star linebacker, was the alternate.

Warren Lahr was the left half, while Tommy James worked at right half. Cliff Lewis was the safety man, with Don Shula, now head coach of the Miami Dolphins, as his alternate. The group registered four shutouts and held the opposition to 152 points in 12 games.

One of the whitewash jobs was against the New York Giants in the season's second game between the rivals. The first game had gone to the Browns, 14-3, in another stirring defensive struggle. The Browns were leading, 10-0, in the closing moments of the second contest when the Giants came close to the goal line. A Giant touchdown would have made no difference in the outcome, but the Browns' proud defensive unit refused to give up a score.

After their opening defeat, Cleveland went on to win 11 straight games, including a tremendous 42-21 victory over the Chicago Bears in the first league meeting between the two teams.

Dub Jones, who had been nicknamed "Six O'Clock" by an out-of-town sports writer because of his long and lean appearance, had his greatest day as a professional halfback against the Bears. Jones handled the ball only six times and scored six touchdowns, equaling a record established by the great Ernie Nevers in 1929.

It was a rough afternoon. The Browns were penalized 21 times for 209 yards, a league record. The Bears drew 100 yards for infractions, and the two-team total of 309 yards went into the record book.

The 11-game winning streak, of course, carried the Browns into another title game, their second straight in the NFL and the sixth in a row since their birth in 1946. Once more the foe was Los Angeles, but this time the site was the Coliseum.

An ill-fated week led up to the championship game. Trouble began with the final scheduled game at Philadelphia. A snowstorm had grounded the chartered airplane that was to return the squad to Cleveland, and the trip was made by train. Poor flying weather continued and charter air travel was not available for the trip to Los Angeles. The team made the trip in two groups, on regularly scheduled flights. Uniforms were late in arriving and the first day's workout was held on a vacant field behind the hotel with the players in sports clothes. There was no privacy the rest of the week at the team's practice field.

Having edged the Rams in an exhibition game and then beaten them handily in the second game of the year, the Browns were a little complacent going into the title game. They fumbled, muffed passes and missed assignments. Cleveland wasn't playing one of its better games. Still, with seven minutes left to play, the score was tied, 17-17. At that point, Rams quarterback Norm Van Brocklin unleashed a long pass to Tom Fears for a touchdown. The Browns couldn't repeat their Hollywood finish of a year before and went down to defeat, 24-17.

Brown summoned a smile in the dressing room when it was over. Graham, whose play had been erratic, walked by and said, "I let you down, Paul." To this Brown replied, "It's part of living. Nothing to do now but forget it and start thinking of next season."

Paul Brown, who had built a reputation of never losing a big one, had been whipped for the first time in a championship game. Counting the Rams' title in 1945, Cleveland had been able to boast a professional football champion for six straight years. Unfortunately for Brown, losing championship games became a habit he didn't easily lick.

In their first two years in the National League, the Browns had won 23 and lost only four, including championship play-offs. They had definitely established themselves as a real powerhouse and now every opponent was pointing for them. And rival coaches, who once had scoffed at Paul

Brown's high-school background, began to copy many of his playing techniques and training methods.

In 1952, their third season in the NFL, it appeared for a time as if the Browns might be whittled down to size. After dropping their last two exhibition games, they opened the season with a stunning 37-7 triumph over the defending champion Rams in a game that cost Joe Stydahar his job as the Los Angeles coach. Cleveland then edged Pittsburgh, 21-20, but lost to New York, 17-9.

It went that way all season. The Browns, rolling up 11 straight the previous season, couldn't get a sustained winning streak under way. Their passing attack was hampered. Lavelli was on the side lines for half the season with a charley horse, and the same ailment kept Cleveland's best running back, Ken Carpenter, out of action for a good part of the season. This combination of mishaps contributed heavily to a somewhat mediocre season for Graham. He completed 181 passes out of 364 attempts for 2,816 yards gained and 24 touchdowns, but his performance was ragged on several occasions. His completion percentage of 49.7 was the lowest of his career. And for the first time in his coaching career Brown was the victim of second-guessing by the Monday morning quarterbacks.

Cliff Lewis, safety man and reserve quarterback, had retired after the 1951 season, and Brown acquired the veteran George Ratterman in a deal with Dallas. The fun-loving Ratterman had been a pro star for five years. Perhaps his greatest season came in 1950 when he kept the New York Yankees in contention for the Western division title.

At Graham's most erratic moments during the 1952 season the crowd began chanting, "We want Ratterman."

Ratterman had a reputation as a practical joker and always could be counted on for a few laughs during the season. There were a few games in which the Browns pulled comfortably ahead, giving the second-string quarterback some exercise. On one of those afternoons, a rookie guard named Joe Skibinski also got a chance to play some offense. Skibinski was acting as one of Brown's messenger guards. Bearing a play from Brown, he broke into the huddle and relayed the message to Ratterman.

"I don't like it," Ratterman snapped. "Go back and get another."

The stunned Skibinski headed for the side lines, but then Ratterman grinned and yelled for him to return, thus averting mutiny.

On another occasion while the Browns were preparing for a road game at their League Park practice field, Ratterman was seen filling a small can with some dirt. When his teammates inquired why he was filling the can, Ratterman quipped that if he got into the game that Sunday, he wanted to rub his hands in some familiar soil before he went in.

As the Browns were heading for New York and their final game of the season, Ratterman arrived at the terminal with an ironing board under his arm. Curious teammates inquired about the excess baggage.

"My wife just had a baby," Ratterman explained. "You always buy your wife a gift when she has a baby, and I'm flying to Cincinnati right after the game in New York to take this gift to her." There were those who suggested it should have been gift-wrapped.

Though it was the Browns' poorest season in seven years of competition, 1952 was a significant year. It marked the arrival of Ray Renfro, Darrell (Pete) Brewster and Bob Gain as rookies. All were to have distinguished careers with the Browns.

Cleveland went into the final game of the season at New York with an 8-3 record and a one-game lead over Philadelphia in the Eastern Conference standings. In their previous six meetings, the Browns and the Giants had staged a series of defensive struggles which produced a total of only 110 points. But that afternoon, the offensive units unleashed all of their frustrations and the Giants wound up on top 37-34. However, Washington, tied for last place with the Chicago Cardinals, upset Philadelphia, and the Browns captured their third straight Conference crown.

Despite the victory, the Browns were in trouble. Speedie and Jones suffered wrenched knees and Kissell also was injured in the New York contest. Though they had two weeks in which to get ready for the championship game with Detroit, none recovered in time for the contest. Renfro, who had done little since scoring a touchdown on a punt return the first time he touched the ball in a pro game, filled in for Jones, and Brewster replaced Speedie.

It was a jittery team that met Detroit for the championship before 50,934 fans at Cleveland Stadium. The Browns made enough errors to drop several games and were defeated, 17-7.

While the teams were deadlocked at 7-7, the Browns were in a position to grab the lead, but a backfield collision resulted in a fumble and the Lions recovered. Detroit capitalized with a 67-yard touchdown run by Doak Walker. Later, a fumble by Ken Carpenter put the Lions in position for the field goal that clinched the decision. Paul Brown had lost his second big one.

In seven years, Arthur McBride had gotten a lot of fun out of football, but losing the last two championship games was a great disappointment to him. "I don't want to win any half championships," he had once said. "I want to win everything. When I can't, it's time to get out."

Early in 1953, McBride was approached by a syndicate headed by Dave R. Jones, a Cleveland industrialist long identified with sports. He had been Cleveland's first boxing commissioner and a stockholder in the Cleveland Indians during Bill Veeck's regime. The approach was made through Dan Sherby, a McBride associate, while McBride was in Florida for the funeral of a good friend. Sherby telephoned McBride in Florida and asked him, "Will you sell the club?"

"I might, if I get what I want," McBride answered

McBride finally set a price tag of $600,000 on the club, a figure twice as large as any professional football franchise had brought in previous transactions. Dan Sherby, Paddy Dunne, and McBride's two sons, all associates in the ownership, were reluctant to sell, but McBride decided to go through with the deal.

Other key members of the syndicate were Ellis Ryan, insurance man and former president of the Cleveland Indians; Saul Silberman, owner of Randall Park Racetrack and Painesville Raceway; and Homer Marshman, industrialist-attorney who had founded the Cleveland Rams back in 1937.

As word leaked to the newspapers that a deal might be pending, Sherby issued a statement on behalf of his long-time associate McBride: "Mr. McBride has said definitely that he will sell only under two conditions: One -- that we get the money out that we put in. We put over one-million dollars into the Browns and we want to get that much out. Two -- that the purchasers are the kind who will continue to give the city of Cleveland the best in football."

Sherby continued, "According to Bert Bell, the commissioner of the National League, the Browns have the highest player and coaching payroll in the league. In the years we have had the Browns we have never taken out one dime. The club has made money, but we didn't get any part of it. Mr. McBride says all he ever got out of it was three free meals. The money went to the coaches, players and staff. Of course, we went into football as a hobby, not for any particular profit. But it has gotten to be too much pressure on us from August 1 to mid-December. McBride and I have become involved in about 25 different enterprises. We spread ourselves so thin that it began to hurt us physically. We took inventory of ourselves and we decided to cut down."

While the final negotiations for the sale were under way, Paul Brown, a minor stockholder in the club, was out of town on a fishing trip.

The deal was consummated on June 9, 1953, in the office of Homer Marshman, who handed McBride a check for $50,000 as a binder on the transaction. The bulk of the money was to be paid later.

If McBride had any regrets about getting out of pro football, it wasn't obvious in his actions during the transactions. He took the $50,000 check from Marshman, tucked it into the breast pocket of his sports coat and said softly, "Well, I came out clean after all. Considering what happened to some of the other fellows who started the old All-America Conference with me, this isn't so bad. I never made anything, but I didn't lose anything either, except maybe a few thousand dollars. I've simply had my fling at pro football and convinced myself that Cleveland will always buy the best. Now I'm getting out. I have a few other things to keep me busy."

There was a touch of bitterness in his voice when he spoke of Paul Brown after the deal was consummated. "It's a relief to know Paul is aware of this deal," McBride said, when hearing that the new owners had been in touch with Brown. "I've been trying to reach him for a week to tell him that we were selling."

McBride's remark raised the suspicion that he had been having trouble with Brown and that was why he decided to get out. While this was denied, the rumors have persisted ever since that one of the main reasons McBride sold was because his relationship with Brown had deteriorated to such a great degree of incompatibility.

Under the new management arrangement Jones took over as president of the new group, while Ryan became vice president. Silberman was chairman of the executive committee, and Marshman, secretary and counsel.

One of the first things the new owners did upon taking control was to take out a large life insurance policy on Paul Brown. They realized he was their biggest asset. Without him, they reasoned, they would have just another professional football franchise.

Under the new ownership, it was business as usual, with Brown running the entire show.

After their relatively poor record in 1952, there were some who were beginning to write off the Browns as being "over the hill." This belief was given some credence when Speedie and Kissell jumped the team to sign with Canadian clubs.

But Brown still had confidence in his team, and he made only minor changes in preparation for 1953. He did make one deal, however, and it was the biggest in his seven-year tenure as a pro coach. He sent ten players to Baltimore in exchange for five of the Colts, a transaction that proved to be of both immediate and future value. Included in the group which went to the Colts were guard Ed Sharkey and halfbacks Bert Rechichar, Carl Taseff and Don Shula. The latter was destined to become head coach of the Baltimore club in 1963 and later of the Miami Dolphins.

Brown acquired tackles Don Colo and Mike McCormack, guard Herschel Forester, linebacker Tom Catlin and halfback John Pettibon in the deal. The Colts needed immediate help and were willing to part with the five players since McCormack, Forester and Pettibon were in military service. The 10 players they got from the Browns were immediately available. Brown was willing to wait for the servicemen.

Colo plugged the gap in the defensive line, replacing Kissell. Catlin was a valuable addition to the linebacking corps. Brewster, the 1952 rookie, moved into Speedie's spot at offensive left end.

Bill Reynolds, a former University of Pittsburgh halfback and a high draft choice, and Chuck Noll, a native Clevelander who had been an outstanding lineman at the University of Dayton, were the most significant rookie additions. Noll, who lasted through 23 rounds of the annual draft, was one of the lowest draft choices ever to make the Browns' team.

Reynolds had a discouraging pro debut. In a pre-season game at San Francisco, Brown inserted him at right halfback. On one play, Bill received a severe jolt and suffered a slight concussion. He was taken to a hospital and held for observation overnight. Awakening in the morning, he gazed into the eyes of a pretty nurse. "Where am I?" he inquired.

"You're at St. Mary's," the nurse answered softly.

"My goodness, I've got to get going," he said. "I'm supposed to be in California with the Cleveland Browns football team."

Reynolds' home was in St. Mary's, *West Virginia.*

If the Browns were ailing seriously at the end of the 1952 season, their troubles were cured by the following September. They opened the season with four straight easy victories, routing Green Bay, 27-0; the Chicago Cardinals, 27-7; Philadelphia, 37-13; and Washington, 30-14.

Their next stop was New York. A heavy rainstorm pelted the city late Saturday afternoon and continued during the night and into Sunday morning. When Brown and his troupe arrived at the Polo Grounds they found that the field had not been covered. The game was played under the worst conditions the Browns had ever encountered. The players wallowed ankle deep in mud and water, and Brown knew his passing attack would be useless. He removed Jones and Renfro as halfbacks and substituted Reynolds and Carpenter, whose running styles were much more suited to slippery footing.

The short yardage gains of the sure-footed halfbacks got the Browns into position for one score, but the attack stalled on the Giant 11-yard line. On fourth down, Groza attempted an 18-yard field goal that was wide. But center Frank Gatski employed one of his little tricks with the ball before the snap and drew the Giants off side. The official stepped off a five-yard penalty, and the Browns had a first down on the six. From there Cleveland moved in for the game's only score and won, 7-0.

Under better field conditions, the Browns got their offense rolling, ripping Washington again, 27-3, and Pittsburgh, 34-16.

The Brownies had a seven-game winning streak on the line when San Franciso came calling. The 49ers had weathered a disastrous exhibition season, but had emerged as a title threat in the Western Conference once regular play had begun. A crowd of 80,698, the largest up to that time, was on hand for the game at Cleveland Stadium.

Misfortune struck the Browns in the second period when Graham was forced out of the game because of an injury. With the Browns out in front, 10-7, Graham faded back to pass from his own 23-yard line. His receivers covered, Graham spotted an opening and started to run. He picked up 19 yards before the 49ers caught him. First, Fred Bruney, a defensive halfback who had played at Ohio State, shoved Graham out of bounds on the 42, right in front of the Browns' bench. Then Art Michalik, a rugged 225-pound rookie middle guard, landed on top of him, his right elbow striking Graham and opening a deep, three inch cut on the left side of his mouth. Dazed and bleeding, Graham didn't know what had hit him. He was helped into the locker room by Dr. Vic Ippolito. Ratterman moved into the quarterback spot and guided the team while Dr. Ippolito used 15 stitches to close Graham's wound.

Graham returned after the start of the second half with a piece of clear plastic stretched across the front of his helmet to protect him against further mishaps. The injury did nothing to mar Graham's effectiveness. The dark-haired passer completed nine out of ten passes before the game was over, and the Browns bagged their eighth win in a row, 23-21

"We got pretty steamed up when Otto got hurt," Captain Tommy Thompson said in the locker room after the game. "Maybe we had no reason to, but we did. If it had been anybody else, it probably wouldn't have made us so mad. But they couldn't do that to Otto and get away with it. Not old Otto."

After the game, Michalik sat in front of his locker, a towel draped

Above: Browns' founder, Arthur B. McBride, leads the all-girl band which provided halftime entertainment in the early years.

Left: Paul Brown, the first coach of the Cleveland Browns

MARVIN GREENE

HERMAN SEID

MARVIN GREENE

Above: All-Time stars of the early years: Tony Adamle; Lou Saban and Marion Motley
Below: Lou "The Toe" Groza and Otto Graham

TONY TOMSIC

TONY TOMSIC

FRED BOTTOMER

Above: Ray Renfro, Len Ford, Bill Willis
Below: Dante Lavelli and Edgar Jones

FRANK KUCHIRCHUK

Down and Up: *There was a time when a player could get up and run after being tackled. In this photo sequence, End Mac Speedie shows how it was done. He catches the ball and is quickly pulled down from the rear, losing his helmet in the process. He scrambles to his feet, and is finally tackled for good.*

THE BROWNS FIRST NFL TITLE GAME
Above: *Quarterback Otto Graham appears to be biting finger of the Rams' Paul Younger as he makes a 12 yard gain in the 1950 title game.* **Below:** *Lou Groza watches his historic kick soar over the goal posts in the closing moments of the game, giving the Browns a 30-28 victory.*

bove: Marion Motley off on a 51-yard
n in third quarter play, the 1946 AAC title
me with New York Yankees. The Browns
on, 14-9.

DUDLEY BRUMBACH

LARRY KEIGHLEY

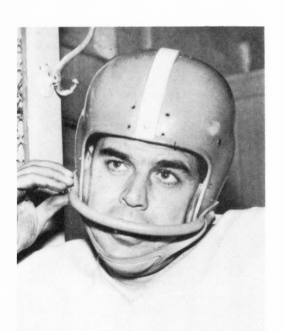

FRED BOTTOMER

Otto wounded! An angry Paul Brown starts after darkshirted 49er, Art Michalik, who collided with his star (on ground), cutting Graham's mouth. Tommy Thompson, with his foot in approved tripping position, holds off an equally angry Pete Brewster. *Left:* Graham displays the protective face mask invented by Paul Brown after the Michalik incident.

around his shoulders and his face in his hands. Both eyes were blackened and he could barely lift his head. The Browns had worked him over.

"I made a dive for Graham and hit him with my elbow," Michalik said. "I hope he's all right. I sure didn't mean to hurt him."

It was this incident which prompted Paul Brown to invent the thin, plastic face guard which for many years was worn across the front of both collegiate and professional football players' helmets. It prevented any opponent from landing a solid blow, with either a fist or an elbow, by accident or on purpose. It was the forerunner of the face mask.

The Browns followed up their 49er victory with a tight 20-16 decision over the Pittsburgh Steelers, and then clinched their fourth consecutive Eastern Conference crown with a 27-16 victory over the Cardinals in Cleveland. They still had two games left to play.

The Browns' next-to-last game was against the Giants in Cleveland. NFL Commissioner Bert Bell had always kept a close eye on gamblers, and when he heard that the odds on the Cleveland-New York game had shifted sharply the day before the game, he frantically called Cleveland to find out what was happening. He discovered that Brown had announced that Ratterman would start at quarterback. Brown had decided to give Graham a rest. This, the gamblers apparently believed, would improve the Giants' chances. But Ratterman threw four touchdown passes, and the Browns rolled up their biggest point total in the National League. They buried the Giants, 62-14.

The Browns went to Philadelphia for the final game of the schedule with a string of 11 consecutive triumphs. A victory over the Eagles would give them the first perfect season in the National Football League since 1942, when the Bears were unbeaten and untied in 11 games.

Cleveland got off to an impressive start and rolled up a 17-0 lead in the first quarter. Hopes were running high. But the Eagles chipped away at the lead, and before the afternoon was over, the Philadelphians powered to a 42-27 victory.

For the second straight year, the championship game opponent was Detroit. The Lions, under Buddy Parker, had finished one game ahead of the San Francisco 49ers with a 10-2 record. The game was scheduled for Briggs Stadium.

Graham had the worst day of his career, completing only two of 15 passes, and at one stage of the game was replaced by Ratterman because of his ineffectiveness. With one completed pass by Ratterman, the Browns finished the day with three completions in 16 tries for a net gain of only nine yards.

Still, Cleveland went into the final four minutes of the game with a 16-10 lead. The scores came on a nine-yard touchdown run by Jagade and Groza's extra point and three field goals.

Detroit quarterback Bobby Layne, one of the game's all-time great scramblers, delivered the *coup de grace* with two minutes remaining. Jim Doran got behind defender Warren Lahr and caught Layne's 33-yard pass in the end zone. Doak Walker kicked the extra point, giving the Lions a 17-16 decision. It was the Browns' third straight play-off loss.

"We tried to rush Graham so that he would have to hurry his passes," Parker pointed out in the Detroit locker room. "That was the key to our defensive strategy."

Of his game-tying catch, Doran said, "I was out in the open, and I just prayed I could hold it."

Paul Brown was obviously bitter in the Cleveland dressing room. "We tried so hard it was pathetic," he commented. "There used to be a time when we were like the New York Yankees. Anything we did turned out right for us. But I guess that's life. I don't even want to think about next year, yet."

But soon Paul Brown was busy planning for another season, one that would return all of the luster to his reputation for winning when it counted.

11

Beating "Father Time"

By 1954, Otto Graham had been playing for the Cleveland Browns for eight years and was acknowledged to be pro football's premier quarterback. He was 32 years old and appeared to have four or five more good years ahead of him.

But each season was getting to be more trying for the brilliant passer. Graham was becoming weary of the tight regimentation of training camp life, which kept him away from his family for six or seven weeks each year. More important, though, was his pride as an athlete. Graham wanted to quit while he was on top so that the fans would remember him for his greatness, rather than as an athlete who battled "Father Time" to the end of the line.

"What if I had retired after the 1953 season, when I played so miserably against the Detroit Lions in the championship game?" Graham asked in a *Sport* magazine article. "If I had quit then, the fans might remember me solely for that game. Look at Sugar Ray Robinson. How many people think of him today as one of the greatest boxers who ever lived?"

So when Graham sat down to sign his contract for 1954, he told Paul Brown that the coming season would be his last.

But Brown had more immediate problems than Graham's pending retirement. The management of the Baltimore Colts, determined to build a winning team, decided that the best way to find a man to head their coaching staff would be to raid the organization directed by the most successful coach in the business. First, they contacted Blanton Collier, who by now was given full credit for the outstanding defensive play of the Browns over the years. Collier turned down the offer. Their next choice was tackle coach Weeb Ewbank. He accepted and before many weeks passed, Collier also departed, taking the head coaching job at the University of Kentucky where he succeeded Paul (Bear) Bryant.

Brown was forced to reorganize his staff. He hired Paul Bixler, his long-time friend and assistant at Ohio State, and Eddie Ulinski, a former Brown who was coaching at Purdue University. Ulinski succeeded Ewbank as tackle coach. Howard Brinker, who had become end coach and chief scout in 1952, replaced Collier as defensive coach, while Bixler assumed the duties relinquished by Brinker. Bixler had worked the previous two years as an assistant at the University of Pennsylvania, and prior to that had served as head coach at both Ohio State and Colgate.

Retirements and defections to the Canadian League cut six important players from the Cleveland roster. Lin Houston, who had played his first football under Brown at Massillon, called it quits after eight years as regular offensive guard. Tommy Thompson, a fine linebacker, had suffered a dislocation of his left knee at Pittsburgh late in the 1953 season, and also decided to end his career. Bill Willis, the middle guard for eight years, Derrell Palmer and Dub Jones also retired.

The 10-for-5 trade with Baltimore in 1953 was helpful in filling some of the vacancies created by the retirements. Tom Catlin assumed Thompson's assignment. Mike McCormick, who Brown knew was a great offensive tackle, was worked into the defense to succeed Willis. Herschel Forester was released from service in time to take Houston's job. The Browns got a real break when John Kissell, after playing two seasons in Canada, decided to return to the United States and asked for reinstatement. He moved into Palmer's spot on defense.

With several new faces in Paul Brown's football machine, it took some time for all parts to start working smoothly. The Browns squeezed past Green Bay by one point in their first exhibition, but then were flattened by the Rams, 38-10, and by the 49ers, 38-21.

During this period of distress, the Browns were quartered in the isolated area surrounding the St. Mary's College campus in California. It was five miles to the nearest store, and no public transportation was available. Arrangements for the 10-day stay had been made by Russell Gestner, the Browns' business manager.

"How did you ever find this place?" asked one of the exasperated players after several days of confinement.

"Just lucky, I guess," Gestner answered.

While the Browns were at St. Mary's, a squabble developed between Don Paul, who had been traded by the Chicago Cardinals to Washington, and George Preston Marshall, the outspoken Redskin owner. Paul jumped the team and returned to his home in Tacoma, Washington. Brown had a leak in his defensive backfield and closed a deal with Washington for Paul. To get him he traded a pair of promising rookies, Dale Atkeson, a powerful runner and end Johnny Carson.

Following the long stay at St. Mary's, the Cleveland team headed for Dallas and a game with the Lions in the Cotton Bowl. The Brownie defense caved in again, and the Lions romped, 56-31

The visit to Texas paid off in other ways, though. Dub Jones visited the team, watched the game and decided to abandon his retirement. Brown also got clearance for Carlton Massey, an All-American end from the University of Texas, to join the club. Massey had been scheduled for a call to military service, but his draft board said the summons could be delayed until January. He eventually became a fine defensive end.

The Browns still were groping for the key to success when they opened the season at Philadelphia and fell to the Eagles, 28-10. Things looked brighter the following week in the home opener, when Cleveland walloped the Chicago Cardinals, 34-7.

But the smiles didn't last. Graham had another miserable day at Pittsburgh. The Steelers, picking off six of his passes, romped to a smashing 55-27 victory. It was the first time Pittsburgh ever had beaten the Browns.

Cleveland, which always had been strong defensively, had lost two of its first three games and had yielded 90 points in the process. One Cleveland columnist was ready to concede that perhaps the Paul Brown success story really should have been credited to Blanton Collier, who had departed as defensive coach.

The Pittsburgh setback shell-shocked the Browns' defensive unit into a closely knit corps. Where it had given up an astronomical 90 points in the first three games, the defense yielded only 110 points in the next nine. Cleveland ran up a string of eight straight victories and had its fifth straight Eastern Conference title in the bag before closing the regular season against the Detroit Lions, who already had captured the Western crown for the third year in a row.

The Browns-Lions game originally had been scheduled for Cleveland in early October, but was postponed until the end of the season because the Indians had won the American League pennant and the football game would have conflicted with the World Series had it gone at least five games. The game really could have gone on as scheduled. The Indians lost four straight to the New York Giants, and there was no fifth Series game on Sunday.

That postponement was perhaps the key to the Browns' season. Had they played the Lions early in the season, it is entirely possible they would have suffered another setback, killing the spirit which marked their stirring comeback.

"The postponement gave us a chance to get our youngsters back into this thing," Brown said. "It was just our run of luck and it helped us give our rookies some experience, which they sorely needed. As far as our coming back after losing two of our first three games is concerned, I'm very proud of these boys. Sometimes a team goes to pieces after getting off to such a poor start, but not this bunch of guys."

The season windup against the Lions figured to be a meaningless game, with the Lions and the Browns slated to meet in Cleveland for the championship the following Sunday. At any rate, most Clevelanders couldn't have cared less. They were waiting breathlessly for a verdict in the trial of Dr. Sam Sheppard, Bay Village osteopath, whose wife had been murdered. The jury had been out for days and was deliberating that Sunday.

The Browns played it cozy and lost another last-minute decision on Bobby Layne's pass to Jim Doran.

If anyone thought that the regular season windup was an omen of things to come, they were badly mistaken. After watching Cleveland blow three straight championship games, the armchair quarterbacks were saying that the Browns had mastered the art of choking up in the big ones.

But during the week prior to the game, the team drilled with deadly seriousness.

Perfect weather greeted the teams in the 1954 championship game. Although there had been either snow or rain for every Cleveland home game that year, the championship contest was played on a warm day in bright sunshine. A crowd of 43,827 was in the stands.

The Browns, who had never beaten the Lions in regular season or in the title play, turned six interceptions and three Detroit fumbles into the worst championship rout since the Chicago Bears buried the Washington Redskins under a 73-0 avalanche in the 1940 title game. Cleveland scored twice in the first quarter, three times in the second, twice in the third and added a final touchdown in the fourth period as dusk settled over Cleveland Stadium. The score was 56-10.

Cleveland's defense limited the Lions to a 36-yard field goal by Doak Walker in the first quarter and a one-foot touchdown run by Bill Bowman in the second period.

In the previous year's title game, Graham had played his worst game as a pro. He was at his best this Sunday. He scored three touchdowns and passed for three. He completed nine of 12 passes for 163 yards. As the clock ticked off the final moments, Brown took Graham out of the game, and the veteran quarterback received a standing ovation the likes of which Cleveland Stadium had seldom heard.

In the locker room, Graham confirmed what had been rumored for weeks. "You've got to quit sometime," said the 33-year-old athlete, "and it's great to quit while you're on top."

Even though Graham had mentioned retirement to Brown in the spring when he signed the contract, the coach had been skeptical. "Otto has said nothing to me about it," Brown explained. "We'll see what happens next summer when the All-Star game rolls around. Why should a guy who did what he did out there today retire?"

Brown was jubilant. He joyfully labeled the 1954 team his "greatest club," and said the day's tremendous triumph resulted "from a great emotional outburst from within."

Raymond (Buddy) Parker, whose Lions had hoped to become the first team ever to win three straight National Football League crowns, wasn't conceding the Browns anything, even in the ruins of a 56-10 shellacking.

"If we could have gotten all the breaks the Browns did, we would have beaten them just as bad," Parker said bitterly. "This sounds funny for a losing coach to say, but I still think we have a better ball club. I hope I never have to go through another one like this. If I do, I'll probably be out picking cotton."

Graham made his retirement stick, at least for a short time. When the Browns went to training camp in the summer of 1955 and began preparing for their second appearance in the All-Star game, the quarterback spot was in the hands of George Ratterman. Challenging him for the post was Bobby Freeman, a rookie from Auburn. However, a law suit developed because Freeman had also signed a contract with a Canadian team. The Browns lost the suit and were barred from using Freeman.

The Browns lost to the All-Stars, 30-27, then edged Green Bay in an exhibition game, 13-7. They dropped three more pre-season games to Los Angeles, San Francisco and Detroit.

The Cleveland quarterbacking was ragged, and Brown sent an S O S to Graham, who answered the distress call and came out of retirement. He rejoined the team the week of the final exhibition game with the Bears at Chicago, where the Browns dropped their fourth straight decision, 24-21.

Graham still was not in shape and hadn't regained his touch when the team opened the season in Cleveland against the Washington Redskins. His timing was off, and he had an uneventful day. He finally was benched in the second half, and Ratterman took over. Ratterman passed for two touchdowns in the second half, but the Browns fell, 27-21.

Only a few months before, Graham had been given a standing ovation as he left the field during the rout of the Lions. On this day, he was loudly booed as he departed from the Washington game. He had completed only three of nine passes and had had two intercepted.

After watching Ratterman's performance, Paul Brown gave very serious consideration to having Ratterman start the next game in San Francisco. But Graham, disgusted with his first game showing, pledged he would make amends. He looked good in practice throughhout the next week, and Brown made the decision to stick with the quarterback who had been so important in the team's nine years of success.

The team stayed at San Francisco's Mark Hopkins Hotel on this western trip on the Saturday night preceding Cleveland's date with the 49ers. Two Western Conference games were being played. A writer traveling with the Browns called a San Francisco paper to get the scores of the two contests, and learned the Baltimore Colts had won their second straight game.

"Wouldn't it be strange if the Colts won the Western Conference title and we met them for the championship with Weeb Ewbank as their coach?" the writer commented to Graham. Then, as an afterthought, he added, "Of course, that is if we get into it."

"What do you mean, IF we get into it?" Graham snapped. "Don't worry about where this team will finish." There was never much doubt in Otto's mind that the Browns ultimately would finish first in the Eastern Conference race.

Graham was on the job and on the beam the next afternoon, hitting on seven of 13 passes. The Browns got some terrific running from Ed Modzelewski and Fred (Curly) Morrison, demolishing the 49ers, 38-3. They were on their way to another championship.

The forward pass was used sparingly, but effectively, that year as the Browns concentrated more on the running power generated by Modzelewski and Morrison. Modzelewski, the ex-Maryland fullback great and elder brother of Dick, was acquired from the Pittsburgh Steelers early in the season in a trade for Marion Motley, the aging, once-invincible Brownie fullback. The Steelers thought that Modzelewski had a chronic back injury and asked the Browns if they would be interested in taking him in exchange for Motley, whom they wanted for blocking on pass protection. Motley retired after the 1953 season, but decided on a comeback in 1955.

"I was interested in finding a job for Marion, so I told them I'd take a look at Big Mo," Brown said.

Brown rested Modzelewski for more than a week. Then he turned him loose in practice. The former Maryland star turned out to be one of the best runners in the league.

Only four of the original Browns were on the 1954 squad -- Graham, Lavelli, Groza and Gatski, the center. The remainder of the team included 15 players acquired in trades, five players signed as free agents, and nine draftees. The squad was a tribute to Brown's ability as a trader.

On the ground, Modzelewski and Morrison rolled up more than 1,400 yards. Modzelewski lugged the ball 185 times for 619 yards, and Morrison carried 156 times for 824 yards.

Graham threw fewer passes than in any other season, attempting only 185 and completing 98. They were good for 1,721 yards and 15 touchdowns. Ray Renfro, the speedster from Texas, became Graham's favorite target. He frequently outran the secondary to get under Graham's deadly floating aerials. Lavelli and Brewster pulled in their share, too.

After the San Francisco victory in the second game of the season, the Browns ran up a streak of five straight triumphs before dropping a 33-17 decision at Philadelphia. They rapped Pittsburgh the following week, 41-14, then battled to a 35-35 tie with the Giants in New York. Cleveland closed the season with a 30-7 win over Pittsburgh and a 35-24 triumph over the Chicago Cardinals to clinch a record sixth straight Eastern Conference crown with nine wins, two losses and a tie.

The Browns had by far the most explosive offense and the tightest defense in the league, rolling up 349 points while yielding 218.

In the 1955 championship game the Browns faced the Los Angeles Rams, who four years before had handed the Browns their first loss in a title game.

Graham was splendid before a crowd of 87,695 at the Coliseum. He nearly duplicated his performance in the 1954 championship game as he threw a pair of touchdown passes and scored two himself to lead the Browns to their second straight crown, 38-14.

The defense had a great day, too, intercepting seven of the the Rams' passes. Six of them were charged to Norm Van Brocklin, whose aerial to Tom Fears had won the title for the Rams against the Browns in 1951.

"Graham is the greatest ever to play the quarterback position in pro football," was Paul Brown's unadulterated praise when the game was over. "He can throw and he can run. More than that, he's a great inspiration for the rest of the team."

Again, Graham had said this would be his last game and someone asked Brown if he would try to get Graham to re-consider his latest retirement plans. Paul said he wouldn't. "I imposed on him once, and that's enough," he said.

In a brilliant 10-year career, Graham had completed 1,464 of 2,626 passes for 23,584 yards and 174 touchdowns.

But it was all over. This time Graham made his retirement stick. The Otto Graham era was history.

12

Mortal After All

The cynics had claimed right along that it wasn't Paul Brown's genius that brought the Browns success year after year. They placed most of the credit in the lap of Otto Graham and his accurate right arm. "Watch the Browns fall apart without Graham in there," they said smugly. To a certain extent they turned out to be right.

Quarterbacks of the quality of Sammy Baugh, Sid Luckman, Otto Graham and Bobby Layne weren't easy to find, and Brown knew it. He realized that one day Graham would hang up his cleats, and he began preparing for it. He began thinking about a successor as early as January, 1954. Cleveland drew the lucky slip out of Commissioner Bert Bell's battered hat at the National Football League draft meeting and named Stanford's Bobby Garrett, the nation's leading college passer in 1953, as their bonus choice.

Early in the 1954 training period, Brown decided to use Garrett as trade bait. He gave the college whiz to the Green Bay Packers in exchange for Vito (Babe) Parilli, who had been an All-American quarterback at the University of Kentucky. The Packers were desperate for a quarterback to back up Tobin Rote, and Garrett appeared to be the answer.

Parilli had had two years of professional experience before entering military service at the end of the 1953 season. The Browns still had Graham as the No. 1 thrower, with Ratterman behind him, and could wait for Parilli's release from service. Parilli drew his separation papers in time to arrive for the opening of the 1956 training camp. Brown installed him as the No. 1 quarterback and again named Ratterman as substitute.

Ratterman had a big advantage. As a result of spending several years of inactivity as a high-priced bench-warmer, he knew the Browns' plays. Parilli was having a great deal of difficuty in mastering the Cleveland offense, and Brown moved Ratterman into the starting position for the College All-Star game at Chicago. Ratterman performed well, and the Browns walked off with an easy 26-0 victory.

Although it had lost Graham and Dub Jones, through retirement, the 1956 Cleveland team was basically the same one that had won the title the previous season. Dante Lavelli also had announced his retirement, but had decided to come back for one more season.

The victory over the All-Stars was one of only two bright spots of the training season. The Browns proceeded to drop five straight exhibition games -- one each to San Francisco, Los Angeles and Green Bay and two to Detroit -- but closed the pre-season schedule with a 24-14 triumph over the Chicago Bears.

In the second exhibition game with Detroit, played at Akron's Rubber Bowl, Paul Brown, the indefatigable innovator, came up with a revolutionary new wrinkle designed to save wear and tear on the messenger guards who carried in every play to the quarterback. He had George Ratterman wired for sound, and, with microphone in hand on the bench, Brown broadcast play assignments to quarterback Ratterman with a citizens' band transmitter on a frequency assigned by the Federal Communications Commission. The receiving set, developed by Clevelander George Sarles in his basement workshop, weighed about a pound. It was installed inside Ratterman's helmet with enough cushioning to protect the delicate equipment. Ratterman could hear Brown's instructions, but could not reply. The electronic system worked all right, but the Browns sputtered and dropped a 31-14 decision to the Lions. And word of Brown's "new look" in football play-calling began to spread across the country like wildfire.

Cleveland opened the season in Chicago. Paul Brown and Ratterman had left their transmitter and receiver at home. The Browns had left their offense there, too. The Cardinals, who had lost 13 straight times to the Browns, turned three field goals by Pat Summerall into a 9-7 victory. Cleveland's only score was a 46-yard touchdown pass from Ratterman to Ray Renfro in the first quarter, followed by Lou Groza's conversion. It was the third straight time the Browns lost the season's opener but nobody was too concerned.

After the game was over, it was revealed that the Cardinals, coached by Ray Richards, had stolen a march on the Browns and had their own electronic communications system in operation throughout the game. Richards disclosed that the Cardinals had buried a wire around the perimeter of the gridiron and had it hooked up to a transmitter. His quarterback and defensive captains were equipped with hearing-aid type receivers. Richards and his assistants sent in about half the plays on offense and helped guide the defenders when the Browns had the ball.

"Those fellows upstairs can see something coming or developing a lot easier than you can on the field, and sometimes they can see things you can't see on the field," Richards said. It obviously helped the Cardinals. They held the defending champions to 215 yards, 106 on the ground.

The electronics were forgotten the following week when the Browns visited Pittsburgh and returned with a 14-10 decision over the Steelers. The victory raised hopes among the players and ignited fan interest.

The biggest crowd in Cleveland Stadium in three years and the second largest since the team entered the National Football League, a gathering of 60,042, was on hand for the home opener with the New York Giants. And Cleveland's newest voice of the airways, Paul Brown, was broadcasting over Station 19A1661 at the start of the game, giving play information to his one listener, George Ratterman. But it didn't help. The Giants, with Alex Webster scoring three times, ripped over the Browns, 21-9, to give Coach Jim Lee Howell his first victory over Cleveland .

In the gloom of the Cleveland locker room, Brown admitted that he had abandoned use of the radio system early in the game. "There was too much crowd noise," Brown said. "George couldn't hear me over the roar of the crowd."

But the Giants had another story when they got back to New York. They claimed that a big receiving set had been utilized on the Giants' bench to intercept Brown's messages to Ratterman. Brown's Hooper Rating was higher than he thought it was, or so it seemed.

"We were able to get the Browns' signals better than they could," Ray Walsh, general manager of the Giants, was quoted in an Associated Press dispatch out of New York. "Finally, after three unsuccessful series of plays, they gave it up. We were seriously warned by Brown before the game that it's a $10,000 fine to anyone found jamming the wave lengths. You see, Cleveland has its own licensed radio station. Other clubs, like the Chicago Cardinals and the Pittsburgh Steelers, have a special wire strung around the field.

"We had Bob Topp on the side lines. He is an end for whom we have asked waivers. And next to him we had Gene Filipski. They had a big receiving set on the bench tuned to the Browns' wave length. Topp could hear Brown's instructions to his quarterback, George Ratterman, very clearly, while Ratterman, with only a little gadget in his helmet, seemed to be having trouble hearing over the roar of the crowd.

"Topp heard Brown give instructions for a pitchout to the left. Topp told Filipski, who yelled to a defensive man on the field, and the word was passed along the line. There was a pitchout to the left and the play lost two yards. The Browns tried three sequences and finally gave up in disgust."

When Paul Brown was informed of the Giants' claim of swiping the signals, his only comment was, "No, they didn't."

The use of electronic devices for calling plays touched off a lively debate among the sports writing fraternity. Milton Gross, in a *New York Post* story, said, "Things have come to such a peculiar pass on the professional gridiron that Bert Bell can't be certain whether he is commissioner of the National Football League or a newly appointed member of the FCC.

"Football has always been the most over-coached sport -- and Paul Brown, the going genius of the Browns, refined it to a point where an original thought on the part of any of his players was regarded as being on the verge of mutiny."

George Preston Marshall, the outspoken Redskins' owner, stepped squarely into the middle of the act when he said he felt all electronic gadgets should be barred, at least for the remainder of the 1956 season. "The subject can then be thoroughly discussed at the next league meeting by all the owners and coaches," Marshall said. "Frankly, it's a potentially dangerous thing -- coaches will run out of alibis if they take the responsibility for all of their offensive and defensive decisions."

Adding fuel to the flames, the Los Angeles Rams complained bitterly when they were denied facilities to operate a radio-controlled, signal-calling system in Detroit. Finally, Bert Bell stepped into the controversy and banned the use of electronic equipment in the helmets of players.

After Bell's announcement, Brown revealed that he was the one who got rid of it. The Cleveland coach and general manager said he called Bell in Philadelphia and told him that "as far as the Browns are concerned you can throw the thing out."

In the *Cleveland News,* Herman Goldstein, veteran football writer, reported that Bell told Brown the Giants had admitted their story of signal-stealing in the Cleveland game was phony. "Bell told me the Giants were against such devices from the start and so they thought they would ridicule the whole thing by planting the story," Goldstein quoted Brown. "They confessed to Bell they never even tried to pick up our signals."

With Paul Brown's attempt to further automate the game of pro football relegated to the history books, the team turned its attention to returning to the winning path after having lost two of their first three games.

At Washington, D. C., trouble came in one large dose. In the first quarter Ratterman, who had spent four years as Graham's understudy and had finally become a regular for the Browns, wrenched a cartilage in his knee. Babe Parilli took over for his ailing teammate, but couldn't light the fuse, and the Browns went down to their third defeat, 20-9.

After the game, Brown said soberly that the injury probably meant the end of Ratterman's professional football career. "It's the knee cartilage and he's out indefinitely. I'd say for good."

He was right. Ratterman never played another pro game.

Cleveland was in bad shape. In four games, the club had scored only 35 points, the worst production in their history. With Ratterman out, Paul Brown was forced to find a reserve quarterback. He settled on Tommy O'Connell, a young Irishman who had been the Big Ten passing champion at Illinois and had played a season with the Chicago Bears. But the Bears, loaded with quarterbacks, had released O'Connell.

Even though he had fine credentials, the 26-year-old O'Connell thought he was through with pro football. Since he had been given his walking papers by the Bears there just didn't seem to be any place in the league for him. In 1952, he had been the nation's leading college passer with 133 completions for 1,761 yards, a sparkling completion percentage of 59.4. In that season, he broke Otto Graham's Big Ten passing records. He leaped at the chance to join the Browns.

Parilli was Ratterman's immediate successor, while O'Connell, an intelligent young man with an abundance of self-assurance, took a cram course on the Browns' offense. With Parilli at the helm, the Browns lost their third straight game (the longest losing streak since they were founded) and their fourth in five starts, bowing to Pittsburgh, 20-16.

Despite the fact that the Browns were not enjoying one of their best seasons, more than 110,000 persons had showed up for their first two home games, prompting Brown to remark, "You might say seeing us lose is an attraction, but I like to believe the reason the fans are willing to pay to see us is that they get a good ball game, whether we win or lose.''

The Browns finally broke their losing streak by taking a 24-7 decision from the Green Bay Packers the next week, but more trouble was around the corner. In Baltimore on the seventh Sunday of the season, Babe Parilli suffered a severe shoulder injury and was side-lined for the remainder of the season. O'Connell, who had been with the team only two and one-half weeks, stepped in as the starting quarterback. The Browns lost to the Colts, 21-7, then bowed the following week to Washington, 20-17, and were mathematically eliminated from title consideration for the first time in 11 years.

But the Browns' new quarterback was learning quickly, and the Browns met with some success the balance of the seaon, winning three of their last four games.

Their biggest moment came in the next to the last game of the season, when they temporarily stalled New York's bid for its first divison championship in 10 years. On a thoroughly miserable afternoon, in which a chilly rain turned to snow and left the field a quagmire of mud, the Browns dumped the Giants, 24-7, before a half-frozen crowd of 27,707 in Yankee Stadium. O'Connell sneaked over for two one-yard touchdowns and passed seven yards to fullback Fred (Curly) Morrison for the other. Lou Groza booted the three extra points and a 41-yard field goal. New York's only touchdown of the afternoon came in the second period when Frank Gifford took a six-yard pass from Charley Conerly.

New York clinched the Eastern Conference crown vacated by the Browns by defeating Philadelphia, 21-7, in the final week of the season.

Cleveland finished the 1956 season with a record of five victories and seven losses, marking its first losing season. The team finished in a tie with Pittsburgh for fourth place. It was the first time since their inception in 1946 that the Browns failed to play in a championship game.

For Paul Brown, it was his first losing season as a professional coach and only the second time in his long career that his team lost more games than it had won. It was a strange feeling, to be sure.

No one in the National Football League shed a tear for the Browns in their misery over their first losing season.

Still, there were some bright signs. The Browns were never overpowered. The defense was solid and allowed the fewest points in the league for the fourth year in a row. But the offense never did function smoothly until O'Connell became a regular. The team scored only 167 points, and only the last-place Philadelphia Eagles had a less-effective attack. There were many who believed, however, that the Browns would have easily made it seven straight Conference titles had O'Connell been with the team at the start of the season.

The 1956 team had begun to feel the inroads of age, and Paul Brown was determined to do an extensive remodeling job before going into another season. He knew the team needed an infusion of youth at several positions, and, despite O'Connell's progress, he was hopeful of landing another quarterback in the National Football League draft. Parilli had been a disappointment.

Three outstanding collegiate quarterbacks were eligible for the draft. They were Paul Hornung of Notre Dame, Len Dawson of Purdue and John Brodie of Stanford. Because of Cleveland's relatively low position in the standings, Brown thought there might be a chance to land one of the three when the first four draft rounds were held in early December.

Fortunately, Lady Luck smiled the other way. Green Bay won the bonus choice and picked Hornung. San Francisco drafted Brodie. The Browns, the Steelers and the Packers were in a three-way deadlock in the won-loss department and a coin flip was used to determine the drafting order. Pittsburgh won the toss and selected Dawson. Paul Brown then decided on a hard-running ball carrier from Syracuse named Jim Brown.

Milt Plum, the great Penn State quarterback who had engineered an upset over Ohio State that fall, was Cleveland's second-round draft choice. Considered to be the most versatile backfield man ever to play for the Nittany Lions, he did the punting, passing and place-kicking as well as his share of running. "He is a flawless ball handler, an excellent passer and has tremendous attitude," his coach, Rip Engle, commented. "Then too, he is capable on defense. He's a deadly tackler and very few ball carriers got past him in the open field."

Paul Brown got an early start on his rebuilding project. He traded six veterans to Green Bay in an unusual deal in which Cleveland acquired Bobby Garrett and Roger Zatkoff. Babe Parilli went back to the Packers in the transaction in which Brown also included Sam Palumbo, Carlton Massey, John Marcelli, John Pettibon and Billy Kinard.

Anxious to get an early line on his quarterback corps, Brown held a special "school," a three-day session at Hiram College early in July. Six quarterbacks came in. Along with O'Connell, they were Plum, Garrett, John Borton of Ohio State University, Bobby Freeman of Auburn and Joe Clark of Santa Clara.

When the regular camp opened three weeks later, it was labeled "New Faces of 1957." Morrison, Lavelli, Gatski, Kissell and Ratterman had retired. Groza was the only member of the original Browns still around. Several of the other veterans were dropped during the training period, and the Browns prepared to enter a new season with the biggest personnel turnover in the team's history.

Fourteen changes were made on the roster that finished the 1956 season. Chet Hanulak, Billy Reynolds and Tom Catlin were released from military service, and 11 rookies made the team. One of these was Jim Brown, who was destined to become pro football's greatest ball carrier.

Rival coaches should have known that, contending with two men named Brown, they stood little chance of making Cleveland a permanent fixture in the lower echelons of the NFL's Eastern Conference.

13

A Rush to the Top

When James Nathaniel Brown arrived at Syracuse University in the fall of 1953, he carried with him the reputation of being the finest athlete Manhassett, Long Island, had ever known. But Brown was at Syracuse without an athletic scholarship, the result of a series of circumstances no fiction writer could ever dream of creating.

Jim was born on February 17, 1936, at St. Simon, Georgia, a tiny island in the Atlantic Ocean just off the mainland. When he was two, his parents' turbulent marriage broke up, and his mother, Theresa, headed for New York to work as a domestic. Nathaniel, as he was known then, was left in the care of his great-grandmother. At the age of seven, he rejoined his mother, who was working for a family in Great Neck, Long Island, outside New York City. He was enrolled in an elementary school at Manhassett, several miles away, and his mother had to send him to school in a taxi, an expense that put a large crimp in the family budget.

Later, Jim's mother felt that their one-room flat was just too small for them both, and the youngster was sent to live with a black family in Manhassett. He saw his mother only on weekends until she left her job with the Great Neck family and took an apartment in Manhassett.

"I was always well cared for," Jim explained years later. "It was like I was a well-off kid. I had nice clothes, and my mother was proud of me. It was hard for her, but she was thrifty and we made out."

All the while, Jim was growing into a big, strong boy who wasn't afraid to use his fists. Sometimes he roamed the streets with a teen-age gang known as the Gaylords. He was the toughest kid in the club, and became its leader. Because of his size and strength, there were few rivals who dared challenge him.

Perhaps the turning point in Jim's life came when Jay Stranahan, who coached several sports at Plandon Road Junior High, convinced the boy to channel his tremendous energy and ability into athletics. From the beginning, Jimmy Brown showed great natural ability. He was a success in every sport he tried.

As a 14-year-old freshman at Manhassett High School, Jim made the first team on the football squad. He continued to pile on weight until, as a senior, he stood six feet one inch and weighed 200 pounds. He was a punishing runner, and averaged 14.9 yards per carry. In basketball, he averaged 38 points per game as a senior, and established a single-game scoring record on Long Island with a 55-point outburst in one game.

While he was setting records in football and basketball at Manhassett, Jim was befriended by a town lawyer, Kenneth Molloy, a Syracuse alumnus who had recruited a number of outstanding athletes for his alma mater. Molloy, a wiry, gray-haired man who described himself as "very Irish-looking," had played lacrosse at Syracuse and was always looking for promising young athletes to send there. But more than his interest in his alma mater, Molloy just liked kids, and he tried to help as many as he could in the Manhassett area. If scholarship aid was not available at Syracuse, he would try elsewhere. Frequently, Molloy reached deep into his pockets to buy clothing for some of the underprivileged athletes in the community.

The word of Jim Brown's accomplishments had spread across the country, and 45 colleges beat a path to his door with scholarship offers. Ed Walsh, Brown's high-school coach, wanted him to go to Ohio State. Molloy wanted Jim to go to Syracuse, not only because of its fine athletic program but also because of academic and social advantages.

Athletic officials at Syracuse were trying to build a big-time football team and were doing most of their recruiting in Pennsylvania. Consequently, they had paid little attention to the boy from Manhassett. Molloy went to Syracuse and tried to sell Brown to the athletic officials, but they had no interest in handing out a scholarship to a black athlete. Forty-five other colleges were willing to give Jim Brown a scholarship, but not Syracuse. Molloy persisted in his selling job and finally won a loose promise that Jim might win athletic aid in January if he proved himself during the freshman football season.

Armed with this half-promise, Molloy told Jim that he had won an athletic scholarship at Syracuse, and convinced him to attend his alma mater. Unknown to Jim Brown, his first semester at Syracuse was being paid for by well-wishing Manhassett businessmen who had been solicited by Molloy. Amazing as it may sound, Jim never learned the circumstances of his admission until after his graduation from Syracuse.

Jim was the only black player on the Syracuse football team, and because he was not on an athletic scholarship, he was largely ignored by the coaches. He did not live in the football players' dormitory, nor did he eat his meals with the other players. He wasn't playing much football, and he began thinking of switching to another school. Molloy and other friends convinced him to stick it out.

"There seemed to be an assumption that I had come to Syracuse for no other reason than to be footloose and fancy free," Jim revealed years later in his autobiography, *Off My Chest.* He said he had the feeling that the coaches viewed him as a potential troublemaker.

The basketball season rolled around and Jim made the freshman squad, but January came and went and still no scholarship. Molloy and other interested men in Manhassett had to come up with another $1,000 to pay Brown's expenses. Playing largely as a substitute, he still managed to break the freshman scoring record. In the spring, Brown made the track team as an all-around performer. About the only things he couldn't do was pole-vault and run the hurdle events.

Just before the end of the school year, football coach Ben Schwartzwalder called Brown into his office and told him the coaching staff was considering switching him from halfback to end. Brown was adamant in refusing. He didn't want to play end. The coaches finally agreed to let him remain a back.

That summer, Molloy suggested to Jim that he try to put all of his track talents together, learn how to pole-vault, run the hurdles and throw the javelin, and then enter the National AAU Decathlon Championships at Atlantic City. Without the benefit of coaching, Jim worked hard on these events and then headed for Atlantic City.

There was a star-studded field of some four dozen competitors at the championships, including many athletes who had trained for months for the event under the watchful eye of track coaches. Included in the field was Rafer Johnson, the splendid black athlete who later won the Olympic decathlon title. In some of the events, Jim Brown had no finesse or style, but on sheer ability alone he finished tenth in the tough field. Molloy calls this the most graphic illustration of Brown's almost unbelievable all-around athletic ability.

There were other examples, too. The first time Jim Brown stepped onto the golf links, he shot in the low 80s for 18 holes. In his first year as a bowler, he had several games over 200. And as a second lieutenant in the Army Reserve, Jim attained a rating as an expert marksman with a rifle.

By the time September, 1954, rolled around, Syracuse athletic officials had decided to give Jim a scholarsip, but when he arrived for the first football practice session, he found himself listed on the fifth team. He had promised Molloy he would hustle in training, and he did. Soon he was on the second team.

Just before the start of the season, Sam Alexander, a senior left halfback, suffered a leg injury, and Jim was named to start the opener with Villanova. Jim fumbled the first time he got the ball, and his brief stint as a starter was over. During the first five games, he played both offense and defense, but longed to get another crack at a regular job. A pair of injuries paved the way. Early in the first quarter of the sixth game, against Cornell, Brown was pressed into service. He scored Syracuse's only touchdown of the day on a 54-yard run, but the Orange lost, 14-6. His 151 yards gained rushing clinched a regular job.

Almost a year and a half of frustration was behind him, and Jim Brown began developing into what Ken Molloy knew he could be, the greatest all-around athlete in Syracuse history. He became a star in football, basketball, track and lacrosse.

His brilliant performances on the gridiron helped propel Syracuse into national football prominence. In his senior year, Brown rolled up 986 yards on the ground for a new Syracuse record. Jim was hailed as "the east's most powerful running back since Army's Doc Blanchard." He was named on most All-American teams.

In the last game of the regular season in 1956, Brown turned in an amazing one-man show, rolling up 43 points as the Orange smothered Colgate. He was great again in the Cotton Bowl at Dallas as Syracuse dropped a 28-27 decision to Texas Christian.

Most observers were duly impressed. An exception was a columnist who wrote: "I can't see the raving over Jim Brown on his work in the Cotton Bowl. He scored three touchdowns and gained considerable yardage on short plays, but never got away on long runs despite the fact that he was sprung into the Texas Christian secondary.

"His press clippings were too much for him. The wire service writers who write their stuff from the box score went nuts over him, but I'll bet the pros watching him will admit much work will have to be done. The Browns will have to teach him to start more quickly. He doesn't knock anybody down, either. If the hole wasn't there in the line, Brown didn't crack through the Texas Christian defense.

"If I were a pro scout, I'd drool over Colorado's John Bayuk, who played in the Orange Bowl."

As it turned out, the Browns later drafted Bayuk, and both he and Brown were candidates for fullback in 1957. Brown made it, but Bayuk was released and never caught on with another pro team.

Paul Brown had really wanted a quarterback as his first draft choice, but he wasn't sorry he landed Brown instead. He dispatched Dick Gallagher to Syracuse to sign Brown, who also was being wooed by the Canadian League. Molloy, who had steered Brown to Syracuse, sat in on the negotiations as Jim's advisor. Before the talks were concluded, Jim had won a pact for $12,000 and a $3,000 bonus. It was the highest salary the Browns had ever paid an untried rookie.

Jimmy wasn't on hand when the Browns opened their 1957 camp at Hiram. He was practicing with the College All-Stars in Evanston, Illinois. Jim had hoped to win a starting halfback role with the All-Stars, but Curly Lambeau, who was coaching the team, wasn't overly impressed with Brown. He started the flashy Jon Arnett, a Southern California star whom Brown had beaten out for All-American honors.

Brown didn't see too much action that night, and it turned out to be one of the biggest disappointments of his career. He was so disgusted that he passed up the party after the All-Star game, packed his bags and drove all night to Hiram.

The Jim Brown who arrived at Hiram was an amazing physical specimen. He was a handsome young man with sharp, rugged facial features and broad shoulders which tapered to a 32-inch waist. He was perfectly proportioned and, although he had a prodigious appetite, there wasn't an ounce of fat on him. He didn't drink or smoke. Jim was quiet and soft-spoken. He knew his place as a rookie and kept his chatter to a minimum. He liked Ivy League clothes, music and big cars.

Unfamiliar with the Cleveland offense, Jim didn't play much in the first exhibition contest with Detroit, but in the second game, against Pittsburgh, the six-foot-two, 220 pounder got his chance at fullback. He put on a dazzling running exhibition, including a 48-yard touchdown run. After the play, Paul Brown called the rookie over and told him, "Well, you're my fullback."

Three other rookies began to impress Paul Brown in the exhibition season. They were quarterback Milt Plum, Vince Costello, a middle linebacker, and Paul Wiggin, an All-American tackle at Stanford, who was made into a defensive end with Cleveland.

The Browns' opener was a rugged one against the World Champion New York Giants, who had trounced the Chicago Bears in the 1956 title game. A few days before the game, Giant Coach Jim Lee Howell was quoted as saying that the Detroit Lions had the best defense in pro football, superior even to his own talented unit. But on this opening day, there were no better defenses in the league than those presented by the Browns and the Giants. Not a touchdown was scored by either team. The Browns won, 6-3, on a pair of field goals by durable Lou Groza, who was starting his twelfth year with the team.

Jim Brown got off to an impressive start, racking up 89 yards in 21 carries. He made a key play in the drive that put the ball in position for Groza's game-winning field goal. With a third and 11 situation and the Giants expecting O'Connell to pass, Brown went roaring up the middle for 15 yards and a first down. It was his longest gain of the day.

The victory over the defending champions gave the youthful and inexperienced Brown a psychological lift, lighting a fire that carried them a long way.

Groza was a conspicuous figure again the following Sunday in Pittsburgh, booting three field goals in a 23-12 triumph over the Steelers. Brown picked up only 39 yards in 15 carries. The next week, he managed 70 yards in 22 tries against the Cardinals as the Browns won, 17-7. The schedule then called for back-to-back games against the Eagles.

In the first game at Cleveland, Brown got only 28 yards in 10 carries, but the Browns won 24-7. He had a better day the next Sunday in Philadelphia, but the Eagles, in a complete reversal of form, stunned the Browns, 17-7, snapping Cleveland's four-game winning streak. Brown picked up 58 yards in 12 carries

Brown had the first 100-yard day of his professional career when the Browns entertained Washington the following week. He chewed up 109 yards in 21 attempts as the Browns got back on the winning path, 21-17.

The Browns at home shut out Pittsburgh, 24-0, then moved into Washington for a return match with the Redskins. O'Connell, who had cemented the job as the No. 1 quarterback, had his best day in a Cleveland uniform. He passed for 318 yards against the Redskins, but it took a field goal by Lou Groza with 17 seconds remaining to pull out a 30-30 tie. Brown got 68 yards in 15 carries.

If there had been any doubt that Jim Brown was destined for stardom in the National Football League, it was dispelled when the Los Angeles Rams came to Cleveland the following Sunday. A crowd of 65,407, largest of the season, was on hand for the game.

In the first quarter, O'Connell was injured and had to leave the field for the rest of the day. It looked as if the Browns' half-game lead in the Eastern Conference was in serious jeopardy. With O'Connell out of action, Jim Brown assumed the offensive burden.

The big fullback had put the Browns in front, 7-0, with a touchdown run early in the first quarter. Now, as Cleveland found itself trying to get something started on its own 31, Plum, on instructions from the bench, called a fullback draw and handed the ball to Brown, who was belted so hard while bolting through the line of scrimmage that his helmet was knocked off. But he kept his balance, turned on the steam and dashed 69 yards for a touchdown!

The Browns had a 14-0 lead, but it didn't stand up for long. The Rams had plenty of big guns, including Norm Van Brocklin at quarterback and two strong runners in Tank Younger and Tommy Wilson. By half-time they had pulled ahead, 21-17.

Early in the third quarter, Brown fumbled on his own 29-yard line. Art House of the Rams grabbed the ball and ran into the end zone, giving the Rams a 28-17 lead. Jim Brown was furious with himself, and there was no stopping him the rest of the afternoon. Within moments, he had bull-dozed his way to two touchdowns, and the Browns were out in front again, 31-28. Before the game was over, Brown's running had set up two more touchdowns and Cleveland triumphed, 45-31.

It had been the greatest single running exhibition in the history of the National Football League. Brown had scored four touchdowns and had rambled to a record 237 yards in 31 carries. (He equaled the 237-yard mark against Philadelphia in 1961.)

That game marked the first time that Brown was asked to carry the ball more than 30 times in a single game. Throughout his career with the Cleveland team, he would do it many more times, reaching a peak of 37 carries in a game against the Cardinals during the 1959 season.

Brown was working hard and enjoying it. Paul Brown continually encouraged the rookie, and the muscular young man thought his new coach was great. This attitude on the part of the workhorse fullback was to change gradually, as Paul Brown began working him more and encouraging him less.

O'Connell was injured again the next Sunday when the Browns closed their home schedule with a 31-0 conquest of the Cardinals. The Browns were within one victory of regaining the Eastern Conference title they had relinquished in 1956 after holding it for six straight seasons. The defending champion New York Giants were the Browns' only rivals for the crown, and they faded from contention the day before the Browns were to play their semi-final game against their perennial nemesis Detroit. The Giants dropped a decision to the Pittsburgh Steelers in a mud bath at Forbes Field, and their hopes of repeating were crushed.

The Browns were champions of the East once again. The game on Sunday with the Lions was academic for the Browns, but the Detroiters needed a victory to remain in contention for the Western Conference crown. With Milt Plum at quarterback, the Browns were ineffective, and dropped a 20-7 decision. But in the final game of the season, Plum redeemed himself and passed the Browns to a 34-28 victory over the Giants. Cleveland had finished with nine wins, two losses and a tie, two and one-half games ahead of the Giants.

The Western race was a hectic one, with the Lions and the San Francisco 49ers finishing in a tie for first place. The two teams met in a play-off in San Francisco. The 49ers had a comfortable half-time bulge, but Detroit fought back and squeezed out a 31-27 victory in a sensational last period comeback.

Detroit, thriving on the momentum built up in the late-season rush to the title, was still smarting over the 56-10 lacing suffered at the hands of the Browns in the 1954 championship game. They were eagerly awaiting this one.

Having clinched their conference crown two weeks before the end of the regular season, the Browns lost some of their steam. They had other problems as well. O'Connell's ankle was tender and there was some question as to how far the league's best passer in 1957 could go against the Lions. Still, Paul Brown had another quarterback in Plum, and he kept Detroit guessing as to which one he would start in the championship game.

Two days before the clash, the Browns suffered a blow that sent them into a battle at Detroit without an able-bodied passer. After the regular practice session had ended, Plum and Ray Renfro participated in an extra passing drill on their own. Milt leaped for one of Renfro's throws and pulled a hamstring muscle.

With both quarterbacks ailing, the Browns were little match for the spirited Lions, who avenged the 1954 debacle and then some. Before the numbers on the Briggs Stadium scoreboard stopped spinning, the Lions had flattened Cleveland, 59-14.

The Lions, too, had quarterback problems. The gifted Bobby Layne was out with a broken leg, but Tobin Rote was an able replacement. He passed for four touchdowns and scored another.

Despite the fact that the Browns were destroyed in the championship game, it was a significant season. Many believe that in rebuilding the team after the losing season in 1956, Paul Brown turned in one of the best coaching jobs of his career.

The season also marked the beginning of Jim Brown's great career. In his first year, he led the league in rushing with 942 yards, and was voted "rookie of the year." His fine season earned him a raise to $17,000 for 1958, and it was the start of a spiral that was to make him pro football's highest paid performer. But despite Jim's instant success as a pro he remained the modest young man who had reported to the Browns' camp in August. He really wasn't as interested in setting records as he was in helping the Browns to win football games. It was an attitude he kept throughout his career.

By the start of the 1958 season, brittle Tommy O'Connell, who had played such an important role in regaining the Eastern Conference title for Cleveland, had retired to take a coaching position at the University of Illinois. Plum assumed the mantle as the team's No. 1 quarterback. Backing up Plum was a youngster named Jim Ninowski, an all-Big Ten quarterback at Michigan State, who had completed 14 of 20 passes to lead the College All-Stars to an upset of Detroit in the 1958 classic at Chicago.

Another young man who had performed brilliantly in that game, Bobby Mitchell, also became a member of the 1958 Browns. Mitchell, a former University of Illinois football and track star, caught two touchdown passes in the All-Star game. He and Ninowski shared the "most valuable player" award that night.

Drafted eighth, Mitchell immediately won a starting spot as a running halfback. With Plum passing well and Brown and Mitchell combining as an "inside-outside" running team, the Browns dashed to five straight victories in the 1958 season. It looked as if Paul Brown was ready to re-establish the dynasty that had been toppled in 1956.

In the first five games, Jim Brown rambled for 815 yards, just 127 shy of his complete rookie-year output, and Mitchell rolled up 413. In the team's fifth game, Brown sprinted for four touchdowns to spark a 38-24 triumph over the Cardinals.

Brown was well on the way to establishing a running dynasty in the National Football League. Commenting on his success, he said, "One thing that helps me is my running style. I don't go into the line in the traditional fullback manner. You don't find me leading with my head. Most of the time the contact is only my shoulder pads. Normally, I start with small steps so I'll be able to turn or slide toward the opening. When the tackler comes at me, I drop the shoulder. The runner's shoulder should be the first thing to hit the tackler."

How true! Opposing players had found out that it frequently took two, three, four and sometimes five men to bring down the powerful runner. It was not an unusual sight to see Brown lumber down the field with a handful of players on his back, picking up valuable extra yardage with his tremendous second effort.

The Browns' sixth opponent of the season was New York and the game drew a crowd of 78,404, at Cleveland. The Browns ran up a 17-7 lead in the third quarter, but the Giants came from behind to win, 21-17, and snapped the Cleveland winning streak.

In the game, Mitchell was guilty of three fumbles, and although none was recovered by the Giants, Bobby fell out of favor with Paul Brown and was demoted to the second team. It was Paul Brown's handling of Mitchell during that season that helped to lead to Jim Brown's disenchantment with pro football's most succesful coach.

The following week, Leroy Bolden, another ex-Michigan State star, was in Mitchell's halfback slot and the Browns lost their second in a row, 30-10, to Detroit.

Lew Carpenter moved into the running back slot against Washington the next week, and the Browns began a four-game winning streak. The offense was far from brilliant, but the defense was outstanding, and the team didn't need a big point production to win football games. Cleveland whipped Washington twice, 20-10, and 21-14, and Philadelphia twice, 28-14 and 21-14, to move into the season's final game against the Giants with a one-game lead over the New Yorkers.

They needed only a tie to sew up the crown, and, with time running out and the score 10-10 in another titanic defensive battle, Pat Summerall kicked a long field goal to give the Giants a 13-10 victory before a crowd of 63,192 in New York. No one ever knew just how far Summerall's unbelievable effort went. The field was covered with snow, but there was no question about the kick. It was a long one into the wind and the driving snow, but it cleared the goal posts with plenty to spare. The best guess was the the kick traveled about 50 yards.

New York and Cleveland were tied at the end of the 1958 season with 9-3 records. A play-off game was set for New York, and 61,174 were there to see it.

The Giants had beaten Cleveland twice during the season in rugged defensive batles. Could they do it again? Jim Lee Howell, the Giant coach, wasn't sure. "This is a great team emotionally, the greatest," he said. "But how many times emotionally can you do this?"

Jim Brown had scored 19 touchdowns and rolled up 1,527 yards in 257 carries for a 5.9 average and easily led the league during the season. In each of the two games against the Giants he gained over 100 yards. In the second meeting, he got away for a 65-yard touchdown run on the first play of the game and ended the afternoon with 148 yards in 26 carries.

The field in New York was frozen, but the Giants' defense was hot. With Sam Huff, the great New York linebacker, dogging Brown on every play, the Giants held pro football's most powerful runner to 18 yards, and won the game 10-0.

About his great performance on defense, Huff said, "Brown was in a tough spot. Cleveland likes to run its plays to perfection. As long as they run the play perfect, they figure your mistakes will beat you. Well, here I was, knowing Jimmy would run and just where he would run. I wasn't about to make any mistakes."

It was a heartbreaking end to a fine season for the Browns.

While the team failed to win the Conference crown, the club had its best year at the gate since 1947. In six games, the Browns played before 370,781 at home, an average of better than 60,000 per game. It marked the second straight season in which attendance topped 300,000. Prior to the 1957 season, Cleveland's best attendance since joining the National Football League was 274,671 in 1953.

After the near-miss in 1958, the Browns settled down to the uncommon role of an also-ran. About the only thing the Cleveland fans had to cheer about was the running of Jim Brown.

With Plum at quarterback, Cleveland lost its first two games in 1959, then rallied for five victories in a row before a pair of one-point losses, to Pittsburgh and San Francisco, knocked the team out of contention. Then the Browns absorbed a 48-7 shellacking at New York before rebounding to beat Philadelphia, 28-21, to tie the Eagles for second place in the East with a 7-5 record. They finished three games behind the New York Giants.

Jimmy Brown grabbed the rushing title for the third straight year with 1,329 yards in 290 carries for a 4.6 average. The Syracuse speedster got 14 touchdowns.

Shortly after the 1959 season ended, a Syracuse fight promotor approached Jimmy Brown and told him that he would guarantee Jim $150,000 in his first year if he would sign to become a professional boxer. Brown had never boxed and didn't know whether he had the ability to become a fighter, but $150,000 was a lot of money and he agreed to consider the offer. (This was not the first time Brown had been offered another job. The previous year, Frank Lane, then general manager of the Cleveland Indians, had offered Jim an opportunity to try out with the Indians at Tucson in the spring of 1959. Brown didn't accept the offer, but the publicity helped him win a $25,000 contract from Paul Brown.)

It so happened that the boxing offer came shortly before Jim was to sit down with Paul Brown to discuss contract terms for the coming season. In the winter of 1960, Brown, an intelligent and articulate young man who had become a shrewd bargainer, leaked out the news of the boxing offer to newsmen, and it received widespread play in newspapers across the country. Naturally, the publicity didn't hurt his bargaining position with Paul Brown, who was as tough across the bargaining table as he was on the football field. Jim Brown's tactics worked. He agreed to a two-year contract calling for $32,000 a season, putting him in the same pay bracket as Baltimore's brilliant quarterback, Johnny Unitas. By 1962, Brown's salary was $45,000 and by 1965 it was reported to be in the neighborhood of $70,000 a season, making him one of the highest paid athletes in the world at that time.

In addition to his football salary, Brown had for several years been drawing a year-round salary from Pepsi Cola. During the off-season, he worked in a marketing capacity for the soft-drink firm. He starred in a Hollywood movie, made personal appearances for sizable fees, was a television sportscaster and engaged in many other activities which helped to swell his bankroll. His total earnings in 1965 were reported to have pushed well over the $100,000 mark. Not bad for a young man who was something of a charity case when at Syracuse University, supported by thoughtful business and professional men who answered Ken Molloy's call for help.

In 1960, Paul Brown made wholesale changes again, and nineteen newcomers made the team. But Brown couldn't duplicate the miracle which had transformed the 1956 team from a loser to a winner. The Browns won their first three and last three games, but couldn't put two victories together in between. They finished the season with eight victories, three losses and a tie to wind up one and one-half games behind the champion Eagles.

Jim Brown made it four rushing crowns in a row, though, rolling up

1,257 yards in 215 carries for a 5.8 average. The big fullback from Syracuse was an established star, but his workhorse performances game after game weren't enough to return Cleveland to the lofty grid pinnacle it once held.

By now Jim was thoroughly disenchanted with Paul Brown. He found him cold and uncompromising. Jim felt that he was just a component in a machine and he didn't like it. He didn't mind the hard work, and he didn't complain about the number of times he was required to carry the ball each Sunday. "I always said I'll run the ball as much as they want me to," was Brown's way of putting it. "I'm getting paid for that and I want to give value received."

Once, after Brown had carried 34 times in a game, someone asked him, "Aren't 34 carries too many? Can't it cut your career?"

"If he says carry 50 times, then I carry 50 times," said Jim softly.

At times Paul Brown was accused of working Jim too hard, and once he admitted, "When you have a big gun you shoot it. I remember a time when Jim smashed into a tackler and got up and walked back to the huddle. The tackler got up and followed Jim into our huddle like a boxer staggering to the wrong corner. His teammates had to get him. Maybe the people who have been trying to stop Jim are taking the beating."

Big Jim never seemed to tire. He had an amazing amount of stamina and never suffered an injury that put him out of commission for more than a period or two. Sometimes when he got up slowly after a tackle and returned to the huddle, it would seem as if he couldn't carry the ball another time. But the appearances were deceiving. He always bounced back with his typical bulldozing power.

It had been three years since the Browns had won a Conference title and five since they had been victorious in a championship game. The fans and experts were beginning to wonder out loud whether Paul Brown had lost the "magic" touch that had produced winner after winner for so many years.

The truth of the matter was that Paul Brown, the great organizer and innovator, had virtually written the textbook on pro football organization, talent-hunting and coaching techniques. Other coaches were quick to recognize and utilize his methods, then improve on them. He had also made some bad trades, which helped other clubs, notably the Green Bay Packers. Defensive end Bill Quinlen went to Green Bay at the end of 1958. Henry Jordan, a defensive tackle, was traded to the same team in 1959, as was Willie Davis, another tackle, in 1960. All of these players were big factors when Vince Lombardi was building the Packers into pro football's most powerful team.

Paul Brown still had the fervent desire to win, but somewhere along the line he appeared to have lost the creative spark that had been the key to his success for so many years.

14

From Madison Avenue to Tower B

Arthur B. Modell, a handsome, dynamic young advertising executive, left his Madison Avenue office in New York City early one evening in October 1960, and was rushing to the elevator on his way to a dinner date when he remembered that he had forgotten something. He hurried back into the office and was about to open his desk when the phone rang.

Modell was in a hurry and nearly didn't answer. After a moment, he picked up the receiver and heard the voice of Vincent Andrews, a New York theatrical agent. Andrews was a friend of Fred (Curly) Morrison, onetime Ohio State University, Chicago Bear and Cleveland Brown fullback and now a television sportscaster for CBS. Morrison had heard that the Cleveland Browns football team was for sale and had called Andrews to find out if he knew anyone who might be interested in acquiring the franchise. Knowing that Modell was a football enthusiast who had dreamed for years of owning a professional team, Andrews called him to report the rumor.

Young Arthur lost no time. He was in Cleveland the next day, talking with the Browns' owners, including President Dave Jones, and stockholders Homer Marshman, Ellis Ryan and Paul Brown. He assembled the details, then went back to New York to put together a syndicate that would buy the team for $3,925,000, nearly six and one-half times more than the Jones group had paid Arthur McBride for the franchise in 1953.

The 36-year-old New Yorker sold a television production company he owned and his partnership in the L. H. Hartman Company, an advertising agency, to help raise a $500,000 down payment. Under the terms of the contract, he had until April 11 to come up with the balance of the money for the franchise. Through other members of his syndicate, principally R. J. Schaeffer, owner of the Schaeffer Breweries of New York, and bankers, Modell met the deadline and took over ownership of the Browns.

Art Modell had come a long way since his teen-age days when he had to scrape together 50 cents each week to see the Brooklyn Dodgers and the New York Giants play football. When he was 14, his father died. A wine dealer who had gone bankrupt during the Depression, the senior Modell left his wife, two daughters and son virtually penniless.

A year later, in 1940, Art lied about his age to obtain a job as an electrician's helper in the Bethlehem Steel Company shipbuilding yards in

Brooklyn for 45 cents an hour. By 1942, he was up to 87 cents an hour. He enrolled in night classes at New York University, but couldn't make ends meet, and was forced to abandon his college courses.

Early in 1943, Modell enlisted in the Air Force and remained in uniform until the end of the war. As he headed home on a train after his separation from service, Art was undecided about his future. Leafing through a magazine, he noticed an advertisement for a television school. He decided to enroll.

"I knew nothing about it," he said later. "But it was so new, neither did anybody else. Therefore, why not start in a business where almost no one has experience?"

While he was still taking the nine-month course, Modell came up with an idea. He wanted to install custom-made television sets in about 200 large supermarkets in the New York area, then feed them a two-hour daytime show aimed at women shoppers. Modell took his idea to the American Broadcasting Company. The network bought it and Art became the show's producer. The program was an instant success, and Art Modell was on his way to a career in a brand new field.

In 1954 the program ended and Art turned to advertising, becoming executive vice-president and a partner in the L. H. Hartman Company. In six years he boosted the agency's annual billing to more than $6.5 million.

Though he was busy during the postwar years building a career and a small fortune, Art never lost his love for professional football. If anything, his zest increased. Watching football was one of his few outlets from the frenzied world of Madison Avenue.

One of the men Art admired most was Paul E. Brown. He had tremendous respect for Brown's coaching ability and business acumen, but Modell, in his role as owner, did not intend to be a nonworking participant in the affairs of the Cleveland Browns.

Arthur McBride had given Paul Brown carte blanche, and as coach and general manager Brown had his fingers in everything -- from advertising and half-time activities to coaching and making travel arrangements. About the only thing Brown didn't do was sell tickets on Sunday. When McBride sold the team to the group headed by Dave Jones in 1953, Brown continued in many of the same roles. Jones and his associates all were wealthy and weren't interested in the day-to-day operation of the club. They left that to Paul Brown.

As negotiations for the sale of the club to Modell and his syndicate began, Brown maintained that he could block the transfer of ownership since he held a sizable hunk of stock, and a majority of the stockholders looked to him for the final word. As coach and general manager, Brown wanted to make sure that his area of responsiblity was clearly defined before he gave his blessing to the deal, which was to net him approximately $500,000 for his share of the stock. Once all were in agreement, the deal went through.

"In consultation with my lawyers, I drew up my contract just as I want it," commented Brown at the time. "Art Modell read it and said, 'That suits me!' He never quibbled on any phase of it. I still will do the hiring and firing as before, and will control factors important to the success of the team. The financial and promotional aspects will be his problems. The loan is his responsibility.''

So Art Modell moved from Madison Avenue to Tower B at Cleveland's Municipal Stadium and assumed the title of Chairman of the Board. Jones remained as president for a year, and then retired. He died in February, 1965, in Bal Harbour, Florida, at the age of 78.

From the day Modell arrived on the scene in Cleveland, he impressed people with his warmth and sincerity and his penchant for hard work. With his personal fortune at stake, he plunged headlong into the promotional activities of the Browns. Meanwhile, Paul Brown began preparing for the 1961 season.

As things turned out, the first season under the Modell regime was more of a financial success than an artistic triumph. With the Minnesota Vikings playing their first season in the league, the schedule was expanded to seven home games. Professional football was booming, and the Browns shared in the prosperity with an all-time record attendance of 426,886.

On the field, the Browns went into the season with the same offensive guns they had used the previous years. Plum was at quarterback, Mitchell was a running halfback, Renfro played at flankerback and the incomparable Jim Brown was again at fullback.

The Browns lost their opener to the defending NFL champs at Philadelphia, then came home for three straight games and rolled up successive victories over St. Louis, Dallas and Washington.

Green Bay's powerhouse, which had lost to Philadelphia, 17-13, in the 1960 championship game, came to town and dismantled the Browns piece by piece before 75,042 at Cleveland Stadium. The Packers had a 21-3 lead at the half and completed the rout in the second half, winning, 49-17. They rolled up 487 yards against the leaky Cleveland defense.

Len Dawson, who had been acquired from the Steelers, started the next game at Pittsburgh in place of Plum, who had suffered a dislocated thumb in the game with Green Bay. But the Steelers had a 14-13 lead going into the final quarter, and Paul Brown called upon Plum for duty. It was a wild fourth quarter. The Browns outscored the Steelers, 17-14. Bobby Mitchell scored twice for Cleveland, but it was Lou Groza's 12-yard field goal with three minutes left that gave the Browns a 30-28 victory.

The following Sunday, the Browns completed the first half of their schedule with a 21-10 victory over St. Louis. The Browns had a 5-2 record and still were very much in contention. But Pittsburgh put a little damper on the Browns' hopes. The Clevelanders blew a 10-point lead and bowed, 17-13, to the Steelers.

In the week prior to the game, Bobby Mitchell was called to active Army duty, and, although his schedule allowed him to participate in games, he wasn't around for practice during the week. He carried the ball only four times and lost eight yards. To make matters worse, Tom Watkins, a rookie halfback who was alternating with Mitchell, dislocated his shoulder. Coupled with Mitchell's Army duties, the injury put a serious crimp in the Browns' running game for the rest of the season.

The Browns dumped Washington, 17-6, and walloped Philadelphia, 45-24, but New York, on its way to another Conference crown, outscored the Browns, 37-21, before 80,455 at Cleveland Stadium. It was the largest NFL crowd of the year.

There was still a slim hope when the Browns defeated the Cowboys, 38-17, at Dallas, but it all ended in Chicago the following Sunday as the Browns bowed to the Bears, 17-14. It marked the first time that the Bears had beaten the Browns in a regular NFL game.

The final game was at New York. The Giants had clinched at least a tie for the Eastern Conference crown, but a Philadelphia victory at Detroit and a Cleveland triumph over New York would force the Giants and the Eagles into a play-off.

The two teams staged another of their patented defensive struggles. The Giants scored in the first period, but the Browns tied it up on a 38-yard touchdown pass from Plum to Leon Clarke in the third quarter. Both teams struggled scorelessly through the final quarter and the game ended in a 7-7 deadlock. The Giants were champions for the fourth time in five years. The Eagles were second and the Browns third with a record of eight wins, five losses and a tie.

Art Modell, an intense man, lived and died emotionally with every play. He was still a fan at heart. But, while it was sometimes hard on his nerves, Modell relished his new role.

Outwardly, the relationship between Brown and Modell had worked just the way the contract said it should, but the lines of communication were starting to break down. Try as he might, Art Modell could not establish a real rapport with his hired hand. Brown, in turn, had been running things his own way for years, and he found it difficult to cooperate with Modell. Resentment began to fester over Modell's friendships with his players.

The pot was boiling, and it wouldn't be many months before the lid blew off.

15

Turmoil at the Top

The files of the National Football league teams are chock-full of the names of highly touted All-American players who have failed to cut the mustard in professional football. To be sure, a player doesn't make the All-American squad on good looks alone, and it helps to have an aggressive school publicity man tooting the horn for him. All-American teams usually are selected by writers or coaches who usually have never seen most of the candidates play. Selections, then, generally are based on how much they have read about various players. This is where the publicity comes in.

Professional football scouts are considerably more scientific in their approach, and they frequently pass up All-American stars in the annual draft in favor of obscure players who have demonstrated the kind of ability that tabs them as a real pro prospects. Even then, pro teams have made mistakes on highly publicized players who have never made the grade.

At Syracuse University in the fall of 1961, there was a young fullback who didn't need a press agent to promote him for All-American honors. His name was Ernie Davis, and his credentials said he was as good or better than Jim Brown was at the same point in his career. Like Brown, Davis had been a terrific high-school athlete. He had led the Elmira, New York, Free Academy to a 52-game winning streak with a 110-yard per game rushing average.

In his first year on the Syracuse varsity, Davis led the Big Orange to an unbeaten season and a victory over Texas in the Cotton Bowl. He rolled up 686 yards on the ground as a sophomore, 877 as a junior and 823 as a senior. In his splendid career at Syracuse, the hard-running, fast-starting halfback scored 35 touchdowns, and his name was entered beside 10 Syracuse records, many of which previously had been held by Jim Brown. He twice was named to the All-American team and, in 1961, he became the first black ever to be awarded the John W. Heisman Memorial Trophy as the outstanding college football player in the land.

Davis, who had exceedingly powerful legs, was just a little lighter in weight than Jim Brown. Both were six feet two inches tall. The handsome, round-faced athlete was the product of a broken home and had grown up in proverty. He was a quiet, shy individual with an infectious smile, a good sense of humor and a pleasing manner which made friends for him wherever he went. He was always reluctant to talk about himself or his many accomplishments, prompting one sports writer to describe Davis as "a fourth-stringer when it comes to talking about himself, but a Heisman Trophy winner on the field."

Davis, an average student at Syracuse, gave much of the credit for his success to his high-school coach, Marty Harrigan. "Harrigan wasn't only my coach, but also my guidance counselor," the soft-spoken Davis said. "He gave me confidence, not only on the field but in the classroom."

Paul Brown decided he wanted Ernie Davis, and was willing to pay dearly for him. He felt that with Davis and Brown in the backfield, Cleveland would have the same type of potent running game that Green Bay, with Paul Hornung and Jim Taylor, was using to smother other National Football League teams.

Because they were mired in the National League's Eastern Division cellar in late 1961, the Washington Redskins were assured of the first draft choice. Bobby Mitchell, the fleet black halfback, was the bait Brown offered to the Washington Redskins in return for the draft rights to the brilliant Davis. Mitchell had become an established National Football League star as a member of the Cleveland backfield. He was a four-year veteran, and among his accomplishments was a team-record 90-yard run from scrimmage in 1959. The Redskins, willing to take a proven veteran in return for a young man who had never played a pro game, accepted Brown's offer.

Brown, whose contract with Art Modell stipulated that he was entirely responsible for playing personnel, didn't bother to tell Modell what he was going to do until the deal was consummated. This failure to discuss an impending deal with a man who had a $4 million investment in the team didn't endear Brown to Modell.

The deal didn't sit well with Cleveland fans or writers, either. They questioned the wisdom of giving up a tried and proven veteran for an unknown quantity.

There was another problem, too. There was some doubt that Davis would even sign with the Browns. The American Football League was in business, and the Buffalo Bills also had drafted Davis. The Browns and the Bills were in a dollar battle for the services of the Syracuse star. However, with the aid of Jim Brown, who had helped sell Davis on Syracuse, the Cleveland club was able to sign Davis to a three-year, $80,000 contract, despite the fact that the Bills were prepared to pay more for his services

After he had signed with the Browns, Davis was asked frequently if he didn't get tired of being compared with Jim Brown all the time. "I haven't let it bother me," he said. "I was out to do a job. I wasn't out to break his records. And I didn't sign with the Browns because Jimmy was there but because it's a wonderful organization. But I'm happy to play with Brown. I think he's the greatest player in the game. One like him comes around every 100 years."

Jim Brown viewed with mixed emotions the deal which brought Davis to Cleveland. Although he was Ernie's friend, he had also been Mitchell's roommate. "I would have been happier if in some way we could have kept Mitchell and obtained a back like Davis," Brown told writer Hal Lebovitz in a magazine interview. "Mitchell is still in our division and he can come back to haunt Cleveland. He always has been tough in Washington, where the weather is warmer and not so wet. The grass is firmer there and helps the runner. On the other hand, I understand Paul Brown's reasoning. Having Davis gives him offensive balance. He can call any play without worrying if the back can go inside or outside. It's now easier from the play-calling view."

While the Browns were successful in getting Davis under contract, they failed to sign another highly touted collegian, Sandy Stephens, the All-American quarterback from Minnesota. Stephens signed a no-cut contract with Montreal of the Canadian League.

Just about the time that the controversy generated over the Davis-for-Mitchell trade was simmering down, Milt Plum, who had been the team's regular quarterback since 1958, did something that few players had ever dared to do while playing for Paul Brown. He publicly criticized the coach. (Plum, a 27-year-old former Penn State star, had the best quarter-backing record in the league in 1961 on the basis of his completion percentage and the lowest percentage of passes intercepted. He had completed 177 passes in 302 attempts for 2,416 yards.) Milt was particularly irritated about the lack of a checkoff system at the line of scrimmage, where the quarterback could change the play to take advantage of defensive changes. This allowed him flexibility in calling plays. Under Paul Brown's system, all of the plays came from the bench.

Plum sounded off in a newspaper interview: "The team is in a rut. We don't get up for the big game most of the time and we have to struggle with the not-so-strong teams." Plum suggested that someone should tell Paul Brown about it, and complained that the coach couldn't get the team to an emotional peak.

"With a little bit of adjustment," Plum continued, "we could be a fine team. There are lots of young players on the club and we could go on for many years. It's time to straighten things out. Our offense has become stereotyped. The quarterback has to have a little more leeway, although nothing to a great extent. The Packers have a few checkoff plays, and the Giants have four or five."

Jim Brown, who had won the rushing title for the fifth straight year with a record 305 carries for 1,409 yards, agreed with Plum, telling sports writers, "I feel that Milt has given it a lot of thought and that he has just about expressed the general opinion of all the players. Similar feelings have been expressed by the players in private many times. We feel that certain things are necessary to get the maximum out of the players. The right of the quarterback to call a few checkoffs and for the players to make a few decisions would mean a lot. The players have the feeling they are playing under wraps all the time. A little freedom would help. Few speak up, but I'm sure all 36 men on the team would agree with most of the things I've said.''

On March 29, 1962, Paul Brown traded the unhappy Plum to the Detroit Lions in a six-player swap. Key man in the deal was Jim Ninowski, who had started his pro career with the Browns. Cleveland also got defensive end Bill Glass and Howard (Hopalong) Cassady, who had been a great running halfback for Ohio State and a Heisman Trophy winner in 1955. Plum wasn't surprised. ''I thought it might come but not this season,'' Plum said. He allowed that his remarks might have hastened his departure. Along with Plum, the Browns sent to Detroit running back Tom Watkins and Dave Lloyd, a center and linebacker. This time, Brown discussed the deal with Modell, and the boss agreed.

Ninowski, who broke in with Cleveland in 1958, played very little that year and was traded to the Lions, wasn't at all happy with the turn of events. The former Michigan State star, who had improved enough to become a regular on a Detroit team which finished second in 1960 and 1961, flatly told Lion Coach George Wilson, ''I don't want to go to the Browns.''

''The job is his,'' Brown said. ''We've been so impressed by his progress that we can give it to him now. We've gone four years without winning, and feel some changes are required. We talked this thing over and over. We looked at it from all angles. We decided that it was a trade that would help us, though we really hated to give up Tom Watkins.

''We didn't have any idea that Jim might be available. One of our coaches was watching a college practice and ran into a Detroit coach. The latter brought up the subject of a quarterback deal. Then I worked around to the subject in trade talks that had been going on with George Wilson. Finally, we agreed on the players. If we thought we could win with the players we had, there wouldn't have been a deal.''

Paul Brown still had an unhappy Ninowski to deal with. The Cleveland coach flew to Detroit and held a two-hour meeting with the quarterback at Detroit Metropolitan Airport. He convinced Ninowski to play for the Browns. ''He'll be No. 1 with us, and I'll tell you he likes the idea,'' Brown said after the meeting.

Meanwhile, the Browns' publicity department came out with a news release pointing out that although Plum had been the league's most effective quarterback the previous season, 70 per cent of his passes had traveled less than seven yards. ''We feel we must throw more effectively downfield next season,'' Brown said.

There were other developments, too, as the Browns moved toward the opening of the 1962 summer camp. Blanton Collier, who had been a Brown assistant for years, left the University of Kentucky and returned to Cleveland as offensive backfield coach.

In April, Modell announced that pro football's first double-header would be played at Cleveland, with Dallas facing Detroit and Cleveland meeting Pittsburgh. The creative Modell had broached the idea of an exhibition double-header at the National Football League meetings in

January. Most of the owners were skeptical of the proposal, claiming that once the fans were treated to a pro football double-header during the exhibition season, they might expect the same fare every year and possibly even during the regular campaign.

Still, there was no vigorous objection, and Modell was left to try to arrange a program, if he so desired. Although Paul Brown was against the proposal, Modell went ahead and tried to line up two other teams to fill out the program on one of the Browns' exhibition dates. He offered the teams sizable guarantees, so there would be no risk involved should the idea fizzle. Finally, after weeks of fruitless discussions, Modell struck pay dirt. The Detroit Lions agreed to switch their exhibiton date with Dallas from Briggs Stadium to Cleveland as the first game of the twin bill.

On May 9, Dave Jones retired as president and as a director of the Browns. Modell assumed the title of president.

Paul Brown had been criticized for some of his recent deals, but on July 13, 1962, he made what eventually was to turn out to be one of the best in the Browns' history. From the Rams, he obtained Frank Ryan, a Phi Beta Kappa and the one-time Rice Institute star, and Tom Wilson, a fine running back, for two future draft choices and rights to Larry Stephens. Brown said he obtained Ryan, a six-foot, 200 pound, three-year veteran, for insurance. In 1961, he had completed 72 of 142 passes for 1,115 yards and five touchdowns. Ryan became expendable when the Rams got rookie Roman Gabriel from North Carolina State. They also had Zeke Bratkowski, who played ahead of Ryan. Wilson, a seven-year veteran, had been signed by the Rams in 1956, and was one of the few players to reach professional stardom without the benefit of college experience. His career total of 2,130 yards rushing was the third best in the Rams' history.

The first order of business in active preparations for the 1962 season was a quarterback camp at Hiram, Ohio, and Brown launched it with the announcement that Ninowski would have more latitude in calling plays. Brown said he would rotate the guards some of the time, but the coaches would set a game plan from which Ninowski would work.

A few days later, the full team, with the exception of rookie Ernie Davis, arrived for the opening of training camp. The team was extensively remodeled again. There were 27 old hands, eight veterans from other clubs and 20 rookies. Eleven members of the 1961 team were missing. Guard Jim Ray Smith, who had retired, agreed to come back for one more season.

The missing rookie Ernie Davis was in Evanston, Illinois, preparing to take part in the All-Star game with the Green Bay Packers. Early in July, Davis, who appeared to be in great shape, had stopped at Hiram to work out for a few days with the quarterbacks, then headed for Evanston. The day after he arrived at the All-Star camp, Davis had two impacted wisdom teeth removed and the after-effects of the oral operation made him quite ill. Shortly afterwards, he suffered a slight pulled muscle in his leg during practice which further hampered his efforts to get off to a fast start with the All-Stars.

On Thursday, July 26, the All-Stars scrimmaged the Chicago Bears at St. Joseph's College in Rensselaer, Indiana. It was a hot, muggy day, and the Bears trampled the All-Stars, 24-7. One of the bright spots that day was the performance of Davis, who flashed some of the style that had made him the nation's top collegiate star the year before. Davis picked up 38 yards on three rushing plays and two receptions and was mobbed by photographers and autograph-seekers at game's end. Davis, obviously tired from the day's activities under the broiling sun, smilingly posed for pictures and signed autographs long after the last of the Bears and the All-Stars had retired to the locker room.

Then, over the weekend, Ernie began to develop a swelling in the glands around his neck, and on Tuesday, July 31 he was hospitalized with what at first was thought to be the mumps. But word soon came from the hospital that it wasn't mumps after all but rather a form of mononucleosis. That diagnosis didn't hold up long, either. Late in the day, Dr. Franklin Kaiser, the attending physician in Evanston, admitted to reporters, "It isn't mononucleosis. I haven't come to any conclusions. I won't know until further tests are made."

The doctors pored over Ernie's blood samples and found unmistakable evidence that he was afflicted by monoclytic leukemia, the worst form of the dread disease. They concluded he could live a year at the longest, probably less.

As the earlier conflicting reports of Davis' illness filtered out of Evanston, a deeply concerned Art Modell telephoned the hospital. The doctors stunned him with their diagnosis. Modell made hasty plans to fly to Evanston the next day with Marsh Samuel, the team's publicity director. "He's undergoing a series of tests," Modell told writers at the airport. "I'm going up there to make sure he has the best of everything. I'm hoping for the best."

Meanwhile, word that Davis had been hospitalized reached the Browns' training camp at Hiram. "We're dead if there is anything seriously wrong with Ernie," was Paul Brown's first alarmed comment. "We're in trouble if he even misses much practice. We're counting so much on him."

On Wednesday morning, Modell and Samuel were joined in Evanston by Tony DeFillipo, Davis' attorney and long-time friend. When Modell and DeFillipo entered Davis' room, they found the disappointed young man sitting on the edge of his bed weeping. Aside from the swelling Davis felt fine and wanted to play football. He couldn't understand why he wasn't being allowed to play. That night, after a long conference with attending physicians and DeFillipo, it was agreed that Ernie must not be told of the grave nature of his illness.

Modell issued a statement to the press. Davis' ailment, he told reporters, had been diagnosed as a blood disorder requiring extended treatment and rest. "At this moment, it appears almost certain that Ernie will not be able to play this season," Modell added sadly. "The long-range future depends on his response to these treatments. Ernie's recovery is the only thing that matters to all of us and everything will be done to speed it. We'll miss him greatly on the field, but maybe the rest of the boys will make up for it by playing harder. I don't understand why we should give up because Davis hasn't played a game yet," Modell said in an obvious rebuff to Brown, who had said the team was "dead" if Davis didn't play. "This boy means more at the moment than the entire football season. We will see him through to the last down." Modell explained that it had been decided to bring Davis back to Cleveland so that further tests and treatment could be taken, guided by Dr. Vic Ippolito, the team physician.

The day of the All-Star game, Friday, August 13, Ernie Davis returned to Cleveland with Modell and Samuel. Shortly after noon, the tall athlete, wearing an open-necked sport shirt and jacket stepped off a jet airliner at the Cleveland Hopkins Airport. About a dozen newsmen were there to greet him.

"Have the doctors told you what the trouble is, Ernie?" asked one newsman.

"No, they haven't told me anything."

"How do you feel?"

"I feel fine. All I can hope and pray is that I get back."

The question and answer period lasted for ten minutes. Then Davis went back up on the steps of the plane to oblige a photographer. Finally, Modell, Samuel and Davis drove off to Marymount Hospital.

That evening, Ernie watched the All-Star game on television. The game was already under way when three of the Browns, tackle John Brown, a teammate at Syracuse, Jim Brown and guard John Wooten, arrived to view the game with him and to help buoy his spirits.

"Howdy, partner," Jim Brown said as he entered the room. "The guys really miss you down there."

The conversation for the rest of the evening revolved mostly around the players in the All-Star game and the Browns' players.

The Packers, after thrashing the All-Stars, 42-20, awarded the game ball to Ernie Davis.

Spurred by Modell's announcement that Davis had a blood disorder, rumors spread that the athlete was suffering with leukemia. Davis' doctors knew they would eventually have to tell the athlete about his condition, but they wanted to wait until the treatment had taken effect and the disease was in a remissive state. Their problem was to keep the word from reaching Ernie via the newspapers, radio and television.

On August 9, a group of Cleveland newspaper, radio and television reporters gathered in Modell's office at Tower B in the Cleveland Stadium. Modell pledged them to secrecy in the interest of protecting Ernie. Then he told them that Davis did have leukemia and that the remainder of his life was numbered in months. The news media in Cleveland honored their commitment to the letter.

The loss of Davis was a jolt to the squad, but, with the exception of the few players who knew him well, there was very little personal involvement. Most of the players had never met him or seen him play football.

He was still a rookie who had not yet proven himself. They felt that it was a tough break for the Heisman Trophy winner, but there was work to do.

The Browns opened the 1962 exhibition season against the Detroit Lions. It was billed as a battle of the traded quarterbacks -- Plum vs. Ninowski. Ninowski completed 15 of 28 passes for 208 yards and two touchdowns as the Browns won, 17-14. Lou Groza, still around after 17 years, made the difference with his 12-yard field goal. Plum completed five of 11 for 69 yards as he shared the quarterback role with Earl Morrall.

"I think Jim did an excellent job," Paul Brown said.

The next week, 77,783 fans, a record for a pre-season game, turned out for pro football's first double-header in Cleveland. It was a whopping success. Detroit beat Dallas, 35-24, and Cleveland edged Pittsburgh, 33-30.

Ernie Davis was allowed out of the hospital for the game and was introduced to the crowd which gave him a standing ovation.

One of the more interesting battles was that between Scales and Wilson for the halfback spot that Davis was to have occupied. Wilson was impressive as the Browns next whipped the 49ers, 34-27, in Portland. He scored two touchdowns on runs of six and 32 yards and set up another with a 41-yard jaunt. He gained 109 yards in eight carries and was well on his way to a starting spot.

The Browns completed their exhibition season with a 26-24 victory over Los Angeles and a 28-24 triumph over the Chicago Bears. On the basis of their five straight victories, the Browns were rated the favorites in the Eastern Conference, with Philadelphia, New York and St. Louis the contenders. In the West, Green Bay again was the choice.

As the Browns readied for their opener with the Giants, Ernie Davis was at the National Institute of Health in Bethesda, Maryland, for treatment of his serious blood ailment.

There were 81,115 on hand in Cleveland as the Browns intercepted three passes and downed the defending champion Giants, 17-7. It was only Cleveland's second victory over the Giants in the last ten meetings between the teams. Ninowski had seen better days, but contributed a 17-yard touchdown pass to Rich Kreitling. The defense appeared solid.

The next week was Bobby Mitchell's "homecoming," and as far as the Browns were concerned, he could have remained in Washington. With a minute and a half left in the game, Mitchell lined up as a halfback instead of a flanker, and took a pass from quarterback Norm Snead. Mitchell went 50 yards for a touchdown, and the Redskins upset the Browns, 17-16. The Davis-for-Mitchell trade had come back to haunt Paul Brown.

In the following game, the Philadelphia Eagles drubbed the Browns, 35-7. Ninowski completed only nine passes in 27 attempts. "Nobody on the team can point a finger at another guy in this one," an angry Paul Brown commented. "It was as poor a game as we've played in a long time."

Meanwhile, doctors had succeeded in arresting the leukemia afflicting Ernie Davis. Although they knew it could very well be a temporary condition, they felt it now was time to tell the courageous athlete the true nature of the disease. There were two prime factors which motivated their decision. First, rumors of Davis' illness had spread throughout the community and on one occasion, Ernie had been subjected to a cruel encounter. Writing in *Sport* magazine, Jim Brown told of an incident that had been related to him by John Brown, the Cleveland lineman.

"John Brown told us Ernie went to a movie and a stranger came up to him and asked him, 'Are you Ernie Davis?'

"According to John, Ernie never wanted anybody to make a fuss over him, so he said, 'No.'

"The man said, 'You're lucky, because Ernie Davis has leukemia and he's going to die in six months.'

"Ernie replied quietly, 'I'm Ernie Davis, and I'm not going to die.'

"He explained to John afterward, 'I didn't want to hurt that man, but it might keep him from being cruel to somebody else'."

The second reason was because Ernie's case was in perfect remission and the doctors felt they could cushion the shock and improve his morale by telling him he could resume workouts.

The painful job of telling Ernie was left to Dr. Austin Weisberger, chief of hematology at Western Reserve University Hospital, who had been treating the stricken athlete. Davis, who had been released from the hospital in early September, and had become an almost daily visitor at the Browns' League Park practice field, was called to Dr. Weisberger's office at University Hospital. Dr. Vic Ippolito and Art Modell were there, too.

Dr. Weisberger, one of the nation's foremost blood specialists, spoke softly. "Ernie," he said, "the time has come to tell you the whole facts regarding your case."

The 23-year-old Davis, looking fit and just one pound over his playing weight of 212, broke into a sweat. It was his only noticeable reaction.

Dr. Weisberger told Ernie that he had a form of leukemia, which was in perfect remission. Ernie's first reaction to the doctor's words were, "Can I lick it?"

The specialist told Ernie that leukemia patients had been known to live normal lives. "You're an intelligent person. You must have had some inkling," Dr. Weisberger said.

"Yes, I thought about the possibility," Ernie answered. "But I made myself stop thinking about it. I made up my mind that whatever I had I was going to have to live with it and make the most of it."

"I don't believe for a minute that he wasn't upset," Dr. Weisberger said later. "But he never showed it. Not once. I can't honestly say that outwardly he was floored by the revelation."

Davis told Modell and Drs. Weisberger and Ippolito that he wanted the nature of his illness kept secret. But Dr. Weisberger told him that, if it were known publicly that he had leukemia, his return to the gridiron would buoy other leukemia victims. They finally agreeed to a carefully worded statement, released the next day, October 5, by Dr. Weisberger.

"Ernie Davis has a form of leukemia. He has responded extremely well to therapy and medication and at the present time his blood findings are entirely normal. As long as he remains in a perfect state of remission, I see no reason why he cannot play professional football."

Dr. Ippolito was placed in charge of Ernie's training program. He explained to newsmen, "His long illness, of course, will mean Ernie will have to start off from scratch physically. We'll start off with some running. And as his wind and muscle tone returns, he can gradually work into regular practice sessions with the team."

Davis' return to regular workouts, allowed solely as a morale-building factor and to give Ernie hope, touched off a medical controversy. Dr. Charles Doan, retired dean of the Ohio State University Medical School, backed Dr. Weisberger but Dr. James Grace, researcher and clinician at Roswell Park Memorial Hospital in Buffalo, disagreed. Dr. Grace explained that he advised leukemia patients to live as near a normal life as possible. "But this is different," he said. "This is hard, tough football. The more I think of it, the more ridiculous it seems."

Ernie Davis resumed his conditioning program, and it was definitely a tonic for his spirits. Day after day, wearing a sweat suit and with a towel draped around his neck, he jogged around the League Park practice field.

Meanwhile the Browns had a 1-2 record as they faced the Dallas Cowboys before 44,041 on Lou Groza Day. In a horribly dull first half, the Browns took a 7-3 lead, with Jim Brown contributing a two-yard touchdown plunge and Groza booting the extra point. The Browns got rolling in the second half. Ninowski, who completed only six of 15 passes in the first two periods, hit on nine of ten in the final two periods, one of them a 50-yard touchdown throw to Brown.

In the first quarter, Jim Brown jammed his left hand, but had it taped and kept playing. It turned out to be a badly sprained wrist, which bothered the star for the remainder of the season. But he played in every game, and the injury was a well-kept secret.

The Browns had a 2-2 record when the Baltimore Colts came to town and destroyed the team, 36-14, before a gathering of 80,132. Jim Brown fumbled three times, losing the ball twice. Tom Wilson fumbled once. Ninowski completed 16 of 32 passes for 223 yards and two interceptions, but the Colt defense held Jim Brown to a net of 11 yards, his worst performance as a pro.

Renfro, an 11 year veteran and one of the finest pass-catching backs in the history of pro ball, had tears in his eyes when he told Blanton Collier, "I'm just not helping the team. I never thought I'd see the day."

"We're not out of it yet," said Paul Brown as he surveyed the wreckage of a team which seemed disorganized and lacking in poise.

As the team prepared for its next game with St. Louis, Brown benched Wilson in favor of Charley Scales and sold Cassady to the Eagles for the $100 waiver price.

"I don't think Paul Brown knows my name," Cassady commented. "All the time I was with the Browns, he never said anything to me."

At St. Louis, Ninowski, playing with a bad knee, completed 19 of 29 passes for 339 yards. Renfro caught six for 152 yards, and Scales was an impressive runner as the Browns routed the Cardinals, 34-7. The game also marked a return to the messenger play-calling system.

"Injuries have hurt us," Brown said after the game. "There's no use complaining about this. We've been tight and on edge ever since that loss to Washington. Maybe we've finally turned the corner. This is the best we've been since the beginning. We haven't put things like this together since the double-header."

In the second quarter at Pittsburgh the following week, the injury jinx hit again. Ninowski suffered a shoulder separation and was lost for the remainder of the season. Ryan stepped in and coolly and confidently completed 11 of 18 passes for 114 yards and two touchdowns. The Browns won, 41-14.

Another big crowd, 63,848, was on hand for the home game with the Eagles on November 4. Ryan, continuing his fine work, gained 80 yards on nine carries and completed 10 passes for 119 yards. But the best the Browns could do was a 14-14 tie.

Ernie Davis had been working out for a month, and it was time for a decision on his chances with Cleveland in 1962. "Ernie is in fine physical and medical shape," Modell said. "He has been getting checkups every two weeks, and if he plays he'll have them even more often."

It was no secret that Modell felt that Davis should be activated as a player. It was his feeling that the doctors really knew what was best for Ernie. But the decision was up to Paul Brown. The players and the team as a whole were in his domain, and Modell wasn't dictating. Brown's decision was final. Ernie Davis would not replace any of the players currently on the squad.

The Browns lost to the Redskins, 17-9, and then routed the Cardinals for the second time, 38-14. Pittsburgh fell, 35-14, but then the team lost its next two games, to Dallas, 45-21, and to New York, 17-13, crushing their hopes of finishing in second place. They wound up the season with a 13-10 victory over San Francisco in Kezar Stadium.

New York won the title with a 12-2 record, while Pittsburgh finished second and Cleveland wound up third for the second straight year. Their record was seven victories, six losses and a tie. In terms of a won-loss record, it was the Browns' worst season since 1956.

For the first time in six years Jim Brown had been dethroned as the league's leading rusher. The quiet fullback gained "only" 996 yards in 230 carries, to finish behind Jim Taylor of Green Bay.

Jim Brown wasn't happy, other players weren't happy and Art Modell wasn't happy. There was a decision to be made.

16

Exile at $82,500 a Year

Cleveland was submerged in the longest newspaper strike in its history as 1962 came to an end. The strike, which closed its two dailies, the *Cleveland Plain Dealer* and the *Cleveland Press,* had begun before the end of the football season, and it was to stretch almost until spring.

Deprived of their newspapers to remind them of what had promised to be a fine season and had turned out otherwise, most folks were content just to forget about it. But there was one man who spent sleepless nights brooding about the Browns. For four weeks, Art Modell rehashed the season in his mind. Mentally, he poured over his disintegrating relationship with Paul Brown and the dissatisfaction which had been expressed by a numbers of players. Unlike tight-lipped Paul Brown, who remained aloof from his players, Modell had become friendly with a number of them. Brown didn't particularly appreciate the blossoming relationships.

"There was a void I tried to fill," Modell explained. "Mostly I try to help them get off-season jobs or help them with their personal problems, such as tax advice, if they need it. I see nothing wrong with this. I think all employers try to give their employees peace of mind, so they can devote their full energies to their work."

Modell was an almost daily visitor to practice sessions in 1961, his first year as an owner, but as the 1962 campaign moved along toward its unhappy climax, he was seen less and less at the League Park workouts.

With the Browns hopelessly out of the title race, several players came to Art Modell and told him their troubles. They found working for Paul Brown intolerable, they confided, and at least seven of them, all valuable players, said they were planning to quit or ask to be traded. They didn't blame Paul entirely for the disappointing season -- he had no control over the injuries -- but they resented his handling of players.

"This past season I knew there was an undercurrent not beneficial to the team," Modell said later. "This wasn't during the heat of battle, but long after we were knocked out of the 1962 race, and it behooved me as an owner to probe into it and decide how I could remedy the situation to the best interest of the team."

Modell weighed the facts, talked with other stockholders and made his decision: Paul Brown must go.

Brown may have been aware of the grumbling by the players, but outwardly he didn't appear worried. He had six years to go on his latest contract at a salary of $82,500 a year. If that wasn't job security in the uncertain business of coaching, what was? He was in for the jolt of his life.

His decision made, a weary Art Modell summoned Brown to his office in the corner of Tower B of Municipal Stadium. It was Monday, January 7, 1963. Modell simply told Brown that he was through. He would collect his pay during the remaining six years of his contract, but he no longer would be coach and general manager of the Browns.

Two days later, on Wednesday, January 9, Art Modell and the club's legal counsel met Paul Brown and his lawyers in an office away from the stadium to further discuss the situation and to arrive at a mutually satisfactory announcement of Brown's dismissal. Marsh Samuel, then the publicity director of the Browns, had prepared a lengthy news release in which Brown was hailed for his many contributions to the game. Brown and his lawyers balked. They wanted a terse, simple announcement, and they got it.

In the announcement, Modell said Brown was being relieved of his duties "in the best interest of the club." The release stated that Brown, who was also a vice-president of the Cleveland organization, would remain with the organization with "other duties." Modell said he had three or four coaching candidates in mind, and he hoped to have a successor in ten days or two weeks.

The announcement ready, it was distributed to the wire services and other news media. No newspapers were being printed in Cleveland, but the news hit the town like a bomb. Football fans were stunned. Some had called for Paul's scalp after the disappointing season, but none had expected to get it. Some of the Browns' luster had worn off in the long period since the team had won its last Conference championship, and fans were divided on the merits of the move.

Paul Brown was strangely silent for a time as he absorbed the full impact of his dismissal. Modell's action "hit him out of the blue," he admitted. But then from his plush Shaker Heights home he fought back. "My position in this thing is simple," he said sharply. "Art Modell, in my mind, has changed the contract which I have. My status is that the matter is in the hands of the lawyers. It may take a few days or weeks to resolve." Brown said he was hired only as a coach and general manager, and that his contract didn't mention the "other duties" Modell had spoken of. "I haven't changed anything," Brown continued. "But I have been asked to. I was asked to remain as a vice-president."

Modell fired back that he had sent Brown a wire saying that in his opinion there had been no breach of contract. He explained that he had offered Brown a terminal settlement of his contract, but that Brown had turned it down as inadequate.

Since the unions had silenced Cleveland's newspapers, Modell was spared from any immediate local criticism from the press for his action. But columnists across the country were busy second-guessing one of the biggest sports stories in years. There was no unanimity among them.

"The dismissal defies comprehension," wrote Arthur Daley, the Pulitzer Prize-winning columnist of the *New York Times.* "The moody genius from the lakefront had achieved an eminence in his profession that lifted him above the pack. . . . His record for success was both fantastic and unparalleled.

"Paul was the cold, efficient machine that turned out victories and championships with assembly line precision. Five years ago, the machine suddenly became human, developed human flaws and frailties. The magic touch was lost amid personnel changes and the image of Brown's invincibility disappeared with it. Critics pounded on the man.

" 'The parade has passed by Paul Brown,' they crowed. 'He refuses to keep pace with a changing game but insists on calling all the plays for his quarterback. He's grown too old and set in his ways.'

"That's a lot of hooey. At the age of 54, Paul is a wiser, smarter coach than he was when he invented the game in 1946."

In the *Philadelphia Bulletin,* Sandy Grady commented: ". . . If they held a convention of players, coaches and fans who dislike Paul Brown, perhaps no stadium could contain the mob. Yet, there wouldn't be a man-jack in the crowd who did not respect the wintery Cossack. Sam Huff told this tourist once, 'There isn't anybody I like to beat as much as that so-and-so Brown -- because he's the best!'

"It is easy to chuckle at the martinets who slip on banana peels. The chucklers, however, should not forget that Paul Brown gave pro football its passion for precision that made it a first-rate spectacle. Every team uses the Brown innovations: the face mask, the grading system, breaking down of game films into statistics, cloistering players before games, specialists for every job. He was the Da Vinci of the pros.

"Even his enemies were joyless at Paul Brown's departure. There isn't a decent villain in sight."

The *Los Angeles Herald-Examiner's* sports columnist, Melvin Durslag, penned: ". . . Brown never has been the most popular coach. Just the most skillful. His record is remarkable. He hasn't won a title in five years, but his teams unfailingly have been tough, and they have finished close at times when they shouldn't have.

"Socially, Brown is a pleasant, interesting person with a wide range of knowledge, as football coaches go. His mind is keen and his philosophy rational. Professionally, he is a little monster whose ego is fed by success in his games. He imposes on his players the same iron discipline to which he subjects himself. He also demands a standard of excellence which, if not met, leaves him in a snappish, angry mood.

"Brown has never before been fired. . . For his first canning, owner Modell has made an auspicious start."

The fans were mixed in their reactions, but in the final analysis those who favored Modell's action seemed to outweigh those who thought Brown got a raw deal. Those who backed Modell claimed that Paul Brown had become dictatorial with his players and that his offense lacked imagination and diversity. It was time for a change, they said. Those critical of the deal claimed that with his tremendous record, Brown deserved better than a sacking. Others speculated that Modell's action signaled the beginning of an era of front-office interference in the operation of the Browns. Whether they favored the firing or not, most of the fans agreed that Paul Brown had given Cleveland a pro football legacy of which they could be everlastingly proud.

Hal Lebovitz, veteran *Cleveland Plain Dealer* sports writer (and now sports editor) tried to fill the void resulting from lack of local newspapers and rushed into print a 36-page booklet which dissected the Brown firing from every angle and featured the comments of Cleveland's top sports writers. It was entitled *Paul Brown -- The Play He Didn't Call.* News-hungry Clevelanders swallowed up 50,000 copies in a few days.

Perhaps the most eloquent description of the firing of Paul Brown was contained in Lebovitz's book in the headline over the column written by Frank Gibbons: "It Was Like Toppling the Terminal Tower." The Terminal Tower is the city's tallest skyscraper.

Some players were quick to comment. Jim Brown, who had threatened to give up pro football unless there was a change in the Cleveland situation, backed Modell. "I felt Modell had good reason to fire Brown," the great fullback said. "Football players don't like to be treated as inferiors. Allie Sherman praised us at the Pro Bowl in a way Paul Brown never did. I wasn't looking forward to playing for him next year."

"Once you think it over," said center John Morrow, "it's a good move for both Paul and us. We all need a change. Now we've got a new lease on life. Actually, I felt sorry for Paul. He had problems of his own, and everybody was working overtime trying to figure out what was wrong with us. All I know is that it wasn't a relaxed team. There were too many mixed-up feelings."

Observed offensive captain Mike McCormack, "I'm sorry he's being knocked," and continued, "As far as I'm concerned, he's the finest coach I ever played for. And yet I'm convinced that the Browns cannot win a title with Paul as coach."

"I checked with my teammates, and I'm virtually certain they were 100 per cent in favor of the change," remarked Bernie Parrish, defensive back and player representative. "I know that five and maybe seven of them would have retired rather than play for Brown next year. I was one of them. I was glad to see Brown go because he failed to develop the attitude we needed to have to win. He kept his football above us. We should have felt we were working with him, not for him. There's nothing personal in my criticism. But we've all felt so frustrated these past four years it has been awful."

A few days after feeling the sharp blade of Modell's axe, Paul Brown returned to the Browns' office and was surprised to see his assistant coaches looking at game movies in the screening room. After his firing, Brown had told them all that they were through. By-laws of the Browns' pension plan stated that in order to be eligible for a year's service, a coach had to be on the payroll until the end of the year. The Browns' fiscal year ended on Februry 28, and Modell had said that all members of the coaching staff would be paid at least through that date. The coaches felt that as long as they were being paid, they should be working. At that point, they didn't know whether or not they would be with the Browns in 1963, but they were going about their jobs as usual.

Brown wasn't exactly pleased at the sight. He quickly picked up some belongings, said a few good-byes and left. Although he was a vice president of the organization, he never again set foot in the Browns office.

The next week, Modell, Brown and their lawyers huddled again. It was agreed that Brown's contract had not been violated. His duties and method of payment were redefined. Paul Brown was to be used as a consultant only at the call of the chief executive officer of the Browns, Art Modell. He was never called. At the meeting, it was stipulated in writing that Brown would not criticize the Cleveland Browns, nor would Modell disparage his former coach.

The meeting over, Paul Brown was a man of leisure for the first time in his adult life. Under terms of the agreement, he couldn't coach any other football team. He was to receive the full $82,500 a year for six years, and still had options to purchase stock each year. He retired to devote full time to his hobby, golf. After spending a year in the Cleveland area, he moved to La Jolla, California, where he could play the year around. With Brown picking up $82,500 a year while playing golf, someone suggested that only two men in the country made more money at that sport -- Arnold Palmer and Jack Nicklaus.

The Brown situation settled, Modell turned his energies to finding a new coach. Several men were mentioned as possibilities, among them Otto Graham, who was coaching at the U.S. Coast Guard Academy, but Art Modell had only one man in mind. He was Blanton Collier. Modell tried to talk with Collier about the vacancy, but the assistant coach refused to discuss it for several days. There were two reasons. First, Collier was extremely loyal to Brown. Second, his protege, Don Shula, had been named head coach of the Baltimore Colts to succeed Weeb Ewbank, and Collier, not knowing what would happen in Cleveland, had accepted an invitation to discuss a job with Baltimore.

Modell finally sat down with Collier and offered him a three-year contract. Collier said he wanted to discuss the matter with his long-time friend and associate, Paul Brown, before making a decision. Collier telephoned Brown at his home and told him of Modell's offer. "Blanton, you have no choice but to accept it," Brown said. "You have your family to think of."

Collier accepted the job. "He's always been fair with me, and I've tried to be fair with him," Collier said of Brown later.

The scholarly looking Collier had started his coaching career in 1928 at the Paris, Kentucky, High School. He was athletic director, coached the football, basketball, baseball and track teams during his years there and also taught algebra.

A graduate of Kentucky's Georgetown College, Collier had enlisted in the Navy in December, 1943, and fate ultimately took him to the Great Lakes Naval Training Station near Chicago, where Paul Brown was coaching the football team. As Brown put his Great Lakes team through its paces late one afternoon, he noticed a sailor leaning on the fence bordering the practice field. Day after day the sailor came back and took his position along the fence to become absorbed in the day's workout. That sailor was Blanton Collier.

One day Commander Alden W. Thompson, head of the Great Lakes Physical Training Department, told Brown, "There's a yeoman over in my office who's a nut on football. What I mean, a complete filbert. Seems to know something, too, as nearly as I can tell. I wonder if you could use him in some minor capacity."

That evening, Yeoman Blanton Collier reported for the interview.

"Oh, it's you!" Brown said, recognizing the sailor as the man who had been hanging on the fence for weeks.

Collier related his background and the two talked football. Brown quickly became convinced that the sailor had one of the finest football minds he ever had encountered. He gave Collier a job, and an enduring professional association and friendship was born.

When Paul Brown moved to Cleveland to launch the Browns, he took Blanton Collier with him. After the successful 1946 campaign, Brown instructed Collier to make a close analysis of the team's season. Collier took the movies of the Browns' games to his Kentucky home and broke down every one of the more than 1,000 offensive plays run by the Browns during the preceding season. He produced a report which showed why -- and how much -- each play had gained, or why it hadn't clicked. It was a minute study of every player and his performance on every play. It pinpointed the effectiveness of each play against various defenses.

"Blanton's survey is the most profound study of a football team's performance ever made," Brown said. "I'd have settled for something half as comprehensive when I told him to do the job. But Collier doesn't do things by halves..."

Brown was so pleased with the study that it was done annually and the technique of grading players' performances by film was born. It is used now by many high school teams and all major college and professional teams in the country.

When the University of Kentucky approached its native son in 1954 to offer him the job vacated by Bear Bryant, who had moved to Texas A & M, Collier sought out his friend and mentor, Paul Brown, for advice. Brown told him to take the job.

It was only natural, then, even though the circumstances were much different, that Collier wanted to seek out his friend for counsel when Modell asked him to succeed Brown.

On January 16, 1963, the Browns called a press conference and Collier's selection was announced. He was the leading candidate and there was no surprise. Modell also announced that he was splitting the job of coach and general manager into two separate jobs. Collier would handle the coaching, he said, and Harold Sauerbrei, who had once covered the Browns as a sports writer for the *Cleveland Plain Dealer* and later became the club's publicity director, had been elevated from business manager to general manager. Operation of a pro football team, with television and countless other details which needed attention, had become too big for one man to handle, Modell pointed out.

Facing the press, Collier had some good news for Paul Brown's other assistants. They were all rehired.

Through all the sound and fury, only Paul Brown was missing. It wouldn't be quite the same without him, but peace and tranquility had returned to the Cleveland Browns.

17

The Beginning of a New Era

Three members of the Cleveland Browns were destined to lose their lives before another football season rolled around.

Ernie Davis lost his courageous battle against leukemia without ever having played a football game for the Cleveland Browns. During the winter of 1962-63, he played a little basketball with a team composed of Browns' players. In his first game against a group of Cleveland-area Catholic high-school coaches, Davis, playing brilliantly, scored 18 points, second only to Jim Brown's 22.

Davis roomed with tackle John Brown on Cleveland's East Side. Despite his illness, he did his share of the cooking and shopping and other chores that were required. And he never complained about his illness.

"If I hadn't known that he had leukemia, I'd never have suspected it," said the big tackle. "He lived like a typical young bachelor. He never slowed down. He lived every day up to the hilt."

Davis went to parties, attended the state high school basketball tournament in Columbus, worked for a soft drink company and helped coach the Syracuse alumni for their annual spring game with the Big Orange varsity. When he occasionally interrupted his routine to enter the hospital for a few days of treatment, he never wanted anyone to know he was going.

"If anybody asks where I am, tell them I went out of town for a few days," Davis advised John Brown.

Ernie kept talking about the future. He bought a new car coat for the coming winter, six months away, and put away his heavy clothes for the summer. He bought a new set of golf clubs, and discussed the new car he would purchase the following year. He even talked about marriage.

On May 16, 1963, Ernie had an appointment with Dr. Weisberger, the blood specialist. As Brown was leaving for his off-season job, he woke up Ernie to remind him of the appointment. Ernie sat on the side of the bed, half asleep.

"Bubbles is feeling pretty bad," whispered ex-Syracuse star Art Baker, a house guest. "Bubbles" was a nickname some of Ernie's good friends had given him.

Before keeping his appointment at University Hospital, Ernie stopped at the Stadium to see Art Modell. Usually he called before coming down. This time he just stopped in unannounced.

"He was here for one hour," Modell recalls. "He told me that he had to go to the hospital, but that it was nothing serious and that he'd be out in a couple of days. His neck was swollen considerably and we all knew what it meant. I think Ernie did, too. He was coming to say good-bye to me and the others. I asked him how he was feeling. All he would say was, 'I've felt better, but it's nothing to worry about. My throat hurts a little.' He was apologetic about having to go to the hospital."

Thirty-seven hours after Ernie Davis entered the hospital, the telephone rang in Art Modell's apartment on the shore of Lake Erie. It was Dr. Austin Weisberger with the news that Ernie's battle with leukemia had finally ended. It was 2 a.m., May 18.

Modell cried when he heard the words that he had expected for so long. "It will be a long time before we see a boy like Ernie Davis again," he said sadly. "He was a great athlete, but more important, he was a great person. He is the finest boy I have ever met in my life."

Modell announced that No. 45 would never be worn again by a member of the Cleveland Browns. As a tribute to Davis, the number that was worn by him only for picture-taking was retired.

Word of Ernie's death plunged Elmira, New York, into mourning. "A SATURDAY OF SORROW: ERNIE DAVIS DIES" was the black-bordered headline atop the Sunday edition of the *Elmira Star Gazette.* Davis' body was returned to Elmira for the funeral and burial. On Tuesday, the body lay in state in the gymnasium of Neighborhood House, where Ernie had played basketball when he was a youngster. During a 12-hour period, 9,000 persons -- black and white alike -- entered the black-draped Dickinson Street entrance of Neighborhood House and filed past the bier. A nine-year-old boy came dressed in a football uniform. Men in work clothes and business suits and women in mink coats and thread-bare dresses came to pay their respects to the young man who had fought the fatal disease so bravely and so unselfishly. Flags flew at half-mast in Elmira on the day of the funeral, and at Free Academy, where Ernie had started his short but brilliant athletic career, home-room classes observed a moment of silence.

Art Modell chartered a United Airlines DC-7 to fly the Cleveland Browns' party to the funeral. The group included Modell, other club officials, nine players, six coaches and newsmen. The players were Lou Groza, Jim Brown, Bob Gain, Rich Kreitling, John Morrow, Dick Schafrath, John Wooten, Mike Lucci and Vince Costello. Marion Motley, the ex-Brown star, came, too. Charley Scales, who had roomed with Davis in Cleveland, drove up from Pittsburgh. Buddy Young, the ex-Illinois great, came from Baltimore, and Bobby Mitchell, for whom the Browns acquired rights to Davis, came from his home.

Toward the end of the service in a church packed with 4,000 mourners, Rev. Latta Thomas unfolded a telegram addressed to Mrs. Arthur Radford, Ernie's mother. "I would like to express my sympathy to you on the occasion of the death of your son," Rev. Thomas read to the congregation. "I had the privilege of meeting Ernie after he had won the Heisman

Trophy. He was an outstanding young man of great character who consistently served as an inspiration to the other people of the country." It was signed "John F. Kennedy."

A few days after the interment services in the Evergreen section of Woodlawn Cemetery in Elmira, an Ernie Davis Leukemia Fund, associated with the American Cancer Society, was launched with a large initial contribution by the Cleveland Browns organization.

Weeks later, Jim Brown wrote in *Sport* magazine: "Why is Ernie's memory being preserved for the ages? Obviously, his illness and his athletic achievements are emotionally involved in his memory. But it is so much more than that. It's the way in which he carried himself through his life. Always humble, but with dignity, pride and strength. And always with an unforgettable selflessness, a compassion for others."

The Browns were just getting over the news of Davis' death when tragedy struck the squad again. On June 4, Don Fleming, who had become a regular safety man after joining the team as a rookie in 1960, was electrocuted while working on a construction project near Orlando, Florida. Fleming, who worked on the construction job to stay in shape during the off-season, and a fellow worker, Walter Smith, died instantly when a crane cable brushed against a 12,000-volt electric line.

Fleming, who had been a star at Shadyside High School near Bellaire, Ohio, was an All-Southeastern Conference choice in both baseball and football at the University of Florida, where he was a teammate and close personal friend of the Browns' Bernie Parrish. He was drafted by the Chicago Cardinals, but was traded to the Browns before the start of his career. Married and with one son, Fleming was recognized as one of the finest defenders in the National Football League, and was named to *Sporting News'* All-NFL team after the 1962 season.

Art Modell had talked with Fleming three weeks before the tragedy, and the defender readily agreed to terms. Ironically, the announcement of his signing for the 1963 season was made the day he was electrocuted.

"I'm at a loss for words," said Modell upon hearing of his death. "Don was a great kid, a fine football player."

For the second time in three weeks, Modell chartered an airplane to take a saddened group of players, coaches, officials and writers to a funeral, this time in Shadyside, Ohio, where services were held for Fleming.

Fleming's death was the third to hit the Browns in five months. An automobile accident in mid-January had taken the life of Tom Bloom, the team's sixth draft choice, before he had even had a chance to meet the members of the team. Purdue University's "most valuable player" as an offensive back during the 1962 season, Bloom had hoped to win a defensive backfield job with the Browns. He was killed in the car he had purchased with the bonus money received for signing with the Browns.

The period between the end of the 1962 season and the opening of a new training camp had been punctuated by turbulence and sadness, but now it was time for the Cleveland Browns to get back to work. For the players who had been with the team for years, it was strange to hear a new man deliver the opening remarks at the start of camp.

Blanton Collier began to speak:

"We're going to be watched by the entire football world in the coming season, and we'll be judged on only one basis -- if we win or lose. It's sort of the law of the range, and I've learned it the hard way. The world doesn't want the nice guys. I think the world would sort of like a winner to be a nice guy -- but first he's got to be a winner. Each year you've got to produce or get out. That's not Collier's law or Modell's law. It's the law of professional sports.

"I won't be mild-mannered and easy-going. I don't know how I acquired that reputation. I'm not a tough person, and I don't try to be. But I do get fired up at things, especially lack of effort and lack of attention. What you do and how soon you do it will indicate how dedicated you are.

"My coaches have worked harder for the last six months than any coaches I've ever known. We've made a lot of adjustments and they gave up much of their vacations to prepare for this camp. Now it's time for everyone to get down to work."

Collier made it clear that one of the major adjustments would be the end of the messenger system for sending in all plays. "Basically, the quarterback will call the plays, but I will reserve the right to call them when the opportunity is there," he said.

Another adjustment would be the use of more checkoff plays by the quarterback. "This gives greater surprise to your offense," explained Collier. "In many instances, defensive football has caught up with the offense, and when the quarterback sees the deck is stacked against a certain play, he can call a checkoff at the line of scrimmage, substitute a new play and take advantage of the shifted defense. We plan to do a considerable amount of this."

Two of Collier's first moves were to shift Jim Houston from defensive left end, where he backstopped Paul Wiggin, to left linebacker, and John Wooten, previously a messenger guard with Gene Hickerson, from right guard to left guard. But the big interest was in the quarterbacking spot and which of the two candidates, Frank Ryan or Jim Ninowski, would get the nod from Collier. Ninowski had been No. 1 in the first half of 1962, but had suffered a shoulder separation and was side-lined for the rest of the year. Ryan had taken over and done a commendable job. Collier said that as a result of his work at the end of 1962, Ryan deserved first shot at the starting role and that's the way it worked out.

The Browns' first game under Collier was a pre-season visit to Detroit. A surprise starter was Larry Benz, the former Northwestern quarterback who had been signed as a free agent. Benz was used in the left safety spot, previously occupied by the ill-fated Don Fleming.

Cleveland absorbed a 24-10 licking at Detroit. When he returned to Hiram College training camp and had a look at the game films, Collier said candidly, "I've said before that movies are humbling. It's usually the case that your team plays a good game, and then the movies deflate what you thought was a good performance. This time it worked in reverse. I thought we smelled the park out, but it turned out we played a pretty good football game. We were better than I thought.''

The next exhibition game was part of Cleveland's second annual pro football double-header. It was a huge success as a sports promotion, with 83,218 turning up for what had been billed as a "dream double-header." In the first game, the New York Giants, the defending Eastern Conference champions, edged Detroit, 24-21. Then Baltimore took Cleveland apart, 21-7. "Our execution was atrocious," was Collier's comment.

Cleveland headed west for exhibition games in San Francisco and Los Angeles. Against the San Francisco 49ers, at the start of the second quarter, Collier reinstituted the messenger system for calling plays. The Browns won, 24-7.

"We showed the quarterbacks what we have in mind," Collier said. "Now when we get back to letting them do the calling, they'll have a better idea of our thinking. Two things encouraged us to call the plays. I thought we were awfully tight, and I thought we were playing too conservatively. Pro football can't be played conservatively, and I don't want my team to play that way."

Frank Ryan took a firmer grip on the quarterbacking job the next Saturday night as the Browns downed the Rams, 23-14. The team seemed to be building to a fast and smooth transition to the regular season when it suddenly went flat. The Browns met the Pittsburgh Steelers in a Hall of Fame game at Canton, Ohio, and turned in a miserable performance in falling 16-7. Things looked so bad that when the Browns started rolling late in the game a radio announcer was moved to remark, "That's the only time Cleveland has been across mid-field except to go to the dressing room at half-time."

Ryan completed 13 passes in a row in the second half and won starting quarterback honors for the 1963 season opener against Washington the following weekend.

A crowd of 57,618 was on hand to see a show they would not soon forget as the Browns buried the Redskins, 37-14. Jim Brown galloped 162 yards on 15 running plays and added another 100 yards with three pass catches. His 262 yards gained represented the fourth highest total ever made by a player in a single NFL game. Brown scored on an 83-yard screen pass and on runs of 80 and 10 yards. At this point, he had 72 career touchdowns on the ground, and set a record each time he scored.

"He gave one of the greatest exhibitions of running you will ever see," said Collier, flushed with his first regular season victory. The general impression was that the big fullback had begun his campaign to prove a point, since Jim had been outspoken in his disapproval of Paul Brown's coaching methods.

Ryan also had a brilliant day with 21 completions in 31 tosses for 334 yards and two touchdowns.

In Dallas the following week, the Browns ran their scoring binge to 78 points with a 41-24 victory over the Cowboys in 100-degree heat. Offensively, the Browns were off to their best start in 13 NFL seasons.

There was one casualty that afternoon. Halfback Ken Webb, obtained from Detroit in exchange for defensive tackle Floyd Peters, suffered a cracked rib. Ernie Green, the former University of Louisville star, moved into the starting spot. Webb never played much from then on and finally was released prior to the start of the 1964 season.

When the Browns faced the Los Angeles Rams in Cleveland the following Sunday, they had an average of nine yards per play, but they ran into some rough going, although winning, 20-6. Rain, high wind and a treacherous turf hampered the offense, and the defense came in for its share of glory. Los Angeles had the ball inside the Cleveland 40-yard line seven times, but could manage only two field goals.

"Some days the offense has to do it, and other days it will be up to the defense," Collier said.

Ryan got two more touchdown passes, and Brown boosted his three-game rushing total to 489 yards.

With three straight Brown victories in the hamper, football fever was beginning to sweep Cleveland. A crowd of 84,684, an all-time attendance record for the Browns, was on hand for a Saturday night meeting with the Pittsburgh Steelers. It turned out to be another razzle-dazzle show for Cleveland fans as the Browns won, 35-23, in the game that saw the lead change hands nine times. One of the highlights of the game was a goal-line stand by the Browns in which the Steelers had six cracks from no farther away than three yards, including four chances from the one-yard line. "We just chain them together," said defensive line coach Dick Evans in describing the six-man goal-line unit. Ryan had three touchdown throws, two to Gary Collins and one to Rich Kreitling. Jimmy Brown tore off 175 yards on 21 carries, and Ryan's throwing, especially in the second half, finished the job as the Browns came from behind four times.

The Browns had rolled up 133 points in four games, and the fans were beginning to wonder how they were doing it. Collier explained that it was partially due to "option blocking" by the offensive line. "It's a tag I've put on a type of blocking based on letting a defensive man block himself out of the play," the coach said. "It involves isolating a defender and blocking him to whichever direction he wants to go. The ball carrier then goes where the hole opens, rather than to a pre-designated spot. If the defensive man doesn't commit himself to going to either side, the blocker then has a priority in the direction he walls him off. Option blocking doesn't involve so much pulling, and it gives the ball carrier more leeway in finding his openings. Jim Brown is especially good at making split-second decisions as he nears the line."

Collier admitted that he didn't invent option blocking. "Other teams have been using it, but we hadn't before this year. It's no panacea, though. But with the stunting defenses of today, specific blocking assignments often are nullified by the time the play gets off. Option blocking gives the lineman and the runner a choice of ways to go."

In New York the next week, the Browns took in a Manhattan movie called "The Running Man" on the Saturday night prior to their date with the Giants at Yankee Stadium. The next day Jim Brown ran over the Giants with 123 yards rushing, 86 receiving and three touchdowns. Included were a 72-yard gallop with a screen pass and a breathtaking 32-yard broken field run. The final score was Cleveland 35, New York 24. And when the Browns returned to Cleveland's Hopkins Ariport, a crowd of some 5,000 was on hand to cheer them.

But Cleveland came back with some personnel problems. Team Captain Galen Fiss and backup man Mike Lucci had suffered leg injuries. To fill the void, Collier signed Stan Szurek, a native Clevelander who had been released during the training camp period, but had remained active with the Cleveland Bulldogs in the United Football League. The Browns had won five in a row, but they had paid a heavy price. As they prepared for their sixth opponent, Philadelphia, ten men were absent from workouts.

Injuries didn't seem to bother the team, however, as the Browns gunned down Philadelphia, 37-7, before 75,174 at the Stadium. Gary Collins caught scoring passes of 35, 18 and 14 yards, and Jim Brown became the greatest ground gainer in NFL history. His 144-yard splurge against the Eagles lifted his season total to 931 for a career total of 8,390 yards gained rushing. The old mark was held by Joe Perry, playing out his final year with San Francisco. Perry compiled his total in 13½ years, Brown in six and one-half.

Collier was ecstatic. "They've got the doggondest spirit and attitude I've ever seen in all my years in football," he commented. And Art Modell, who had fired Paul Brown ten months earlier, was being hailed as a full-fledged genius.

The Browns' next date was a return match with the New York Giants in Cleveland. Another staggering crowd of 84,213 was on hand for the game, but left mumbling as the Giants pricked the bubble of Cleveland's invincibility, 33-6.

A fumble by Jim Brown, recovered by Sam Huff of the Giants on the Cleveland 30, started it. The Giants couldn't move the ball and settled for a 29-yard field goal by Don Chandler. On the first play after the kickoff, Jim Patton interecepted a Ryan pass and ran to the Cleveland 23. Y. A. Tittle immediately connected with Del Shofner, Chandler kicked the extra point and the Giants led 10-0, with the game only three minutes old. The Giants, led by Tittle's passing and Chandler's kicking, scored the first seven times it got the ball and so dominated the game that they ran 78 plays to the Browns' 38.

"The Browns were up for six weeks in a row and at times the emotional well runs dry," Collier noted in a vain attempt to explain away the Browns' first setback.

Obviously still shaken by the events of the previous week, the Browns needed three Eagle fumbles and vital interceptions to hammer out a 23-17 victory at Philadelphia. Cleveland's margin of victory was provided by Lou Groza, who booted three field goals.

In the ninth week of the season, the streaking New York Giants finally pulled into a first-place tie with the Browns in the Eastern Conference, as

Cleveland sputtered and lost, 9-7, at Pittsburgh. Defensively the Browns were great. The Steelers had 42 plays in Brown territory and managed only a nine-yard scoring pass from Ed Brown to young Gary Ballman. A safety, called when Jim Brown was trapped in the end zone on a disputed play, was the margin of victory.

At this point, the Cleveland aerial attack had so faltered that Ryan completed only 16 of 43 throws for a slim 157 yards in three weeks. Collier was desperate to get the offense rolling again, and he promoted Jim Ninowski to the starting role for the game with the St. Louis Cardinals.

Otto Graham, never one to pass up a chance to be quoted, was asked in Washington what he thought of Cleveland's chances. "In my humble opinion, the Browns have had it," he said. "The Giants have the momentum and are the better team. Y. A. Tittle is fabulous."

Graham was right. With Ninowski in the saddle, the Browns lost to the Cardinals, 20-14, before 75,932 at the Stadium. More importantly, they lost the lead to the Giants. It was the Cards' first victory over the Browns since 1956. Ninowski had his troubles, but some others shared the blame. Rich Kreitling, Ernie Green, and Ray Renfro all dropped important throws, and the Browns' defensive line was unable to stop the Cards' blitzing. Jim Brown scored on a dazzling 59-yard run on the second play of the game and finished the day with 154 yards. But Cleveland couldn't score again until late in the game.

With Frank Ryan back in his old job, the Browns regained a share of first place with a 27-17 victory over the Dallas Cowboys before 55,096 at the Stadium. St. Louis throttled New York, 24-17, and the Browns, Giants and Cardinals shared first place with 8-3 records.

The crowd that day was larger than expected, coming as it did just two days after the assassination of President John F. Kennedy in Dallas. There had been some talk of postponing the week's NFL schedule, but the seven-game slate went on as planned. In Cleveland, halftime ceremonies to honor Ray Renfro were cancelled.

The game wrapped up Cleveland's home schedule, and the Browns finished with a total attendance of 487,430, the biggest gate in their history. Counting the whopping turnout for the exhibition double-header, the Browns drew 570,648 for eight home dates, almost surpassing the attendance of the Cleveland Indians in their 81-game home schedule.

The Eastern Conference race was moving to a spectacular climax, with Cleveland, New York and St. Louis all in the running.

The Browns jolted St. Louis' title chances the next week by turning in a 24-10 victory at Busch Stadium. Much of the credit for the victory went to defensive tackle Frank Parker who stalked Cardinal quarterback Charley Johnson all afternoon. With Parker leading the way, Johnson's net passing yardage was a mere 19 for the afternoon.

Verve and dash returned to the Cleveland offense as the Browns picked up 403 yards. Jim Brown broke his own National League rushing record of 1,527 yards set in 1958. He gobbled up 179 yards to push his total to 1,677 for the season. His biggest play -- and the run that shattered the mark -- came when the Browns were backed up on their own three-yard line. Jim sprung loose for 61 yards.

"That was a big play," said Cardinal Coach Wally Lemm. "It took Cleveland out of the soup."

There were only two games left and the Browns still had a share of first place with the Giants. Detroit and Washington were the last two opponents on the Browns' schedule, while the Giants had to contend with Washington and Pittsburgh.

One thing the Browns had never been able to do since they began playing in the National Football League was to beat the Detroit Lions in regular season play. They had lost five in a row to the Detroiters, in addition to three out of four championship games and a flock of exhibition contests.

For all intents and purposes, Detroit took care of the Browns' title hopes, taking Cleveland apart, 38-10, at Detroit, while the Giants surged past Washington, 44-14, to take sole possession of first place. Detroit ran and passed the Browns into the ground. Dan Lewis and Nick Pietrosante gained huge chunks of yardage, and Earl Morrall had a big passing day by completing 13 of 25 passes for 271 yards. In his frustration, Collier finally substituted Ninowski for Ryan, but between the two quarterbacks only 11 passes were completed.

"They just sat there and waited for us to come at them," said Lion defensive tackle Floyd Peters, an ex-Brown, in explaining the ineptness of his former teammates.

Collier was beside himself. "I can't explain it. It was obvious from the start that we were accepting the Lions' line charge both offensively and defensively without fighting back."

Two days after the hapless showing in Detroit, Collier was asked for his analysis of the crusher. "I'm reminded of an article by a golf pro about pressure. He said there are numerous golfers with great potential, enough to be as good as Arnold Palmer and the other top ones. But playing on the tournament trail did something to them. They were unable to play their normal game. Something like that seemed to happen to us. I know we wanted to win, wanted to play. But we couldn't play our normal game." In other words, the Browns cracked under pressure.

The odds were long, but the Browns still had a chance for the title after losing four of their last seven games. A victory over Washington combined with a New York defeat by Pittsburgh would again throw the race into a deadlock and force a play-off.

Cleveland edged Washington, 27-20, but the Giants didn't crack. They walloped Pittsburgh, 33-17, to clinch the 1963 championship, their third consecutive Conference crown and their sixth in eight years.

The victory over Washington gave the Browns a second-place finish with a total of ten victories for the first time since 1953, and qualified them to meet the Green Bay Packers in the Play-off Bowl Game in Miami, an extravaganza arranged for the runner-up teams in each conference.

At Washington, Gary Collins snared touchdown passes of 34 and 9 yards to finish the season with 13, a new club record. Jim Brown plowed for 125 yards and finished the season with the astounding total of 1,863 in 291 carries, an average of 6.4 yards per carry. Brown became the first player in professional football history to amass more than a mile on the ground in a single season. In total yards gained on the ground, he out-rushed 11 other clubs in the league.

And Frank Ryan, who was working for his doctorate in mathematics on geometric function theory, finished the season with 25 touchdown passes to tie a team record set twice by Otto Graham in 1947 and 1948. In Miami, where the Browns dropped a 40-23 play-off bowl decision to the Packers, Ryan predicted boldly, "I'll be a Y. A. Tittle in two or three years. If I had four years with the Browns rather than with Los Angeles, I'd be a Tit-tle today. Now that I'm here, I'll still be one in two or three years. I learned more this year than any previous year. Considering how well the team did starting from scratch this year, I can't help feeling good about the outlook for next year."

- 18 -

Return to Glory

A steady, bone-chilling rain pelted New York City as the Cleveland Browns and their supporting entourage walked out of the Waldorf-Astoria Hotel on Park Avenue about 11:00 a.m. on Saturday, December 14, 1964. Rookies, press members and club officials boarded the first bus, while veterans climbed into the second. The skies were lead gray and the rain was so heavy that those inside could hear it pinging against the metal skin of the buses. The gloom of the day made the trip seem longer than it was as the buses rolled slowly through the congested Manhattan streets. There was no merriment, no animated coversation. The players were deadly serious -- some concentrating on what lay ahead, others pondering the past, wondering what had gone awry, what cruel hoax had been perpetrated on a team that just a few weeks prior had seemed in such command of its destiny.

This was to be the final game of a long season which had begun five months before at Hiram, Ohio, where the Browns held their summer camp. It had been a long, tough season and now the fruits of all the weeks of labor would be determined by what happened in Yankee Stadium that afternoon, when they faced the New York Giants.

The Browns had parlayed a stout defense, more than a little luck, a dashing passing attack and the vicious running of brooding Jim Brown into a seemingly invincible lead in the Eastern Conference race. Suddenly, they were on the verge of losing it all. They needed a victory over the New York Giants to clinch their first Conference title since 1957.

Those in the buses whose thoughts drifted back over the 13 games played to date during the regular season could recall a hundred thrills -- and some very crushing disappointments.

After winning four of five exhibition games, the Browns had opened their season against the Redskins in Washington. A lot of defense, a lot of luck and a lot of Jim Brown brought about a 27-13 victory on a cold, wet, muddy day.

Brown carried 23 times for 89 yards and scored two touchdowns as the Clevelanders overcame an early 10-0 deficit. Just before the half Brown again put the team ahead with a one-yard touchdown slash and then padded the margin by plunging a yard for his second score nine minutes into the third quarter.

In the first quarter of that game, Frank Parker, the Browns' 265-pound defensive right tackle, suffered torn ligaments in his left knee. The injury kept him out of action practically all season, except for goal-line stands. Dick Modzelewski, who had been traded to the Browns after spending seven years as a key defender for the Giants, replaced Parker and did such an outstanding job that his new teammates presented him with the game ball as a token of their appreciation. "It's my first game ball in 12 years as a pro," a tired but happy Modzelewski said after the game. "The Giants never gave them to the slobs on the line." Modzelewski was aided in his tremendous first game effort by four other Cleveland defensemen, Mike Lucci, Ross Fichtner, Vince Costello and Walter Beach, each of whom recovered Washington fumbles.

In their home opener the next week at Cleveland Stadium, before 76,954, the Browns and the St. Louis Cardinals staged one of the most thrilling games seen on the shores of Lake Erie in many years. With 88 seconds remaining, the Cardinals had a 30-26 lead. Lou Groza, in his eighteenth season with the team, had tied his own club record with four field goals, and Frank Ryan, the team's brainy quarterback, had tossed two touchdown passes. But Charley Johnson's passing and Jim Bakken's three field goals (one a 51-yarder) kept the Cardinals ahead in scoring.

The clock was ticking and the Browns had a fourth down on the Cardinals' 45-yard line. Coach Blanton Collier sent in a play from the side lines but Ryan waved incoming Clifton McNeil, a flanker, back. Ryan faded back to pass and unleashed a long "bomb." Flanker Gary Collins, who had gone down the right side, cut toward the goal post and made a diving desperation catch at the two. A few seconds later, Jim Brown skirted right end for the touchdown and Groza's extra point put Cleveland ahead, 33-30.

But Charley Johnson wasn't ready to concede. With just 42 seconds until the final gun, the Cardinals received the ball on their own 28. Three quick Johnson passes moved them to the Cleveland 21 and Bakken parted the uprights with his fourth field goal of the game to give the Cards a 33-33 tie.

Inside the St. Louis dressing room, Cardinal safety man Larry Wilson took the blame for Collins' big catch. "Everybody in the park knew they were going to throw long and it was my job to make sure nobody got behind me. So I let Collins get by and gave the game away," he said. At the end of the season, that was to turn out to be the Browns' biggest play of the year .

Just after the Cardinal game, *Look* magazine began a two-part serialization of Jim Brown's book, *Off My Chest*, in which the black fullback told his personal story, a graphic description of his early life and rise to become the greatest running back in pro-football history. He let the chips fall where they may and created a stir with his bold statements on many controversial subjects. Brown's remarks received widespread attention in newspapers across the country.

Reaction to Brown's comments among Cleveland football fans was mixed. Most welcomed the book's sincerity, but others were unhappy about Jim's statements concerning inter-racial relationships among players on the team when he wrote " 'Don't try to clown to win friendship,' I've told young players. 'Don't seek false friendship by being something a white man wants you to be. Generally he expects you to be a jolly fellow, always laughing. When he wants to talk foolishness he comes to you, but when he wants to talk seriously he goes to a white man.' "

The players' reactions to Jim Brown's views were much less complicated. "When the whistle blows, the only color you see is on the opponent's jersey," remarked one member of the squad. There was widespread fear that the timing of the book might cause a serious morale problem for the team. Art Modell was extremely unhappy and insisted that he had not seen the text before it was published. It was feared for a time that the Browns might have a serious public relations problem on their hands which could hurt the team at the box office.

Cleveland's third game of the season was in Philadelphia where Jim was greeted by a round of boos for the first time in his career when introduced prior to the game. He answered the boos with 104 yards rushing and 53 with passes for nearly half of the team's yardage as Cleveland slipped by the Eagles, 28-20, before 60,671.

In the meantime, a number of newspaper columnists jumped to Jim's defense, claiming that he had every right to express his private feelings. The incident soon became ancient history. The fans really were interested in Brown's performance on the playing field and not in his views on race relations. Throughout the season he gave them plenty to cheer about.

Jim was involved in another controversy of sorts -- but not of his making -- early in the season, when Otto Graham stirred up a hornets' nest in a speech at Canton. Graham suggested that Brown was not much of a blocker or faker, just a runner. "If I were the Browns' coach, I would tell the fullback that I would trade him if he didn't block and fake," Graham told the audience. He went on to say that the Browns would not win a title as long as Jim Brown was the fullback. He stated that while Brown was a "great athlete and a great runner," Marion Motley was the best all-around man at the position.

Head Coach Blanton Collier rose to Brown's defense. "Don't blame Brown for things until we ask him to do them -- and consistently," Collier explained. "Blame me, not him." Then he pointed out that Brown carried the ball on 74 per cent of Cleveland's running plays in 1963 and couldn't block more than six or seven times a game for other backs. Several of the players also came to Brown's defense and typical of the comments was that of Ryan who said, "It sounds like the game has passed Graham up."

Frank Ryan fired three touchdown passes in Cleveland in the fourth game of the campaign as 72,062 saw the Browns win easily over the Dallas Cowboys, 27-6. Ryan's best target of the day was Paul Warfield, the Ohio State star who was Cleveland's first draft choice for 1964. The speedy flanker back had five catches for 123 yards and one touchdown.

Although the victory enabled the Browns to keep pace with the Cardinals in the East, it was costly. Bob Gain, the veteran tackle, fractured a leg and was out for the season. Fichtner suffered a concussion and was lost for several weeks. Safety Larry Benz damaged his hip, an injury which bothered him for weeks, and tackle John Brown ran into knee trouble.

But with four weeks of the season behind them, the Browns and the Cardinals, each with three wins and a tie, were the only unbeaten teams in the National Football League.

Despite their injuries, the Browns were solid 12-and-one-half point favorites when the Steelers came to town for a Saturday night game. A crowd of 80,530 saw Pittsburgh temporarily belt the Browns out of first place, 23-7. The Cardinals lost Monday night and the two teams were once again even in the standings.

Led by John Henry Johnson, who had one of his finest games in eleven years as a professional, the Steelers punctured the Cleveland defense for 354 yards on the ground. Johnson's contribution was 200 yards gained in 30 carries and three touchdowns on runs of 33, 46 and 5 yards. "I just started running and nobody stopped me," he quipped.

The game again cost the services of Frank Parker, sent in to relieve second-year tackle Jim Kanicki, who received the brunt of Johnson's thrusts. Parker re-injured the knee that had kept him out of action since the first quarter of the opening game.

Although the Browns rebounded the following week in Dallas, there really wasn't much to cheer about. With just under seven minutes remaining and the Browns trailing, 16-13, Bernie Parrish picked off one of Don Meredith's passes and streaked 54 yards for a touchdown. Groza kicked the extra point and the Browns lucked out a 20-16 triumph before 37,456 in the Cotton Bowl.

The Cowboys went on the march again, but Beach tackled Tommy McDonald 18 inches short of a first down to nip a Dallas drive on the Browns' 28-yard line with three minutes remaining.

A near-riot erupted at the end of the game when Ryan fell on the ball twice trying to run out the clock. He was roughed up on the first try and, when Dallas end George Andrie tried to land on the quarterback during the second play, Jim Brown went after him. Several fans jumped out of the stands and raced for the playing field. Players and fans moved into position for what would have been a free-swinging affair, but police acted quickly and dispersed the growing mob. "Andrie was trying to put a knee into Ryan, so we went at it," Brown explained after the shoving was over.

The Browns had done it with mirrors against Dallas, but that didn't stop 81,050 from showing up at the Stadium in Cleveland the next Sunday when the limping New York Giants moved into the arena. The Giants, with a record of only one win, five losses and a tie, needed a victory to avert the worst mid-season record in their history, but Blanton had a rabbit's foot in his pocket again.

New York outgained the Browns, 426 to 225 yards. Fortunately, games are decided by the final score. The Browns turned two of three interceptions and two of three Giant fumbles into touchdowns and emerged with what looked on the scoreboard to be an impressive victory, 42-20.

Against Pittsburgh the next week, the Browns didn't need even a touch of luck as they gained revenge for the earlier setback, 30-17. The Cleveland running game clicked on both cylinders as Ernie Green tore off 86 yards on 17 carries and Brown lugged the ball 23 times for 149 yards, boosting his league-leading total to 813 yards. On the first play of the second half, Brown became the first player in NFL history to gain 10,000 yards on the ground.

With eight games out of the way, the Browns had a record of six victories, one loss and a tie and a comfortable two-game lead over the Cardinals. They did nothing to hurt their position against Washington the following week before 76,385 at Cleveland.

After spurting to a 13-3 lead in the first half, they battled the Redskins on even terms in the last two periods to wind up with a 34-24 victory, their seventh in nine starts. Ryan tossed a 13-yard touchdown pass to Collins and then a 62-yard "bomb" to Warfield in the third quarter to put the game out of the Redskins' reach. Offensively, it was the Browns' second best showing of the season. They rolled up 385 yards on the ground and in the air.

George Wilson's Detroit Lions came to town next and there was cause for concern. The Browns had not beaten the Lions in five regular season games. A curious crowd of 83,064 came to see if they would finally do it. They did, 37-21, in a free-wheeling affair that really wasn't settled until the fourth quarter.

The Browns had a 27-21 lead over the Lions in the final period when Groza booted his third field goal of the game, a 36-yarder, to give the team a nine-point margin. Then Walter Beach put frosting on the cake by racing 65 yards with an intercepted pass for a touchdown. Brown rolled up 147 yards running and scored his first two touchdowns against Detroit in a game that really counted.

With only four games left, the Browns had a two-and-one-half game lead. But memories of 1963, when the team had won its first six games, only to collapse and give the Giants the championship, still haunted them.

Despite an 8-1-1 record and five straight victories, the Browns were underdogs for the first time in the season as they prepared to face the Green Bay Packers, who had been beaten five times in ten games. The game was scheduled for Milwaukee and the Packers were the choice by three points.

The Browns had a 14-7 lead at halftime and things were going quite well. On the first series of plays in the third quarter, the Packers had a short yardage situation on their own 44-yard line. Cleveland expected a run and Collier sent the six-man goal-line unit into the game to stop it. But the Packers, out of contention in the Western Conference, shot the works. Bart Starr fired down the middle to end Max McGee, who beat Beach on the play, and the speedy Packer ran down to the Cleveland one-yard line before he was hauled down from behind. Jim Taylor slammed over for the score. The Packers scored two more quick touchdowns before the stunned Browns recovered. The game was already out of reach.

It was generally conceded that even in defeat the Browns had turned in one of their best performances of the season. But the Cardinals won their third straight game, and the Browns' lead was shaved to a game and a half with three contests left to play. Still, just one Cleveland victory and one Cardinal setback would make the Browns champions of the Eastern division for the first time since 1957.

A crowd of 79,289 was on hand for the final home game of the season against the Philadelphia Eagles. Things started going awry for the Philadelphians on the very first play. Groza's kickoff was short and the Eagles bobbled the ball. A dozen Browns and Eagles had their hands on the slippery pigskin before it finally squirted nine yards into the end zone where Cleveland's Roger Shoals fell on it for a touchdown. A few minutes later, Sid Williams blocked a punt by the Eagles' Sam Baker deep in Philadelphia territory and recovered it in the end zone. Then just before the end of the half, Jim Houston picked off a pass and raced 42 yards for the defensive unit's third touchdown of the game. The Browns went to the dressing room with a comfortable 21-3 lead. The Eagles outscored the Browns, 21-17, in the final two quarters but the Browns triumphed, 38-24.

The big crowd helped the Browns shatter their home attendance record. Counting their exhibition double-header, the team drew 633,070 spectators in eight dates. The total was 69,000 more than the Cleveland Indians had drawn in all of 1963, and within 22,000 of the Tribe's 1964 home attendance.

For a time, it looked as if the Browns would clinch the Conference crown that Sunday. The scoreboard showed the Pittsburgh Steelers ahead of the Cardinals in the fourth quarter, but the Cards put on a stirring rush in the dying moments to pull the game out of the fire and preserve their championship hopes.

Cleveland's game-and-a-half lead with two games remaining still looked fairly comfortable. But the sports world, already treated to one miracle during the baseball season when the Philadelphia Phillies blew a big lead in the final weeks of the season and the St. Louis Cardinals streaked to the National League pennant, looked for another. St. Louis fans were hopeful that their football Cardinals could duplicate the heroics and bring the city its first professional gridiron crown. The Cardinals had won four games in a row and their next encounter was a head-to-head clash with Cleveland in Busch Stadium. A Cardinal victory would reduce the Browns' margin to a razor-thin half game and send the Eastern Conference race down to the final week of the season.

The Browns went to St. Louis confident they would beat the Cardinals on their own home ground and clinch the crown and a date with the Baltimore Colts, early winners in the Western Division, in the NFL championship game. Four cases of champagne had been ordered and placed on ice at the Bel Air West Motel in St. Louis. A taxicab was ready to take the bubbling stuff to the Cleveland locker room for a celebration the moment it appeared certain the Browns had defeated the Cardinals. "Fortunately, someone in the Cleveland organization had the discretion to order the champagne on consignment," wrote Edwin Shrake in *Sports Illustrated* after the game. "By Sunday night the four cases were on their way back to the liquor store."

It was a bitterly cold day in St. Louis. The temperature stood at 12 degrees and snow banked the edges of the field. By the end of the afternoon, no St. Louis fan cared about the cold.

Midway in the first quarter, Parrish gathered in one of Charley Johnson's passes and took it all the way to the St. Louis 32-yard line. The Browns drove to the St. Louis 15, but stalled, and Groza booted a 22-yard field goal to give his team a 3-0 lead. Holding the Cleveland offense to one field goal after spotting the ball on the 32 ignited a spark in the Cardinals, and for the rest of the afternoon they blitzed Ryan as Johnson short-passed the Browns to death.

In the second quarter, Johnson fired a strike to Joe Childress going down the middle and the hard-running fullback went into the end zone on a 46-yard touchdown run. Before the half was over, Johnson sneaked for a one-yard touchdown and then passed seven yards to Billy Joe Conrad for another score. The only other score the Browns could muster in the first half was a second field goal by Groza. The Cards went to the locker room ahead by 21-6.

Groza cut three points off the Cardinals' lead in the third quarter with a 17-yard boot, but Johnson engineered another drive and capped it with a one-yard sneak in the same period and the Cardinals had a 28-9 lead. The Browns picked up another ten points in the final quarter on Groza's fourth field goal, a 36-yarder, and a 30-yard touchdown pass from Ryan to Green. The final score was 28-19.

Johnson wound up the day by completing 15 of 22 passes for 167 yards. He ran for two touchdowns and passed for two more. Ryan had 15 completions in 33 tries for 242 yards, and Warfield caught six passes for 91 yards, but it was all academic. Johnson had made the big plays; Ryan had not. That was the gist of Blanton Collier's summation in a quiet Cleveland dressing room.

"The Cardinals took advantage of their opportunities," he said. "We weren't able to make the plays. No, they didn't show us anything unusual. They simply executed."

The Browns' once-fat, two-and-a-half-game lead had evaporated to just a half game. The race had gone down to the wire and the Browns' chances for a Conference crown rested on the outcome of play in the final weekend of the season. Their final opponents were the hapless Giants in a rare Saturday afternoon game in New York. The Cards would have to sweat out that one on television, then play the Eagles on Sunday.

"We deserve to be the champions," said Cardinal defensive end Joe Robb. "We have a better team than Cleveland, especially if you take that big guy [Jim Brown] out of their backfield. If Y.A. Tittle can beat the Browns, we'll vote him a full share of the championship money."

When the Browns reported for practice the week of the Giant game,

Collier didn't show his squad the movies of the Cardinal disaster. He wanted the team to concentrate only on the Giants. Preparations were made on the assumption that Tittle would be the Giant quarterback, and, as the week drew on, Sherman confirmed that the Browns would be looking at the veteran Y.A. from the outset.

It was to face Tittle, an eventual pro football Hall of Fame choice and a proud, but undermanned New York Giants team that the Browns had traveled by bus through the streets of New York for what seemed an eternity. When they reached the "House that Ruth Built," which stands beside the Major Deegan Expressway, they filed slowly off the buses, went through the gate and walked down to the playing field. A few stopped and examined the turf to check on the footing. Most went to the locker room and began putting on their armor.

Meanwhile, the steady rain did not deter the faithful Giants fans. They came in droves, pouring from subway trains, buses and automobiles. Thousands of other fans, not fortunate to have season tickets for the Giants' games, fled to Connecticut, southern New Jersey or upstate New York, and checked into hotels for the afternoon to catch the game on television, blacked out within a 75-mile radius of the city, by NFL rules. In Cleveland, 500 miles to the west, thousands of people flicked on televison sets and sat back apprehensively. They were joined by millions of viewers watching on a nationwide hookup.

The Giants, after winning three straight Eastern Conference championships, were hopelessly out of the race. They had won only two games, lost nine and tied two. They weren't alone in their fall to rags from riches. The Chicago Bears, who had defeated the Giants 14-10 in the 1963 NFL championship game, were sixth in the seven-team Western Division.

New York fans had found little to cheer about all season. Injuries, inexperienced rookies and aging veterans had reduced the once-powerful Giants to the patsies of the East. It seemed finally that the old warrior Y.A. Tittle, 37, who had come from the 49ers to pass the Giants to three straight Conference championships, had finally played out the string. There had been speculation all week that the game would be Tittle's last, the Bald Eagle's 176th as an NFL quarterback. The fans -- 63,007 of them -- had come to Yankee Stadium hoping that the marvelous old athlete had one more great day left and could inspire his injury-riddled team to kill the hopes of their bitter rivals, the Cleveland Browns.

There was no oration in the Cleveland dressing room as Blanton Collier and his assistant coaches quickly reviewed the game plan. As the moment drew near for the team to head for the field and the pre-game introductions, Collier said simply, "I don't have to say anything to you. You know what you have to do out there today."

First the Browns were introduced to the crowd. Then, one by one, the Giants trotted onto the field. Finally, the announcer called the name of the Giant quarterback, Y. A. Tittle. A thunderous ovation erupted. It continued until Tittle reached the Giant players' bench.

Groza kicked off and the Giants had the ball. Tittle handed off twice for running plays, but the Browns' defense didn't yield an inch. Then Tittle tried a pass, but Joe Morrison couldn't hang on to it. New York punted, and the Browns began moving the football. Cleveland stalled on the New York 32-yard line and Groza was called upon for his specialty. He booted a 39-yard field goal to put Cleveland out in front, 3-0.

Early in the first quarter, Dick Modzelewski broke through the Giant defense and tossed his old teammate Tittle for a long loss. As the two veterans were getting up, Modzelewski turned to the New York quarterback and said, "Isn't it time you hang 'em up?" Tittle, shaken from the hard tackle that spilled him, looked up at Modzelewski and answered slowly, "Maybe you're right."

Neither team could get anything going in the remainder of the first quarter. Early in the second period, Tittle began looking like the Y.A. of old. With some accurate throwing and the help of a 15-yard penalty, he moved the Giants to the Browns' nine-yard line. New York picked up two yards on a running play and then Tittle missed connections on a pass. On the third play, he whipped a short toss to Dick James in the end zone. Don Chandler's kick was good and the Giants were out in front, 7-3.

There were some long faces in the Cleveland press box contingent, but not for long. The Browns took the kickoff and in nine plays, eight of them running, took the lead. Ryan, who faded back to pass and couldn't find a receiver open, carried the ball the remaining 12 yards for the score. He fumbled as he fell across the goal line. Although the Giants recovered the pigskin, the officials ruled that the ball had crossed the line before the bobble. Groza's extra point made the score 10-7. The Giants argued that Ryan had not scored, but their protests were brushed off by the officials.

Two interceptions of Tittle passes in the second quarter turned the game into a rout. Parrish grabbed the first and Ryan capitalized by tossing an 11-yard touchdown pass to Collins. The young quarterback flipped a one-yard pass to Green for another touchdown with 17 seconds remaining in the half. An interception by Costello set that one up. At halftime, the Browns held a commanding 24-7 lead.

During the season, when Cleveland enjoyed more than its share of luck, it was suggested by a New York newspaper writer that if the Browns won the Conference title, they'd be "laugh champs." The remark stung.

"These guys don't look like laugh champs, do they?" asked Modell, flushed with the comfortable lead at halftime. "I've got a good team."

In the second half, the Browns did nothing to spoil the boss's confidence. Sherman started Wood at quarterback, but the Browns' tide was rolling and there was no stopping it. Before the third period was over, Cleveland had three more touchdowns on the scoreboard and it was 45-7. Ryan, gaining confidence with every play, first passed 25 yards to Green for his second touchdown, then fired a seven-yard scoring pass to Warfield. Finally, Ryan and Brown connected on an eight-yard scoring play.

In the fourth quarter, Collier inserted Jim Ninowski to mop up after Ryan had staged one of the greatest passing exhibitions in NFL history. He had completed 12 of 13 passes for 202 yards and five touchdowns. He had "arrived" as a big-time quarterback.

New York outscored the Browns in the fourth quarter, 13-7. Wood connected twice for the Giants on touchdown throws and a 24-yard Ninowski pass to Roberts gave Cleveland its sixth scoring aerial of the afternoon.

As the game neared its end, New York fans mobbed the field. On what turned out to be the final play, Wood tossed a one-yard pass to Aaron Thomas in the end zone. There was still time left on the clock, but the officials called it a game without the try for the extra point. There were just too many fans on the field. The Browns won it, 52-20.

At the end, Tittle, who had given New Yorkers more than their share of thrills, was a pathetic figure, kneeling in the mud in front of the Giants bench, a blue hood thrown over his shoulders. As he left the Yankee Stadium field after what was to be his final game, a fan came up to him and expressed his condolences.

"I'm sorry I couldn't give you something better," Tittle answered. "You people here have been awful nice to me."

It was all over. The Browns were Eastern Conference champions for the first time since 1957, when Jim Brown was a rookie. When the chips were down, they won, and there could be little doubt of their qualifications to represent the East in the championship game against Baltimore.

There were many heroes in addition to Ryan -- Parrish and Costello, who made the big second-quarter interceptions; Brown who chugged 99 yards in 20 carries; and Warfield, who caught five passes for 103 yards -- to name a few. Basically, however, it was a team effort.

Groza's two field goals and seven points gave him a total of 115 points for the season, a new career high. Not bad for a man of 40, still playing football while many of his contemporaries had long since retired to their easy chairs.

There was no big celebration in the Cleveland dressing room. This time there was no champagne ordered, and aside from an occasional howl and the inevitable backslapping of well-wishers, the scene was relatively quiet. The Browns had struck early, and by the time the game was over, much of the exhilaration had turned to just plain satisfaction.

Newsmen gathered around Brown and Ryan while waiting for Collier to finish a television interview. Brown was asked how he would compare the thrill of winning the 1964 crown with the title the team won in 1957.

"This one meant a lot more to me than the first one," he said, seated on a stool in front of his locker, his face marked by bruises suffered during the hard afternoon's labors. "I was a rookie then and a rookie doesn't realize the significance of it like a veteran does.

"We won it when we had to do it, and we won it big," was Brown's summation of the day's activities.

Modzelewski, the old New York Giant who received a standing ovation when he was introduced in a Cleveland uniform at the start of the game, said after it was over that "the attitude of everybody was just like it used to be with the Giants."

Finally, Collier strolled in. He was the calmest of all as he addressed writers in a small room off the main locker room.

"Our ball club played a great football game today," he said, in the understatement of the year. "These kids have taken a lot of guff. They were a dedicated group of boys the entire week and this dedication paid off. I think we played awfully well and certainly put more things together than we had done all season."

Once airborne on the return trip to Cleveland, two stewardesses produced a surprise for the happy group. They passed out goblets and proceeded to fill them with champagne. The glasses had been put aboard the plane in Cleveland, and the bubbling stuff had been stored in a refrigerator at Newark, pending the outcome of the game. There were shouts and cheers and many toasts, and, over the din, Art Modell, an extremely emotional man, was heard to shout that this was "the biggest thrill of my life. I couldn't be happier. And the best thing about it, we won it in major league style." In the midst of the jubilance, the group found time to dine on filet mignon.

Two hours after take-off from Newark, the plane touched down at Cleveland's Hopkins Airport to a tumultuous welcome, reminiscent of the one which greeted the Cleveland Indians after they had clinched the American League pennant in a play-off at Boston in 1948.

The players moved slowly through the mob into the terminal and were greeted by a shower of confetti, more back-slapping and loud greetings. Finally, the married players were reunited with their wives in a special VIP room at the airport.

It was a welcome none would forget. It would be 16 years until another Cleveland team received such an ovation.

The Browns' supercharged win over New York in the season finale still didn't do much for their nationwide image insofar as the experts were concerned. They had beaten an injury-riddled New York team that finished the season with only two victories and two ties in 14 games. The Giants had been beaten handily by other teams in the league. As a result, the experts didn't accord the Browns much chance of harnessing the potent Baltimore Colts, who had wrapped up the Western Conference crown three weeks before the end of the season. Aside from the Browns' on-and-off performances all season, there was the matter of long-standing Western Conference supremacy over the East in the title game.

Six of the seven title contests since 1957 had gone to the Western Conference representative. The Detroit Lions had walloped the Browns in their last championship effort, 59-14. Then Baltimore handled the Giants twice, 23-17 and 31-16. In 1960, the Philadelphia Eagles provided the only bright spot for the East by edging the Green Bay Packers, 17-13. Since then, it had been the West every year. The Packers destroyed the Giants, 37-0, in 1961, and won, 16-7, over the New Yorkers in 1962. In the last title clash, the Bears edged out the Giants, 14-10.

There certainly was some statistical evidence for rating the Colts favorites over the Browns. On their record alone, the Colts, who had won 12 and lost two, rated an edge. The Browns finished with a mark of ten wins, three losses and a tie. Offensively, Baltimore outscored Cleveland by only 12 points in 14 games -- 427 to 415 -- but defensively, it was another story. Baltimore had yielded only 215 points, while the generous Browns gave up 239. Taking all things into consideration, the odds-makers made the Browns seven-and-one-half-point underdogs.

During the two weeks between the end of the season and the championship game, the experts began dissecting the two teams piece by piece. The big edge, they conceded, was Johnny Unitas, the bold Baltimore quarterback, who had been the hero of the Colts' successive championships in 1958 and 1959. Unitas, they said, could do everything well and, with a 51.8 completion average, figured to conveniently prick Cleveland's pass defense all afternoon.

Unitas had plenty of help in the backfield. Lenny Moore had made a spectacular comeback as a runner and pass receiver, and he had help in the running department from Jerry Hill and a sparkling rookie, Tony Lorick. End Ray Berry and flanker Jimmy Orr, two guys with some of the best moves in pro football, made Unitas' passing game look easy.

In short, the Colts were described as a team without any offensive weaknesses. Defensively, they made frequent use of the blitz, and this, the experts said, would bother the Browns as it had done all season. Gino Marchetti and Jim Parker made life miserable for quarterbacks.

As for Cleveland, the Browns' offense had Jim Brown, the greatest runner in pro football, some fine receivers in Collins and Warfield and an on-and-off quarterback in Ryan, who could be either very good or very bad. If Ryan were clicking, as he was in the victory over New York, Cleveland might be tough to handle. Cleveland's zone defense had been porous at critical times during the season. The Browns had not been able to put on the big rush on enemy quarterbacks and blitzed only occasionally. Given time to pass, Unitas could be murder.

The consensus, then, was that Baltimore had the edge at quarterback and in the defense department, and these advantages figured to make them a solid favorite.

The experts' opinions didn't faze Collier and the Browns. They just went to work to prove them wrong. Collier's first move after the glowing victory over New York was to give his team a long rest. Then he assembled the players at their League Park practice site for what he thought would be a week and half of intensive work. So much of the time was devoted to television and radio interviews and sessions with photographers that on Saturday, with the game eight days away, he finally put his foot down and said there would be no more distractions. He wanted the final week devoted to total concentration for the battle with Baltimore.

Meanwhile, the Browns, hosting the contest, were deluged with tens of thousands of ticket requests. Within a few days, a sellout was assured.

A side light on the impending clash was the relationship betwen Collier and Don Shula, the Colts' young coach. Collier had coached the former John Carroll University star when he was a defensive back with the Browns in 1951 and 1952. Later, when Collier went to the University of

Kentucky as head football coach, Shula was one of his assistants. So it would be teacher against pupil in the championship clash.

The days of preparation ticked off. Four days before the contest, owner Art Modell surprised Collier with a new, three-year contract. Collier had a year to go on the original three-year pact he had signed when Paul Brown was fired, but Modell tore up the old document and replaced it with a new, richer one. It was a vote of confidence for Collier. Win or lose in the title game, there was no question about his future.

A few days before the game, Jim Kanicki, the 22-year-old, second-year tackle who had a lot to learn about professional line play, was pushing his cart through a supermarket in suburban Euclid.

"Hey, you gonna show up for that game Sunday?" the manager of the store asked him. "I just read a magazine article that says the Colts are gonna run at you every time they need five yards."

Kanicki, vulnerable in the Cleveland defense on numerous occasions during the season, was scheduled to play opposite Jim Parker, the 275-pound, All-Pro Baltimore tackle.

Outwardly, the giant Kanicki, a regular customer at the store, passed off the manager's remarks as more of the good-natured ribbing that had taken place on previous occasions. Inwardly, the words made an indelible impression on the young tackle and reinforced his desire to make the magazine writer eat his words.

The night before the game, the Browns' offensive unit huddled without coaches present to review in total their individual assignments.

While the offense was meeting in the Pick-Carter Hotel, where the Browns were quartered for the night, Parrish, who called the signals for the defensive unit, was trying to pick up something that might stall the Baltimore passing game. In his room, he poured over Baltimore play diagrams and notes he had made on previous evenings while viewing movies of the Colts' games. Parrish suddenly found the answer. The outspoken, six-year NFL veteran from Florida University remembered that Baltimore opponents were most effective when they played the Colt receivers tight. He reasoned that the Baltimore passing attack's success was based more on the time in which the plays were executed than by the individual patterns of the receivers. Parrish felt that the Browns' secondary could break up Baltimore's precise timing sequence by moving in closer to the Colt receivers. This would force the receivers to alter their style or pattern slightly and cut down on Unitas' effectiveness. He also reasoned that Lenny Lyles, one of Baltimore's best defenders, had become extremely proficient at his job by playing slick Ray Berry tight in practice sessions. That, he felt, was how Lyles had made the Baltimore team in the first place.

Elated with his "find," Parrish, who had done some part-time coaching of the Browns' defenders during the season, spread the word to his teammates. Move in close to the Colt receivers and stay close was his advice to the linebackers and defensive backs. His eleventh-hour observation was to prove to be one of the decisive factors in the game.

When Sunday morning rolled around it was cool and cloudy and a brisk wind whipped the downtown Cleveland area. Johnny Unitas expressed concern about the wind as he left his hotel for church.

The Browns assembled for their pre-game meal in the dining room of the Pick-Carter and then separated into groups.

When the meetings were over, the players gathered their belongings and left for Cleveland Stadium in their own cars.

As Jim Brown was walking to his auto in a parking lot near the hotel, a group of Baltimore fans recognized him and began to chide him. "Laugh champs," they taunted. "Marchetti will rub your face in the dirt." "The Eastern Conference is a joke." "Too bad, Jim, you're going to be a loser again." Brown half-smiled, got into his car and left for the ball park.

At the Stadium, the Browns began dressing for the game. Grounds-keeper Harold Bossard came into the locker room. "The snow's stopped and the field isn't frozen," he reported.

The Browns, as a whole, seemed to be relaxed. Perhaps the most poised was Dick Modzelewski, the ex-Giant, a veteran of championship games. "I'm glad we're underdogs," he said. "I like it that way. We're gonna surprise a lot of people."

It was just a few minutes before 1 p.m. when Collier cleared the club-house of outsiders. He talked privately to a few players, patted Jim Brown on the back and then called the squad together. His remarks were brief: "It's time now to go out and loosen up. There's really nothing for me to say. You know what you have to do." Without further comment or com-motion, the Browns turned and ran through the tunnel, out of the Cleve-land Indians' dugout and onto the field. The stands were about half full.

The brief workout over, the team returned to the dressing room for a final few moments. "We won the toss and will receive at the west goal," Collier said. "That means the first quarter we'll be facing the wind. Be in the dugout at 1:37 for the introductions." Collier wished the players good luck and left the locker room.

Captain Galen Fiss summoned the team together. "There's no point in making speeches," he said. "Let's say our prayers." Then Fiss led the en-tire squad in the Lord's Prayer.

The players turned and headed for the dugout to be introduced before 79,544 people in the stands and millions more across the country, who watched on television over a 336-station network. CBS had paid $1.8 million for the rights, a staggering figure when compared with the paltry $75,000 the DuMont Television Network shelled out for the first televised NFL championship game in 1951 between the Los Angeles Rams and the Browns.

Some 9,000 fans from Baltimore cheered lustily as field announcer Les Clark introduced the Colts. As the Baltimore players huddled around Coach Don Shula for a last word, Clark bellowed, "Introducing the Cleveland Browns . . . ." The fans went wild and, in the confusion, the Browns made their first and only mistake of the day.

"At center, from the University of Michigan, John Morrow," Clark shouted into the microphone. His words were lost in the din. Instead of Morrow trotting out to mid-field, Paul Warfield, the splendid rookie left end from Ohio State, raced from the dugout.

During the course of the season, the offensive team had been introduced from left end across the line and Warfield was always first. For the title game, the Browns decided to change things and Warfield got his signals crossed. Clark, seeing the mistake, changed back to the regular format.

Left tackle Dick Schafrath of Ohio State, left guard John Wooten of Colorado, center John Morrow, right guard Gene Hickerson of Mississippi, right tackle Monte Clark of Southern California, right end John Brewer of Mississippi, left halfback Ernie Green of Louisville, flanker back Gary Collins of Maryland, quarterback Frank Ryan and fullback Jim Brown were introduced to enthusiastic applause.

The turf was in good condition and appeared to offer neither team an advantage. It was cloudy and cold. The lights had been turned on. The wind -- destined to be a decisive factor -- was swirling inside the giant horseshoe on the lake at approximately 17 miles an hour, with occasional gusts of up to 30 miles an hour.

Collier sent in his kickoff return unit to accept the opening boot. Leroy Kelly and Walter Roberts, a pair of speedsters, were in the deep spots. Tom Gilburg kicked off for the Colts and Walter Roberts returned it to the Browns' 21-yard line. The game was on. Ryan faked to Brown and handed off to Green on the first offensive play. Green knifed for two yards. Brown carried on the second play and went for eight yards and a first down. Cleveland bogged down for a moment and lost yardage. On third down, with 18 yards to go, Ryan and Brown combined on a flare pass good for a first down on the Browns' 46. But the team could negotiate only five yards in its next three plays and was forced to punt.

Before the first quarter was over the two teams traded a fumble and an interception and the Colts were on the move. Unitas, doing more running than passing, moved his team to the Browns' 19, where the attack ran into an unyielding Cleveland defense. Lou Michaels was called in to try a field goal. The snap from center was poor and Michaels never got a chance to boot the ball. The Browns defense had passed its first stern test.

After the unsuccessful Colt field goal attempt, the Browns began to move and marched to the Colt 35. Jim Brown sliced for 10 more yards, but a penalty pushed the team back to the 40. Ryan was spilled back to the 49, and the drive ran out of steam. Gary Collins finally punted into the end zone, and the Colts took over on their own 20.

Unitas got his team moving again, but the going was rough. The Browns' forward wall was exerting great pressure on the free-wheeling Baltimore quarterback and he was having to hurry his passes or run with the ball. Hitting on two crucial third-down passes to Berry and Orr, Unitas moved the Colts to a first down on the Cleveland 46. A running play netted four yards. On second down, Unitas, under pressure from the Cleveland line, fired long to end John Mackey, but Vince Costello intercepted at the 30 for the Browns.

The fans had come to see an offensive struggle and they were seeing just the opposite. At halftime, the game was scoreless. With the Cleveland front four putting on a great rush, the Browns' linebackers were able to help the defensive backs crowd the Baltimore receivers. Parrish's strategy was paying off.

Kicking off to start the second half, ageless Groza booted the ball out of the end zone. Baltimore took over on its own 20, but Cleveland's defense yielded only three yards. Gilburg punted on fourth down, and the ball went out of bounds on the Baltimore 48 -- a 25-yard kick into the wind.

Brown lost five yards on Cleveland's first play, but gained 14 on a pass from Ryan. Brown got another yard, but Ryan missed connections on two consecutive passes. Groza, playing in his eighth title game, trotted onto the field. With the 17-mile-an-hour wind at his back, Groza kicked a 43-yard field goal. The ice was broken; the Browns led, 3-0.

Groza, again helped by the wind, put the next kickoff deep into the end zone to prevent a Colt runback. Unitas went to the air on the first play and missed. On the second play, Kanicki dropped Unitas for a two-yard loss. A third-down pass gained five yards, but the Colts had to punt into the gale again. This time Gilburg's punt went to the Cleveland 32.

The Browns had been very successful during the season on their end sweeps, but during the first half had refrained from calling the play because they knew the Colts were prepared for it. Now they were ready to use it.

Jim Brown had driven to the 36-yard line on the first play. Now Cleveland lined up in a double-wing. Ryan pitched out to Brown, and the big fullback raced around the left side and sprinted all the way to the Colts' 18 -- a 46-yard run that brought the partisan crowd to its feet.

"This was probably the most important decision I had to make all afternoon," Ryan said after the game. "We had established tremendous momentum. The running was going. We had just gained 46 yards on a running play, and I was tempted to call another sweep. But maybe I would call a sweep into an outside blitz and they would throw Jim for a long loss. Then maybe we'd go inside, but if they pinched in and cut off the inside we wouldn't gain, and the momentum could go from us to them. I knew they had been playing Gary Collins for a hook pass all afternoon. I decided to call a hook-and-go to Collins and when he went he was open."

The six-foot four-inch, 210-pound former University of Maryland star got loose in the end zone and Ryan fired a strike. Groza kicked the extra point and the Browns had a 10-0 lead. The fans went wild.

Groza, who was getting plenty of exercise for a man of 40, kicked off again. This time Lorick got the ball, but Leroy Kelly nailed him at the 12-yard line with a vicious tackle. A clipping penalty forced the Colts back to their own five. The best Baltimore could do was pick up seven yards on three plays, and Gilburg again was called upon to punt. The ball went out of bounds on the Baltimore 40.

On the first Browns' play, Warfield was spilled for a three-yard loss on a reverse. Ryan decided to pass. The Browns came out in a strong left formation, but Jerry Logan, the Baltimore defensive back, misread the formation and thought it was strong right. With a large hunk of real estate uncovered, Collins broke into the open. He took Ryan's pass at the 15 and dashed into the end zone for his second touchdown. Groza kicked the extra point and the Browns had the mighty Colts on the ropes, 17-0.

Late in the third quarter, Wiggin recovered a Lenny Moore fumble on the Cleveland 48. A pass from Ryan to John Brewer, a 23-yard run by Brown and a Ryan to Warfield aerial moved the ball quickly to the Colts' two-yard line, but the Browns couldn't push it over. They settled for Groza's nine-yard field goal to make it 20-0 early in the fourth quarter.

The Browns' defense refused to let Unitas get something going. Twice in the next series of downs the Colts' quarterback was thrown for losses, and Gilburg punted from the Baltimore 39.

Walt Roberts returned the punt to the Cleveland 36 and the Browns were off to the races again. Ryan and Collins collaborated on their third touchdown of the afternoon on a 51-yard pass play. Collins, on a down-and-in pattern, caught the ball on the 10, scored, and Groza's extra point made the score 27-0.

Six minutes remained in the game. The Colts tried desperately to avert their first shutout since November, 1962, but were throttled again by the Browns' defense. Walter Beach picked off one of Unitas' passes on the Cleveland 43 to end all Baltimore hopes of scoring.

As the final seconds ticked off, hysterical Cleveland fans stormed onto the field. With 26 seconds on the clock, both teams headed for the clubhouse. The Browns were champions of the football world for the first time in nine years.

Collier and Shula met on the field, and the one-time pupil offered his congratulations. Collier couldn't say he was sorry about the way things turned out.

The Browns pushed their way through the fans on the field and finally reached the clubhouse. It was a jungle of television cables and cameras and smiling fans. In a few moments, reporters were admitted and the questions came thick and fast. Jim Brown, his arms and face bruised and lacerated, was surrounded by reporters. One writer asked him if he had believed before the game that Cleveland would win.

"Yes, but not this bad," answered the superbly built athlete, who had run 27 times for 114 yards and caught three passes for 37 yards.

"What was the turning point?" someone inquired.

"When we held them scoreless the first half," Brown answered. "We proved to ourselves they were human, not supermen. There was pleasure in knowing we could give them a hard time, fight them toe-to-toe."

One player who seemed to be taking it all in stride in the steamy surroundings was Groza, who contributed two field goals and three extra points in his eighth National Football League championship game. "I still get a kick out of it," he said. Groza had played on every one of Cleveland's championship teams. His nine points lifted his championship total to 49 -- more than any other player in NFL history. It was Groza's biggest payday in a championship game. Each winning player received a little more than $8,052, while the Colts got a shade over $5,571. No wonder the din in the clubhouse was deafening.

Another individual who was outwardly calm was Collier, who had captured a championship in his second year as head coach. "We played a great game both ways," he said after wading through dozens of well-wishers. "The defense took care of the Colts until we could get our offense going." Collier singled out Ryan for playing a "real tough game," but added: "If anybody deserves credit, it's the defense."

Cleveland's defense, the league's most generous during the regular season, gave up only 171 yards. Unitas, who had been expected to eat up large chunks of yardage with his precision passes, completed only 12 of 20 for 95 yards. He was on the seat of his pants during a great part of the game in one of his most frustrating afternoons. Time after time, when his protection broke down or his receivers were covered, Unitas tried to run with the ball. And frequently he ran into Galen Fiss, the rugged, 233-pound Cleveland linebacker, who kept reminding the All-Pro quarterback, "Just keep running, Johnny. They don't pay a guy like you that much to run."

"Most of all it was the front four who broke down the Colts' offense," said Nick Skorich, the Cleveland line coach. The front four was composed of ends Bill Glass and Paul Wiggin and tackles Jim Kanicki and Dick Modzelewski. Kanicki, who had been expected to be fodder at the hands of Jim Parker, outplayed the great All-Pro star most of the afternoon. Kanicki was generous in his praise of Modzelewski, who had helped him develop into a first-class defensive tackle.

"Everybody picked us to lose," said Modzelewski in the Cleveland dressing room. "And we shut them out, that's the best part of it."

"I don't know how we got Modzelewski," Collier told the reporters. "I don't know how they [the Giants] could give him up. But we were lucky we got him."

As Modzelewski emerged soaking wet from the shower, Collier embraced him. "Thanks, Mo," he said. "Thanks."

"It was a good trade," Dick Modzelewski answered. "I never had a better season."

In the gloomy Baltimore dressing room, Shula, who suffered his first shutout in two seasons as head coach, was generous in his praise of the Browns, but he was just plain disgusted with his team's offense.

"Their defense did a heck of a job," he conceded, "but when you say that, you also have to mention our complete lack of offense. We couldn't get anything done. We had zero points on the scoreboard. I wasn't satisfied with anyone."

Shula insisted that the Cleveland team showed him nothing new or anything he had not expected by way of defensive strategy.

"They used a lot of man-to-man coverage and mixed it up pretty well," he explained. "And they used some unusual spacing in the line, but they had shown it before."

Unitas, whose passing had made the Colts the third-highest scoring team in NFL history during the regular season, admitted he had trouble seeing any target beyond his well-covered primary receiver on each play. "It just wasn't our afternoon. They just beat us is about all you can say," he said.

The outcome of the game and the manner in which the Browns dismantled the supposedly invincible Baltimore Colts left many in a virtual state of shock.

"We sure stank out the joint," said Don Kellett, general manager of the Baltimore team. "I still can't believe this is the same team I've been watching all season, even though I can't help but say that the Cleveland defense was magnificent."

Joe Kuharich, coach and general manager of the Philadelphia Eagles, called the outcome "bizarre" and added, "This was so weird an outcome that it is almost beyond belief. The top team on offense in the league faces the one with the weakest defense. Not only does the club with the supposedly weak defense stop the Colts cold, but shuts them out. How can you explain it?"

Some of the euphoria of the Browns' victory disappeared a few weeks later in the Pro Bowl Game when Baltimore's Gino Marchetti thundered into Frank Ryan on the first play of the second half, causing a severe shoulder separation. The West eventually won the game, 34-14, but Marchetti was accused in various quarters of taking a "cheap shot" at Ryan to atone for Baltimore's flop in the title game. Defending himself, Marchetti commented, "I'd like to say that I've only had one 15-yard penalty for roughing the passer in my 13 years as a pro -- and the ref made a mistake on that one."

At first, the doctors felt that Ryan might need surgery to repair his talented passing arm. However, when he returned to Cleveland, specialists decided on a more conservative approach, an upper body cast with straps over the front and back of his stomach and over the clavicle. Ryan spent six weeks in the cast, underwent an extensive rehabilitation program and was pronounced fit when he reported to training camp that July.

In addition to the Ryan injury, there had been some other distracting news in the period between the victory over Baltimore and the start of a new season. Early in the year, Bernie Parrish had publicly suggested that NFL Commissioner Peter Rozelle be ousted because it was felt by many of the players that he did not represent them as he should. Parrish wanted to replace Rozelle with Paul Brown.

Art Modell was furious. He called Parrish's remarks "outrageous and disgraceful," and added: "If Parrish is unhappy with conditions that prevail in the NFL, then I suggest he seriously consider retirement. If it is just a condition in our local picture with which he is unhappy, then I will try to accomodate him by trading him."

In mid-July Parrish announced his retirement, saying he had lost the desire to play. "The fun has gone out of it," the six-year veteran explained. "I don't think I could enjoy it this season. I'd only be hurting the team and my family." For a time, the Browns were threatened with the loss of their defensive captain, who had been a solidifying factor in an otherwise average defensive backfield. He changed his mind several days later and was fined $100 a day for missing practice.

Meanwhile, Jim Brown was not in camp when training began. A young woman named Brenda Ayres had accused him of slapping her in an east side Cleveland motel and he was ordered to stand trial. In late July, a jury acquitted the superstar of the charges and he was free to rejoin the team.

One of the prizes the Browns received for winning the NFL championship was a date with the College All Stars in Chicago in early August. The Browns won the game, 24-16, but lost the services of Paul Warfield, who fractured a shoulder and was sidelined for 10 weeks.

Despite the job the Browns had done defensively on Baltimore the previous December, there still was concern about the club's defensive prowess, especially in the secondary. The Browns moved boldly to correct this during the pre-season by engineering a three-way deal with the New York Giants and the Detroit Lions. The Browns gave up linebacker Mike Lucci to the Detroit Lions, who sent quarterback Earl Morrall, a 10-year veteran, to the New York Giants. The Browns got a gem in Erich Barnes, a four-time All-Pro defensive back from the New York Giants.

Even though the Browns were defending NFL champions, they were not the unanimous favorites of the experts to win the Eastern Conference crown, who were about evenly divided between St. Louis and Cleveland in the east and solidly for Green Bay in the west.

In the season's opener, the Browns were splendid defensively on a sweltering 100-degree day in Washington, ravaging the Redskins, 17-7. Blanton Collier called it "one of the best defensive jobs I've ever seen." He spoke too soon.

The following week, the Browns made their home debut before 80,161 at the Stadium and were buried by the St. Louis Cardinals, 49-13. Quarterback Charley Johnson plundered the Cleveland secondary with six touchdown passes to help administer one of the worst defeats in the team's history.

Cleveland bounced back with four straight victories over Philadelphia, Pittsburgh, Dallas and New York before running into Minnesota at the Stadium, where the Vikings held Jim Brown to only 39 yards rushing in a 27-17 win. At the mid-point in the season, the Browns were 5-2 and had a one-game lead over St. Louis.

The Browns went on another tear, beating Philadelphia, New York, Dallas, Pittsburgh and Washington in succession. Their fourth straight win was a 42-21 win over Pittsburgh which clinched their ninth Eastern Conference crown in 16 NFL seasons. There would be no repeat of the fold-up in 1963, and the near disaster of 1964. The Browns had it salted away with three games left to play.

Jim Brown was marvelous against the Steelers. The former Syracuse star scored four touchdowns and gained 146 yards in 20 carries to put him over the 1,000 yard mark for the seventh straight season.

There was a bit of agony and ecstasy in the final two games. Los Angeles buried the Browns 42-7, in Game No. 13, but Cleveland came back to edge St. Louis, 27-24, partially atoning for the humiliating defeat in the second game of the season.

Cleveland, 11-3, finished with the best record in the NFL and far outstripped its nearest rivals in the conference -- Dallas and New York, which tied for second with 7-7 records. Much of the credit for the Browns' second straight trip to the NFL championship game went to Jim Brown, who scored a club record 21 touchdowns and gained 1,544 yards. It was the second best rushing season for the 29-year-old fullback, exceeded only by his 1,863-yard performance in 1963.

The Browns took their hopes for a second straight NFL championship to Lambeau Field in Green Bay, Wisconsin, to face pro football's most successful team since the start of the 1960s. Under Vince Lombardi, who was fast becoming a legend, the Packers had made the title game in four out of six years. They lost to Philadelphia, 17-13, in 1960, then whipped the Giants, 37-0, and 16-7, in 1961 and 1962. The next two seasons the Packers finished second in the Western Conference and now were back in the championship game once again.

The odds-makers favored the Packers by three points, mainly on the basis of an offensive backfield that included savvy quarterback Bart Starr and two extraordinary talents in Jim Taylor and Paul Hornung. Green Bay also had the NFL's stingiest defense, a unit that grudgingly yielded an average of only 16 points per game, compared to 23 for Cleveland.

There was also the momentum factor. While the Browns "ho-hummed" their way through the final three games of the regular season, the Packers were in a war with Baltimore. The two teams tied with regular season records of 10-3-1, and hammered it out in a sudden death overtime play-off which finally was won by Green Bay, 13-10.

Mother Nature pulled out all the stops for this one before a crowd of 50,852 fanatics in Green Bay. In the course of this late December afternoon, the spectators and players were subjected to snow, sleet, rain and fog. The playing field was turned into a sea of mud.

Most of the excitement was generated in the first half. The Packers scored first when Starr fired a 47-yard touchdown pass to end Carroll Dale. Don Chandler's extra point made it 7-0. The Browns came back with a 17-yard Frank Ryan to Gary Collins touchdown pass, but a missed extra point left the lead in Packer hands, 7-6. Lou Groza's 24-yard field goal put the Browns on top, 9-7, but the ever-accurate Chandler kicked a pair of field goals, making it Green Bay, 13-9. Just before the half, Groza booted a 28-yarder in what was becoming a war of field goals, to shave the margin to 13-12.

Green Bay took command after the intermission with a crunching 90-yard drive capped by Hornung's 13-yard run. Chandler's point-after made it 20-12. The Green Bay place kicker put the icing on the cake that frosty day with a 29-yard fourth quarter boot. The final score was Green Bay 23, Cleveland 12.

Much of the credit went to a pair of Green Bay defenders named Ray Nitschke, a linebacker, and Willie Davis, a defensive lineman who had formerly played for Cleveland. The pair keyed on Jim Brown and were instrumental in holding Cleveland's primary offensive threat to 50 yards in 12 carries.

In the Green Bay locker room, the gruff Lombardi was asked if he thought that Cleveland's clinching the Eastern Conference title so early had hurt the Browns.

"Who the hell knows," barked Lombardi. "I think Blanton Collier gave the best answer before the game when he said: 'If we win, people will say it's because we were well rested. If we lose, people will say it was because we laid off so long!' "

Unknown to all as dusk settled on Green Bay, Wisconsin, that day, the game marked the end of an unforgettable era in Cleveland Browns football and it was the last time the NFL champion could automatically proclaim it was on top of the football world.

19

Close, But No Cigar

There was a war in the United States in the early to mid-60s. The combatants in this struggle didn't use bullets and other sophisticated weapons. The artillery in this battle was cash, cold hard cash. It began in 1960 when a Texas millionaire named Lamar Hunt decided it was time the National Football League had some competition. Hunt and a group of gentlemen, many of whom were financially well-heeled, founded the American Football League, to begin play in the fall of 1960.

The new league was bent on going head-to-head with the established NFL in four cities. The New York Titans (later to become the Jets) were organized on the home turf of the New York Giants. The Dallas Texans were set to vie for football fan loyalty with the NFL Dallas Cowboys, also scheduled to play their first NFL season in 1960. In Los Angeles, a team called the Chargers was sent into an area that had been the private reserve of the Los Angeles Rams ever since they fled Cleveland in 1946. And, across the bay from San Francisco, the AFL positioned the Oakland Raiders. There were also four teams in markets that had not yet been claimed by the NFL -- Houston, Buffalo, Boston and Denver.

As they had done when the All-America Conference was founded in the mid-1940s, the smug NFL owners looked down their noses at this upstart league. It was all sort of gentlemanly, though. The two leagues reached a verbal agreement not to tamper with players under existing contracts. However, when it came to the draft, it was open season.

That great source of talent the NFL had been tapping for years -- the nation's college football stars -- now was up for grabs to the highest bidder. A draftee, who once had a choice of signing with an NFL team or playing in the Canadian Football League, suddenly found himself on a veritable auction block where his talent usually went to the team that put up the most cash. Of course there often was another consideration: Many of the college super stars preferred to cast their lot with the more established NFL. Still, in this war, the losses were not counted in human terms, but in thousands and thousands of dollars.

The American Football League had a decided advantage over the defunct All-America Conference -- a thing called "the tube." Television was just finding its way out of the laboratory in the late 1940s when the

All-America Conference was struggling for survival. Now television was *the* media and sports was a very large part of its programming. ABC-TV gave the AFL immediate legitimacy in 1960, when it coughed up a tidy sum to broadcast selected games.

The AFL played a more wide-open type of football than the NFL. In the new league, the pass was the thing. To hell with defense. The upstarts also had another wrinkle -- the two-point conversion. If you kicked the ball through the goal posts after a touchdown, you got an extra point. But a run or completed pass over the goal line was worth two points.

The battle heated up on another front when the AFL filed a $10,000,000 anti-trust suit against the NFL in federal court. The litigation took three years before the old league was absolved of the monopoly charges.

Not all of the franchises in the AFL did well artistically and financially. After one season in Los Angeles, the Chargers decided to move down the coast to San Diego. The Texans spent three years in Dallas and then became the Kansas City Chiefs. After an infusion of fresh cash from new owners, the New York Titans changed their name to the Jets and shelled out $400,000 to a young quarterback named Joe Namath.

In 1964, the AFL got a financial break that seemed to secure its future. NBC-TV signed a $36,000,000, five-year contract with the new league, assuring each team $900,000 a year beginning in 1965. Two years later, the fighting between the leagues reached its peak. In the first six months of 1966, they spent a whopping $7,000,000 to sign new draftees and the AFC began launching a program to lure established NFL stars away from their existing teams with lavish sums of money. It was time for sanity.

On June 9, 1966, the two leagues announced they would merge, bringing to an end the most costly war in sports history. The agreement, coming with dramatic suddenness, called for a common draft after the 1966 college football season. Because of television commitments -- the NFL with CBS and the AFL with NBC -- the actual merging of the two leagues would not take place until the 1970 season, though exhibition games would be played between AFL and NFL teams.

As far as the fans were concerned, the most exciting piece of news was the fact that the champions of the two leagues would play for the real world title in a post-season extravaganza to be called the Super Bowl, the first of which would be held in January, 1967, at Los Angeles. Members of each winning team would get about $15,000 and the losers about $7,500.

Art Modell was stunned at the suddenness of the announcement. "I was absolutely certain it wouldn't happen so soon," he said. "I knew they were working on it, but I had no idea the agreement had been reached. Apparently so many rumors had been flying, when they got together they decided to announce it right away." Modell said he was in total accord with the merger and called it a step forward for pro football and a means of exposing the game to a wider audience.

Shortly after the announcement, the Browns' chances of making it to Super Bowl I plummeted sharply. Jim Brown aspired to a career in the movies and about the time the Browns were ready for pre-season drills, the durable fullback was in London working on a movie called *The Dirty Dozen*. The shooting would not be completed for several weeks.

During those weeks, Modell was aware that Brown might report late for summer practice and tried without success to reach the star in London by telephone. Finally, the frustrated owner said that Brown would be fined for every day he was late. Furthermore, he said, the Browns were making alternate plans should the big fullback fail to report at all.

On July 14, Jim Brown -- at the peak of his career -- announced he was quitting football for good. "I had intended to play this season because Art wanted me to," Brown said in a London press conference. The brilliant performer was in the final year of a three-year contract. "However," he continued, "Art pointed out to me that my reporting late would put the team in an awkward position. My original reason for returning vanished. I am no longer prepared mentally to play football. I've committed myself to other things."

It was a devastating blow to the Browns. How do you replace a man who in nine season had scored 126 touchdowns and rushed for a pro football record 12,312 yards in 2,359 carries?

Blanton Collier was philosophic. "I don't expect to replace him," Collier said. "Runners such as he come along once in a lifetime. But I do expect someone from this squad to make a name for himself."

When the Browns opened the 1966 season, Bernie Parrish was gone, released at his own request. There were two new faces in the starting offensive lineup. One was rookie Milt Morin, a 250-pound tight end from the University of Massachusetts, Cleveland's No. 1 draft choice. Big and quick, Morin had earned 12 letters in four sports in high school and had gone on to set several pass receiving records in college where he played both offense and defense for two seasons.

The other newcomer was Leroy Kelly, a 200-pound, 6' running back who had joined the Browns in 1964, after being drafted eighth. In 1964 and 1965, Kelly was a superb kick-off and punt return artist for the Browns. The previous season, he averaged 25.9 yards per kick-off return in 24 tries, but in two seasons rushed only 43 times and gained 151 yards.

Leroy had grown up in Philadelphia where he attended Simon Gratz High School and starred in both baseball and football. He was named an All City quarterback and shortstop. When Leroy arrived at Morgan State College in Baltimore, he was shifted to running back and won four letters.

Collier teamed Kelly with former Louisville star, Ernie Green, starting his fifth season with the club.

The Browns did not win the Eastern Conference in 1966, but they did find a spectacular replacement for Jim Brown. Leroy Kelly exploded for 1,141 yards in 209 carries for an impressive 5.5 yard average, scored 15 touchdowns and caught 32 passes for 366 yards. Leroy lost out to Gale Sayers of the Chicago Bears in a bid for the NFL rushing title on the final day of the season. The surprising running back was held to only 19 yards in a 38-10 win over the St. Louis Cardinals, while Sayers piled up 197 against the Minnesota Vikings. In his first year as a starter, the Morgan State product was named All Pro and was selected to play in the annual NFL Pro Bowl Game.

Ernie Green accumulated 750 yards rushing, giving the starting Cleveland rushing tandem a total of nearly 1,900 yards. At the same time, the brainy Ryan had his best year as a pro quarterback and set several single season records for the club. They included: most touchdown passes (29), most yardage (2,974), most attempts (382), and most completions (200). All had been held by the incomparable Otto Graham. Art Modell rewarded him with a new three-year contract.

The Browns were in the thick of the Eastern Conference race until the 11th game of the season, when they were punished by Dallas, 26-14, a defeat which left them with a 7-4 record at that point. The Cowboys eventually won the title with a 10-3-1 mark, leaving Cleveland and Philadelphia, both 9-5, a game and a half behind. Green Bay flattened the Cowboys in the NFL championship game and then defeated Kansas City, 35-10, in Super Bowl I.

Once again there was disquieting news about Ryan in the off-season. The prematurely-greying athlete had been complaining of pain in his forearm and elbow. After extensive examinations, doctors decided to perform exploratory surgery and ultimately repaired torn muscles, stretched ligaments and considerable scar tissue in his right elbow. His arm was in a cast for nearly two months and he underwent an intensive weight-lifting program to regain strength in his throwing arm.

There was a lot of other off-season news which kept football in the headlines. The NFL added another expansion team called the New Orleans Saints and held a draft among existing teams to stock the new franchise. The Saints took regular center John Morrow, a 10-year Cleveland veteran, and flanker Walter Roberts, as well as first-year tackle Jim Battle.

The American Football League, which had inducted the Miami Dolphins in 1966, awarded a new franchise to Cincinnati and a group headed by Paul Brown. The Cincinnati Bengals would begin play in the 1968 season. It was a triumphant year for Brown, the original architect of the Cleveland team. He was also named to the Pro Football Hall of Fame in Canton. His nemesis, Art Modell, was elected president of the NFL by fellow owners.

Modell had some severe personnel problems prior to the start of the 1967 season, when five black players struck and refused to report to training camp until contracts were renegotiated. The quintet included Leroy Kelly, defensive back Mike Howell, guards Sid Williams and John Wooten and tackle John Brown. An impasse that lasted for several days was finally settled.

The NFL had a new look for the 1967 season and a new way to determine the league champion and representative in the Super Bowl. Each of the two conferences was split into two divisions. In the Eastern Conference, the Browns were teamed in the Century Division with the New York

Giants, St. Louis Cardinals and the Pittsburgh Steelers. Dallas, Philadelphia, Washington and the New Orleans Saints made up the Capital Division. The Western Conference Coastal Division had Los Angeles, Baltimore, San Francisco and Atlanta, while the Central Division took in Green Bay, Chicago, Detroit and Minnesota. Under the new arrangement, the division winners in each conference would meet in a play-off game to determine the conference representative in the NFL title game.

The Browns got off to an inauspicious start in 1967, losing back-to-back games to Dallas and Detroit. It was the first time in their history they lost the first two games. After scoring only 28 points in the two losses, the Browns got their offense untracked against the fledgling New Orleans Saints and romped to a 42-7 win, the first of four straight victories. Cleveland's winning streak came to an end against the New York Giants, 38-34. One of the Giant heroes was Vince Costello, a veteran Cleveland linebacker who had been traded to the New York club earlier in the season. "It did feel good to beat them," Costello said after the game. "It was like playing against your brother. You would try to beat him, too." At midseason, the Browns were 4-3.

After defeating Pittsburgh, 34-14, the Browns went to Milwaukee to face the defending Super Bowl champion Green Bay Packers. The Packers, who went into the game as 5½ point favorites, riddled Cleveland for 35 points in the first quarter, and sent the Browns home on the short end of a 55-7 humiliation, the worst defeat in Cleveland history. After the game, owner Art Modell went directly to the dressing room and addressed the team. "It was the first time I ever spoke to the team after a game," he said. "I cleared it with Blanton first. I spoke in a positive nature. There was no indictment of anyone. I still believe this is the best Browns team since I bought the club in 1961."

Whatever Modell said must have provided some inspiration because the Browns rattled off four straight victories to capture the Century Division crown, the clincher being a 20-16 decision over St. Louis.

The Browns bowed to Philadelphia, 28-24, in the regular season finale, but it didn't matter. Cleveland finished with a 9-5 record, the same as Dallas, winner in the Capital Divison and the Browns' first play-off foe on the road to the Super Bowl. Much of the credit for the run to the play-offs went to Leroy Kelly, who led the NFL in rushing with 1,205 yards in 235 carries, a 5.1 yard average. Kelly and guard Gene Hickerson, one of his primary blockers, were named to the All-NFL team. Frank Ryan was not nearly as effective as in the record-breaking 1967 season, primarily because of a series of nagging injuries that did not keep him out of play but hampered his performance.

Blanton Collier kept Ryan out of the Philadelphia game so that the veteran could mend a bit for the Christmas Eve date with the Cowboys in Dallas. It didn't matter. The Cowboys really put it to the Browns before a crowd of 70,786 at the Cotton Bowl. Dallas took the opening kickoff and put together a 13-play touchdown drive that was culminated on a three-yard pass from Don Meredith to substitute running back Craig Baynham.

The Browns were never in the ball game and left the Cotton Bowl on the short end of a 52-14 drubbing. Frank Ryan spent most of the afternoon running for his life. It was nearly as bad as the Green Bay debacle earlier in the season.

Modell was livid. The owner cancelled plans to visit his family in New York for the holidays and said he would spend the time pondering changes in the Cleveland organization. "We're not going to push the panic button, though," he cautioned.

The final humiliation of the season was a 30-6 loss to the Los Angeles Rams at Miami, in a meaningless post-season game called the Play-Off Bowl, featuring the losers in the division play-offs. Green Bay edged Dallas, 21-14, in the NFL championship game and then buried Oakland, 33-14, in Super Bowl II.

Modell and Collier put the team under the microscope during the ensuing weeks and came up with the conclusion that the Browns indeed needed help. Despite the fact that Ryan had played with a series of injuries, there were some nagging feelings that perhaps he had peaked as a pro quarterback. In a bold move to provide back-up insurance and perhaps a quarterback for the future, veteran tackle Frank Parker and back-up quarterback Dick Shiner were traded to the Pittsburgh Steelers for Bill Nelsen, a 195-pound, 6' veteran from the University of Southern California who had spent five years with the Steelers. The Browns also received a defensive back named Jim Bradshaw.

Nelsen, a cool, confident performer became the Steelers starting quarterback in 1965, but was plagued with injuries for three seasons. The Los Angeles native missed parts of all three seasons due to knee injuries and underwent surgery twice in that time.

In another deal, this one aimed at bolstering the defensive line, the Browns acquired defensive end Ron Snidow from the Washington Redskins for a second round draft choice. Snidow, a 250 pound, 6'6" end from the University of Oregon, was slated for the defensive slot vacated by retiring Paul Wiggin.

The most important change for the Browns as they started the 1968 season was the fact that they had a new place-kicker. Time had finally run out on veteran Lou Groza, one of the original Browns. His replacement was Don Cockroft, drafted in the third round out of Adams State, Colorado, in 1967. Cockroft made a try at ousting Groza during that season, but the ace kicker hung in for his 22nd season. Cockroft was placed on the taxi squad and came back to win the battle this time.

Groza's final statistics were staggering. During 18 NFL seasons he attempted 659 extra points and made 641 -- talk about automatic! He connected on 234 of 404 field goal attempts and totaled 1,349 points. Counting four years in the All-America Conference, the prolific kicker had a total of 1,603 career points.

In addition to kicking off and making field goals, Cockroft had a second advantage. He also punted and took over that role from Gary Collins.

Cleveland fattened up on New Orleans, 24-10, in the 1968 opener and then ran smack into the two teams that helped the Browns to end the 1967 season on such a downbeat note -- Dallas and Los Angeles. The Cowboys were rude at Dallas, beating the Browns, 28-7, and then Los Angeles buried them in Cleveland, 24-6, for their first victory at the Stadium since moving to the West Coast in 1945.

Blanton Collier had trouble sleeping that night. He knew that the Browns had an excellent receiving corps with Paul Warfield, Gary Collins and Milt Morin and a solid running attack with Kelly. Yet the offense had produced only 13 points against Dallas and Los Angeles.

At 3 a.m., Collier made a decision. Ryan would be benched and replaced by Nelsen, gimpy knees and all. On Monday morning, the soft-spoken coach called Ryan into his office and told him about the change. "He was hurt but understood," said Collier of the veteran's reaction. On Tuesday, he pulled the 27-year-old Nelsen aside and said, "I want you to know you're my quarterback."

Nelsen made his debut against his former teammates and guided the Browns to a 31-24 victory, completing 16 of 25 passes for 190 yards and a touchdown. The Browns had evened their record at 2-2. Nelsen was brilliant at the Stadium the next week, but a second-half comeback failed and the Browns fell to the St. Louis Cardinals, 27-21. Nelsen passed for two touchdowns -- one a 65-yard bomb to Warfield -- and scored another.

With Nelsen at the throttle, the Browns ticked off eight successive victories over Baltimore, Atlanta, San Francisco, New Orleans, Pittsburgh, Philadelphia, New York and Washington to clinch their second straight Century division title in the the 13th week of the season. St. Louis broke the string with a 27-16 victory to wind up a half game behind, but the Browns finished with a 10-4 record, and a date against the Cowboys at Cleveland in the divisional play-offs.

The Browns were prolific offensively. In seven of their eight straight victories they had scored 30 or more points. Leroy Kelly was devastating on the ground and rolled up 1,239 yards to lead the NFL for two years in a row. A master at following blockers on sweeps and traps, Kelly also scored 16 touchdowns. He became only the third man in NFL history to rush for over 1,000 yards in three seasons. One of the others, of course, was his former teammate, Jim Brown. With Bill Nelsen, the passing game thrived. The newcomer passed for 2,366 yards and 19 touchdowns and had only ten interceptions. His favorite receiver, Paul Warfield, caught 50 passes for 1,067 yards, most by a Cleveland Player since the team entered the NFL in 1950. Milt Morin caught another 43 for 792 yards. Gary Collins was injured in the fourth game of the season and was out of action for the remainder of the regular season. Eight members of the team, including Kelly, Warfield, and Milt Morin, were selected to play in the Pro Bowl Game. In addition, two of Kelly's primary blockers, guard Gene Hickerson and tackle Dick Schafrath, as well as defensive backs Ernie Kellerman and Erich Barnes and mountainous defensive tackle Walter Johnson, who was emerging as one of pro football's best at that position, also played in the post-season game. Kelly, Hickerson and Warfield were named to the All-NFL team as well.

Tom Landry, the stone-faced coach of the Dallas Cowboys, was impressed with the rejuvenated Browns, a team which Dallas had manhandled, 28-7, in the second game of the season, and said the Cleveland club was vastly improved from that early meeting.

As the Browns launched their bid for the NFL championship and a berth in the Super Bowl, a short man with a big heart stood up in the locker room and began speaking. He was Tommy McDonald, one-time great receiver for the Philadelphia Eagles who had been acquired by the Browns when Collins was injured. McDonald, one of the smallest men in professional football and in the twilight of his career, spoke softly. "I didn't earn my way here," he said. "I'm here because Gary Collins got hurt. I'm proud to be wearing this uniform. I'm proud to be a Brown." As McDonald continued, his voice became louder and soon he was screaming encouragement to his new teammates. Most players couldn't remember much of what McDonald said. They sat there in silence as he stoked their emotional fires. "It was like Knute Rockne," Gary Collins said later. "It was one of the most inspirational speeches I've ever heard."

The Browns, who had lost four straight to the Cowboys, battled the visitors on even terms during the first half. Nelsen connected on a 45-yard touchdown pass to Leroy Kelly, to erase a 10-3 Dallas lead and sent the two teams to the dressing room tied at the intermission at 10-all.

Dale Lindsey put the Browns on the board quickly in the second half when he grabbed a Don Meredith pass at the Cowboy 27 and ran into the end zone. After the kick-off, Ben Davis picked off another pass by Dandy Don, setting up a 35-yard touchdown run by Kelly. With 2:31 gone in the second half, the Browns had a 24-10 lead and the Cleveland Stadium was in bedlam. Several minutes later a two-yard touchdown run by Ernie Green put the game out of reach for the Cowboys. The Cowboys, who had led the NFL in offense during the regular season, could only muster a field goal and a touchdown in the remaining 30 minutes of play -- and the TD came in the final seconds of the game. In one of the finest performances in history, the Browns picked off four Dallas passes and won, 31-20, to advance to the NFL championship game against the Baltimore Colts, 24-14, winners over Minnesota in the Western Conference play-off.

One more victory and the Browns would be in Super Bowl III. It did not come. In a reverse of their 1964 meeting, the Browns were flattened 34-0, by the team coached by Don Shula, who had played his college football at Cleveland's John Carroll University and was a former member of the Cleveland Browns. The hero for the Colts was another local man, Tom Matte, who had played at East Cleveland's Shaw High School and for Woody Hayes at Ohio State. Matte, a quarterback in high school and college and a pro halfback, scored three touchdowns to lead the rout. The Baltimore defense was superb in shutting down the Cleveland offense and limiting Kelly to only 28 yards rushing.

"We found out how they felt in 1964," said tackle Monte Clark of a wipeout that cost each member of the Browns as much as $20,000.

Typically, Collier was philosophical and did not dwell on the defeat. "I still have confidence in our team. It's a young club with a good future," he said. The Colts went on to make history. They became the first NFL team to lose a Super Bowl. A super quarterback named Joe Namath predicted before the game that the New York Jets would beat the NFL's best and they did, 16-7, at the Orange Bowl in Miami.

The Browns bid farewell to three players who had been much a part of their recent history as they readied for the 1969 season. Ernie Green and defensive end Bill Glass retired and Frank Ryan was dropped, ending a seven-year association with the Browns that produced 11 team passing records. Ryan, who eventually was picked up by the Washington Redskins, became expendable when the Browns acquired Jerry Rhome of Tulsa University, who had seen little action during the previous four years as a back-up quarterback for the Dallas Cowboys.

Bill Nelsen seemed none the worse for wear after knee surgery in the off-season and got the Browns off to one of their best starts in recent history. During the first seven games they posted a record of five wins, one loss to Detroit and a 21-all tie with St. Louis. The high point of the first half of the season came in the seventh game when they buried the favored Dallas Cowboys, 42-10.

The next weekend, the Browns were caught napping at Bloomington, Minnesota, where the Vikings administered one of the worst beatings any Cleveland team had ever suffered. Minnesota destroyed the Browns, 51-3, embarrassing them in every way possible. The Vikes had 31 first downs to Cleveland's eight, 454 yards offense to the Browns 151. Nelsen had three passes intercepted, Rhome one, and Kelly could muster only 24 yards in six carries. "We went from one of our best games (against Dallas the previous week) to one of the worst in the history of the club," intoned Nick Skorich, Cleveland's offensive coach. Collier, the master of understatement, simply said, "These things happen, they are part of football."

The Browns pulled themselves off the turf in Bloomington and ran a streak of five straight victories to chalk up their third Century Division championship. For the third consecutive year, they lost the final regular game of the season, this time to the New York Giants, 27-14, who wound up in second place four and half games behind the Browns. Cleveland finished with a record of 10-3-1 and for the third time in as many years had a date with the Dallas Cowboys in the Eastern Conference play-off game. Like the Browns, the Cowboys (11-2-1) had clinched their division title long before the end of the regular season.

At the Cotton Bowl in Dallas, the Browns proved rather conclusively that the 42-10 pasting they had handed the Cowboys earlier in the season was no fluke. On a damp day in Texas, the Browns spurted to a 17-0 halftime lead and kept the Cowboys from crossing midfield in the first two periods. Cleveland tacked on another 21 points in the second half to beat the Cowboys, 38-14, and once again advance to the NFL championship game.

One of the heroes on that day in Dallas was Robert "Bo" Scott, a former Ohio State star who had initially passed up NFL football and played four seasons in the Canadian Football League where he was the top rusher each year. Scott scored two touchdowns for the winners. Paul Warfield also had a spectacular day with 99 yards on eight catches.

Once again there was glory and big money on the line for the Browns. Once again they were only one step from the elusive Super Bowl. The hurdle they had to overcome this time was Minnesota, which defeated Los Angeles, 23-20, in the Western Conference play-off. In three seasons, the Vikings had come from the basement of the Central Division to be champions of the Western Conference.

When the Browns were pummeled by Minnesota, 51-3, at mid-season, Collier spared the players the distaste of watching the game films the next week, saying that "there would be nothing gained by it." But as a psychological ploy prior to the NFL title game, Collier pulled that horror movie out of the can and showed it to his team. The Browns apparently liked it so much they tried to repeat it at Bloomington, Minnesota, in the title clash.

Behind big, rangy quarterback Joe Kapp, the tenacious running of Dave Osborne and the sensational pass catching of Gene Washington, the Vikings sprinted to a 24-0 lead on a cold, sunny day. The field was frozen and slick and the Browns slipped and skidded on the turf. Bill Nelsen suffered an arm injury in the second quarter and couldn't throw effectively and the Browns seemed to lack pursuit and determination.

Cleveland outscored Minnesota, 7-3, in the second half, but the damage had been done. The Vikings had their first NFL title and a trip to the Super Bowl.

For Cleveland, the pot of gold turned out to be a mirage once again. The decade was over and the Browns were one of the NFL's winningest teams. But since that stirring victory over Baltimore in 1964, the story for the Browns had been "close, but no cigar." They had been in the championship game three more times and had come up empty.

It was time to find some new playmates.

20

Out of the Frying Pan and into the Fire

National Football League owners were in a quandary in the spring of 1969. The amalgamation of the NFL and the American Football League was to be completed in time for the 1970 season and there was much work to be done to homogenize the two leagues. The NFL had 16 teams and the AFL 10 and some realignment was necessary to create two 13-team conferences. One basic premise had been decided. If possible, there would be no wholesale scrambling of teams. The most expeditious manner of creating the two separate entities would be to shift three teams from the NFL to the AFL grouping. There was one problem: No teams from the NFL came forward and volunteered to move.

Art Modell was wearing two hats, of course. He was president and principal owner of the Browns and also president of the National Football League. An impasse developed. Modell suggested that the last three teams to join the NFL -- Atlanta, New Orleans and Minnesota -- move over to what would become the American Football Conference. That was rejected primarily because the addition of Atlanta and New Orleans to the AFL's other warm-weather teams -- San Diego, Miami, Oakland and Houston -- would have created a climatic imbalance between the two conferences.

On his own, according to Modell, NFL Commissioner Pete Rozelle made an offer he felt some owners could not refuse. Rozelle said the league would give $3,000,000 to each of the three teams that decided to move into the AFC.

One night at dinner with Rozelle and Tex Schramm, owner of the Dallas Cowboys, Modell made a proposal that he believed might break the impasse. He shocked his companions by suggesting that Cleveland, Pittsburgh and St. Louis of the Century Division be shifted to the AFC, leaving only the Giants to find another competitive home.

St. Louis balked, and the issue was complicated by the fact that Baltimore rather quickly decided to take $3,000,000 and move to the AFC. Modell then reiterated his offer to switch the Browns to the AFC, providing Pittsburgh would come along and that Cincinnati would be placed in the same division, to create a Pittsburgh-Cleveland-Cincinnati triangle and which would make for natural rivalries.

Modell felt a strong kinship with the Steelers. "I was their meal ticket for many years when they played at Pitt Stadium and Forbes Field," he recalled. "We were their biggest draw of the year, and they were a big draw in Cleveland. I wasn't going to dump them to move with two other teams of no consequence."

During the course of the meetings, Modell developed severe stomach bleeding and was rushed from the St. Regis Hotel in New York City, site of the meetings, to Doctors Hospital where he was confined for several days. The bleeding was diagnosed as an ulcer, caused in part by overwork from handling the two jobs.

The issue of moving Cleveland, Baltimore and Pittsburgh to the AFC was put on the table at the NFL meetings. Baltimore and Cleveland had already agreed, but there was the matter of Pittsburgh as well as getting the approval of the New York Giants, who had been one of the Browns' great rivals.

During a recess in the league meetings, Art Rooney, Sr., and his son, Dan, owners of the Pittsburgh Steelers, and Wellington Mara, owner of the New York Giants, visited Modell at Doctors Hospital. The discussion quickly turned to the proposed shifts. Dan Rooney objected, saying he thought the Steelers ought to remain in the NFC. But his white-haired father turned to him and said, "Dan, you can stay in Pittsburgh, I'm going with Art Modell."

Modell thanked the elder Rooney, but then turned his attentions to Mara, who said he was reluctant to give up the 20-year rivalry with the Browns. Mara explained flatly that he didn't like the idea, but would agree to it if the Browns and the Giants could play an occasional pre-season game to keep the relationship alive.

The stalemate was broken. Cleveland, Pittsburgh and Baltimore would move to the American Football Conference. The Browns were put into the Central Division with Pittsburgh, Cincinnati and Houston. "If I had known that Buffalo was going to have a new facility, I would have asked for Buffalo instead of Houston," Modell explained. "But Buffalo was playing in an old barn up there and I wanted no part of it."

Why did Modell decide to make the switch? Certainly the lure of $3,000,000 in cash had to be part of it, but Modell had several other reasons. First, he thought that a continued stalemate might cause the owners to opt for a total realignment of the teams in both conferences, which he felt would have been destructive to pro football. In total realignment, Cleveland might wind up in a divison with such teams as Boston, Miami and Denver.

"I just felt that it was going to be good for Cleveland," Modell said, "that we would bring in some new teams. We would be preserving our rivalry with Pittsburgh and be starting what promised to be a great rivalry with Cincinnati. And, frankly, I had more than a passing notion that we were going to dominate for a while."

The announcement was made on May 10, 1969, after the NFL and AFL owners conducted a marathon, 36-hour negotiating session to hammer out details. It was greeted with shock and dismay in Cleveland. The *Cleveland Press* ran a poll among its readers and they rejected the the shift by a 2-1 margin. One man who was extremely happy was Cincinnati Bengals' coach Paul Brown, who said, "I never dreamed we'd end up so well. I think the Cleveland fans will like their new affiliation. I think for all of us, this will work out worthwhile."

One voice of reason in Cleveland was *The Press*, which editorialized: "Why did it happen? The only possible answer is that Art Modell is convinced that, in the end, the move will be good for the Browns and pro football. Don't bet against the instincts and savvy of Modell. He has proved himself a smart operator many times over since taking over the Cleveland franchise. And a man who worked himself into an ulcer trying to straighten out the realignment of the two football leagues must be doing something right."

Had Art Modell known what the outcome of Super Bowl IV would be in January, 1970, he might have had some second thoughts about the move and his feeling that the Browns might dominate the AFC. The Kansas City Chiefs, champions of the AFL, flattened Minnesota, 23-7, at Tulane Stadium in New Orleans. After four Super Bowls, the AFL and the NFL were tied at two victories each. It was obvious that the Browns were not going into a "Mickey Mouse" conference.

The shock of Kansas City's stunning upset was still reverberating throughout the football world when the Browns released some disquieting news of their own. Paul Warfield, who had been named all-pro in 1969 with Leroy Kelly and Gene Hickerson, was traded to the Miami Dolphins for a first round draft choice. Warfield was surely one of pro football's premier receivers. In six years with the Browns, the fleet speedster had made 215 catches for 4,346 yards -- a 20.2 yard per catch average -- and had scored 44 touchdowns!

The Browns were incredulous and the fans were incensed. "You're kidding?" asked Gary Collins. "I'm as shocked as everyone else," said Bill Nelsen. "I feel as though I was the one traded. There is no finer receiver than Paul. We're losing an awful lot. If you had time to throw, Paul was always open."

At the same time, the Browns traded seven-year defensive tackle Jim Kanicki, rookie fullback Ron Johnson from Michigan and a reserve linebacker named Wayne Meylan to the New York Giants for receiver Homer Jones, who had very impressive statistics himself. In six years with the Giants, Jones had caught 214 passes for an average of 22.6 yards per catch and 35 touchdowns.

The *Plain Dealer* reported that 95 percent of the calls it received regarding the deal were negative.

In getting the draft choice from Miami, the Browns picked up the third selection in the NFL lottery and they used it to select Mike Phipps, the sensational quarterback from Purdue University. The Pittsburgh Steelers, who had finished with a dismal 1-13 record in 1969, had the first choice in the draft and selected a big, strong quarterback named Terry Bradshaw out of Louisiana Tech. Green Bay picked Mike McCoy second and the Browns grabbed Phipps.

The strategy in the trade of Warfield for the draft choice had been obvious. The Browns knew that Phipps would be available by choice No. 3, and they wanted a quarterback for the future, considering the state of Bill Nelsen's wobbly knees. Phipps had excellent credentials. He had been a consensus All-American in 1969, when he played in eight of 10 games and passed for more than 2,000 yards. During his career at Purdue, the Boilermakers had won 22 of the 27 games in which he played. The native of Shelbyville, Indiana, also had been named to the Big Ten All-Academic squad. He could not only pass well, he apparently had brains, too.

The Browns did fairly well in the rest of the draft. Their regular first round draft produced 260-pound offensive tackle Bob McKay of Texas. In two second round choices they got Jerry Sherk, a 245-pound, 6'4'' defensive tackle from Oklahoma State, and Joe Jones, a 240-pound, 6'5'' defensive end from Tennessee A & I. McKay was slated eventually to fill the slot vacated by the retirement of Monte Clark, who took a coaching job with Miami.

Preparations for the start of the 1970 season were hampered for a time by the first player strike in NFL history. The rookies reported to the Browns training camp, but veterans set up their own training facility at John Carroll University in a suburb of Cleveland and worked out for nearly two weeks until the labor problem was settled on August 3.

The Browns split in their first two exhibition games against traditional NFL foes -- Los Angeles and San Francisco -- and then got a taste of the best team in the football world, the Kansas City Chiefs, defending Super Bowl champs. Cleveland played brilliantly and the issue was in doubt until the final 51 seconds when Jan Stenerud kicked his third field goal of the game to provide the Chiefs with a 16-13 margin.

The next week, the Browns played a game for which everyone had been waiting -- an exhibition clash with the Cincinnati Bengals in their brand new Riverfront Stadium. To everyone concerned, it was a lot more than an exhibition contest. On the one hand there were the Cincinnati Bengals, whose uniforms looked like they were cloned from the Browns' and who were playing in only their third season under coach and general manager Paul Brown. On the other side was Blanton Collier, the man who had succeeded Brown after he was unceremoniously dumped by Modell eight years before. Here was Cleveland, a team that had made it to the NFL championship game little more than eight months before, against a Cincinnati team that had won only four of 14 games.

The Browns took a 14 point lead and it looked like a piece of cake. Blanton Collier put in his second team defense. The Bengals responded with 17 unanswered points in the second quarter and went to the dressing room with a 17-14 lead. The Browns never regained their momentum and were beaten, 31-24, before a delirious sell-out crowd of 57,112 at Riverfront. After the game, an elated Paul Brown stood in the locker room and fondled the game ball presented by his players. "This one," he said with more emotion than he usually showed, "I'll keep. I didn't know if we had a prayer. I didn't know if we could make it a contest. Everyone knows they have a great team."

The Browns won two of their first three games in the 1970 season and then had a date with Cincinnati at Cleveland Stadium. This time it counted. Bill Nelsen, who had been injured in the second game of the campaign, a 34-31 loss to San Francisco, returned to action against the Bengals after sitting out the Pittsburgh game in which Mike Phipps led the Browns to a 15-7 victory.

Cincinnati stunned Cleveland with 10 quick points to take a 10-0 lead before a crowd of 83,520 on a gray, mild day. The Browns rallied with two touchdowns and a safety but a Cincinnati touchdown gave the River City club a 17-16 halftime lead. The Browns outscored the Bengals, 14-13, in the second half to emerge with a 30-27 victory that wasn't salted away until the final moments. Offensively, it was a big day for both Nelsen and Kelly. Nelsen passed for two touchdowns and 226 yards. Kelly caught one touchdown pass, ran for another and combined for 163 yards running and receiving. It was Cincinnati's third straight loss. Cleveland fans, who once admired Paul Brown, booed him vigorously as he hurried to the locker room at the end of the game, refusing to cross the field and shake hands with Blanton Collier. He had turned his back on Collier at Cincinnati, too. In the dressing room, Brown said he was sorry that the fans didn't understand why he shunned the post-game ceremony. "I haven't done it after a game for years," he explained. In the meantime, the Browns presented owner Art Modell with the game ball as a symbol of a victory which obviously meant so much to him.

By the time the Browns and the Bengals hitched up for the return engagement in Cincinnati, Cleveland's record had slipped to 4-4, but the Browns were still tied with Pittsburgh for the division lead. Meanwhile, the Bengals had snapped a six-game losing streak the previous week and now had a dismal 2-6 record.

Mike Phipps made his first start at quarterback and looked like a winner on the first series as the Browns drove for a touchdown by Leroy Kelly. Don Cockroft kicked a 15-yard field goal and the Browns had a 10-0 lead. Cincinnati's Virgil Carter passed to Jess Phillips in the second quarter to shave Cleveland's margin to three points at the half.

Cincinnati shut down the Cleveland scoring machine in the second half and put together an 85-yard touchdown drive, capped by Paul Robinson's one-yard smash, to clinch its first regular season victory over the Browns, 14-10. The Browns' pride was hurt, but they still were on top of the Central with Pittsburgh, which also had lost.

Paul Brown was in tears after the game. "Satisfied, that's the way I feel," he gushed. "This is my best victory. This victory somehow makes coming back worthwhile."

The Bengals, only in their third year, ran off a streak of six straight victories, to take the lead in the divison with a 7-6 record and one game left to play. The Browns had dropped to 6-7, and needed a Cincinnati loss in Boston coupled with a victory over Denver to win the division and a berth in the play-offs. The Browns' hopes were crushed in Boston even before they took the field to play the Broncos. The Bengals ripped Boston, 45-7, to capture the Central crown with their seventh straight victory. Despite the disappointment, Cleveland beat Denver, 27-13, to finish with a 7-7 record, the second worst ever for a Cleveland team.

It was Blanton Collier's last game as head coach of the Browns. The soft-spoken, scholarly mentor whose hearing was failing, had decided to retire, leaving behind a splendid record of 79 wins, 38 losses and two ties, counting play-off games. He had taken the Browns to the NFL championship game four times in eight seasons and won it all once.

Art Modell had picked out Collier's successor long before the likeable Kentuckian decided to call it quits. Prior to hiring Chuck Noll (who has led Pittsburgh to four Super Bowl crowns), Steelers owner Art Rooney, Sr., told Modell he wanted to hire Cleveland Assistant Nick Skorich and asked permission. Modell turned him down, saying that when Collier retired Skorich would be the third head coach in the team's history. Modell announced Skorich's appointment during the first week of January, 1971. "I haven't spoken to anyone but Nick," he said. "I predict a return to peak performances the Browns enjoyed under Blanton Collier."

Skorich, 49, a native of Bellaire, Ohio, was no stranger to professional football. After winning All-American mention as a guard at the University of Cincinnati and spending three years as a commissioned officer in the U.S. Navy, Skorich decided to give pro football a try. He spent three years with the Pittsburgh Steelers and then quit to become a high school football tutor. In 1953 he became head coach at Rensselaer Poly in Troy, New York. A year later, he rejoined the Steelers as line coach, a post he held until 1958 when Green Bay made him offensive line coach and offensive coordinator. After a year in Green Bay, Skorich moved back east to the Philadelphia Eagles where Coach Buck Shaw put him in charge of the running game. When Shaw retired, Skorich was elevated to head coach in 1961. The Eagles posted a 10-4 record that season, missing the Eastern Conference title by a half-game. After losing seasons in 1962 and 1963, Skorich was fired by the Eagles and was hired by Collier as an assistant.

"I don't think we're too far away from being champions," said Skorich, who had been Cleveland's line coach and in charge of overall offense.

A more productive performance from Leroy Kelly would be one key to a better season. After three straight 1,000-yard plus seasons, Kelly had slipped to 817 yards in 1969, and 656 in 1970, when ankle injuries hampered his cutting ability.

The Browns picked corner back Clarence Scott from Kansas State in the first round of the draft, a surprise since Ohio State's All-American defensive back, Jack Tatum, was still available when the Browns selected Scott. Tatum went to Oakland and became one of the NFL's best defensive backs. Cleveland's sixth-round choice in 1971, was Doug Dieken, a 237-pound tackle from Illinois.

In the off-season, the Browns traded receiver Homer Jones to the St. Louis Cardinals. The man who had come from the New York Giants to replace Paul Warfield caught only 10 passes for 141 yards in 1970.

HENRY BARR FRED BOTTOMER

TONY TOMSIC

Above: Running back Bobby Mitchell and Ernie Davis; **clockwise from upper right:** Ernie Green and Jim Brown; Leroy Kelly; Paul Warfield; Jim Brown

TONY TOMSIC

ONY TOMSIC

TONY TOMSIC

Gary Collins

TONY TOMS

Frank Ryan

TONY TOMSIC

Blanton Collier

TONY TOMSIC

A delirious crowd celebrates the Browns' victory in the 1964 Championship Game, Cleveland Stadium.

TONY TOMSIC

Left: Milt Morin
Clockwise, starting below: Don Cockroft;
Bill Nelsen; Nick Skorich; Art Modell

PAUL TEPLEY

TONY TOMSIC

PAUL TEPLEY

Clockwise, from left: Don Cockroft and
Forrest Gregg; Dick Schafrath and Jim Brown;
the 1964 Browns Championship defensive line;
Gene Hickerson

TONY TOMSIC

TONY TOMSIC

Brian Sipe sets up for a long pass.

Right: Mike Pruitt,
Oakland Play Off Game, 1981

Left: Dave Logan in action

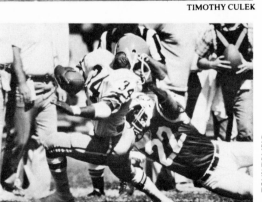

Left: Greg Pruitt face masked
by Burgess Owens (Jets)

TONY TOMSIC

ght: Sam Rutigliano after the
ond Bengals game, 1980.
ockwise, starting below:
gie Rucker; "Siper Bowl 81";
g Pruitt; Charles White

TAMI TOMSIC

TIMOTHY CULEK

TIMOTHY CULEK

TONY TOMSIC

*Oakland's Mike Davis and Ozzie Newsome battle for the ball
on the final offensive play of the 1980 season!*

"Kardiac Kids" fever

"Browns teams used to be the ones to beat," Skorich told his players at the opening of training camp. "They earned that regard over the years. There has been a winning tradition here but we have little to be proud of, reflecting on the 1970 season. It was the second worst record ever for the Browns. We are out to regain that old prestige. We start with horizons unlimited. A unique joy and ecstasy comes from winning. We must win. We're going to win. Our primary goal will be the Central Division title."

It was a strange season. The Browns won four of their first five games, including a 27-24 victory over Cincinnati. Then they fell apart, dropping successive games to Denver, Atlanta, Pittsburgh and Kansas City. After three straight losses, Skorich decided to start Phipps instead of Nelsen. But when the Browns generated very little offense in dropping a 13-7 decision at Kansas City to drop to 4-5, Nelsen was back in the starting lineup for Game No. 10, and in a surprising turnabout, Cleveland won five in a row to capture the Central Divison crown with a 9-5 record and win a place in the play-offs. Despite an aching right knee that was supported by an aluminum brace, Nelsen passed for 2,319 yards and 13 touchdowns. Wide receiver Frank Pitts, who had been acquired from Kansas City just before the start of the season, turned out to be the Browns' most effective receiver. The 9.5 speedster caught 27 passes for 487 yards and four touchdowns to lead all Cleveland receivers. Kelly had his best season since 1968, with 865 yards on the ground and another 252 yards on 25 receptions.

After missing the play-offs for one year, the Browns were back -- this time against the Baltimore Colts, who had finished second to Miami by half a game in the AFC East and earned a "wild card" spot. This was essentially the same Baltimore team that had edged Dallas, 16-13, in Super Bowl V. The Colts, 4½-point favorites, demolished the Browns, 20-3, before 74,082 on a drab, grey day at Cleveland Stadium. The score was nowhere indicative of the beating the Browns took. Nelsen was sacked four times for 34 yards and the Browns gained only 145 yards for the day, 49 rushing and 96 passing. Much of the offensive destruction was created by Baltimore's Don Nottingham of nearby Ravenna, Ohio, who smashed over on touchdown runs of one and seven yards and gained 92 yards for the day. Jim O'Brien kicked two extra points and two field goals to complete the Colt scoring. Cleveland's only score was a 14-yard field goal by Cockroft in the third quarter.

The Browns had nine months to think about the Baltimore debacle, which again nipped them on the road to the Super Bowl. If anything, they were just as bad when they opened the 1972 season by losing to Green Bay, 26-10, in what generally was conceded to be one of their worst openers in history.

During the pre-season schedule, Skorich had been alternating Mike Phipps and Nelsen at quarterback. Nelsen got the call for the opener, but was on the bench when the Browns faced Philadelphia. He never started another game. Phipps won his first game as a starter for the Browns at Philadelphia. The one-time Purdue star passed for one touchdown and ran four yards for another in a 27-7 victory. Over the next three games, there was no consistency. They beat the Bengals, 27-6, then scored only seven points while losing to Kansas City and Chicago. Then things started to come together. The Browns beat Houston, Denver, Houston and San Diego to boost their record to 6-3. The next week, they pulled one out of the hat against a vastly improved Pittsburgh team when Cockroft kicked a 26-yard field goal with 13 seconds left to erase a one-point Pittsburgh lead and win the game, 26-24. They made it six straight victories by measuring Buffalo and O. J. Simpson, 27-10

Now it was time to play Pittsburgh again and both teams were tied for the AFC Central lead with 8-3 records. "If we don't beat the Steelers we don't deserve the title," Skorich said. "We can't wait for the next guy to do it for us." Pittsburgh won, 30-0, and the Browns had lost another big game, a contest which saw Cleveland gain only a net 27 yards passing. Cleveland didn't lose another game in regular season play and neither did Pittsburgh. The Steelers, 11-3, won their first division title in history and the Browns, 10-4, got into the play-offs on a "wild card."

They did not draw an easy opponent. The Miami Dolphins, now coached by former Brown Don Shula, had lost Super Bowl VI to the Dallas Cowboys, 24-3. They had not dropped a game since and had finished the regular NFL season with a perfect, 14-0, record. The Dolphins were devastating. They had the most productive offense in the league, including a running game that featured bruising fullback Larry Csonka of Stow, Ohio, near Cleveland, and sidekicks Mercury Morris and Jim Kiick. They also had the stingiest defense in pro football.

Cleveland was a 13-point underdog when it took the field in the Orange Bowl in Miami, primed to become the Dolphins' 15th victim. But a strange thing happened. The Browns were playing a magnificent defensive game and held a 14-13 lead late in the game. It happened this way: The Dolphins took a 10-0 first half lead when Charley Babb blocked and recovered Don Cockroft's punt and scored from the five yard line and Garo Yepremian kicked a 40-yard field goal. Phipps put the Browns on the board in the third quarter on a five yard run, but the Dolphins came back in the fourth period to make it 13-7 on Yepremian's second field goal of the game. With 8:11 remaining in the game, Mike Phipps tossed a 27-yard touchdown pass to wide receiver Fair Hooker and Cockroft booted the extra point to put Cleveland out in front.

Miami came back and drove 80 yards, with Jim Kiick rushing the final eight to give Miami a 20-14 margin. With time running out, the Browns tried gamely to tie the score and reached the Miami 34. Phipps then pitched his fifth interception of the day and the Browns lost a heartbreaker. Miami went on to beat Pittsburgh in the AFC championship game and Washington in the Super Bowl to finish with an incredible 17-0 record. It was the first time in the history of the NFL that a team had put together a perfect season without a loss or a tie. The Browns took some consolation in the fact that they had taken the Dolphins down to the wire. However, if anyone had suggested that it would be 1980 before the Browns made another appearance in the NFL play-offs, a strait jacket would have been in order.

Cleveland had high hopes for 1973. Bill Nelsen had retired, and the role he assumed beginning in the second game of 1972 -- backup quarterback -- now was filled by Don Horn, a 1967 first round draft choice of the Green Bay Packers. Horn had served as the man behind Bart Starr until 1971, when he was traded to Denver. The Browns acquired him after the 1972 season. Brian Sipe, who had hoped he might fall in behind Mike Phipps, eventually was placed on the taxi squad. Sipe had been drafted the previous season. He spent that campaign working in practice, but sat in the stands at gametime.

One of the extremely bright spots during pre-season practice was a rookie named Greg Pruitt, who was small as pro backs went. Though only 5'10'' and 190 pounds, the Oklahoma running back had finished second in the Heisman Trophy voting after the 1972 season. He was a consensus All-American and was named Player of the Year by the Washington, D. C. Touchdown Club.

The Browns were a very inconsistent team in the first half of the 1973 season, and their 4-2-1 record showed it. Things seemed to be going worse when they opened the second half of the AFC campaign with a dismal 26-3 loss to the Vikings. But then Greg Pruitt exerted his presence. The speedster dashed for a 53-yard touchdown as the Browns dealt Houston a 23-13 loss. After Cleveland edged Oakland, 7-3, Pruitt's 19-yard dash provided the winning points in a 21-16 win over a Pittsburgh team which had creamed the Browns, 33-6, earlier in the season. The following week at Kansas City, the youngster sprinted for a 65-yard touchdown and gained 112 yards as the Browns fell behind, 20-6, and then came back to tie at 20-all.

With two weeks left in the campaign, the Browns shared the AFC Central lead with Pittsburgh and Cincinnati as they paid a visit to Riverfront Stadium in the Queen City. A victory would insure a play-off berth for the third straight year. It was not to be. Cincinnati riddled the Browns, 34-17, and eventually won the AFC Central title. The Browns finished at 7-5-2 and missed the play-offs.

There was trouble prior to the start of the next season. The World Football League, a new competitor, had been formed and was ready to play that season. Unlike the American Football League, the latest entry decided to stock its teams with several established players from the NFL. The Toronto Northmen had pulled off a blockbuster when they signed Larry Csonka, Paul Warfield and Jim Kiick, who had contributed mightily to Miami's back-to-back Super Bowl wins in 1972 and 1973. The Browns were not immune. Charles "Chip" Glass, a back-up tight end, tackle Bob McKay and wide receiver Fair Hooker all inked WFL contracts to play in the 1975 season. The new conference also coveted Jerry Sherk, but the big defensive end decided to stay with the Browns. The WFL lasted just one season!

Prior to the start of the training camp, the Browns bid farewell to Leroy Kelly who was put on waivers and eventually claimed by Oakland. Kelly was the NFL's fourth leading all-time rusher with 7,274 yards for a 4.2 average. The veteran from Morgan State had scored 74 touchdowns for the Browns.

And labor problems hit the NFL in the summer of 1974. Veterans around the league struck the various training camps and it took nearly three weeks for both sides to reach a compromise to end the walkout. Because of the strike, the Browns used mostly rookies in their first pre-season game, losing to a rookie-dominated Los Angeles team, 24-14.

The Browns never got on the track in the regular season. After splitting their first two games, they lost four in a row and found themselves out of contention with the season less than half over. In mid-October, it was obvious that Skorich's tenure was in jeopardy. Modell refused to give him a vote of confidence, but did state "I'm not going to act hastily for a one-shot headline."

Brian Sipe, who had finally made the team as Mike Phipps' back-up quarterback after two seasons on the taxi squad, pulled the Browns out of their tailspin. With the Browns trailing 21-9 in the fourth quarter, the rookie from San Diego State engineered two touchdown drives and scored both times to lead the team to a 23-21 upset over the Broncos. Cleveland won only two more games during the 1974 season and Sipe was instrumental in both. He was one of the few bright spots in the worst campaign in the club's history. The Browns finished 4-10, marking only the second losing season in 27 years. Their previous losing season had been in 1956 when they finished 5-7.

On December 12, Nick Skorich was fired after four seasons as head coach. "Nick and I came to a mutual understanding," said Art Modell. "It was in the best interest of the Browns. He felt that he had run his course, that we had failed. He'd been around for a long time and he took it with grace and dignity. To show you what kind of man he is, Nick insisted on being at the press conference when I announced he was leaving as head coach." Modell offered Skorich another job with the Cleveland organization but the outgoing coach chose instead to take a position in NFL headquarters.

The Cleveland Browns were a shambles and Art Modell was now faced with the task of finding the right man to pick up the pieces.

21

A Chip Off the Lombardi Block

Art Modell has a basic business philosophy: You build from within. When Paul Brown was fired, he tapped Blanton Collier and met with tremendous success. When Collier retired, he elevated Nick Skorich and for two years the Browns were in the play-offs. "I believe in rewarding people for their loyalty, for being here," Modell explained. "I think the strength of an organization is in internal growth, not in grabbing outside people all the time. I was determined once more to try inside the organization."

The man he selected was Forrest Gregg, a legend as a pro football tackle with the Green Bay Packers and a relative newcomer to the Cleveland staff. A native of Birthright, Texas, the 41-year-old Gregg played for Southern Methodist University before going to the Packers in 1956. The big and burly 240-pound, 6'4" Gregg was the NFL's best offensive tackle year after year. An eight-time all-pro choice, Gregg earned two Super Bowl rings with the Packers and one with the Dallas Cowboys, where he finished out his career in 1971. During his final two years at Green Bay, he had served as a player-coach. Gregg's first full-time coaching assignment was at San Diego, where he was offensive line coach in 1972 and 1973. The following season, he took a similar position with the Cleveland Browns.

"I'm delighted and optimistic," Modell said as he announced that Gregg had been signed to a three year pact. "There's no doubt in my mind that Forrest Gregg will make an outstanding coach in the NFL."

Once in the job, Gregg, who had played for the late Vince Lombardi -- one of the toughest taskmasters of all -- did not mince words. "Some of the players did not play up to their potential last season. We're not going to ease into this. People who aren't in shape will be left behind." Gregg also left no doubt that his coaching personality was largely influenced by the late Lombardi. The Browns found out quickly that Gregg was a tough, demanding coach. "As a player," he explained, "I always felt there was only one way to go. You had to beat the other guy physically."

Forrest Gregg did not get off to a very good start. In fact, the Browns lost their first nine games. No Cleveland team had ever come close to that mark. Gregg started the season with Phipps at quarterback. After the losing streak reached six, he switched to Sipe, and after nine losses went back to Phipps, who finally passed the Browns to a 35-23 win over the Bengals to break the streak. Cleveland won three of its final five games, but wound up with a 3-11 record, worst in team history. It was the first time the Cleveland Browns had ever had posted two straight losing seasons.

The fans were dismayed and they showed it at the turnstiles when only 390,440 showed up for seven home dates, an average of 55,777. It was the worst total attendance since 1960, when 337,972 had seen six games at Cleveland Stadium for a per game average of 56,328.

There was plenty of blame to go around for the Browns' collapse. Their drafting had been poor. They had made several bad deals, like the Warfield trade to Miami, and there were charges that the team's overall management lacked imagination and had become tired.

After the second straight disastrous year, Modell moved to strengthen the organization by hiring 32-year-old Peter Hadhazy as his executive assistant. Hadhazy's last job had been as assistant general manager of the New England Patriots under Chuck Fairbanks.

"I'm not surrendering my prerogatives or interests in any way," Modell was quick to point out. "What Pete's job will grow into I don't really know. I want a fresh look at everything. I'm afraid the organization has become somewhat inbred."

The Browns went into the NFL Draft looking for offensive help and came out with running back Mike Pruitt of Purdue as their No. 1 draft choice and wide receiver Dave Logan of Colorado as the No. 3 pick. There were some raised eyebrows when the team passed Archie Griffin, the two-time Heisman Trophy winner from Ohio State. The explanation was that with Greg Pruitt emerging into stardom, the Browns didn't need another small back.

In April, Forrest Gregg had a malignant mole removed from his thigh and it was a matter of some days before doctors knew whether they had removed all of the cancerous tissue. Gregg was philosophical after the scare. "I know this will help me in many things," he said. "Yes, my coaching, too. All has been put into better perspective."

Cleveland's primary goal in 1976 was to get back on a winning beat. Since Gregg had taken over as coach, there was a huge turnover in personnel. Only 18 players were on hand who had been with the club when the former Green Bay star assumed the head coaching job.

Among the new faces was Paul Warfield, who returned to the Browns after the World Football League folded. Reggie Rucker, an outstanding wide receiver, had been acquired the previous season from New England and led all Browns receivers in 1975 with 770 yards. Cleo Miller, a running back from Arkansas-Pine Bluff, had joined the offense late in 1975 as a free agent after playing briefly with the Kansas City Chiefs. Miller earned a starting spot with Greg Pruitt in the backfield, giving the Browns a potent running combination. Pruitt gained 1067 yards in 1975 for a 4.9 average per carry.

Despite a challenge from Sipe in training camp, Phipps again won the role as the Browns' No. 1 quarterback. However, after passing the Browns to a 21-10 halftime lead over the New York Jets, Phipps suffered a shoulder separation in the third quarter. Sipe stepped in and threw touchdown passes to Reggie Rucker and Steve Holden to insure the victory, 38-17.

The Browns lost their next three games and looked horrible doing it. They fumbled six times in a 31-14 thrashing by the defending Super Bowl champion Steelers and they were buried 49-13 by the Broncos. Hadhazy, the newcomer, was livid; calling the team a "disgrace," he shouted, "You want [running back] Larry Poole? You want Brian Sipe? Take them. There are some others you can have, too, but I can't give you their names because we might want to trade them."

When asked to comment on his young assistant's verbal blast, Modell commented, "Hadhazy said some things out of frustration but perhaps things were said that should not have been said. In retrospect, obviously, I wish they had not been said."

The following week the Browns were buried again, this time by the Cincinnati Bengals, 45-24!

However, seven days later, the fans were treated to one of the Browns' biggest wins in recent years when they edged the super Steelers, 16-13, at Cleveland Stadium. Sipe was knocked groggy in the second quarter, left the game and spent the night in the hospital. Dave Mays, the backup quarterback, brought the Browns from a 10-6 halftime deficit and the team went on to win three games straight before the Bengals brought them back to earth, 21-6, and left them with a 4-4 record.

The Browns didn't lose again until the final game of the season. They tore off five successive victories over Houston, Philadelphia, Tampa Bay, Miami and Houston again.

When the Browns traveled to Kansas City for the finale, they had no chance of making the play-offs. Still, they had the opportunity to finish with a 10-4 record, which would have tied them with Pittsburgh and Cincinnati on a won-loss basis. Sadly, they reverted to their old ways and lost, 39-14, finishing with a 9-5 record.

Particularly disgusted with the play against the Chiefs, Gregg told reporters that the Browns' 9-5 mark might be deceiving, the team probably not being as good as the record indicated.

"This team was hot and cold all year," he said. "This is not the trademark of a good team. Good teams win the games they are supposed to win. We looked like a bunch of people ready to go home, and I have no idea why. This absolutely takes the glow out of all we did before."

Despite Hadhazy's comments earlier in the season, Sipe proved he could play in the National Football League. The San Diegan started 12 games and completed 178 of 312 passes for 2113 yards and 17 touchdowns. Although hobbled part of the season with a sprained right ankle, Greg Pruitt gained an even 1000 yards on 209 carries for a 4.9 average. Defensive end Jerry Sherk was named All-Pro. Forrest Gregg was named AFC Coach of the Year by the Associated Press and runner-up by United Press International for bringing the Browns back to respectability. The next spring he was also inducted into the Pro Football Hall of Fame.

In spite of Gregg's success on the field, a rupture began to develop between the coach and the team's top management -- Modell and Hadhazy. It started at the height of the 1976 season when Gregg closeted himself with Modell and Hadhazy at the team's Stadium offices. Gregg forcefully asked for a raise and for an extension of his contract beyond the 1977 season. According to Hadhazy, Gregg claimed that a new agreement would reinforce his position with the players. They would know that he had a solid position with management and that he would not have to go through the 1977 season perhaps perceived as a "lame duck" coach. He argued that an extension would enable him to maintain greater player discipline. Hadhazy was incensed at the timing of the Monday morning discussion. Recalling his conversation, he said: "I asked Forrest, 'Do you know what the other 27 NFL coaches are doing now? They're reviewing game films and making plans for the next game. Your mind should be on the next game, not on your contract.' "

The meeting lasted for several minutes and at times the conversation became heated. Finally, a frustrated Modell said, "You guys work it out!" Hadhazy recalls that Gregg stormed from the room. "It was the way he came in and demanded it that annoyed me," Hadhazy said. "I felt like a high school principal disciplining one of his pupils."

In February Hadhazy and Gregg hammered out a new contract which called for a one-year extension through 1978 and an increase in salary. Hadhazy had the new contract typed and sent over to Gregg at the team's Baldwin-Wallace College training center in suburban Berea. It was a long time before Gregg signed and returned it and, in the meanwhile, Hadhazy was promoted to executive vice president and general manager.

The long experiment to make Mike Phipps the Browns' quarterback of the future ended in the spring of 1977 when he was traded to the Chicago Bears for a fourth round draft choice that year and for a first round pick in 1978. Phipps had previously said that he would welcome being traded because he didn't think he could accept being the Browns backup quarterback. "It's in the best interest of the Browns and myself that I get a fresh start someplace else." Mike had started 51 games, of which the Browns won 23, lost 26 and tied two. He threw only 40 touchdown passes but had 81 interceptions.

On paper, the Browns' 1977 draft looked good. Their first choice was Robert L. Jackson, a 230-pound, 6'1" linebacker from Texas A & M who was described as the most highly rated player the Browns had selected in many years. The second pick was Tom Skladany, a sensational punter and place kicker from Ohio State. Modell was especially excited about Skladany and said "Tom could give us an established kicker for the next ten years." Skladany hired west coast attorney Howard Slusher to negotiate a long-term contract and Hadhazy, who had previously negotiated with the short, heavy-set lawyer, knew there might be trouble. There was! The two sides started miles apart but began to narrow their differences. Skladany refused to report to the Browns' training camp pending the outcome of the negotiations. The punting duties were turned over to Greg Coleman who had been drafted by Cincinnati in 1976, dropped from the Bengals' roster and then signed as a free agent by Cleveland. Coleman boomed punts during the practice sessions, causing club officials to worry a little less about Skladany's future.

Still, the Browns wanted to sign the talented Ohio State graduate and undertook a last-ditch effort. Prior to the first exhibition game, Hadhazy held an all-night session at the Pittsburgh Airport Hilton Hotel. Young Skladany was there with his father, Tom, and Howard Slusher. Oddly enough, the meeting took place in the "Steelers Room." Tom showed up with his suitcases and was ready to head for camp if the negotiations with Hadhazy proved fruitful. After exchanging pleasantries, Slusher asked the Skladanys to leave the room while he and Hadhazy worked out the details. "After a long discussion I thought we had agreed on a base salary, incentive clauses and a signing bonus in the $50,000 range," Hadhazy recalled. "Slusher went over the details and Tom and his father seemed very excited." Though he declined to name a specific figure, Hadhazy indicated that the three-year deal would have netted the youngster more than $200,000. "After he had finished going over the proposal, Slusher looked up and said, 'Give me $10,000 more in bonuses and you've got a deal'," Hadhazy remembered. "You could have knocked me off the chair."

Hadhazy insisted that the offer he had made was final. Thus the Browns began the season with Greg Coleman as their punter. But the story of the negotiations with Skladany has an epilogue. Coleman experienced problems by mid-season and Hadhazy, Slusher and the Skladanys met again. "The conversation lasted all of about five minutes," Hadhazy recalled. "They asked that Tom be paid for the five or six games he missed. I said, 'See you later,' and left." Skladany sat out the entire season and eventually was dealt to the Detroit Lions, who were able to sign him.

The Browns jumped off to a pair of quick victories in 1977. In the opener, the defense was superb in whipping Cincinnati, 13-3, at Riverfront Stadium. The following Monday night the Browns made their first appearance in four years on ABC Monday Night Football against the New England Patriots. The home crowd of 76,418 was treated to a thriller of rare proportions. The Browns, down 24-17 midway in the fourth quarter, tied the score on an eight-yard pass from Sipe to Greg Pruitt. Don Cockroft kicked a 37-yard field goal with 55 seconds left in the game to put the Browns ahead by three points. New England bounced back on a John Smith field goal, tying the game as time ran out in regulation play. With 4:45 gone in the overtime period, Cockroft salted away the victory with a 35-yard boot.

The Browns lost their next two games to Pittsburgh and Oakland before running off three straight victories, reaching mid-season in first place in the AFC Central. Then things got tough. Cincinnati edged the Browns, 10-7, and Sipe fractured his shoulder blade in a 35-31 heartbreaker at Pittsburgh. He was finished for the season. The quarterbacking duties fell to long-throwing Dr. David Mays, the dentist/football player from Texas Southern, who engineered a Browns victory over New York, 21-7. It was, however, the Browns' last win of the season. They finished with four successive losses to wind up the campaign with a 6-8 mark.

Even before the tailspin and the injury to Sipe, Modell had second thoughts about Gregg's abilities. It was more a problem of style than anything else. Modell called it "human chemistry." Gregg would yell, insult and badger his players when they did something wrong. It was a tactic he had learned from the legendary Lombardi. While it may have worked in the 1960s, his style didn't seem appropriate for the 1970s. Several players approached Hadhazy and Modell to complain about Gregg's heavy-handed coaching style and his post-game tirades. When the complaints reached epidemic proportions, according to Hadhazy, top management knew there was a problem!

The beginning of the end for Gregg came against Los Angeles when the Browns were shut out for the first time since 1972, 9-0. At San Diego the next week, the Chargers barged to a 27-0 lead before the Browns ended a seven-quarter scoring drought which allowed their opponents to win 37-14. Modell called the game a "disgrace," and added, "You couldn't put what I am thinking in a family newspaper." At his Monday press conference, Gregg was asked if he needed that kind of heat. "There's heat every day and it will always be that way with this business because the name of the game is winning," he answered. "And, if you don't win you're going to get heat regardless of the circumstances. As to what Mr. Modell meant, you have to ask him. I have no idea, so I would gather that he wasn't talking about me. You can ask him."

The writers, asking if Gregg would be back the next year, were told by Modell "I will say nothing about next year." He continued sharply, "Our goal is to finish as respectable as possible with an 8-6 record. Then I will have plenty of time to reflect." Queried as to whether there was an open rift with Gregg, Modell would neither confirm nor deny.

When the Browns dropped a 19-15 decision to Houston in the next to last game and fell into the cellar of the AFC Central, that was it. Modell summoned the coach and told him he was fired, adding that the team would handle the situation in any manner Gregg might suggest and would announce Gregg's departure as a "resignation," though he would be paid through the 1978 season.

At a news conference, Modell announced Forrest Gregg had "resigned." Later, however, the deposed coach made it clear that he had been fired. According to Hadhazy, when the axe fell, Gregg reached into his desk at Baldwin-Wallace College, pulled out the contract they had negotiated the previous February, signed it and sent it over to the Browns' offices. He had coached 13 games without a signed contract, and even though it was signed and delivered after his dismissal, he was paid in full.

The players viewed the firing with mixed emotions. "He was affecting my career, my life," said defensive back Thom Darden, a former University of Michigan star. "My background is such that I don't need to be kicked to perform." Greg Pruitt, who had gained at least 1000 yards each season under Gregg, said, "He's a hard man and there are a lot of things I disagreed with him about. But I also agreed with many things and some guys overlook the fact that he did apologize at times for things he said."

Second-year running back Mike Pruitt, who had been on the receiving end of some of Gregg's outbursts after fumbling, commented that the coach's tirades "sometimes weren't necessary. We're grown men and we're paid to do a job. We don't need a coach to scold or chastise us like second and third graders. Maybe it was like that in the days of Vince Lombardi, but players are more mature now."

Gregg left Cleveland a bitter man and spent two months as an assistant coach for San Diego in 1978, then sat out the rest of the season. In 1979, he was named head coach for the Toronto Argonauts of the Canadian Football League, and after Paul Brown fired Homer Rice at the end of the 1978 season, he turned to Gregg to rebuild the Cincinnati Bengals.

Modell has been reluctant to discuss Forrest Gregg, though he has said "He can be as bitter as he wants, but if it wasn't for me he might still be an assistant coach. I gave him that opportunity to be a head coach. I gave him that forum where he could be heard and seen, and go to Canada and then come back and go to Cincinnati. I feel that I did what I could to help the man, not by design but by happenstance. For him to be so bitter is beyond comprehension."

Forrest Gregg did not coach the last game of the 1977 season. That chore was turned over to Dick Modzelewski, the defensive coordinator. The Browns lost to Seattle, 20-19, to complete their third losing season of the past four.

As Modell began his search for a new coach, he was sure that it was now time to clean house.

22

Modell Rolls the Dice

Months before Forrest Gregg was given the gate as head coach of the Cleveland Browns, Art Modell picked up the telephone in his handsome Stadium office and placed a call to State College, Pennsylvania. The man on the other end was Joe Paterno, highly successful coach of the Penn State Nittany Lions, a man whose talents had been coveted by several professional football organizations. Paterno had turned down a number of lucrative offers to leave the college ranks for what certainly would have been greener financial pastures.

Modell told Paterno that he had some ideas he would like to discuss and arranged to meet him at the Pittsburgh Airport Hilton Hotel a few days later. Even after Gregg posted the 9-5 record in 1976, Modell hadn't been totally comfortable with the situation with his coach. "I wasn't too sure Forrest was totally at fault for this feeling I had and felt that maybe he needed some help -- that perhaps we were deficient in not giving it to him."

When Modell and Paterno met in Pittsburgh, the Cleveland owner outlined a proposal. He offered Paterno an opportunity to join the Browns in an executive role, during which time he would have the opportunity to work with Gregg and to counsel him. "I didn't know whether Gregg would eventually remain with us or not," Modell said later, "but I wanted some help in making that judgment." He told Paterno that after evaluating the coach, he felt that Gregg was not the man for the job, Paterno had the option of taking the coaching post himself. Paterno pondered the situation and eventually told Modell that if he came to Cleveland and helped Gregg to become a better coach, he would then preclude himself from doing what he really wanted to do most -- teach and coach. He turned down the proposal.

Modell presented the same proposition to Ara Parseghian, who had retired from coaching after several successful seasons at Notre Dame. Parseghian had walked away from the pressures of the coaching game and now had a successful insurance business and was as well color commentator on the ABC-TV college football telecasts. After several telephone conversations, Parseghian told Modell that he did not want to get back into football.

After Gregg was fired, Modell decided it was time to go outside. "What had happened before was not working," he explained. "I needed a fresh perspective, a fresh slant, new ideas; not the same scouts, not the same assistant coaches, not the same way of doing business." Modell went back to the drawing board. He called Paterno and Parseghian, both of whom had turned down executive positions, and asked whether they would be interested in coaching the Cleveland Browns. Paterno said he preferred to stay at Penn State and Parseghian said he was still happy confining his association in football to weekend telecasts. Modell also talked with several other men who had head coaching experience in college and professional football. Then he began to look around for a good assistant coach.

"It was a gamble," Modell stressed. "You never know what you get until they become a head coach. One never knows what's lurking out there.

"You think Carroll Rosenbloom [late former owner of the Baltimore Colts and Los Angeles Rams] was so smart when he hired Don Shula? He gambled. Success in this league does not come from name coaches. They became names after they had achieved success. Whoever heard of Lombardi when he was an assistant coach with the Giants? Landry, an assistant coach with the Giants? Knox, Noll, Shula?"

Modell had one particular assistant coach in mind. His name was Sam Rutigliano, who was then an assistant to Hank Stram at New Orleans. Peter Hadhazy had worked with Sam at New England and thought highly of him. "Peter's judgment was important to me," Modell explained. Modell had dined with Rutigliano one night in 1970, when the Browns were in Denver for a game, and was impressed. The leading candidate was invited to spend three days with Modell at his Waite Hill home before Christmas. He spent hours talking with Modell and his wife, Pat. He viewed movies with Modell, Hadhazy and Nixon, who gave him high marks for football intellect. "He came off strong. We got along fine," Modell said. "I was looking for someone I could be happy with. It's tough enough to be happy when you win, let alone when you lose. The greatest experience of all for me came in the Blanton Collier years. In Sam, my instincts told me I had a young Collier. Blanton was mentally and intellectually honest. Sam is, too."

Rutigliano, the son of an Italian immigrant truck driver, had grown up in the Sheepshead Bay section of Brooklyn, New York. A star end at Erasmus High School, he went to East Central Junior College in Decatur, Mississippi, and earned junior All-American honors. Next he enrolled at Tennessee and played on the Vols' 1951 national championship team. Then it was on to Tulsa, where he also lettered in football. Sam Rutigliano didn't stay in one place very long. His first coaching job was in high school, where he taught and coached during the day and earned his master's degree in education at Columbia University at night. After several years in the schoolboy set, Sam moved into the college ranks, first at the University of Connecticut and then at Maryland as an aide to Lou Saban, a former Cleveland Brown. When Saban became head coach and general manager of the Denver Broncos, Sam went with him. Then there were jobs with the Patriots, the Jets and finally, the Saints.

"I want you to know, this man's record was not very good," Modell said one day three years later. "He bounced around pretty good."

In light of the measure of success Gregg had had for at least one season, Modell knew that Cleveland fans would not have put up with any more failure. They would not have displayed much patience with Art Modell had the Browns failed to start moving quickly into a positive direction.

Still, Modell decided to go out on a limb, to play a hunch, to -- as he said -- take the biggest gamble since firing Paul Brown.

At 3 p.m. on December 28, 1977, Sam Rutigliano was introduced to the media at a Stadium Club press conference. "He's a teacher by background," Modell told the press, "just the way Blanton Collier was. I feel I have a new Blanton Collier. Beyond that, he relates with today's attitudes. He's contemporary in his relationship with players.

"Sam is an assistant coach with a proven record in all phases of the game," the owner continued. "I could have gotten a name coach and made a big headline, but that's not what I wanted."

Rutigliano, dressed in a navy blue suit, vest and red tie, impressed the audience with his soft, articulate and humorous manner. "My way," he said of his coaching philosophy, "is to somehow, someway reach a person. That could come from putting an arm around one man, and applying harsher methods to another."

When Browns fans got the word that a man whose only head coaching experience had been in high school was the new boss of the Cleveland Browns, they asked incredulously, "Sam who?"

Modell gave Rutigliano carte blanche to clean house among the assistants. The new coach stressed that his new assistants would be men who are "great teachers, communicators and knowledgeable, coaches who will be involved in patiently bringing players along."

The only man retained from Gregg's staff was Rod Humenuick, offensive line coach, who was to play a major role in developing the pass protection for Brian Sipe.

Sam decided he would take his time in evaluating the talent. "I thought there had been a motorcade of changes in players in Cleveland," Rutigliano recalls. "There's an old saying that a new broom sweeps clean. I believe that, but I also think it takes an old one to get into the corners. I said to Art and Peter and all the principal guys, even the guys who handle the equipment, and the trainers: 'Look, I appreciate everything you're going to tell me about all these players, but I would prefer not to hear anything negative, because I want to find out for myself'."

With the draft upcoming, Rutigliano knew what he wanted most to put his offensive game plan into operation -- a tight end with the speed and moves of a wide receiver. Then, on obvious passing downs, the Browns would not have to substitute a wide receiver for a relatively slow tight end. It would also enable Sipe to pass more frequently and more effectively to the running backs, adding a new dimension to the Cleveland attack.

The Browns had two choices in the first round. Clay Matthews, a 231-pound, 6'1" linebacker from Southern California, was their initial selection. Next, they took Ozzie Newsome, a 232-pound, 6'2'' tight end from Alabama, who had been described by Crimson Tide coach Bear Bryant as ''the finest receiver we've ever had.''

Other key players drafted in 1978 included Johnny Evans, a quarterback/punter from North Carolina State and Keith Wright, a 176-pound wide receiver from Memphis State, a fearless young man with great speed.

When Sam assembled the players for pre-season practice he found out that what he had seen on the screen in Modell's basement was not a mirage. There were plenty of talented people there, who, if channeled in the right direction, could carry the team a long way. There was a crop of good defensive backs in Oliver Davis, Tony Peters, Thom Darden, Ron Bolton and Clarence Scott. Dick Ambrose and Charlie Hall were solid linebackers and, of course, Jerry Sherk was just about the best in the business as a defensive tackle.

Offensively, the talent was there, too, in players like Reggie Rucker, Dave Logan, Sipe, Greg Pruitt, Doug Dieken, Tom DeLeone, Henry Sheppard and Robert E. Jackson. And, of course, there was Mike Pruitt, Purdue's most valuable player in 1975, who spent most of his time on the bench since joining the club as the No. 1 draft choice in 1976. Pruitt had developed a reputation as a fumbler, had frequently drawn the enmity of Forrest Gregg, and had carried the ball only 99 times in two seasons.

When the team went to its Kent State University training camp, Sam Rutigliano had a chat with Pruitt. He told the young running back that he had been studying the films and saw nothing that should keep Pruitt on the bench. ''Now you'll have an opportunity to play,'' Sam said.

There were some players on the team who did not share Rutigliano's assessment that Sipe was the man who could take the Browns a long way, but it did not matter. Brian was Sam's man. And he put the handsome quarterback in the hands of Jim Shofner, star defensive back for the Browns during the 1958-1963 seasons. Shofner had been hired as quarterback coach on Sam's new staff. Sipe would later state that the hiring of Shofner ''was the greatest decision Sam ever made as it relates to my career.''

The players at the Kent training camp found the scenario to be vastly different from the days of Forrest Gregg. There was a calm, cool approach to things. The players thought of Sam as a patient, fatherly man with an uncommon touch and a wonderful sense of humor.

The NFL had dictated a major change beginning in the 1978 season. Teams would be limited to four exhibition games and the regular season was expanded from 14 to 16 games.

The Browns were impressive in Sam's debut, putting together an outstanding team effort to beat the San Francisco 49ers, 34-7, before a crowd of 68,973 at Cleveland Stadium. Greg Pruitt had his 13th 100-yard game, rookie Ozzie Newsome dazzled the fans with a 33-yard touchdown on a reverse and Sipe and Reggie Rucker combined on a 65-yard scoring pass. Meanwhile, the Cleveland defense swarmed over the incomparable O. J. Simpson, limiting the former Southern Cal star to just 78 yards rushing. Seven days later, the Browns treated another home crowd to a come-from-behind, 13-10, overtime victory against the Bengals. Don Cockroft's 27-yard field goal did the trick. However, Greg Pruitt suffered a calf injury in the game and was sidelined for a month. At Atlanta, the following week, the Browns made it three in a row with a hair-raising 24-16 win. Sipe scored a touchdown with 1:19 remaining to erase a 17-16 Atlanta Margin.

Sam suffered his first loss the next week in a game the Browns should have won. The Browns and the Steelers had tied 9-9 at the end of regulation play and the game went into overtime. On the kick-off, Steeler Larry Anderson's fumble on the Pittsburgh 22 was recovered by Ricky Feacher for the Browns. The officials, however, ruled incorrectly that Anderson's knee had touched the ground an instant before the fumble. The ball was awarded to the Steelers, robbing Cleveland of a field goal opportunity. The Steelers turned the break into a 79-yard touchdown drive, culminating in a 37-yard touchdown pass from Terry Bradshaw to Bennie Cunningham on a trick play. The Steelers won, 15-9.

Prior to the next game, against Houston in Cleveland, the Browns signed a 31-year old free agent, Calvin Hill. A former Yale star, Hill was the Cowboys' No. 1 draft choice in 1969 and became an immediate star for the Texans. In six years with Dallas, he gained 5,009 yards rushing, 1,359 receiving and scored 45 touchdowns. The highly intelligent Hill played out his option with the Cowboys in 1974, signed with Hawaii of the World Football League in 1975, then moved on to Washington, where he was used sparingly in 1976 and 1977.

A 19-yard field goal by Tony Fritsch with 44 seconds remaining dealt the Browns another heartbreaking blow that week and they bowed to Houston, 16-13. The Browns were done in by another disputed play. A 44-yard pass from Dan Pastorini with 54 seconds left was ruled simultaneously caught by Houston's Ken Burrough and Cleveland's Ron Bolton. The Oilers were awarded the ball on the Cleveland four, thus setting the stage for the field goal. The Browns argued that Burrough had committed a foul by reaching over Bolton to get the ball, but the "zebras" would hear none of it. Fans in the bleachers began throwing cans filled with beer at players and officials. After a 10-minute delay, the men in stripes moved the teams to the closed end of the field for the remaining plays. After the game, Modell banned all cans and bottles from the park.

Ron Bolton was furious. "The officials are the only guys who can rob you and then get away with a police escort," he fumed after the game.

At the Superdome in New Orleans the following week the Browns did not have to wait until the last minute. Cleo Miller dashed 61 yards for a touchdown, then Calvin Hill trotted for another 57-yard score as the Browns won handily, 24-16. Ron Bolton fractured a bone in his forearm and was sidelined for seven weeks.

The season began to deteriorate from that point. Losses on successive weeks to Pittsburgh and Kansas City dropped the Browns to a 4-4 record. After rebounding against Buffalo, the Browns dropped to 5-6 with back-to-back losses to Houston and Denver. Strong offensive performances against Baltimore and Los Angeles renewed their play-off hopes, but chances for a "wild card" berth vanished when they lost to Seattle, 47-24, at the Kingdome. A 21-yard overtime field goal by Don Cockroft provided the 37-34 margin of victory over the New York Jets, lifting the Browns to 8-7 with one game remaining.

Prior to the final game of the season, Art Modell extended Rutigliano's three-year contract through 1983, because "Sam is a winner," as Modell said. The Browns responded with one of their worst performances that year as they were buried by the Cincinnati Bengals 48-16, to break even for the season.

A look at the statistics showed that Rutigliano's offensive blueprint was beginning to take shape. There was a wide variety in the passing attack. The Browns regular receiving corps of Rucker, Logan and Newsome accounted for 118 catches, while the principal running backs -- Gregg Pruitt, Calvin Hill, Mike Pruitt and Cleo Miller -- accounted for another 103 receptions. Brian Sipe had his best year to date with 222 completions in 399 tries for 2,906 yards and 15 touchdowns. Despite missing four weeks, Gregg Pruitt had 960 yards rushing. Mike Pruitt ran for 560 yards, his best showing in three seasons.

In the off-season, Modell moved to strengthen what had been the Browns' weakest link -- the draft. Tommy Prothro, who had a wealth of experience as a college and professional coach, was hired as executive vice-president, director of player personnel. In 16 years at Oregon State and UCLA, Prothro's teams had won 104 and lost 55. He also spent more than five years in head coaching assignments with the Los Angeles Rams and San Diego Chargers. "Tommy has complete power to get us the best 45 players," Modell said.

With Prothro on the job, the Browns went looking for defensive help in the 1979 draft. Though the first choice was a wide receiver named Willis Adams out of the University of Houston, Cleveland did get some help in defensive backs Lawrence Johnson of Wisconsin and Clinton Burrell of Louisiana State. As it turned out the team did not come up with any strong defensive linemen who could help. Fortunately, however, there was help around the corner.

Jack Gregory, a 254-pound, 6'5" defensive end who had left Cleveland in 1972 for the New York Giants after a contract dispute with Modell, was re-acquired from the Giants for a 1980 draft selection. The Browns also picked up an unexpected prize. Lyle Alzado, a nine-year veteran and two-time All-Pro was having contract difficulties with the Denver Broncos. His problems had followed an exhibition boxing match with Muhammed Ali in July, which the 250-pound, 6'6" Alzado had lost.

When Alzado, who had 157 final hits and 80 assists in the past two seasons, became available, Modell jumped at the chance and in return gave the Broncos draft choices for 1980 and 1981. Alzado signed a five-year contract with the Browns and Rutigliano was ecstatic. "This is another major step by Art Modell to bring Cleveland a winner."

The Browns, who had flirted with last-minute heroics in 1978, were ready to make it a regular practice and win the nickname of "The Kardiac Kids." They started in the very first game, at Shea Stadium, when Don Cockroft kicked a 27-yard field goal in overtime to beat the New York Jets, 25-22. The next week they squandered a 20-0 lead over Kansas City, trailed 24-20, and came from behind when Sipe threw a 21-yard touchdown pass to Rucker with 52 seconds remaining. It was more of the same when Sipe and Newsome combined on a 74-yard pass play to set the stage for a 28-yard Don Cockroft field goal to break a 10-10 tie with 1:51 remaining, and give the Browns a 13-10 win over Baltimore.

They did not need a Kardiac job when they hosted the Cowboys in a Monday Night spectacular. Cleveland scored 20 points in the first seven minutes en route to a 27-6 rout of the Cowboys, who had lost a four-point decision to Pittsburgh in the Super Bowl the previous January. Even Howard Cosell was impressed.

The Browns were 4-0, but not for long. They were bombed at Houston, 31-10, then took a 51-35 whipping at the hands of the Steelers in an offensive bloodbath in Cleveland. Terry Bradshaw threw three touchdown passes and Franco Harris churned up 153 yards and scored twice as Pittsburgh cut through the Cleveland defense like a hot knife through butter. It was little consolation that Sipe fired five touchdown passes. "I'm absolutely appalled they scored 51 points on our defense," said Rutigliano. Alzado was more succinct. "I'm ashamed, embarrassed," the big man said.

Rutigliano shook up the defense. Alzado was moved from right defensive end to the left side. Jack Gregory was installed as the regular defensive right end. Mike St. Clair, who had occupied that spot, was miffed and didn't show up for practice one day. Cleveland's losing streak continued against Washington. The Browns' tenuous 9-6 lead was erased on an 80-yard touchdown drive with 27 seconds remaining and the Browns lost their third in a row, 13-9.

It looked like the Browns were on their way to another setback when they fell behind Cincinnati, 20-7, in the third quarter. But Sipe finished with four touchdown passes for the day and Mike Pruitt exploded for 135 yards on the ground as the Browns edged their bitter rivals, 28-21, at Cleveland Stadium.

It was an especially meaningful victory for Modell. The week of the Cleveland-Cincinnati game marked the official publication date of Paul Brown's long awaited autobiography entitled, *PB: The Paul Brown Story*, written with free-lancer Jack Clary. Paul Brown came to town and made appearances to promote the book, which was serialized in *The Plain Dealer*.

Brown was not very kind to Art Modell in the book. Among other things, he accused the owner of undermining his powers after Art bought the team and of breaching the authority given him in his contract. He charged that Modell asked him to play Ernie Davis, who was dying of leukemia, for publicity purposes. Modell maintained a stoic silence, but did complain to league Commissioner Pete Rozelle that his former coach had violated NFL rules by publicly criticizing a fellow owner. In the meantime, the newspapers were filled with stories quoting others close to the situations referred to in Brown's book. Many of the sources sought to refute Brown's charges, especially as they related to the Ernie Davis situation.

Rozelle eventually fined Brown $10,000 for the comments he made about his former boss, now a fellow owner.

To this day, Modell still refuses to make extensive comments about the book, except to say: "I feel sorry for Paul Brown in writing that book. I will not say anything in my own defense, but others who knew the true story did speak up, unsolicitedly -- people who knew the man and knew the relationship. It is sad and somewhat disquieting that all his [Paul Brown's] references in the book were either dead or unnamed."

The following week the Browns exploded for 21 points in the fourth quarter against St. Louis to riddle the Cardinals, 38-20, and push their record to 6-3. The victory was costly. Gregg Pruitt tore knee ligaments with just 23 seconds gone in the contest and was lost for the season. It was miracle time again in Philadelphia. With less than four minutes remaining and the Browns trailing, 19-10, Sipe passed five yards to Newsome to cut the margin to 19-17. Then the brilliant quarterback engineered a 71-yard drive, which was capped by a 24-yard touchdown run by Mike Pruitt with 55 seconds remaining. With their 7-3 record, the Browns appeared headed for the play-offs.

Their next date was against Seattle at Cleveland Stadium, but they got some bad news. Jerry Sherk suffered a staph infection in his knee and was knocked out for the rest of the season. They lost to the Seahawks, 29-24.

Sipe had the best day of his career to date against Miami at the Stadium seven days later and he needed it, as the Browns pulled out another one in overtime, 30-24. A 35-yard Sipe to Newsome touchdown pass evened the score at 24-all with 1:21 remaining in regulation play. In the extra period, Sipe needed less than two minutes to engineer a 74-yard drive that was completed on a 39-yard scoring pass to Rucker.

They went into overtime again the next week at Three Rivers Stadium, where they had never won a game. This time the powerful Steelers, headed for their fourth Super Bowl title, reversed the scenario. With the clock showing 24 seconds left in regulation time, Pittsburgh's Matt Bahr tied the score at 30-all with a 21-yard field goal. The two teams traded thrusts for 14 minutes and 47 seconds in the extra session until Bahr exploded a 37-yard field goal with 13 seconds remaining.

It was Mike Pruitt's day against Houston. The former Purdue star scored two touchdowns and topped the 1,000 yard mark for the first time in his career as the Browns edged the Oilers, 14-7, to keep their play-off hopes alive. With two games remaining the Browns had a 9-7 record. Pruitt was brilliant against Oakland, gaining 149 yards on the ground and scoring two touchdowns (one on a 77 yard jaunt), but the Browns lost, 19-14. Sipe was sacked five times.

There was still a glimmer of hope for a play-off berth as the Browns headed for Cincinnati and their final regular season game. The Bengals were struggling and had won only three of 15 games under Coach Homer Rice. However, there was no miracle on this day. On the final play of the game, with Cleveland on the Cincinnati four-yard line, trailing 16-12, Sipe's pass went off the finger tips of Ricky Feacher in the end zone.

In many ways it had been a remarkable season. The Browns had beaten four teams who were on their way to the play-offs. They had proved they were solid contenders. Brian Sipe had proved he was among the best at his craft in the NFL. He tossed for a club record 3,793 yards and 28 touchdowns. He also set a team record with 26 interceptions. Mike Pruitt had emerged as one of the NFL's leading fullbacks with 1,294 yards and a 4.9 average. In Rutigliano's gambling run-and-gun offense, he had also caught 41 passes for 372 yards. His outstanding performance earned him a trip to the Pro Bowl. Ozzie Newsome, the young man fans called "The Wizard of Oz," was named All-Pro on the strength of a sensational performance during which he caught 55 passes for 781 yards. And Sam Rutigliano was named AFC Coach of the Year by the United Press International.

In 12 of Cleveland's 16 games, the issue was in doubt until the final seconds. The Browns had made it interesting all season long and the fans loved it. But not as much as they did in 1980, when Sam and the Kardiac Kids finally got Cleveland into the play-offs in a season that gave Greater Cleveland an unbelievable psychological lift.

Cleveland was a winner once again, but can it remain one?

23

Sam, Sipe, and the Future

The Browns' 14-12 loss to Oakland on that bitter cold day at Cleveland Stadium surely hurt. Just when it seemed that fate would shine kindly one more time on the Kardiac Kids, the pacemaker went dead. But the Browns went down in style, with class, trying as they had done time after time to work one more miracle.

It is basic to Sam Rutigliano's philosophy that you do not look back. You look to the future. And even in the wreckage of the Browns' hopes on the frozen turf of Cleveland Stadium there is great hope. The team that defeated them by just two points was no ordinary team. It was, as future events would show, the very best team in the National Football League.

On another day, when hands were not frozen, the field not slick, the temperature not bitter cold, the outcome might have been different. What the Browns did show in winning the AFC Central and in taking the Super Bowl Champion Raiders down to the final seconds is that they are among the best teams in the National Football League, that they have the talent to play with and beat the best. And remember, they made the best showing of all the play-off teams against the Raiders. Sam Rutigliano and his staff have brought consistency and stability to the Cleveland Browns, creating a climate in which the Browns can play up to their potential.

It should be recognized that one season does not mean a great deal in the context of time. One trip to the play-offs is not the end, it is the beginning. The next five or 10 years will tell whether people like Sam Rutigliano, Brian Sipe and other members of the supporting cast can be mentioned in the same breath as the enduring stars of the past. If you want to know what heritage they carry, the goals for which they must grasp, you need only walk through the hallowed corridors of the Pro Football Hall of Fame in Canton, Ohio. There you will find the bronzed busts of former members of the Cleveland Browns whose performances have stood the test of time: Paul Brown, Otto Graham, Marion Motley, Dante Lavelli, Lou Groza, Bill Willis, Lenny Ford, Jim Brown.

Brian Sipe has broken a lot of Otto Graham's passing records. At age 31, he still has many, many more productive years ahead if he stays healthy. But to put Brian Sipe's 1980 performance into context, consider these facts: When Otto Graham retired after leading Cleveland to a second straight world title in December, 1955, he had just turned 34. In the

10 seasons he quarterbacked the Browns (counting four in the All-America Conference), Cleveland never failed to make it to a championship game. In his six seasons in the NFL, the Browns won three championships. As the busts in Canton graphically illustrate, Otto Graham had an excellent coach, and an unparalleled supporting cast.

Many of those ingredients are here now. Sam Rutigliano is a man for the times, thoughtful, intelligent, smart and with a sense of adventure, a man who knows how to handle the temperamental stars of today, most of whom earn a lot more than the coach. He is a gambler at heart, not afraid to take chances, win or lose. He has molded the Browns into a caring, family unit, with a spirit that hasn't been seen in a Cleveland Browns team in years. His second consecutive AFC Coach of the Year award is an indication that others recognize his superb talents.

Sipe was acknowledged in 1980 as the NFL's Player of the Year, a heady honor that is not worn lightly. It was just one of a bushel full of honors heaped upon the modest young man from San Diego who really did not know whether he wanted to make pro football a career or not. Now, Sipe says he sees no end to his career. "It's going to be way down the line. I'm not going to speculate in years. I'm still in my prime physically and feel as good now as I ever have."

As a measure of what others think about the cast of characters that helped make the Browns tick in 1980, Sipe and four other players from the offensive squad were named to the 1981 Pro Bowl Game in Hawaii. Included were Doug Dieken and Joe DeLamielleure, two of the men responsible for providing Sipe with the best pass protection in the league. Sipe and the two linemen were named starters, while Mike Pruitt and center Tom DeLeone were selected for the squad. A lot of extraordinary players, including Newsome, Logan, Rucker and Gregg Pruitt, stayed home.

The only player honored from the defense was Lyle Alzado and he was selected as an alternate. In assessing the future, the Browns must concentrate on the defense. Much was made of the success of the switch to the 3-4 defense in the 1980 season, but it is deceiving. Sam switched to the 3-4 because he wanted to bolster Cleveland's defense against the rush. It worked. The Browns had the third best average in the AFC against the rush, a 110.1 yards per game average. But they gave up considerably more yardage per game in passing and finished dead last in the conference, with an average of 241.6 yards per game. One of the reasons the Browns had to scramble late in many games after taking comfortable leads was because the pass defense broke down. The opposing quarterbacks, not pressured by a three-man rush, were able to pick apart the Cleveland secondary.

The Cleveland kicking game is being overhauled. When Johnny Evans was kicking knuckle balls against Oakland in the play-offs, the presence of Tom Skladany surely would have been welcome.

As 1980 indicated, the Browns certainly had their act together on the playing field. The only consistent flaw in the entire organization for the past several years has been in drafting. The Browns have been poor judges of talent in both the draft and in trading. If they hope to remain in the National Football League's elite, they must do a much better job. Coaching is only part of the equation and Art Modell recognizes this. Teams like Pittsburgh, Oakland, and Dallas have remained on top by being remarkably astute at assessing promising talent. They have to be better than anyone else because they usually draft at the bottom of the heap.

However, the man who will probably have more to say about where the Browns are going in the 1980s is Brian Sipe, and he is very optimistic. "Believe it or not, we have a lot of room for improvement," he says. "It's nice to know we can accomplish what we did even though we have not really hit stride. I'm looking forward to considerable improvement personally and to our team getting better collectively. Consequently, the sky's the limit as far as the Cleveland Browns are concerned."

Statistical Appendix

All-time Browns' Roster
1946-1980

Adamle, Tony (Ohio State)............47-51, 54
Adams, Chet (Ohio U.)...................46-8
Adams, Pete (So. California).............74, 76
Adams, Willis (Houston).................79-80
Agase, Alex (Illinois)...................48-51
Akins, Al (Wash. State)....................46
Aldridge, Allen (Prairie View)..............74
Allen, Ermal (Kentucky)....................47
Alzado, Lyle (Yankton).................79-80
Ambrose, Dick (Virginia)................75-80
Amstutz, Joe (Indiana).....................57
Anderson, Preston (Rice)...................74
Andrews, Billy (S.E.Louisiana)..........67-74
Athas, Peter (Tennessee)...................75
Atkins, Doug (Tennessee)................53-4

Babich, Bob (Miami-Ohio)...............73-8
Baker, Sam (Oregon State)...............60-1
Barisich, Carl (Princeton)...............73-5
Barnes, Erich (Purdue)..................65-71
Barney, Eppie (Iowa State)...............67-8
Bassett, Maurice (Langston)..............54-6
Battle, Jim (Southern U.)...................66
Beach, Walter (Central Mich.)............63-6
Beamon, Autrey (E. Texas St.)..............80
Benz, Larry (Northwestern)...............63-5
Bettridge, Ed (Bowling Green)..............64
Beutler, Tom (Toledo)......................70
Biedermann, Leo (California)...............78
Blandin, Ernie (Tulane)..................46-7
Boedeker, Bill (No College).............47-9
Bolden, Leroy (Mich. State).............58-9
Bolton, Ron (Norfolk State).............76-80
Borton, John (Ohio State)..................57
Bradley, Harold (Iowa)...................54-7
Bradley, Henry (Alcorn State)...........79-80
Brewer, Johnny (Mississippi)............61-7
Brewster, Darrell (Purdue)...............52-8
Briggs, Bob (Heidelberg).................71-3
Brooks, Clifford (Tenn. State)...........72-4
Brown, Dean (Ft. Valley State).............69
Brown, Eddie (Tennessee)................74-5
Brown, Jim (Syracuse)...................57-65
Brown, John (Syracuse)..................62-6
Brown, Ken (No College).................70-5
Brown, Stan (Purdue).......................71
Brown, Terry (Oklahoma State).............76
Buehler, George (Stanford)..............78-9
Bumgardner, Rex (West Va.)..............50-2
Bundra, Mike (So. California)..............64
Burrell, Clinton (Louisiana St.)........79-80

Caleb, Jamie (Grambling)...............60, 65
Campbell, Milt (Indiana)...................57
Carollo, Joe (Notre Dame)...............72-3
Carpenter, Ken (Oregon St.).............50-3
Carpenter, Lew (Arkansas)...............57-8
Carpenter, Preston (Arkansas)...........56-9
Cassady, Howard (Ohio State)...............62
Catlin, Tom (Oklahoma).........53-4, 57-8
Caylor, Lowell (Miami-Ohio)................64
Cheroke, George (Ohio State)..............46

Clark, Monte (So. California)............63-9
Cline, Ollie (Ohio State)...................48
Cockroft, Don (Adams State).............68-80
Cole, Emerson (Toledo)...................50-2
Colella, Tom (Canisius)..................46-8
Coleman, Greg (Florida A & M).............77
Collins, Gary (Maryland)................62-71
Collins, Larry (Texas A & I)...............78
Colo, Don (Brown)........................53-8
Conjar, Larry (Notre Dame).................67
Connolly, Ted (Tulsa)......................63
Copeland, Jim (Virginia)................67-74
Coopage, Alton (Oklahoma).................46
Cornell, Bo (Washington).................71-2
Costello, Vince (Ohio U.)...............57-66
Cotton, Fest (Dayton)......................72
Cowan, Bob (Indiana).....................47-8
Cowher, Bill (Pittsburgh)..................80
Craig, Neal (Fisk).......................75-6
Craig, Reggie (Arkansas)...................77
Craven, Bill (Harvard).....................76
Crespino, Bob (Mississippi)..............61-3
Crews, Ron (Nevada-L.V.)...................80
Cureton, Will (E. Texas State).............75
Cverko, Andy (Northwestern)................63

Daniell, Jim (Ohio State)..................46
Darden, Thom. (Michigan)........72-4, 76-80
Darrow, Barry (Montana).................74-8
Davis, Ben (Defiance)...........67-8, 70-3
Davis, Dick (Nebraska).....................69
Davis, Oliver (Tenn. State).............77-80
Davis, Willie (Grambling)................58-9
Dawson, Len (Purdue).....................60-1
DeLamielleure, Joe (Mich. St.).............80
DeLeone, Tom (Ohio State)...............74-80
Dellerba, Spiro (Ohio State)...............47
DeMarco, Bob (Dayton)....................72-4
Demarie, John (Louisiana St.)...........67-75
Dennis, Al (Grambling)...................76-7
Dennison, Doug (Kutztown St.)..............79
Denton, Bob (College of Pacific)...........60
Deschaine, Dick (No College)...............58
Devrow, Billy (So. Mississippi)............67
Dewar, Jim (Indiana).......................47
Dieken, Doug (Illinois)..................71-80
Dimler, Rich (So. California)..............79
Donaldson, Gene (Kentucky).................53
Dunbar, Jubilee (Southern U.)..............74
Duncan, Brian (So. Methodist).............76-7
Duncan, Ron (Wittenberg)...................67

East, Ron (Montana State)..................75
Edwards, Earl (Wichita)..................76-8
Ellis, Ken (Southern U.)...................77
Engel, Steve (Colorado)....................70
Evans, Fred (Notre Dame)...................46
Evans, Johnny (N. Carolina St.)........78-80

Fairchild, Greg (Tulsa)....................78
Feacher, Ricky (Miss. Valley)...........76-80
Fekete, Gene (Ohio State)..................46

Browns' Colleges

Abilene Christian 1	Jackson State 2	Sam Houston State 1
Adams State 1	John Carroll 2	San Diego State 3
Alabama 2	Kansas 3	San Francisco State 1
Alcorn 1	Kansas State 2	San Jose State 2
Arizona 2	Kent State 2	Santa Clara 1
Arizona State 5	Kentucky 7	Shaw University 1
Arkansas 3	Kutztown State 1	South Carolina State 1
Arkansas AM & N 1	Langston 1	Southeastern Louisiana 1
Auburn 2	Louisiana State 4	Southern California 9
Baylor 2	Louisville 1	Southern Methodist 5
Boise State 1	Marquette 3	Southern Mississippi 1
Boston College 2	Marshall 2	Southern U. 6
Boston U. 1	Maryland 6	Southwest Texas State 2
Bowling Green 2	Maryland-E. Shore 1	Southwestern 1
Brown 1	Massachusetts 2	Stanford 3
California 1	Memphis State 2	Superior Teachers 1
California Poly 1	Miami 1	Syracuse 2
California State (L.A.) 2	Miami-Ohio 4	Temple 1
Canisius 1	Michigan 9	Tennessee 8
Carson-Newman 1	Michigan State 7	Tennessee-Martin 1
Case Tech 1	Mississippi 8	Tennessee A & I 1
Central Michigan 1	Mississippi Valley 1	Tennessee State 6
College of Pacific 3	Missouri 5	Texas 4
Colorado 6	Montana 1	Texas A & I 3
Colorado State 1	Montana State 1	Texas A & M 2
Dayton 3	Morgan State 2	Texas Arlington 1
Defiance 1	Nebraska 5	Texas Christian 3
Delta State 1	Nevada 3	Texas-El Paso 1
Detroit 1	Nevada-Las Vegas 1	Texas Southern 2
Duke 5	New Mexico 2	Texas Tech 1
Duquesne 1	Niagara 1	Toledo 3
East Texas State 1	No College 6	Trinity-San Antonio 1
Edinboro State 1	Norfolk State 1	Tulane 4
Findlay 1	North Carolina State 2	Tuskegee 1
Fisk 1	North Dakota 1	UCLA 2
Florida 2	North Texas State 2	Utah 1
Florida A & M 3	Northwestern 5	Vanderbilt 1
Florida State 3	Notre Dame 15	Villanova 1
Ft. Valley State 1	Ohio State 27	Virginia 4
Georgia 2	Ohio U. 3	Wake Forest 1
Georgia Tech 4	Oklahoma 6	Wayne-Neb. 1
Glassboro State 1	Oklahoma State 5	Waynesburg 2
Grambling 7	Oregon 1	West Virginia 1
Harvard 1	Oregon State 2	West Chester State 1
Heidelberg 2	Pennsylvania 1	West Texas State 1
Henderson State 1	Penn State 2	Western Kentucky 1
Hofstra 1	Pittsburgh 5	Western Reserve 1
Houston 5	C. W. Post 1	Wichita 1
Idaho 1	Prairie View 1	William & Mary 1
Illinois 7	Presbyterian 1	Wisconsin 2
Indiana 9	Princeton 1	Wittenberg 1
Iowa 1	Purdue 16	Wyoming 1
Iowa State 2	Rice 4	Yale 1
Iowa State Teachers 1	St. Vincent 1	Yankton 1

CLEVELAND BROWNS' ALL-TIME
INDIVIDUAL AND TEAM RECORDS

Note: The following individual records relate to service with the Cleveland Browns only. They include National Football League statistics only.

INDIVIDUAL RECORDS
SERVICE

Most Seasons

Career	17	Lou Groza (1950-59, 61-67)
	15	Gene Hickerson (1958-60, 62-73)
	14	Bob Gain (1952, 1954-66)
	13	Jim Houston (1960-72)
	13	Dick Schafrath (1959-71)
	13	Don Cockroft (1968-80)

Most Games

Career	216	Lou Groza (1950-59, 61-67)
	202	Gene Hickerson (1958-60, 62-73)

Most Consecutive Games

	188	Don Cockroft (1968-80)
	168	Walter Johnson (1965-76)

SCORING
Most Total Points

Career	1,349	Lou Groza (1950-59, 61-67) 641 PAT, 234 FG, 1 TD
	1,080	Don Cockroft (1968-80) 432 PAT, 216 FG
	756	Jim Brown (1957-65) 126 TD
	540	Leroy Kelly (1964-73) 90 TD
Season	126	Jim Brown (1965)
	120	Leroy Kelly (1968)
Game	36	Dub Jones (11-25-51 vs. Chi. Brs), 6 TD
	30	Jim Brown (11-1-59 vs. Balt.), 5 TD

Most Consecutive Games Scoring

	107	Lou Groza (1950) 9-(1959) 2

Most Touchdowns

Career	126	Jim Brown (1957-65)
	90	Leroy Kelly (1964-73)
	70	Gary Collins (1962-71)
	55	Ray Renfro (1952-63)
Season	21	Jim Brown (1965)
	20	Leroy Kelly (1968)
Game	6	Dub Jones (11-25-51) vs. Chi. Brs.)
	5	Jim Brown (11-1-59 vs. Balt.)

Most Consecutive Games Scoring Touchdowns

	10	Jim Brown (1965)
	9	Leroy Kelly (1968)

Most Points After Touchdown

Career	641	Lou Groza (1950-59, 61-67)
	432	Don Cockroft (1968-80)
Season	51	Lou Groza (1966)
	49	Lou Groza (1964)
Game	8	Lou Groza (12-6-53 vs. N.Y.)

Most Consecutive PATs Made

Career	138	Lou Groza (1963-66)

Most PATs Attempted

Career	658	Lou Groza (1950-59, 61-67)
	458	Don Cockroft (1968-80)
Season	52	Lou Groza (1966)
	50	Lou Groza (1964)
Game	8	Lou Groza (12-6-53 vs. N.Y.)

Most Field Goal Attempts

Career	405	Lou Groza (1950-59, 61-67)
	328	Don Cockroft (1968-80)
Season	33	Lou Groza (1952, 64)
	31	Lou Groza (1962)
	31	Don Cockroft (1973)
Game	7	Don Cockroft (10-19-75 vs. Den.)

Most Field Goals

Career	234	Lou Groza (1950-59, 61-67)
	216	Don Cockroft (1968-80)
Season	23	Lou Groza (1953)
	22	Lou Groza (1964)
	22	Don Cockroft (1972, 73)
Game	5	Don Cockroft (10-19-75 vs. Den.)

Longest Field Goal (Yards)

	57	Don Cockroft (10-29-72)
	52	Lou Groza (10-12-52 vs. N.Y.)

Most Consecutive Games Field Goals Made

	14	Lou Groza (1950) 10-(1951).4

Most Consecutive Field Goals

	16	Don Cockroft (1974)
		11-(1975) 5

RUSHING
Most Rushing Attempts

Career	2,359	Jim Brown (1957-65)
	1,727	Leroy Kelly (1964-73)
Season	305	Jim Brown (1961)
	291	Jim Brown (1963)
Game	37	Jim Brown (10-4-59 vs. Chi. Cards.)
	34	Jim Brown (10-12-58 vs. Chi. Cards.)
	34	Jim Brown (11-19-61 vs. Phil.)

Most Yards Rushing

Career	12,312	Jim Brown (1957-65)
	7,274	Leroy Kelly (1964-73)
Season	1,863	Jim Brown (1963)
	1,544	Jim Brown (1965)
Game	237	Jim Brown (11-24-57 vs. L.A.)
	237	Jim Brown (11-19-61 vs. Phil.)
	232	Bobby Mitchell (11-15-59 vs. Wash.)
	232	Jim Brown (9-22-63 vs. Dall.)
	214	Greg Pruitt (12-14-75 vs. K.C.)

Longest Rushing Plays (Yards)

	90	Bobby Mitchell (11-15-59 vs. Wash.) TD
	80	Jim Brown (9-15-63 vs. Wash.) TD

Most Touchdowns Rushing

Career	106	Jim Brown (1957-65)
	74	Leroy Kelly (1964-73)
Season	17	Jim Brown (1958, 65)
	16	Leroy Kelly (1968)
Game	5	Jim Brown (11-1-59 vs. Balt.)
	4	Dub Jones (11-25-51 vs. Chi. Brs.)
	4	Jim Brown (11-24-57 vs. L.A.)
	4	Jim Brown (10-26-58 vs. Chi. Cards.)
	4	Jim Brown (11-19-61 vs. Phil.)
	4	Jim Brown (11-18-62 vs. St. L.)
	4	Leroy Kelly (12-1-68 vs. N.Y.)

Most Consecutive Games Touchdowns Rushing

	9	Leroy Kelly (1968)
	7	Jim Brown (1957) 1, (1958) 6, (1962) 2, (1963) 5

Best Rushing Average (At Least 450 Attempts)

Career	5.22	Jim Brown (1957-65) 2,359-12,312
	4.77	Greg Pruitt (1973-80) 1,127-5,372
Season	6.40	Jim Brown (1963) 291-1,863
	5.94	Jim Brown (1958) 257-1,527
Game	17.09	Marion Motley (10-29-50 vs. Pitt.) 11-188
	16.57	Bobby Mitchell (11-15-59 vs. Wash.) 14-232

PASSING

Most Passing Attempts

Career	2,191	Brian Sipe (1974-80)
	1,755	Frank Ryan (1962-68)
Season	554	Brian Sipe (1980)
	535	Brian Sipe (1979)
Game	49	Otto Graham (10-4-52 vs. Pitt.)
	46	Brian Sipe (10-26-80 vs. Pitt.)

Most Passes Completed

Career	1,239	Brian Sipe (1974-80)
	907	Frank Ryan (1962-68)
Season	337	Brian Sipe (1980)
	286	Brian Sipe (1979)
Game	30	Brian Sipe (12-7-80 vs. N.Y.J.)
	28	Brian Sipe (10-26-80 vs. Pitt.)

Most Consecutive Completions

	13	Brian Sipe (9-28-80 vs. T. Bay)
	12	Brian Sipe (11-28-76 vs. Mia.)

Most Yards Passing

Career	15,207	Brian Sipe (1974-80)
	13,499	Otto Graham (1950-55)
Season	4,137	Brian Sipe (1980)
	3,793	Brian Sipe (1979)
Game	401	Otto Graham (10-4-52 vs. Pitt.)
	391	Brian Sipe (10-19-80 vs. G.B.)

Longest Pass Plays (Yards)

	87	Bill Nelsen (11-24-68 s. Phil.) to M. Morin
	86	Milt Plum (10-23-60 vs. Phil.) to L. Clarke, TD

Most Touchdown Passes

Career	134	Frank Ryan (1962-68)
	107	Brian Sipe (1974-80)
Season	30	Brian Sipe (1980)
	29	Frank Ryan (1966)
Game	5	Frank Ryan (12-12-64 vs. N.Y.)
	5	Bill Nelsen (11-2-69 vs. Dall.)
	5	Brian Sipe (10-7-79 vs. Pitt.)

Most Consecutive Games TD Passes

	23	Frank Ryan (1965) 1-(1967) 8
	18	Milt Plum (1959) 1-(1961) 5

Most Passes Had Intercepted

Career	94	Otto Graham (1950-55)
Season	26	Brian Sipe (1979) 535 atts.
	24	Otto Graham (1952) 364 atts.
Game	5	Otto Graham (10-17-54 vs. Pitt.) 29 atts.
	5	Frank Ryan (11-6-66 vs. Pitt.) 37 atts.

Most Consecutive Attempts None Intercepted
208   Milt Plum (1959-60)

Fewest Passes Had Intercepted
Career   39   Milt Plum (1957-61)
Season   5   Milt Plum (1960) 250 atts.
         7   Frank Ryan (1962) 194 atts.
Game   0   Brian Sipe (10-3-76 vs. Cin.)
               42 atts.
         0   Brian Sipe (11-18-79 vs.
               Mia.) 42 atts.

Highest Passing Percentage
Career   57.9 Milt Plum (1957-61)
               1,083-627
         56.5 Brian Sipe (1974-80)
               2,191-1,239
Season   64.7 Otto Graham (1953) 258-167
         60.8 Brian Sipe (1980) 554-337
Game   82.1 Brian Sipe (10-24-76 vs.
               S.D.) 28-23
         78.6 Otto Graham (10-17-54 vs.
               Pitt.) 28-22

PASS RECEIVING

Most Receptions
Career   331   Gary Collins (1962-71)
         283   Reggie Rucker (1975-80)
Season   63   Mike Pruitt (1980)
         62   Mac Speedie (1952)
Game   11   Mac Speedie (11-9-52 vs.
               Chi. Cards.)
         10   Dub Jones (12-10-50 vs.
               Wash.)
         10   Greg Pruitt (12-7-80 vs.
               N.Y.J.)

Most Consecutive Games Receptions
         36   Dave Logan (1978) 8-(1980)
               12

Most Yards Receiving
Career   5,508 Ray Renfro (1952-63)
         5,299 Gary Collins (1962-71)
Season   1,067 Paul Warfield (1968)
         982   Dave Logan (1979)
Game   182   Darrell Brewster (12-6-53 vs.
               N.Y.) 7
         177   Reggie Rucker (11-18-79 vs.
               Mia.) 9

Longest Reception (Yards)
         87   Milt Morin (11-24-68 vs.
               Phil.) B. Nelsen
         86   Leon Clarke (10-23-60 vs.
               Phil.) M. Plum - TD

Most Touchdowns Receiving
Career   70   Gary Collins (1962-71)
         52   Paul Warfield (1964-69,
               76-77)
Season   13   Gary Collins (1963)
         12   Gary Collins (1966)
         12   Paul Warfield (1968)
Game   3   Mac Speedie (11-25-51 vs.
               Chi. Brs.)
         3   Darrell Brewster (12-6-53 vs.
               N.Y.)
         3   Ray Renfro (11-22-59 vs.
               Pitt.)
         3   Gary Collins (10-20-63 vs.
               Phil.)
         3   Reggie Rucker (9-12-76 vs.
               N.Y.)
         3   Larry Poole (11-3-77 vs.
               Pitt.)
         3   Calvin Hill (11-19-78 vs.
               Balt.)

Most Consecutive Games TD Receptions
         7   Gary Collins (1963) 2-(1964)
               5
         6   Paul Warfield (1968)

Best Receiving Average
Career   19.6 Ray Renfro (1952-63) 281
         19.2 Paul Warfield (1964-69,
               76-77) 271
Season   29.0 Ray Renfro (1957) 21-589
         23.9 Ray Renfro (1958) 24-573
Game   39.3 Fair Hooker (10-27-70 vs.
               S.F.) 4-157
         34.3 Dante Lavelli (10-4-53 vs.
               Chi. Cards) 4-137

INTERCEPTIONS

Most Interceptions
Career   42   Thom Darden (1972-74,
               76-80)
         40   Warren Lahr (1950-59)
Season   10   Thom Darden (1978)
         9   Tommy James (1950)
Game   3   Tommy James (11-15-50 vs.
               Chi. Cards.)
         3   Tommy James (11-1-53 vs.
               Wash.)
         3   Bobby Franklin (12-11-60 vs.
               Chi. Brs.)
         3   Bernie Parrish (12-3-61 vs.
               Dall.)
         3   Ross Fichtner (10-23-66 vs.
               Dall.)
         3   Ron Bolton (11-27-77 vs.
               L.A.)

Most Yards, Interceptions Returned

Career	752	Thom Darden (1972-74, 76-80)
	581	Ross Fichtner (1960-67)
Season	238	Bernie Parrish (1960)
	200	Thom Darden (1978)
Game	115	Bernie Parrish (12-11-60 vs. Chi. Brs.) 2
	98	Ross Fichtner (10-23-66 vs. Dall.)

Longest Interception Returns (Yards)

92	Bernie Parrish (12-11-60 vs. Chi. Brs.), TD
88	Ross Fichtner (10-1-67 vs. N.O.), lateral from Erich Barnes

Most Touchdowns on Interceptions

Career	5	Warren Lahr (1948-59)
	4	Ken Konz (1953-59)
Season	2	Warren Lahr (1950, 51)
	2	Ken Konz (1954)
	2	Bobby Franklin (1960)
	2	Jim Houston (1967)
Game	2	Bobby Franklin (12-11-60 vs. Chi. Brs.)

Highest Average Gain on Interceptions

Career	21.5	Ross Fichtner (1960-67) 27
	19.2	Bernie Parrish (1959-66) 29
Season	39.7	Bernie Parrish (1960) 6
	32.0	Erich Barnes (1966) 4
Game	57.5	Bernie Parrish (12-11-60 vs. Chi. Brs.) 2
	41.5	Ken Konz (11-2-58 vs. N.Y.) 2

Most Consecutive Games Interceptions

7	Ben Davis (1968)

PUNTING

Most Punts

Career	651	Don Cockroft (1968-80)
	385	Horace Gillom (1950-56)
Season	90	Don Cockroft (1974
	82	Don Cockroft (1973, 75)
Game	12	Horace Gillom (12-3-50 vs. Phil.)
	11	Horace Gillom (10-4-53 vs. Chi. Cards.)
	11	Gary Collins (12-12-65 vs. L.A.)

Highest Average Yardage Punting

Career	43.8	Horace Gillom (1950-56) 385
	42.6	Sam Baker (1960-61) 108
Season	46.7	Gary Collins (1965) 65
	45.7	Horace Gillom (1952) 61
Game	54.8	Horace Gillom (11-28-54 vs. N.Y.) 4
	54.3	Gary Collins (10-17-65 vs. Dall.) 6

Longest Punts (Yards)

80	Horace Gillom (11-28-54 vs. N.Y.)
75	Horace Gillom (10-29-50 vs. Pitt.)

PUNT RETURNS

Most Punt Returns

Career	94	Leroy Kelly (1964-73)
	68	Ken Konz (1953-59)
Season	37	Keith Wright (1978)
	32	Rolly Woolsey (1977)
Game	7	Chet Hanulak (11-7-54 vs. Wash.)

Most Yards, Punt Returns

Career	990	Leroy Kelly (1964-73)
	659	Greg Pruitt (1973-80)
Season	349	Greg Pruitt (1974)
	295	Dino Hall (1979)
Game	109	Leroy Kelly (11-28-65 vs. Pitt.) 4
	101	Ken Carpenter (11-30-52 vs. Wash.) 4

Longest Punt Returns (Yards)

78	Bobby Mitchell (12-6-59 vs. N.Y.) TD
74	Leroy Kelly (10-24-71 vs. Den.)

Best Average Punt Returns

Career	11.8	Greg Pruitt (1973-80) 56
	11.2	Bobby Mitchell (1953-61) 54
Season	15.6	Leroy Kelly (1965) 17
	12.9	Greg Pruitt (1974) 27
Game	27.7	Bobby Mitchell (10-8-61 vs. Wash.) 3
	27.3	Leroy Kelly (11-28-65 vs. Pitt.) 4
	27.3	Greg Pruitt (10-27-74 vs. Den.) 3

Most Touchdowns, Punt Returns

Career	3	Bobby Mitchell (1958-61)
	3	Leroy Kelly (1964-73)
Season	2	Leroy Kelly (1965)
Game	1	By Several Players

KICKOFF RETURNS

Most Kickoff Returns

Career	82	Dino Hall (1979-80)
	76	Leroy Kelly (1964-73)
Season	50	Dino Hall (1979)
	32	Dino Hall (1980)
Game	9	Dino Hall (10-7-79 vs. Pitt.)
	8	Dino Hall (11-25-79 vs. Pitt.)

Most Yards Kickoff Returns

Career	1,781	Leroy Kelly (1964-73)
	1,705	Dino Hall (1979-80)
Season	1,014	Dino Hall (1979)
	789	Keith Wright (1978)
Game	172	Dino Hall (10-7-79 vs. Pitt.)
	165	Greg Pruitt (11-3-74 vs. S.D.)

Longest Kickoff Returns (Yards)

	104	Carl Ward (11-26-67 vs. Wash.) TD
	102	Leroy Bolden (10-26-58 vs. Chi. Cards.) TD

Best Average Kickoff Returns

Career	28.9	Bo Scott (1969-73) 25
	26.5	Keith Wright (1978-79) 45
Season	28.9	Bo Scott (1969) 25
	28.3	Greg Pruitt (1973) 16
Game	42.0	Keith Wright (9-2-79 vs. N.Y.J.) 3
	37.0	Leroy Kelly (9-26-65 vs. St. L.) 3

Most Touchdowns, Kickoff Returns

Career	3	Bobby Mitchell (1958-61)
	1	By Several Players
Season	1	By Several Players
Game	1	By Several Players

COMBINED NET YARDS GAINED

Attempts

Career	2,658	Jim Brown (1957-65)
	1,987	Leroy Kelly (1964-73)
Season	354	Jim Brown (1961)
	323	Jim Brown (1965)
Game	39	Jim Brown (10-4-59 vs. Chi. Cards.)
	38	Jim Brown (11-19-61 vs. Phil.)

Combined Yardage

Career	15,459	Jim Brown (1957-65)
	12,239	Leroy Kelly (1964-73)
Season	2,131	Jim Brown (1963)
	2,014	Leroy Kelly (1966)
Game	313	Jim Brown (11-19-61 vs. Phil.)
	299	Leroy Kelly (12-4-66 vs. N.Y.)

Average Gain

Career	8.84	Bobby Mitchell (1958-61) 669-5,916
	6.58	Greg Pruitt (1973-80) 1,495-9,836
Season	9.25	Bobby Mitchell (1961) 163-1,508
	9.03	Greg Pruitt (1974) 196-1,769
Game	14.95	Leroy Kelly (12-4-66 vs. N.Y.) 20-299
	14.82	Bobby Mitchell (11-15-59 vs. Wash.) 17-252

TEAM RECORDS

SCORING

Most Points

Season	415	(1964)
Game	62	(12-6-53 vs. N.Y.)
	62	(11-7-54 vs. Wash.)

Most Points Against

Season	372	(1975)
Game	55	(10-17-54, Pitt.)
	55	(11-12-67, G.B.)

Fewest Points

Season	167	(1956 - 12 games)
	218	(1975 - 14 games)

Most Points, Both Teams

Game	89	(12-4-66, Cleve. 49 vs. N.Y. 40)
	86	(10-7-79, Pitt. 51 vs. Cleve. 35)

Fewest Points, Both Teams

Game	6	(10-1-50, N.Y. 6 vs. Cleve. 0)
	6	(11-21-54, Cleve. 6 vs. Phil. 0)

Most Touchdowns

Season	54	(1966)
Game	8	(12-6-53 vs. N.Y.)
	8	(11-7-54 vs. Wash.)

Most Touchdowns Against

Season	48	(1975)
Game	8	(10-17-54, Pitt.)

Fewest Touchdowns

Season	19	(1956 - 12 games)
	24	(1973, 75 - 14 games)

Fewest Touchdowns Against

Season	19	(1950 - 12 games)
	24	(1973 - 14 games)

Most Touchdowns Rushing

Season	24	(1958)
Game	6	(11-24-57 vs. L.A.)

Most Touchdowns Rushing Against

Season	21	(1975)
Game	6	(10-15-61, G.B.)

Fewest Touchdowns Rushing

Season	8	(1956)

Fewest Touchdowns Rushing Against

Season	4	(1954)

Most Touchdowns Passing

Season	33	(1966)
Game	6	(12-12-65 vs. N.Y.)
	6	(10-30-66 vs. Atl.)

Fewest Touchdowns Passing

Season	7	(1975)

Most Touchdowns Passing Against

Season	31	(1965)
Game	6	(9-26-65, St. L.)

Fewest Touchdowns Passing Against

Season	7	(1956)

Most Points After Touchdown
Season   52   (1966)
Game   8   (12-6-53 vs. N.Y.)
          8   (11-7-54 vs. Wash.)

Fewest Points After Touchdown
Season   18   (1956)

Most Points After Touchdown Against
Season   45   (1975)
Game   7   (10-17-54, Pitt.)
          7   (11-12-67, G.B.)

Fewest Points After Touchdown Against
Season   18   (1950, 51)

Most Field Goals
Season   23   (1953)
Game   5   (10-19-75 vs. Den.)

Fewest Field Goals
Season   5   (1959)

Most Field Goals Against
Season   29   (1973)
Game   4   (10-12-75 - most recently by
               Hou.)
          4   (by 10 other clubs)

Fewest Field Goals Against
Season   2   (1953)

Most Points, Each Quarter
1st: 21   (12-3-61 vs. Dall.)
2nd: 24   (11-8-63 vs. Pitt.)
3rd: 24   (12-6-53 vs. N.Y.)
4th: 28   (10-25-64 vs. N.Y.)

FIRST DOWNS

Most First Downs
Season   350   (1979)
Game   34   (10-30-77 vs. K.C.)

Most First Downs by Opponents
Season   340   (1980)
Game   36   (11-25-79, Pitt.)

Most First Downs, Both Teams
Game   58   (11-25-79 vs. Pitt.)

Most First Downs Rushing
Season   135   (1963)
Game   21   (12-13-59 vs. Phil.)

Most First Downs Rushing by Opponents
Season   136   (1979)
Game   20   (10-10-64, Pitt.)

Most First Downs Passing
Season   207   (1980)
Game   21   10-26-80 vs. Pitt.)

Most First Downs Passing by Opponents
Season   197   (1980)
Game   21   (12-14-80 vs. Minn.)

Most First Downs by Penalty
Season   36   (1979)
Game   7   (10-23-77 vs. Buff.)

Most First Downs by Penalty by Opponents
Season   38   (1978, 80)
Game   9   (11-25-51, Chi. Brs.)

NET YARDS

Most Net Yards Gained
Season 5,772   (1979)
Game   550   (11-25-51 vs. Chi. Brs.)

Fewest Net Yards Gained
Season 3,020   (1956)
Game   60   (10-24-71 vs. Den.)

Most Net Yards Gained by Opponents
Season 5,650   (1979)
Game   606   (11-25-79, Pitt.)

Fewest Net Yards Gained by Opponents
Season 2,658   (1954)
Game   64   (11-7-54, Wash.)

RUSHING

Most Yards Gained Rushing
Season 2,639   (1963)
Game   338   (10-29-50 vs. Pitt.)

Fewest Yards Gained Rushing
Season 1,558   (1971)
Game   5   (9-17-67 vs. Dall.)
        6   (11-6-60 vs. N.Y.)

Most Yards Gained Rushing by Opponents
Season 2,604   (1979)
Game   361   (10-7-79, Pitt.)
        354   (10-10-64, Pitt.)

Fewest Yards Gained Rushing by Opponents
Season 1,050   (1954)
Game   4   (11-28-54, N.Y.)

Most Rushing Attempts
Season 559   (1978)
Game   60   (10-2-55 vs. S.F.)

Fewest Rushing Attempts
Season 379   (1953)
Game   10   (11-9-69 vs. Minn.)

Most Rushing Attempts by Opponents
Season 577   (1979)
Game   64   (10-10-64, Pitt.)

Fewest Rushing Attempts by Opponents
Season 372   (1954)
Game   15   (9-19-71, Hou.)

PASSING

Most Yards Gained Passing
Season 4,132   (1980)
Game   401   (10-4-52 vs. Pitt.)

Fewest Yards Gained Passing
Season 1,175   (1956)
Game   0   (12-3-50 vs. Phil.)

Most Yards Gained Passing by Opponents
Season 4,089   (1980)
Game   401   (12-16-59, N.Y.)

Fewest Yards Gained Passing by Opponents
Season   1,103   (1956)
Game   3   (11-18-56, Phil.)

Most Passes Attempted
Season   554   (1980)
Game   49   (10-4-52 vs. Pitt.)

Fewest Passes Attempted
Season   195   (1957)
Game   0   (12-3-50 vs. Phil.)

Most Passes Attempted by Opponents
Season   536   (1980)
Game   56   (9-28-80, T. Bay)

Fewest Passes Attempted by Opponents
Season   226   (1956)
Game   7   (11-24-76, Buff.)

Most Passes Completed
Season   337   (1980)
Game   30   (12-7-80 vs. N.Y.J.)

Fewest Passes Completed
Season   105   (1956)
Game   0   (12-3-50 vs. Phil.)

Most Passes Completed by Opponents
Season   336   (1980)
Game   38   (12-14-80, Minn.)

Fewest Passes Completed by Opponents
Season   105   (1957)
Game   1   (11-24-74, Buff.)

INTERCEPTIONS

Most Interceptions
Season   32   (1968)
Game   7   (12-11-60 vs. Chi. Brs.)

Fewest Interceptions
Season   10   (1975)

Most Interceptions by Opponents
Season   31   (1977)
Game   6   (10-17-54, Pitt.)
          6   (9-26-65, St. L.)

Fewest Interceptions by Opponents
Season   5   (1960)

Most Yards Interceptions Returned
Season   624   (1960)
Game   213   (12-11-60 vs. Chi. Brs.)

Fewest Yards Interceptions Returned
Season   107   (1975)

Most Yards Interceptions Returned by Opponents
Season   453   (1971)
Game   147   (10-17-54, Pitt.)

Fewest Yards Interceptions Returned by Opponents
Season   58   (1960)

Most Touchdowns by Interceptions
Season   6   (1960)
Game   3   (12-11-60 vs. Chi. Brs.)

Most Touchdowns by Interceptions by Opponents
Season   4   (1970)
Game   2   (10-17-54, Pitt.)
         2   (10-18-70, Det.)

PUNTING

Most Punts
Season   90   (1974)
Game   12   (12-3-50 vs. Phil.)

Most Punts by Opponents
Season   82   (1978)
Game   11   (11-18-51, N.Y.)
         11   (10-4-52, Pitt.)
         11   (11-18-73, Oak.)

Fewest Punts
Season   45   (1962)

Fewest Punts by Opponents
Season   46   (1960)

Highest Punting Average
Season   45.7   (1952, 65)
Game   54.8   (11-28-54 vs. N.Y.)

Highest Punting Average by Opponents
Season   45.5   (1960)
Game   57.5   (11-20-60, Pitt.)

PUNT RETURNS

Most Punt Returns
Season   61   (1954)
Game   8   (11-7-54 vs. Wash.)
          8   (11-28-54 vs. N.Y.)
          8   (11-18-56 vs. Phil.)

Fewest Punt Returns
Season   20   (1962, 64)

Most Punt Returns by Opponents
Season   68   (1974)
Game   12   (12-3-50, Phil.)

Fewest Punt Returns by Opponents
Season   15   (1962)

Most Yardage Punt Returns
Season   523   (1974)
Game   137   (11-17-74 vs. Pitt.)

Fewest Yardage Punt Returns
Season   96   (1968)

Most Yardage Punt Returns by Opponents
Season   705   (1974)
Game   149   (9-22-74, Hou.)

Fewest Yardage Punt Returns by Opponents
Season   39   (1959)

Most Touchdowns by Punt Returns
Season   2   (1965)
Game   1   (11 times)

Most Touchdowns, Punt Returns by Opponents
Season   3   (1977)
Game   2   (9-26-77, Den.)

KICKOFF RETURNS

Most Kickoff Returns
Season   75   (1979)
Game   9   (10-17-54 vs. Pitt.)
          9   (10-7-79 vs. Pitt.)

Most Kickoff Returns by Opponents
Season   75   (1964)
Game   9   (11-7-54, Wash.)

Most Kickoff Return Yardage
Season 1,697 (1978)
Game   256 (11-7-65 vs. Phil.)

Most Kickoff Return Yardage by Opponents
Season 1,517 (1964)
Game   236 (12-15-63, Wash.)
          236 (12-4-66, N.Y.)

Most Touchdowns, Kickoff Returns
Season   2   (1958)
Game   1   (7 times)

**Most Touchdowns, Kickoff Returns by
  Opponents**
Season   2   (1966, 67)
Game   1   (several times)

PENALTIES

Most Penalties
Season   128 (1978)
Game   21   (11-25-51 vs. Chi. Brs.)

Most Penalties by Opponents
Season   131 (1978)
Game   16   (11-25-51, Chi. Brs.)

Fewest Penalties
Season   36   (1959)

Fewest Penalties by Opponents
Season   32   (1959)
Game   0   (9 times)

Most Penalty Yards
Season 1,170 (1978)
Game   209 (11-25-51 vs. Chi. Brs.)

Most Penalty Yards by Opponents
Season 1,110 (1978)
Game   165 (11-25-51, Chi. Brs.)

FUMBLES

Most Fumbles
Season   50   (1978)
Game   7   (10-25-53 vs. N.Y.)
          7   (12-12-71 vs. N.O.)

Most Fumbles by Opponents
Season   39   (1972)
Game   8   (11-12-50, S.F.)
          8   (10-5-58, Pitt.)

Most Fumbles Lost
Season   29   (1978)
Game   5   (12-12-71 vs. N.O.)

Most Fumbles Lost by Opponents
Season   22   (1969)
Game   6   (11-12-50, S.F.)

SHUTOUTS

Most Shutouts
Season   4   (1951)

Most Shutouts Against
Season   2   (1972)

BROWNS IN PRO FOOTBALL HALL OF FAME

Otto Graham	1965	Lou Groza	1974
Paul Brown	1967	Dante Lavelli	1975
Marion Motley	1968	Len Ford	1976
Jim Brown	1971	Bill Willis	1977

Browns' Championship
Playoff Scores — NFL

1950........CLEVELAND 30, Los Angeles 28
1951........Los Angeles 24, CLEVELAND 17
1952.......Detroit 17, CLEVELAND 7
1953........Detroit 17, CLEVELAND 16
1954........CLEVELAND 56, Detroit 10
1955........CLEVELAND 38, Los Angeles 14
1957.......Detroit 59, CLEVELAND 14
1964.......CLEVELAND 27, Baltimore 0
1965........Green Bay 23, CLEVELAND 12
1968........Baltimore 34, CLEVELAND 0
1969........Minnesota 27, CLEVELAND 7

Browns' Conference Playoff
Game Scores

1950........CLEVELAND 8, New York 3
1957........New York 10, CLEVELAND 0
1967.......Dallas 52, CLEVELAND 14
1968.......CLEVELAND 31, Dallas 20
1969........CLEVELAND 38, Dallas 14

Browns' Divisional Playoff
Game Scores

1971........Baltimore 20, CLEVELAND 3
1972.......Miami 20, CLEVELAND 14
1980........Oakland 14, CLEVELAND 12

Browns' College All-Star
Game Scores

1951........CLEVELAND 33, All-Stars 0
1955........All-Stars 30, CLEVELAND 27
1956.......CLEVELAND 26, All-Stars 0
1965.......CLEVELAND 24, All-Stars 16

ATTENDANCE DATA

10 Largest Stadium Crowds*

85,703	New York Jets	1970
85,532	Doubleheader	1969
84,918	Doubleheader	1968
84,850	Dallas	1969
84,721	Dallas	1966
84,684	Pittsburgh	1963
84,349	Pittsburgh	1970
84,285	Oakland	1971
84,236	Doubleheader	1967
84,213	New York Giants	1963

*There have been 64 crowds over 80,000.

10 Largest Road Crowds

92,180	Chicago All-Star	1951
87,695	Los Angeles	1955
80,010	Miami	1972
77,045	New Orleans	1967
76,251	Dallas	1965
75,504	Dallas	1966
75,313	Miami	1970
75,283	Detroit	1975
75,000	Chicago All-Star	1955
75,000	Chicago All-Star	1956

NFL CLUB RECORDS IN CLEVELAND

Atlanta	76,825	1971
Baltimore	80,628	1968
Buffalo	70,104	1972
Chicago	83,224	1980
Cincinnati	83,520	1970
Dallas	84,850	1969
Denver	81,065	1980
Detroit	83,577	1970
Green Bay	83,943	1966
Houston	80,243	1980
Kansas City	83,819	1972
Los Angeles	82,514	1968
Miami	80,374	1979
Minnesota	83,505	1965

New England	76,418	1977
New Orleans	70,125	1968
New York Giants	84,213	1963
New York Jets	85,703	1970
Oakland	84,285	1971
Philadelphia	79,289	1964
Pittsburgh	84,684	1963
St. Louis	81,186	1969
San Diego	80,047	1970
San Francisco	80,698	1953
Seattle	72,440	1979
Washington	82,251	1969

BROWNS' RECORDS IN EACH CITY — NFL

Atlanta	57,235	1966
Baltimore	60,238	1968
Buffalo	60,905	1977
Chicago	48,773	1954
Cincinnati	60,284	1971
Dallas	76,251	1965
Denver	62,973	1976
Detroit	75,283	1975
Green Bay	50,852	1965
Green Bay (Milwaukee)	50,074	1967
Houston	51,514	1980
Kansas City	70,296	1973
Los Angeles	87,695	1955
Miami	80,010	1972
Minnesota	47,900	1969
New England	57,263	1974
New York Giants	72,576	1977
New York Jets	62,614	1972
New Orleans	77,045	1967
Oakland	54,463	1970
Philadelphia	71,237	1950
Pittsburgh	54,563	1980
San Diego	54,205	1972
St. Louis	47,845	1979
San Francisco	52,219	1951
Seattle	62,262	1978
Tampa Bay	65,540	1980
Washington	53,041	1971

1980 ATTENDANCE SUMMARY

HOME

1	Pre-Season Game...................	54,986
8	League Games....................	620,496
1	Playoff Game....................	74,655
	Total Home Attendance........	753,137

ROAD

3	Pre-Season Games................	143,005
8	League Games....................	419,834
	Total Road Attendance..........	562,839
	TOTAL ATTENDANCE......	1,315,976

ATTENDANCE DATA
1946-1980

Year	Home Games	Home Attendance	Road Attendance	Pre-Season Attendance	Playoffs & Championship	Total Attendance
1946	7	399,962	206,060	35,964	40,469	682,455
1947	7	392,760	270,619	33,106	61,879	758,364
1948	7	318,619	270,728	43,279	22,981	655,607
1949	6	189,604	211,565	63,997	39,820	504,986
1950	6	200,319	232,361	125,642	62,805	621,127
1951	6	231,414	231,854	259,359	57,540	780,167
1952	6	240,204	200,656	116,310	50,934	608,104
1953	6	274,671	183,272	189,571	54,577	702,091
1954	6	183,476	200,101	182,255	43,827	609,659
1955	6	251,444	220,892	247,200	87,695	807,231
1956	6	221,648	161,887	302,221	......	685,756
1957	6	324,165	222,185	226,348	55,263	827,961
1958	6	370,781	264,375	224,602	61,174	920,932
1959	6	338,380	257,990	191,477	......	787,847
1960	6	337,972	234,767	*197,513	......	770,252
1961	7	426,886	268,909	173,603	......	869,398
1962	7	422,043	289,807	240,081	......	951,931
1963	7	487,430	331,642	*267,807	......	1,086,879
1964	7	549,334	337,929	218,544	79,544	1,185,351
1965	7	557,283	369,055	254,591	50,852	1,231,781
1966	7	544,250	389,783	246,708	......	1,180,741
1967	7	544,807	402,976	*295,514	70,786	1,314,083
1968	7	527,107	366,524	291,232	162,125	1,346,988
1969	7	578,360	380,442	283,248	117,221	1,359,271
1970	7	567,377	379,082	347,558	......	1,294,017
1971	7	541,505	381,467	334,051	74,082	1,331,105
1972	7	528,591	382,182	397,140	80,010	1,387,923
**1973	7	490,406	382,124	329,183	......	1,201,713
1974	7	424,412	319,684	200,904	......	945,000
1975	7	390,440	358,175	180,338	......	928,953
1976	7	472,602	310,340	183,434	......	966,376
1977	7	480,805	380,166	248,178	......	1,109,149
1978	8	510,046	397,891	127,918	......	1,035,855
1979	8	593,821	400,029	169,623	......	1,163,473
1980	8	620,496	419,834	197,991	77,655	1,315,976
		14,533,420	10,617,353	7,426,490	1,351,239	33,928,502

* Includes Miami Playoff games at end of season.
** First year of new method for announcing attendance.

OPPONENTS'
BEST SINGLE GAME MARKS VS. BROWNS

SCORING

Most Points

24　Ray Matthews, Pitt., Oct. 17, 1954
24　Jim Taylor, G.B., Oct. 15, 1961
24　Donny Anderson, G.B., Nov. 12, 1967

Most Touchdowns

4　Same as above

Most PATs Attempted

8　Paul Held, Pitt., Oct. 17, 1954
8　*Jim Martin, Det., Dec. 29, 1957
8　Paul Hornung, G.B., Oct. 15, 1961

Most PATs Made

8　*Jim Martin, Det., Dec. 29, 1957
7　Paul Held, Pitt., Oct. 17, 1954
7　Paul Hornung, G.B., Oct. 15, 1961
7　Don Chandler, G.B., Nov. 12, 1967

Most Field Goals Attempted

6　Roy Gerela, Pitt., Nov. 7, 1971
6　Chester Marcol, G.B., Sept. 17, 1972
6　Skip Butler, Hou., Oct. 12, 1975

Most Field Goals Made

4　10 times by seven players including Roy Gerela three times and Don Chandler twice; last accomplished by Skip Butler, Hou., Oct. 12, 1975.

Longest Field Goal Made (Yards)

53　Jim Turner, Den., Oct. 19, 1975

RUSHING

Most Attempts

30　John Henry Johnson, Pitt., Oct. 10, 1964

Most Yards Gained

200　John Henry Johnson, Pitt., Oct. 10, 1964

Highest Average Gain (Yards)

11.6　Tim Brown, Phil., Nov. 7, 1965

Longest Gain (Yards)

80　Essex Johnson, Cin., Dec. 5, 1971

Most Touchdowns

4　Jim Taylor, G.B., Oct. 15, 1961

PASSING

Most Attempts

56　Doug Williams, T. Bay, Sept. 28, 1980

Most Completions

38　Tommy Kramer, Minn., Dec. 14, 1980

Most Yards

456　Same as above

Passing Efficiency

88.2　Bart Starr, G.B., Oct. 15, 1961 (15 completions in 17 attempts)

Longest Completion (Yards)

99　George Izo, Wash. (to Bobby Mitchell), Sept. 15, 1963
99　*Bart Starr, G.B. (to Tom Moore) Jan. 5, 1964

Most TD Passes

6　Charley Johnson, St. L., Sept. 26, 1965

Most Interceptions

6　*Bobby Layne, Det., Dec. 26, 1954
6　*Norm Van Brocklin, L.A., Dec. 26, 1955
5　Zeke Bratkowski, Chi., Dec. 11, 1960

PASS RECEPTIONS

Most Receptions

11　Raymond Berry, Balt., Nov. 1, 1959 (156 yards)
11　Charley Taylor, Wash., Nov. 26, 1967 (123 yards)

Most Yards

235　Buddy Dial, Pitt., Oct. 22, 1961
200　Tommy McDonald, L.A., Dec. 12, 1965
200　Charlie Joiner, Cin., Nov. 23, 1975

Average Gain (Yards)

48.0　John Gilliam, St. L., Oct. 26, 1969 (4 catches for 192 yards)

Longest Gain (Yards)

99　Bobby Mitchell, Wash. (from George Izo), Sept. 15, 1963
99　*Tom Moore, G.B. (from Bart Starr), Jan. 5, 1964

Touchdowns

3　By 7 players; last accomplished by Isaac Curtis, Dec. 9, 1973

INTERCEPTIONS

Most Interceptions

3　By 6 players; last accomplished by Bobby Bryant, Minn., Nov. 9, 1969

Interception Yardage

115　Larry Wilson, St. L., Dec. 19, 1965 (3 returns)

Average Gain

38.3　Same as above

Longest Interception Return (Yards)

96　Same as above

Touchdowns
1 By many players

PUNTING
Number
11 Charley Conerly, N.Y., Nov. 18, 1951
11 Ray Guy, Oak., Nov. 18, 1973

Most Yards
491 Ray Guy, Oak., Nov. 18, 1973

Highest Average (Yards)
57.5 Bobby Joe Greene, Pitt., Nov. 20, 1960
(4 for 230 yards)

Longest (Yards)
75 Verl Lillywhite, S.F., Sept. 30, 1951

PUNT RETURNS
Number
7 Russ Craft, Phil., Dec. 3, 1950

Most Yards
125 Rick Upchurch, Den., Sept. 26, 1976

*Denotes post-season playoff or championship game.

Highest Average (Yards)
31.1 Rick Upchurch, Den., Sept. 26, 1976 (4 returns)

Longest (Yards)
87 Billy Johnson, Hou., Oct. 16, 1977

Touchdowns
2 Rick Upchurch, Den., Sept. 26, 1976

KICKOFF RETURNS
Number
6 Rick Upchurch, Den., Oct. 19, 1975

Most Yards
197 Same as above

Highest Average (Yards)
86.0 Travis Williams, G.B., Nov. 12, 1967 (2 returns)

Longest (Yards)
105 Tim Brown, Phil., Sept. 17, 1961

Touchdowns
2 Travis Williams, G.B., Nov. 12, 1967

BROWNS' BIGGEST DAYS
RUSHING
237 - Jim Brown vs. Los Angeles, Nov. 24, 1957 (31 carries)
237 - Jim Brown vs. Philadelphia, Nov. 19, 1961 (34 carries)
232 - Bobby Mitchell vs. Washington, Nov. 15, 1959 (14 carries)
232 - Jim Brown vs. Dallas, Sept. 23, 1963 (20 carries)
223 - Jim Brown vs. Philadelphia, Nov. 3, 1963 (28 carries)
214 - Greg Pruitt vs. Kansas City, Dec. 14, 1975 (26 carries)

PASSING
401 - Otto Graham vs. Pittsburgh, Oct. 4, 1952 (21 of 49)
391 - Brian Sipe vs. Green Bay, Oct. 19, 1980 (24 of 39)
369 - Otto Graham vs. Chi. Cards., Oct. 15, 1950 (22 of 35)
367 - Frank Ryan vs. St. Louis, Dec. 17, 1966 (17 of 30)
358 - Brian Sipe vs. Miami, Nov. 18, 1979 (23 of 42)
351 - Brian Sipe vs. Pittsburgh, Oct. 7, 1979 (22 of 41)

RECEIVING
182 - Pete Brewster vs. New York, Dec. 6, 1953 (7 catches)
177 - Reggie Rucker vs. Miami, Nov. 18, 1979 (7 catches)
166 - Ray Renfro vs. New York, Nov. 26, 1961 (7 catches)
161 - Dub Jones vs. Washington, Dec. 10, 1950 (10 catches)
161 - Mac Speedie vs. New York, Oct. 12, 1952 (8 catches)
161 - Ray Renfro vs. Pittsburgh, Nov. 22, 1959 (5 catches)
161 - Paul Warfield vs. St. Louis, Dec. 17, 1966 (6 catches)

THE LAST TIME . . .

PUNT RETURNED FOR TD
By Browns - Ben Davis (52 yards) vs. Pittsburgh, Nov. 5, 1967.
By Opponent - Billy Johnson, Houston (72 yards), Dec. 11, 1977.

KICKOFF RETURNED FOR TD
By Browns - Greg Pruitt (88 yards) vs. New England, Nov. 10, 1974.
By Opponent - Larry Anderson, Pittsburgh (95 yards), Oct. 15, 1978.

INTERCEPTED PASS RETURNED FOR TD
By Browns - Thom Darden (39 yards) vs. Dallas, Sept. 24, 1979.
By Opponent - Ray Griffin, Cincinnati (52 yards), Dec. 21, 1980.

FUMBLE RETURNED FOR TD
By Browns - Joe Jones (0 yards, recovered in end zone) vs. Tampa Bay, Nov. 21, 1976.
By Opponent - Steve Neils, St. Louis (72 yards), Oct. 28, 1979.

PUNT BLOCKED
By Browns - Joe Jones vs. Kansas City, Dec. 14, 1975.
By Opponent - Larry Braziel, Baltimore, Sept. 16, 1979.

SHUTOUT SCORED
By Browns - Cleveland 7, San Francisco 0, Dec. 1, 1974.
By Opponent - Los Angeles 9, Cleveland 0, Nov. 27, 1977.

PAT UNSUCCESSFUL
By Browns - Don Cockroft vs. Minnesota, Dec. 14, 1980.
By Opponent - Rick Danmeier, Minnesota, Dec. 14, 1980.

BROWNS ON MONDAY NIGHTS

*Sept. 21, 1970	CLEVELAND 31, New York Jets 21	at Cleve.
Dec. 7, 1970	CLEVELAND 21, Houston 10	at Hou.
Oct. 4, 1971	Oakland 34, CLEVELAND 20	at Cleve.
Nov. 13, 1972	CLEVELAND 21, San Diego 17	at S.D.
Oct. 15, 1973	Miami 17, CLEVELAND 9	at Cleve.
Sept. 26, 1977	CLEVELAND 30, New England 27 (OT)	at Cleve.
Sept. 24, 1979	CLEVELAND 26, Dallas 7	at Cleve.
Sept. 15, 1980	Houston 16, CLEVELAND 7	at Cleve.
Nov. 3, 1980	CLEVELAND 27, Chicago 21	at Cleve.

W 6, L 3

*First game ever on Monday night TV.

ALL-TIME BROWNS' SCORING (NFL)

	TD	PAT	FG	TOT.
Groza	1	641	234	1,349
Cockroft		432	216	1,080
J. Brown	126			756
Kelly	90			540
G. Collins	70			420
Renfro	55			330
Warfield	53			318
G. Pruitt	39			234
B. Mitchell	38			228
E. Green	35			210
Graham	34			204
Lavelli	33			198
W. Jones	32			192
Rucker	31			188
B. Scott	24			144
M. Pruitt	23			138
Brewster	19			114
K. Carpenter	17			102
Hill	16			96
Logan	16			96
Newsome	16			96
Kreitling	15			90
C. Miller	15			90
Baker		44	12	80
Bassett	11			66
E. Modz'l'ski			66	
Phipps	11			66
Sipe	10	1		61
K. Brown	9			54
Roan	9			54
Speedie	9			54
Plum	8	2		50
Motley	8			48
Hooker	8			48
Brewer	7			42
Hanulak	7			42
Jagade	7			42
R. Johnson	7			42
F. Morrison	7			42
L. Carpenter	6			36
P. Carpenter	6			36
L. Clarke	6			36
McKinnis	6			36
C. White	6			36
B. Reynolds	6			36
Konz	5	3		33
Bumgardner	5	3		33
Feacher	30			30
C. Glass	5			30
Lahr	5			30
McNeil	5			30
Parris	5			30
Poole	5			30
Roberts	5			30
Scales	5			30
R. Smith	5			30
J. Houston	4	1		25
Holden	4			24
R. Morrison	4			24
Nagler	4			24
Parrish	4			24
Phelps	4			24
Ryan	4			24
Barnes	3			18
Darden	3			18
Fichtner	3			18
Franklin	3			18
Gillom	3			18
Howard	3			18
O'Connell	3			18
Paul	3	18		
Ratterman	3			18
Richardson	3			18
C. Scott	3			18
K. Wright	3			18
W. Johnson	2			*14
Noll	2			*14
Barney	2			12
Costello	2			12
Crespino	2			12
B. Duncan	2			12
B. Glass	2			12
V. Green	2			12
Grigg		9	1	12
C. Hall	2			12
Hutchinson	2			12
H. Jones	2			12
Michaels	2			12
Moriarty	2			12
Taseff	2			12
Wiggin	2			12
Gain	1		1	9
Ford	1			*8
Wren	1			*8
Young	1			*8
Andrews	1			6
Beach	1			6
Bolden	1			6
Bolton	1			6
Briggs	1			6
Caleb	1			6
Campbell	1			6
Cole	1			6
L. Collins	1			6
B. Davis	1			6
O. Davis	1			6
Ferguson	1			6
Gault	1			6
Gorgal	1			6
D. Hall	1			6

	TD	PAT	FG	TOT.			TD	PAT	FG	TOT.
Harraway	1			6	Oristaglio	1			6
Helluin	1			6	Roman	1			6
J. Hill	1			6	Shoals	1			6
Howton	1			6	B. Smith	1			6
Irons	1			6	Staroba	1			6
T. James	1			6	Stephens	1			6
J. Jones	1			6	Sumner	1			6
Kellerman	1			6	Ward	1			6
Kinard	1			6	Watkins	1			6
Leigh	1			6	S. Williams	1			6
Lindsey	1			6	Dieken				*2
Luck	1			6	East				*2
McDonald	1			6	Kissell				*2
M. Miller	1			6	M. Mitchell				*2
W. Miller	1			6	C. Reynolds				*2
Minniear	1			6	Sherk				*2
Nelsen	1			6	Snidow				*2

*Includes safety.

1,191	1,133	464	9,695

BROWNS' LEADERS — 1946-1980

RUSHING

	ATT.	YDS.	AVG.		ATT.	YDS.	AVG.
1946				**1965**			
Motley	73	601	8.2	J. Brown	289	1544	5.3
1947				**1966**			
Motley	146	889	6.1	Kelly	209	1141	5.5
1948				**1967**			
Motley	157	964	6.1	Kelly	235	1205	5.1
1949				**1968**			
Motley	113	570	5.0	Kelly	248	1239	5.0
1950				**1969**			
Motley	140	810	5.8	Kelly	196	817	4.2
1951				**1970**			
W. Jones	104	492	4.8	Kelly	206	656	3.2
1952				**1971**			
Motley	104	444	4.3	Kelly	234	865	3.7
1953				**1972**			
Jagade	86	344	4.0	Kelly	224	811	3.6
1954				**1973**			
Bassett	144	588	4.0	K. Brown	161	537	3.3
1955				Kelly	132	389	2.9
Morrison	156	824	5.3	**1974**			
1956				G. Pruitt	126	540	4.3
P. Carpenter	188	756	4.0	McKinnis	124	519	4.2
1957				**1975**			
J. Brown	200	942	4.7	G. Pruitt	217	1067	4.9
1958				McKinnis	71	259	3.6
J. Brown	257	1527	5.9	**1976**			
1959				G. Pruitt	209	1000	4.8
J. Brown	290	1329	4.6	C. Miller	153	613	4.0
1960				**1977**			
J. Brown	215	1257	5.8	G. Pruitt	236	1086	4.6
1961				C. Miller	163	756	4.6
J. Brown	305	1408	4.6	**1978**			
1962				G. Pruitt	176	960	5.5
J. Brown	230	996	4.3	M. Pruitt	135	560	4.1
1963				**1979**			
J. Brown	291	1863	6.4	M. Pruitt	264	1294	4.9
1964				**1980**			
J. Brown	280	1446	5.2	M. Pruitt	249	1034	6.0

SCORING

	TD	PAT	FG	TOT.		TD	PAT	FG	TOT.
1946					**1966**				
Groza..............	0	45	13	84	Kelly..............	16	0	0	96
1947					**1967**				
Groza..............	0	39	7	60	Kelly..............	13	0	0	78
1948					**1968**				
Groza..............	0	51	8	75	Kelly..............	20	0	0	120
1949					**1969**				
Motley.............	8	0	0	48	Cockroft...........	0	45	12	81
1950					**1970**				
Groza..............	1	29	13	74	Cockroft...........	0	34	12	70
1951					**1971**				
Groza..............	0	43	10	73	Cockroft...........	0	34	15	79
1952					**1972**				
Groza..............	0	32	19	89	Cockroft...........	0	28	22	94
1953					**1973**				
Groza..............	0	39	23	108	Cockroft...........	0	24	22	90
1954					Phipps.............	5	0	0	30
Groza..............	0	37	16	85	G. Pruitt...........	5	0	0	30
1955					**1974**				
Groza..............	0	44	11	77	Cockroft...........	0	14	19	71
1956					K. Brown...........	6	0	0	36
Groza..............	0	18	11	51	**1975**				
1957					Cockroft...........	0	21	17	72
Groza..............	0	32	15	77	G. Pruitt...........	9	0	0	54
1958					**1976**				
J. Brown...........	18	0	0	108	Cockroft...........	0	27	15	72
1959					Rucker.............	8	0	0	48
J. Brown...........	14	0	0	84	**1977**				
1960					Cockroft...........	0	30	17	81
Baker..............	0	44	12	80	C. Miller...........	5	0	0	30
1961					Parris.............	5	0	0	30
Groza..............	0	37	16	85	**1978**				
1962					Cockroft...........	0	37	19	94
J. Brown...........	18	0	0	108	Rucker.............	8	0	0	48
1963					**1979**				
J. Brown...........	15	0	0	90	Cockroft...........	0	38	17	89
1964					M. Pruitt...........	11	0	0	66
Groza..............	0	49	22	115	**1980**				
1965					Cockroft...........	0	39	16	87
J. Brown...........	21	0	0	126	Hill...............	6	0	0	36
					M. Pruitt...........	6	0	0	36
					White..............	6	0	0	36

PASSING

	Att.	Comp.	Yds.	Int.	TD		Att.	Comp.	Yds.	Int.	TD
1946						**1964**					
Graham.......	174	95	1834	5	17	Ryan	334	174	2404	19	25
1947						**1965**					
Graham.......	269	163	2753	11	25	Ryan	243	119	1751	13	18
1948						**1966**					
Graham.......	333	173	2713	15	25	Ryan	382	200	2974	14	29
1949						**1967**					
Graham.......	285	161	2785	10	19	Ryan	280	136	2026	16	20
1950						**1968**					
Graham.......	253	137	1943	20	14	Nelsen	293	152	2366	10	19
1951						**1969**					
Graham.......	265	147	2205	16	17	Nelsen	352	190	2743	19	23
1952						**1970**					
Graham.......	364	181	2816	24	20	Nelsen	313	159	2156	16	16
1953						**1971**					
Graham.......	258	167	2722	9	11	Nelsen	325	174	2319	23	13
1954						**1972**					
Graham.......	240	149	2141	18	11	Phipps........	305	144	1994	16	13
1955						**1973**					
Graham.......	185	98	1721	8	15	Phipps........	299	148	1719	20	9
1956						**1974**					
O'Connell.....	96	42	551	8	4	Phipps........	256	117	1384	17	9
1957						**1975**					
O'Connell.....	110	63	1229	9	8	Phipps........	313	162	1749	19	4
1958							Sipe	88	45	427	3	1
Plum	189	102	1619	11	11	**1976**					
1959						Sipe	312	178	2113	14	17
Plum	266	156	1992	8	14	Phipps........	37	20	146	0	3
1960						**1977**					
Plum	250	151	2297	5	21	Sipe	195	112	1233	14	9
1961						Mays	121	67	797	10	6
Plum	302	177	2416	10	18	**1978**					
1962						Sipe	399	222	2906	15	21
Ryan	194	112	1541	7	10	**1979**					
1963						Sipe	535	286	3793	26	28
Ryan	256	135	2026	13	25	**1980**					
						Sipe	554	337	4132	14	30

RECEIVING

	NO.	YDS.	TD		NO.	YDS.	TD
1946				**1965**			
Lavelli	40	843	8	Collins	50	884	10
1947				**1966**			
Speedie	67	1146	6	Collins	56	946	12
1948				**1967**			
Speedie	58	816	4	E. Green	39	269	6
1949				**1968**			
Speedie	62	1028	7	Warfield	50	1067	12
1950				**1969**			
Speedie	42	548	1	Collins	54	786	11
1951				**1970**			
Lavelli	43	586	6	Scott	40	351	4
1952				**1971**			
Speedie	62	911	5	Hooker	45	649	1
1953				**1972**			
Lavelli	45	783	6	Pitts	36	620	8
1954				**1973**			
Lavelli	47	802	7	Pitts	31	317	4
1955				**1974**			
Brewster	34	662	6	McKinnis	32	258	0
1956				**1975**			
Brewster	28	417	1	Rucker	60	710	3
1957				G. Pruitt	44	299	1
Brewster	30	614	2	**1976**			
1958				Rucker	49	676	8
P. Carpenter	29	474	1	G. Pruitt	45	341	1
1959				**1977**			
Howto	39	510	1	C. Miller	41	291	1
1960				G. Pruitt	37	471	1
Mitchell	45	612	6	Rucker	36	565	2
1961				**1978**			
Renfro	48	834	6	Rucker	43	893	8
1962				Newsome	38	589	2
J. Brown	47	519	5	G. Pruitt	38	292	2
1963				**1979**			
Collins	43	674	13	Logan	59	982	7
1964				**1980**			
Warfield	52	920	9	M. Pruitt	63	471	0
				Rucker	52	768	4

BROWNS' SCORES
ALL-AMERICA CONFERENCE

CLE.	OPP.	CLE.	OPP.

1946

CLE.		OPP.	CLE.		OPP.
44	Miami (60,135) (N)	0	20	San Francisco (70,385)	34
20	at Chicago (51,962) (N)	6	16	at Los Angeles (24,800)	17
28	at Buffalo (30,302)	0	14	at San Francisco (41,061)	7
24	New York (57,084) (N)	7	51	Chicago (60,457)	14
26	Brooklyn (43,713)	7	42	Buffalo (37,054)	17
7	at New York (34,252)	0	34	at Miami (9,083) (N)	0
31	Los Angeles (71,134)	14	66	at Brooklyn (14,600)	14

CHAMPIONSHIP: 14   New York (40,469)   9

WON 12   LOST 2   **POINTS: 423   OPPONENTS: 137**

1947

CLE.		OPP.	CLE.		OPP.
30	Buffalo (63,623) (N)	14	14	at San Francisco (54,483)	7
55	at Brooklyn (18,876) (N)	7	28	at Buffalo (43,167)	7
28	Baltimore (44,257)	0	13	Brooklyn (30,279)	12
41	at Chicago (18,450)	21	37	San Francisco (76,504)	14
26	New York (80,067)	17	28	at New York (70,060)	28
10	Los Angeles (63,124)	13	27	at Los Angeles (45,009)	17
31	Chicago (35,266)	28	42	at Baltimore (20,574)	0

CHAMPIONSHIP: 14   at New York (61,879)   3

WON 12   LOST 1   TIED 1   **POINTS: 410   OPPONENTS: 185**

1948

CLE.		OPP.	CLE.		OPP.
19	Los Angeles (60,193) (N)	14	35	New York (46,912)	7
42	at Buffalo (35,340)	13	28	Baltimore (32,314)	7
28	at Chicago (30,874)	7	14	San Francisco (82,769)	7
21	Chicago (37,190) (N)	10	34	at New York (52,518)	21
14	at Baltimore (22,359) (N)	10	31	at Los Angeles (60,031)	14
30	Brooklyn (31,187)	17	31	at San Francisco (59,785)	28
31	Buffalo (28,054)	14	31	at Brooklyn (9,281)	21

CHAMPIONSHIP: 49   Buffalo (22,981)   7

WON 14   LOST 0   **POINTS: 389   OPPONENTS: 190**

1949

CLE.		OPP.	CLE.		OPP.
28	at Buffalo (31,839)	28	61	at Los Angeles (27,247)	14
21	Baltimore (21,621)	0	30	San Francisco (72,189)	28
14	New York (26,312)	3	35	Chicago (16,506)	2
28	at Baltimore (36,387)	20	7	Buffalo (22,511)	7
42	Los Angeles (30,465)	7	31	at New York (50,711)	0
28	at San Francisco (59,720)	56	14	at Chicago (5,031)	6

PLAYOFF: 31   Buffalo (17,270)   21
CHAMPIONSHIP: 21   San Francisco (22,550)   7

WON 9   LOST 1   TIED 2   **POINTS: 340   OPPONENTS: 171**

NATIONAL FOOTBALL LEAGUE
1950

CLE.		OPP.	CLE.		OPP.
35	at Philadelphia (71,237) (N)	10	45	Pittsburgh (40,714)	7
31	at Baltimore (15,201)	0	10	at Chicago Cards (38,456)	7
0	New York (37,647)	6	34	San Francisco (28,786)	14
30	at Pittsburgh (35,590)	17	20	Washington (21,908)	14
34	Chicago Cards (33,774)	24	13	Philadelphia (37,490)	7
13	at New York (41,734)	17	45	at Washington (30,143)	21

PLAYOFF: 8   New York (33,054)   3
CHAMPIONSHIP: 30   Los Angeles (29,751)   28

WON 10   LOST 2   **POINTS: 310   OPPONENTS: 144**

1951

10	at San Francisco (52,219)............14	24
38	at Los Angeles (67,186)...............	23
45	Washington (33,968)...............	0
17	Pittsburgh (32,409)...............	0
14	New York (56,947)................	13
34	at Chicago Cards (19,742)............	17

CHAMPIONSHIP: 17

WON 11   LOST 1

37	Los Angeles (57,832)...............	7
21	at Pittsburgh (27,923)................	20
9	New York (51,858)................	17
49	at Philadelphia (27,874)...............	7
19	Washington (32,496)................	15
6	at Detroit (56,029)....................	17

CHAMPIONSHIP: 7

WON 8   LOST 4

27	at (Mil.) G.B. (22,604)................	0
27	at Chicago Cards (24,374).............	7
37	Philadelphia (45,802) (N)............	13
30	at Washington (33,963)...............	14
7	at New York (30,773)................	0
27	Washington (47,845)................	3

CHAMPIONSHIP: 16

WON 11   LOST 1

10	at Philadelphia (26,546)................	28
31	Chicago Cards (24,101).............	7
27	at Pittsburgh (33,262)................	55
35	at Chicago Cards (23,823).............	3
24	New York (30,448)................	14
62	Washington (25,158)...............	3

CHAMPIONSHIP: 56

WON 9   LOST 3

17	Washington (30,041)...............	27
38	at San Francisco (46,150).............	3
21	Philadelphia (43,974)...............	17
24	at Washington (29,168)...............	14
41	Green Bay (51,482)................	10
26	at Chicago Cards (29,471).............	20

CHAMPIONSHIP: 38

WON 9   LOST 2   TIED 1

7	at Chicago Cards (20,966).............	9
14	at Pittsburgh (35,398)................	10
9	New York (60,042)................	21
9	at Washington (23,332)................	20
16	Pittsburgh (50,358)................	24
24	at Green Bay (28,590)................	7

WON 5   LOST 7

6	New York (58,095)................	3
23	at Pittsburgh (35,570).............	12
24	Philadelphia (53,493).............	7
7	at Philadelphia (22,443).............	17
17	at Chicago Cards (26,341).............	7
21	Washington (52,936).............	17

CHAMPIONSHIP: 14

WON 9   LOST 2   TIED 1

20	Philadelphia (36,571)...............	17
10	at New York (52,215)................	0
42	Chicago Bears (40,969).............	21
49	Chicago Cards (30,550).............	28
28	at Pittsburgh (24,229)................	0
24	at Philadelphia (16,263)...............	9

at Los Angeles (57,540)   24

POINTS: 331   OPPONENTS: 152

1952

28	Chicago Cards (34,097).............	13
29	Pittsburgh (34,973)................	28
20	Philadelphia (28,948)................	28
48	at Washington (22,679)................	24
10	at Chicago Cards (24,541).............	0
34	at New York (41,610)................	37

Detroit (50,934)   17

POINTS: 310   OPPONENTS: 213

1953

34	Pittsburgh (35,592)...............	16
23	San Francisco (80,698).............	21
20	at Pittsburgh (32,904)................	16
27	Chicago Cards (24,499).............	16
62	New York (40,235)................	14
27	at Philadelphia (38,564)................	42

at Detroit (54,577)   17

POINTS: 348   OPPONENTS: 162

1954

39	at Chicago Bears (48,773).............	10
6	Philadelphia (41,537)................	0
16	at New York (45,936)................	7
34	at Washington (21,761)................	14
42	Pittsburgh (28,064)................	7
10	Detroit (34,168)....................	14

Detroit (43,827)   10

POINTS: 336   OPPONENTS: 162

1955

24	New York (56,524)................	14
17	at Philadelphia (39,303)................	33
41	Pittsburgh (53,509)................	14
35	at New York (45,699)................	35
30	at Pittsburgh (31,101)................	7
35	Chicago Cards (25,914).............	24

at Los Angeles (87,695)   14

POINTS: 349   OPPONENTS: 218

1956

7	Baltimore (42,404)....................	21
16	at Philadelphia (25,894)...............	0
17	Washington (22,878)................	20
17	Philadelphia (20,654)................	14
24	at New York (27,707)................	7
7	Chicago Cards (25,312).............	24

POINTS: 167   OPPONENTS: 177

1957

24	Pittsburgh (53,709)....................	0
30	at Washington (27,722)................	30
45	Los Angeles (65,407)...............	31
31	Chicago Cards (40,525).............	0
7	at Detroit (55,814)....................	20
34	at New York (54,294)................	28

at Detroit (56,263)   59

POINTS: 269   OPPONENTS: 172

1958

30	at Los Angeles (69,993)............27
45	at Pittsburgh (31,130)............12
35	Chicago Cards (65,403)............28
27	Pittsburgh (66,852)............10
38 ،	at Chicago Cards (30,933)............24
17	New York (78,404)............21

PLAYOFF: 0   at New York (61,174)   10

WON 9   LOST 3

7	at Pittsburgh (33,844)............17
34	at Chicago Cards (19,935)............ 7
6	New York (65,534)............10
17	Chicago Cards (46,422)............ 7
34	Washington (42,732)............ 7
38	at Baltimore (57,557)............31

WON 7   LOST 5

41	at Philadelphia (56,303)............24
28	Pittsburgh (67,692)............20
48	at Dallas (28,500)............ 7
29	Philadelphia (64,850)............31
31	at Washington (32,086)............10
13	New York (82,872)............17

WON 8   LOST 3   TIED 1

20	at Philadelphia (60,671)............27
20	St. Louis (50,443)............17
25	Dallas (43,638)............ 7
31	Washington (46,186)............ 7
17	Green Bay (75,042)............49
30	at Pittsburgh (29,266)............28
21	at St. Louis (26,696)............10

WON 8   LOST 5   TIED 1

17	New York (81,115)............ 7
16	Washington (57,491)............17
7	at Philadelphia (60,671)............35
19	Dallas (44,041)............10
14	Baltimore (80,132)............36
34	at St. Louis (23,256)............ 7
41	at Pittsburgh (35,417)............14

WON 7   LOST 6   TIED 1

37	Washington (57,618)............14
41	at Dallas (28,710)............24
20	Los Angeles (54,713)............ 6
35	Pittsburgh (84,684) (N)............23
35	at New York (62,986)............24
37	Philadelphia (75,174)............ 7
6	New York (84,213)............33

WON 10   LOST 4

27	at Washington (47,577)............13
33	St. Louis (76,954)............33
28	at Philadelphia (60,671)............20
27	Dallas (72,062)............ 6
20	at Dallas (37,456)............16
42	New York (81,050)............20

CHAMPIONSHIP: 27   Baltimore (79,544)   0

WON 10   LOST 3   TIED 1

10	Detroit (75,563)............30
20	at Washington (32,372)............10
28	at Philadelphia (51,319)............14
21	Washington (33,240)............14
21	at Philadelphia (36,773)............14
10	at New York (63,192)............13

POINTS: 302   OPPONENTS: 217

1959

28	Philadelphia (58,275)............ 7
31	at Washington (32,266)............ 7
20	Pittsburgh (68,563)............21
20	San Francisco (56,854)............21
7	at New York (68,436)............48
28	at Philadelphia (45,952)............21

POINTS: 270   OPPONENTS: 214

1960

28	St. Louis (49,192)............27
10	at Pittsburgh (35,215)............14
17	at St. Louis (26,146)............17
27	Washington (35,211)............16
42	Chicago (38,155)............ 0
48	at New York (56,517)............34

POINTS: 362   OPPONENTS: 217

1961

13	Pittsburgh (62,723)............17
17	at Washington (28,975)............ 6
45	Philadelphia (68,399)............24
21	New York (80,455)............37
38	at Dallas (23,500)............17
14	at Chicago (38,717)............17
7	at New York (61,084)............ 7

POINTS: 319   OPPONENTS: 270

1962

14	Philadelphia (63,848)............14
9	at Washington (48,169)............17
38	St. Louis (41,815)............14
35	Pittsburgh (53,601)............14
21	at Dallas (24,226)............45
13	at New York (62,794)............17
13	at San Francisco (35,274)............10

POINTS: 291   OPPONENTS: 257

1963

23	at Philadelphia (60,671)............17
7	at Pittsburgh (54,497)............ 9
14	St. Louis (72,932)............20
27	Dallas (55,096)............17
24	at St. Louis (32,531)............10
10	at Detroit (51,382)............38
27	at Washington (40,865)............20

POINTS: 343   OPPONENTS: 262

1964

30	at Pittsburgh (49,568)............17
34	Washington (76,385)............24
37	Detroit (83,064)............21
21	at (Mil.) G.B. (48,065)............28
19	at St. Louis (31,585)............28
52	at New York (63,007)............20

POINTS: 415   OPPONENTS: 293

1965

17	at Washington (48,208)	7	38	Philadelphia (72,807)	34
13	St. Louis (80,161)	49	34	New York (82,426)	21
35	at Philadelphia (60,579)	17	24	at Dallas (76,251)	17
24	Pittsburgh (80,187) (N)	19	42	at Pittsburgh (42,757)	21
23	Dallas (80,432)	17	24	Washington (77,765)	16
38	at New York (62,864)	14	7	at Los Angeles (49,048)	42
17	Minnesota (83,505)	27	27	at St. Louis (29,348)	24

CHAMPIONSHIP: 12   at Green Bay (50,852)   23

WON 11   LOST 3   **POINTS: 363   OPPONENTS: 325**

1966

38	at Washington (48,643)	14	6	at Pittsburgh (39,690)	16
20	Green Bay (83,943)	21	27	Philadelphia (77,968)	7
28	St. Louis (74,814)	34	14	Washington (78,566)	3
28	at New York (62,916)	7	14	at Dallas (75,504)	26
41	Pittsburgh (82,687) (N)	10	49	New York (61,651)	40
30	Dallas (84,721)	21	21	at Philadelphia (58,074)	33
49	at Atlanta (57,235)	17	38	at St. Louis (47,721)	10

WON 9   LOST 5   **POINTS: 403   OPPONENTS: 259**

1967

14	Dallas (81,039)	21	34	at Pittsburgh (47,131)	14
14	at Detroit (57,383)	31	7	at (Mil.) G.B. (50,074)	55
42	at New Orleans (77,045)	7	14	Minnesota (68,431)	10
21	Pittsburgh (82,949) (N)	10	42	Washington (72,798)	37
20	St. Louis (77,813)	16	24	New York (78,594)	14
24	Chicago (83,183)	0	20	at St. Louis (47,782)	16
34	at New York (62,903)	38	24	at Philadelphia (60,658)	28

PLAYOFF: 14   at Dallas (70,786)   52

WON 9   LOST 5   **POINTS: 334   OPPONENTS: 297**

1968

24	at New Orleans (74,215)	10	33	at San Francisco (31,359)	21
7	at Dallas (68,733)	28	35	New Orleans (70,125)	17
6	Los Angeles (82,514)	24	45	at Pittsburgh (41,572)	24
31	Pittsburgh (81,865) (N)	24	47	Philadelphia (62,388)	13
21	St. Louis (79,349)	27	45	New York (83,193)	10
30	at Baltimore (60,238)	20	24	at Washington (50,661)	21
30	Atlanta (67,723)	7	16	at St. Louis (39,746)	27

PLAYOFF: 31   Dallas (81,497)   20
CHAMPIONSHIP: 0   Baltimore (80,628)   34

WON 10   LOST 4   **POINTS: 394   OPPONENTS: 273**

1969

27	atPhiladelphia (60,658)	20	3	atMinnesota (47,900)	51
27	Washington (82,581)	23	24	atPittsburgh (47,670)	3
21	Detroit (82,933)	28	28	New York (80,595)	17
27	atNew Orleans (71,274)	17	28	atChicago (45,050)	24
42	Pittsburgh (84,078) (N)	31	20	Green Bay (82,137)	7
21	St. Louis (81,186)	21	27	atSt. Louis (44,924)	21
42	Dallas (84,850)	10	14	atNew York (62,966)	27

PLAYOFF: 38   at Dallas (69,321)   14
CHAMPIONSHIP: 7   at Minnesota (47,900)   27

WON 10   LOST 3   **POINTS: 351   OPPONENTS: 300**

1970

31	New York Jets (85,703) (N)	21	20	at Oakland (54,463)	23
31	at San Francisco (37,502)	34	10	at Cincinnati (60,007)	14
15	Pittsburgh (84,349) (N)	7	28	Houston (74,723)	14
30	Cincinnati (83,520)	27	9	at Pittsburgh (50,214)	28
24	Detroit (83,577)	41	21	at Houston (50,582) (N)	10
28	at Miami (75,313)	0	2	Dallas (75,458)	6
10	San Diego (80,047)	27	27	at Denver (51,001)	13

WON 7   LOST 7   **POINTS: 286   OPPONENTS: 265**

1971

31	Houston (73,387)	0	9	at Pittsburgh (50,202)	26
14	at Baltimore (56,837)	13	7	at Kansas City (50,388)	13
20	Oakland (84,285) (N)	34	27	New England (65,238)	7
27	Pittsburgh (83,391)	17	37	at Houston (37,921)	24
27	at Cincinnati (60,284)	24	31	Cincinnati (82,705)	27
0	Denver (75,674)	27	21	at New Orleans (72,794)	17
14	Atlanta (76,825)	31	20	at Washington (53,041)	13

PLAYOFF: 3   Baltimore (74,082)   20

WON 9   LOST 5   **POINTS: 285   OPPONENTS: 273**

1972

10	Green Bay (75,771)	26	20	61,985)	0
27	at Philadelphia (65,720)	17	21	at San Diego (54,205) (N)	17
27	Cincinnati (81,564)	6	26	Pittsburgh (83,009)	24
7	Kansas City (83,819)	31	27	Buffalo (70,104)	10
0	Chicago (72,339)	17	0	at Pittsburgh (50,350)	30
23	at Houston (38,113)	17	27	at Cincinnati (59,524)	24
27	at Denver (54,656)	20	26	at New York Jets (62,614)	10

PLAYOFF: 14   Miami (80,010)   20

WON 10   LOST 4   **POINTS: 268   OPPONENTS: 249**

1973

24	Baltimore (74,303)	14	3	at Minnesota (45,590)	26
6	at Pittsburgh (49,396)	33	23	at Houston (37,230)	13
12	N. Y. Giants (76,065)	10	7	at Oakland (47,398)	3
17	Cincinnati (70,805)	10	21	Pittsburgh (67,773)	16
9	Miami (72,070) (N)	17	20	at Kansas City (70,296)	20
42	Houston (61,146)	13	17	at Cincinnati (58,266)	34
16	San Diego (68,244)	16	17	at Los Angeles (73,948)	30

WON 7   LOST 5   TIED 2   **POINTS: 234   OPPONENTS: 255**

1974

7	at Cincinnati (53,113)	33	35	at San Diego (35,683)	36
20	Houston (58,988)	7	21	at New England (57,263)	14
7	at St. Louis (43,472)	29	16	Pittsburgh (77,739)	26
24	Oakland (65,247)	40	10	Buffalo (66,504)	15
24	Cincinnati (70,897)	34	7	San Francisco (24,559)	0
16	at Pittsburgh (48,100)	20	17	at Dallas (48,754)	41
23	Denver (60,478)	21	24	at Houston (33,299)	28

WON 4   LOST 10   **POINTS: 251   OPPONENTS: 344**

1975

17	at Cincinnati (52,874)	24	10	at Detroit (75,283)	21
10	Minnesota (68,064)	42	17	at Oakland (50,461)	38
6	Pittsburgh (73,595)	42	35	Cincinnati (56,427)	23
10	Houston (46,531)	40	17	New Orleans (44,753)	16
15	at Denver (52,590)	16	17	at Pittsburgh (47,962)	31
7	Washington (56,702)	23	40	Kansas City (44,368)	14
7	at Baltimore (35,235)	21	10	at Houston (43,770)	21

WON 3   LOST 11   **POINTS: 218   OPPONENTS: 372**

1976

38	New York Jets (67,496)	17	6	at Cincinnati (54,776)	21
14	at Pittsburgh (49,169)	31	21	at Houston (39,328)	7
13	at Denver (62,973)	44	24	Philadelphia (62,120)	3
24	Cincinnati (75,817)	45	24	at Tampa Bay (36,390)	7
18	Pittsburgh (76,411)	16	17	Miami (74,715)	13
20	at Atlanta (33,364)	17	13	Houston (56,025)	10
21	San Diego (60,018)	17	14	at Kansas City (34,340)	39

WON 9   LOST 5   **POINTS: 267   OPPONENTS: 287**

1977

13	at Cincinnati (52,847)	3
30	New England (76,418) (N) (OT)	27
14	Pittsburgh (80,588)	28
10	Oakland (80,236)	26
24	at Houston (47,888)	23
27	at Buffalo (60,905)	16
44	Kansas City (60,381)	7

WON 6   LOST 8

24	San Francisco (68,973)	7
13	Cincinnati (72,691) (OT)	10
24	at Atlanta (56,648)	16
9	at Pittsburgh (49,513) (OT)	15
13	Houston (72,776)	16
24	at New Orleans (50,158)	16
14	Pittsburgh (81,302)	34
3	at Kansas City (41,157)	17

WON 8   LOST 8

25	at New York Jets (48,472) (OT)	22
27	at Kansas City (42,181)	24
13	Baltimore (72,070)	10
26	Dallas (80,123) (N)	7
10	at Houston (48,915)	31
35	Pittsburgh (81,260)	51
9	Washington (63,323)	13
28	Cincinnati (75,119)	27

WON 9   LOST 7

20	at New England (49,222)	34
7	Houston (80,243) (N)	16
20	Kansas City (63,614)	13
34	at Tampa Bay (65,540)	27
16	Denver (81,065)	19
27	at Seattle (61,366)	1
26	Green Bay (75,548)	21
27	Pittsburgh (79,095)	26

PLAYOFF: 12   Oakland (77,655)   14

WON 11   LOST 5

7	Cincinnati (81,932)	10
31	at Pittsburgh (47,055)	35
21	at N. Y. Giants (72,576)	7
0	Los Angeles (70,352)	9
14	at San Diego (37,312)	37
15	Houston (30,898)	19
19	at Seattle (61,583)	20

POINTS: 269   OPPONENTS: 267

1978

41	Buffalo (51,409)	20
10	at Houston (45,827)	14
7	Denver (45,341)	19
45	at Baltimore (45,341)	24
30	Los Angeles (55,158)	19
24	at Seattle (62,262)	47
37	New York Jets (36,881) (OT)	34
16	at Cincinnati (46,985)	48

POINTS: 334   OPPONENTS: 356

1979

38	at St. Louis (47,845)	20
24	at Philadelphia (69,019)	19
24	Seattle (72,440)	29
30	Miami (80,374) (OT)	24
30	at Pittsburgh (48,773) (OT)	33
14	Houston (69,112)	7
14	at Oakland (52,641)	19
12	at Cincinnati (42,183)	16

POINTS: 359   OPPONENTS: 352

1980

27	Chicago (83,224) (N)	21
28	at Baltimore (45,369)	27
13	at Pittsburgh (54,563)	16
31	Cincinnati (79,253)	7
17	at Houston (51,514)	14
17	New York Jets (78,454)	14
23	at Minnesota (42,202)	28
27	at Cincinnati (50,048)	24

POINTS: 357   OPPONENTS 310

PRE-SEASON GAMES

1950 (5-0)

G.B. at Toledo (10,000)............... 38-7
Balt. at Cin. (21,000)................. 34-7
Det. at Akron (23,670)............... 35-14
Chi. Brs. at Cleve. (51,076)............ 27-23
Pitt. at Buff. (15,259)................ 41-31

1951 (4-1)

College All-Stars (92,180)............. 33-0
N.Y. Yks. at Akr. (25,820)............ 52-0
Det. at Det. (35,165)................. 20-21
Chi. Brs. at Chi. (67,342)............. 32-21
L.A. at Cleve. (38,851)............... 7-6

1952 (2-2)

G.B. at G.B. (22,215)................ 21-14
Chi. Brs. at Cleve. (37,976)............ 14-7
Det. at Syracuse (26,000)............. 21-28
S.F. at Akron (30,119)............... 31-35

1953 (4-1-1)

S.F. at S.F. (36,273)................. 20-7
L.A. at L.A. (21,440)................. 9-27
Det. at Det. (39,985)................. 24-24
Balt. at Akron (20,000)............... 23-21
Chi. Brs. at Chi. (36,796)............ 20-14
G.B. at Cleve (22,336)............... 21-13

1954 (2-3)

G.B. at G.B. (15,747)............... 14-13
L.A. at L.A. (58,567)............... 10-38
S.F. at S.F. (46,877)................. 21-38
Det. at Dallas (42,000)............... 31-56
Chi. Brs. at Cleve. (17,631)........... 35-7

1955 (1-5)

College All-Stars (75,000)............. 27-30
G.B. at Akron (22,000)............... 13-7
S.F. at S.F. (41,604)................. 14-17
L.A. at L.A. (35,948)................. 21-38
Det. at Cleve. (29,581).............. 3-19
Chi. Brs. at Chi. (43,067)............ 21-24

1956 (2-5)

College All-Stars (75,000)............. 26-0
S.F. at S.F. (38,741)................. 17-28
L.A. at L.A. (40,175)................ 6-17
G.B. at Cleve. (15,456)............... 20-21
Det. at Det. (48,105)................. 0-17
Det. at Akron (28,201).............. 14-31
Chi. Brs. at Chi. (56,543)............ 24-14

1957 (2-4)

Det. at Det. (40,150)................. 10-20
Pitt. at Akron (26,669).............. 28-13
S.F. at S.F. (32,840)................. 17-21
L.A. at L.A. (45,011)............... 14-20
Det. at Cleve. (34,369)............... 23-7
Chi. Brs. at Chi. (47,354)............ 3-29

1958 (3-3)

Pitt. at Akron (27,202).............. 10-0
Det. at Det. (36,662)................. 7-17
L.A. at L.A. (41,387)................ 13-10
S.F. at S.F. (31,339)................. 16-21
Chi. Brs. at Chi. (52,669)............ 31-42
Det. at Cleve. (35,343)............... 41-7

1959 (2-4)

Pitt. at Pitt. (27,432)................ 20-34
Det. at Akron (22,654)............... 3-9
S.F. at S.F. (24,737)................ 14-17
L.A. at L.A. (55,883)................ 27-24
Det. at Det. (33,435)................ 28-31
Chi. Brs. at Cleve. (25,316)........... 33-31

1960 (5-1)

Det. at Det. (24,620)................. 28-14
Pitt. at Pitt. (16,360)................ 27-24
L.A. at L.A. (48,175)................ 17-22
S.F. at Portland (25,898)............. 26-24
Chi. at Akron (21,568).............. 16-10
Det. at Cleve. (25,911)............... 14-10
Jan. 7, 1961 Playoff Bowl
Det. at Miami (34,981)............... 16-17

1961 (3-2)

Det. at Det. (25,602)................ 7-35
S.F. at S.F. (38,759)................. 27-24
L.A. at L.A. (40,086)................ 34-17
Pitt. at Akron (27,758).............. 38-6
Det. at Cleve. (41,374)............... 17-35

1962 (5-0)

Det. at Det. (34,241)................ 17-14
Pitt. at Cleve. (77,683).............. 33-10
S.F. at Portland (27,161)............. 34-27
L.A. at L.A. (43,118)................ 26-24
Chi. at Chi. (57,878)................. 28-24

1963 (2-3)

Det. at Det. (83,248)................ 10-24
Balt. at Cleve. (83,218).............. 7-21
S.F. at S.F. (28,335)................. 24-7
Pitt. at Canton (18,462).............. 7-16
Jan. 5, 1964 Playoff Bowl
G.B. at Miami (54,921)............... 23-40

1964 (4-1)

S.F. at S.F. (27,404)................. 7-26
L.A. at L.A. (43,183)................ 56-31
Pitt. at Akron (27,255).............. 42-7
Det. at Det. (36,946)................ 35-14
G.B. at Cleve. (83,736)............... 20-17

1965 (5-1)

College All-Stars (68,000)............. 24-16
S.F. at S.F. (22,000)................. 37-21
L.A. at L.A. (29,508)................ 21-19
Det. at Det. (28,803)................ 28-14
G.B. at Cleve. (83,118)............... 14-30
Pitt. at Akron (23,162).............. 28-16

1966 (3-2)

L.A. at L.A. (63,285)............... 6-16
S.F. at S.F. (27,867)................ 28-17
Atl. at Atl. (48,548)................ 42-3
Balt. at Cleve. (83,418).............. 17-24
Pitt. at Birming. (23,590)............ 13-10

1967 (1-5)

Phil. at Canton (17,500)............. 13-28
S.F. at S.F. (27,482)................ 14-42
L.A. at L.A. (36,942)............... 17-24
Atl. at Atl. (52,240)................ 31-34
G.B. at Cleve. (84,236)............. 21-30
Minn. at Minn. (40,012)............ 42-14
   Jan. 7, 1968 Playoff Bowl
L.A. at Miami (37,102)............. 6-30

1968 (2-3)

L.A. at L.A. (64,020)............... 21-23
S.F. at S.F. (26,801)............... 31-17
N.O. at N.O. (70,045)............... 27-40
Buff. at Buff. (45,448).............. 22-12
G.B. at Cleve. (84,918)............. 9-31

1969 (3-2-1)

S.F. at Seattle (32,219)............. 21-16
L.A. at L.A. (54,937)............... 10-7
S.D. at S.D. (36,005)............... 19-19
G.B. at Cleve. (85,532)............. 17-27
Wash. at Wash. (45,994)........... 20-10
Minn. at Akron (28,561)............ 16-23

1970 (2-4)

L.A. at L.A. (71,559)............... 17-30
S.F. at Tampa (41,851)............. 17-10
K.C. at Memphis (31,532)........... 13-16
Cin. at Cin. (57,112)................ 24-31
Minn. at Cleve. (83,043)............ 21-24
N.Y. Giants at N.Y. (62,461)......... 30-29

1971 (1-5)

S.F. at S.F. (40,000)................ 24-38
L.A. at L.A. (52,503)............... 5-17
Dal. at Dal. (69,099)................ 15-16
Chi. at South Bend (43,568).......... 19-20
N.Y.G. at Cleve. (82,710)........... 30-7
St. L. at St. L. (46,171)............. 13-27

1972 (0-6)

L.A. at L.A. (64,803)............... 3-13
S.F. at S.F. (58,364)............... 13-20
Det. at Ann Arbor (58,422).......... 7-34
Minn. at Minn. (70,583)............ 17-20
Cin. at Columbus (84,816)........... 21-27
N.Y.G. at N.Y. (60,152)............ 21-28

1973 (2-3-1)

S.F. at Cleve. (65,707)............... 16-27
L.A. at L.A. (54,385)............... 21-21
Cin. at Columbus (73,421)........... 24-6
Atl. at Knoxville (40,831)............ 20-17
Det. at Cleve. (64,088).............. 13-16
N.Y.G. at Akron (30,751)........... 10-21

1974 (2-4)

L.A. at L.A. (28,021)............... 21-24
S.F. at Cleve. (24,008).............. 21-20
Balt. at Tampa (25,116)............. 3-37
Wash. at Cleve. (44,528)............ 17-20
Cin. at Columbus (36,326)........... 21-17
Det. at Det. (42,905)................ 7-21

1975 (2-4)

S.F. at S.F. (45,560)................ 13-17
Phil. at Cleve. (35,769)............. 14-6
Wash. at Wash. (15,513)............ 14-23
Buff. at Cleve. (31,155).............. 20-34
N.Y.G. at Seattle (20,000)........... 24-20
Det. at Cleve. (32,341).............. 24-27

1976 (4-2)

Balt. at Lincoln (20,304)............. 0-21
Atl. at Stillwater (24,227)........... 31-7
Minn. at Cleve. (44,336)............ 31-7
Phil. at Phil. (20,600)............... 21-17
N.E. at Cleve. (36,016).............. 30-27
Buff. at Buff. (37,951).............. 10-28

1977 (3-3)

Wash. at Cleve. (32,554)............ 14-16
Minn. at Minn. (45,370)............ 33-34
St. L. at Cleve. (31,308)............ 19-10
Chi. at Cleve. (36,598).............. 14-7
G.B. at G.B. (53,180)............... 19-14
Det. at Det. (49,168)................ 20-24

1978 (2-2)

N.Y.G. at Cleve. (30,636)........... 7-21
Buff. at Buff. (23,241).............. 20-10
Det. at Cleve. (31,345).............. 14-10
N.E. at N.E. (42,696)............... 10-21

1979 (2-2)

N.Y.G. at N.Y. (30,905)............ 7-27
Balt. at Cleve. (43,056)............. 24-3
Det. at Det. (55,623)................ 10-21
Wash. at Wash. (40,039)............ 21-9

1980 (1-3)

K.C. at K.C. (38,055)............... 0-48
Wash. at Cleve. (54,986)............ 3-12
Chi. at Chi. (57,688)................ 33-31
Minn. at Minn. (47,262)............ 16-38

FUTURE STATISTICS

FUTURE STATISTICS

FUTURE STATISTICS

FUTURE STATISTICS

FUTURE STATISTICS

FUTURE STATISTICS

FUTURE STATISTICS